Consolidating Mexico's Democracy

Consolidating Mexico's Democracy

The 2006 Presidential Campaign
in Comparative Perspective

Edited by
Jorge I. Domínguez
Chappell Lawson
Alejandro Moreno

The Johns Hopkins University Press
Baltimore

The Johns Hopkins University Press
2715 North Charles Street
Baltimore, Maryland 21218-4363
www.press.jhu.edu

Library of Congress Cataloging-in-Publication Data

Consolidating Mexico's democracy : the 2006 presidential campaign
in comparative perspective / edited by Jorge I. Domínguez, Chappell
Lawson, Alejandro Moreno.
    p. cm.
    Includes bibliographical references and index.
    ISBN-13: 978-0-8018-9251-6 (hardcover : alk. paper)
    ISBN-10: 0-8018-9251-1 (hardcover : alk. paper)
    ISBN-13: 978-0-8018-9252-3 (pbk. : alk. paper)
    ISBN-10: 0-8018-9252-X (pbk. : alk. paper)
    1. Presidents—Mexico—Election—2006. 2. Political
campaigns—Mexico—History—21st century. 3. Mexico—Politics
and government—2000– I. Domínguez, Jorge I., 1945– II. Lawson,
Chappell H., 1967– III. Moreno, Alejandro.
    JL1292.C648 2009
    324.972´0841—dc22   2008044015

A catalog record for this book is available from the British Library.

*Special discounts are available for bulk purchases of this book. For
more information, please contact Special Sales at 410-516-6936 or
specialsales@press.jhu.edu.*

The Johns Hopkins University Press uses environmentally friendly
book materials, including recycled text paper that is composed of at
least 30 percent post-consumer waste, whenever possible. All of our
book papers are acid-free, and our jackets and covers are printed on
paper with recycled content.

Contents

Figures

Tables

Preface

Mexico's 2006 presidential election provided high drama during the campaign, a near tie on election day, and confirmation that the Mexican electorate had moved well past seven decades of domination by a single political party. Mexico's democratic politics displayed vigorous contests across the nation. The country's three large political parties—the National Action Party (PAN), the Institutional Revolutionary Party (PRI), and the Party of the Democratic Revolution (PRD)—also dominated the races for Congress, confirming a pattern, first established in the 1997 election, that no party controlled a majority of either chamber.

There is no single date signaling when the Mexican democratic transition began. Its construction has taken place over the past quarter century, and the democratization of Mexico's civilian, one-party regime was protracted. Only after the 2000 election could most Mexicans assert that their political regime had changed decisively. And only in the 2006 election could they assess how well their polity would handle a presidential election entirely outside of the context of single-party rule.

In this book we seek to understand how a campaign might shape the results of a national election in a relatively new democracy. Our primary goal is to assess public opinion and voting behavior during the 2006 presidential campaign in Mexico in the light of the pertinent scholarship in the United States and other countries. But we also seek to inform larger theoretical debates about campaigns and voting behavior, thus making this volume a valuable resource for people who do not follow Mexican politics.

Most of the chapter authors have worked with one another over the years and on past collaborative studies of Mexican public opinion and voting behavior, including an edited book on the 2000 election (Domínguez and Lawson 2004). The scholarly team in this volume has developed and deepened the study of electoral behavior in Mexico, placing it on par with similar studies of elections in the long-established democracies.

This book draws heavily on the Mexico 2006 Panel Study, a three-wave survey of ordinary voters conducted during the 2006 campaign. The National Science Foundation provided the largest portion of funding for the project (SES-0517971), specifically with regard to the surveys in the field. The University of Texas at Austin provided support for a workshop at a crucial early stage of our project, where details of the survey design and instrumentation could be finalized. Harvard University's Weatherhead Center for International Affairs hosted a conference at which many of the draft chapters in this volume were presented for the first time. Domínguez in particular thanks the Weatherhead Center for general support of his research. Lawson likewise thanks the Massachusetts Institute of Technology for general research support and for covering certain costs of project planning and administration. We both thank Kathleen Hoover (Weatherhead Center) for her excellent work in the production of this manuscript, as well as Alexander Noonan (Weatherhead Center) and Michael Myers (MIT) for their work on the project.

As the book went into production, our colleague Wayne Cornelius announced his retirement. We salute and honor his many splendid contributions to scholarship, and certainly to this book and its predecessor (Domínguez and Lawson 2004).

We owe a great debt to *Reforma* newspaper, which conducted the polling for the Mexico 2006 Panel Study and covered approximately half of the cost of that work. *Reforma* deserves its distinction as a private media outlet that takes its public role seriously. Domínguez and Lawson also wish to acknowledge the leadership and skill shown by our colleague, Alejandro Moreno, at *Reforma* in conducting a massive panel survey under extremely challenging circumstances.

Finally, we thank the Mexicans who agreed to be interviewed for this project, both in formal surveys or informal interviews. Whether the Mexican voter was the crucial actor in that country's political transition may be debatable; that ordinary voters were the key to this project is not.

A Note on Spanish Surnames: In Spanish-speaking countries, people use two surnames, with the father's surname appearing before the mother's surname. Felipe Calderón Hinojosa's last name, as far as English speakers may be concerned, is Calderón, not Hinojosa. When the paternal surname is uncommon, people are often known by that name alone. Thus Felipe Calderón Hinojosa is often referred to as Felipe Calderón. Where the paternal surname is very common, however, the maternal surname is typically included. For instance, Andrés

Manuel López Obrador is normally referred to as López Obrador rather than simply López.

When writing in English, some scholars hyphenate the two surnames to indicate that the first is the principal one; our colleague Francisco Flores Macías goes by Francisco Flores-Macías in this volume to avoid being cited by future scholars as "Macías 2009." We have elected not to follow this approach for the names of Mexican politicians. As a result, we refer to some individuals using only their paternal surname (e.g., Felipe Calderón and Roberto Madrazo) and to others using both surnames (e.g., Andrés Manuel López Obrador or Alberto Cárdenas Jiménez), counting on the context to make clear which is the paternal surname.

States won by Felipe Calderón of the National Action Party

States won by Andrés Manuel López Obrador of the Coalition for the Good of All

Consolidating Mexico's Democracy

CHAPTER ONE

Introduction

The Mexican 2006 Election in Context

Chappell Lawson

On July 2, 2006, a narrow plurality of Mexican voters chose Felipe Calderón as their next president. It was the closest national election in Mexican history, with Calderón edging out leftist candidate Andrés Manuel López Obrador by less than 0.6 percent of the 42 million ballots cast. In fact, it would be more than two months before the Federal Electoral Court, after massive street protests and charges of electoral irregularities by López Obrador's supporters, certified the outcome (for results from the 2006 elections, see table 1.1).

Calderón's victory was a remarkably improbable event. He was not the favorite to win his party's nomination, and he trailed López Obrador by 5–10 percentage points for most of the race. Some pundits and scholars initially predicted that he would finish third, behind both López Obrador and Roberto Madrazo, the candidate of the once-dominant Institutional Revolutionary Party (Partido Revolucionario Institucional, or PRI). And yet he won. (A detailed timeline of major events surrounding the 2006 presidential election can be found in the supporting materials for this volume, which are posted on the website for the Mexico 2006 Panel Study, http://web.mit.edu/polisci/research/mexico06/book .html.)

This book analyzes the campaign that ended in a virtual tie between two men who offered very different visions of their country's political future. It addresses the social divisions that characterized Mexico on the eve of the election, the tactics of the main political parties, the choices of ordinary voters, and the place of the campaign in a larger context of democratic consolidation. In doing so, it sheds light on a crucial event in Mexican political development.

Its theoretical ambition, however, is broader. This volume endeavors to advance the comparative study of elections, which has now spread well beyond

Table 1.1   Election returns in 2006

Party	Coalition	Vote for president (IFE)	Vote for president (Court)	Vote for Senate (party list)	Vote for Chamber (party list)
National Action Party (PAN)	—	35.89%	35.89%	33.63%	33.41%
Party of the Democratic Revolution (PRD) Democratic Convergence (*Convergencia*) Labor Party (PT)	For the Good of All	35.31%	35.33%	29.70%	28.99%
Institutional Revolutionary Party (PRI) Green Ecologist Party of Mexico (PVEM)	Alliance for Mexico	22.26%	22.23%	27.99%	28.18%
New Alliance Party (PANAL)	—	0.96%	0.96%	4.04%	4.55%
Social Democratic Peasant Alternative (*Alternativa*)	—	2.70%	2.71%	1.91%	2.05%
Valid votes as percentage of total		97.12%	97.12%	97.27%	97.18%
Total votes cast		41,791,322	41,557,430	41,762,798	41,531,750

Sources: Instituto Federal Electoral, *Elección de Presidente de los EUM de 2006 por entidad federativa*, July 11, 2006, www.ife.org.mx/documentos/computos2006/ReportePresidenteEUM.html; Tribunal Electoral del Poder Judicial de la Federación, *Dictamen relativo al cómputo final de la elección de Presidente de los Estados Unidos Mexicanos, declaración de validez de la elección y de presidente electo*, September 5, 2006, www.trife.org.mx/acuerdo/dictamen.pdf.

Note: Vote shares are given as a percentage of the total vote. The first column of figures indicates the results of the final count (district count) as reported by the Federal Electoral Institute (IFE). The second column of figures gives the vote share for each candidate after the Federal Electoral Court annulled the results at certain polling stations where they found evidence of irregularities. In the district count for president, 2.16% of the ballots were null and 0.71% were cast for unregistered candidates. Turnout in the presidential race, based on the IFE's figures, was 58.55%; the effective turnout rate was a few points higher, given the fact that several million potential voters reside in the United States.

the United States. In other words, it is meant to be relevant and accessible to those who care about campaigns and voting behavior but may know or care little about Mexico. One way it does so is by combining analyses of internal party dynamics and strategies (part II) with methodologically sophisticated analyses of changes in the mass public (part III). Readers can thus see how and why candidates chose the tactics they did and, in turn, how and why voters chose among the candidates.

Within this overall framework, individual chapters offer their own theoretical innovations for comparative research on electoral behavior. For instance, they shed light on the role of social cleavages in partisan politics, the consequences of intraparty factionalism, the extent of ideological reasoning in the mass public, the relationship between mass and elite attitudes, the nature of economic voting, and the role of social networks in reinforcing voters' preferences. Scholars wishing to dig deep into specific topics in the study of campaigns can use these contributions as a conceptual springboard for work on other countries.

Paralleling the structure of the book, this introductory chapter focuses first on Mexico and then generalizes from that experience. It begins by describing the political context in which the 2006 campaign took place. It next summarizes the main events of the 2006 campaign, closing with a brief discussion of why public opinion shifted toward Calderón. It then discusses the consequences of the election for Mexican democracy. The final section speculates on the implications of the findings from this study for research on campaigns and elections around the world. These include the magnitude and nature of campaign effects, the mechanics of persuasion, the effectiveness of negative advertising, and the effect of intraparty dynamics on campaign strategy and electoral success.

Background to the 2006 Campaign

During the late 1980s and early 1990s, Mexico made a gradual transition from an autocratic, one-party-dominant regime to a more competitive system. Opposition parties—principally, the conservative National Action Party (Partido Acción Nacional, or PAN) and the leftist Party of the Democratic Revolution (Partido de la Revolución Democrática, or PRD)—overcame decades of fraud and official harassment to wrest state, local, and legislative offices from the ruling party. In 1996, after almost fifteen years of economic volatility and corruption scandals had accentuated demands for reform, President Ernesto Zedillo signed off on constitutional amendments that gave the PAN and the PRD a chance to compete with the ruling PRI on an equal footing (Eisenstadt 2004;

Lawson 2000). In the 1997 midterm elections, the PRI lost control of the lower house of Congress, the Chamber of Deputies. Three years later, PAN presidential candidate Vicente Fox defeated the PRI's nominee, Francisco Labastida, as well as three-time leftist standard-bearer Cuauhtémoc Cárdenas (Domínguez and Lawson 2004). What followed was the first peaceful transfer of power between leaders of different political parties in Mexico's 200-year history.

Through the 2000 campaigns, most Mexicans saw elections as a contest between the government and its opponents (Domínguez and McCann 1995, 1996; Paolino 2005). Indeed, this view of political life was central to Fox's victory, as many Mexicans who had not necessarily been sympathetic to the PAN voted for Fox in the name of change (Domínguez and Lawson 2004). With the old regime gone, however, differences between the PAN and the PRD loomed much larger. Mexican voters thus had to grapple with the more complex political reality of a true three-party system in which the country's main political groupings could be plausibly arrayed on a left-right spectrum (McCann and Lawson 2003). When the 2006 presidential campaign began, many voters were still sorting themselves out.

As Joseph Klesner discusses in Chapter 3, Mexico's three main parties draw their support from somewhat different social groups: the PRI from older, rural, and less educated voters; the PAN from northerners, Catholics, and urban professionals; and the PRD from urban working class voters, southerners, and residents of Mexico City. Collectively, however, these factors do not predict individual voting decisions with much precision. All three of Mexico's parties are multiclass coalitions that enjoy support across demographic categories. The contribution by McCann, Cornelius, and Leal (chapter 5) indicates that these same generalizations apply to Mexican expatriates, who have not been exposed to recent campaigns.

Of the demographic factors that influence voting behavior, the most important is not class, but region. As chapter 3 shows, the PRI and the PAN remain the primary competitors in areas of the country north of Mexico City, while the PRI and the PRD tend to dominate in many southern states (see also Hiskey and Canache 2005). This regional divide reflects long-standing cultural differences between North and South, which in turn influenced long-term patterns of party building during the period of PRI rule. It also reflects geographical disparities in growth over the last two decades, in which the northern part of the country has benefited much more from economic integration with the United States than did the southern portion or Mexico City. Today, as Andy Baker explains in chapter 4, interpersonal communication about politics reinforces regional asymmetries in partisan support (see also Baker et al. 2006).

Federalism also affects the party system. Competition in state and local elections, which are rarely held on the same dates as federal contests, forestalled the nationalization of the party system. It also helped to sustain the PRI long after the electoral reforms of the mid-1990s effectively eliminated electoral shenanigans in national contests. Governors in Mexico control substantial discretionary resources in the form of financial assistance via transfers from the federal government. Higher oil prices during the Fox administration led to greater federal revenues and thus increased federal transfers. This infusion of funds enabled some bosses to build—or rebuild—political machines. Combined with the PRI's selection of strong candidates in a number of states, the old ruling party was able to remain highly competitive in subnational contests (see chapter 7).

One crucial result, discussed by both Klesner (chapter 3) and Roderic Camp (chapter 2), is the persistence of a three-party system at the national level. In the midterm elections of 2003, the PRI-led coalition garnered 37 percent of the vote, the PAN 31 percent, and the PRD 18 percent. The PRD's leftist allies, running separately, captured almost 5 percent of the vote; the PRI's coalition partner, the center-right Green Ecologist Party (Partido Verde Ecologista de México, or PVEM), which ran separately in some districts, captured an additional 4 percent. In October 2005, 27 percent of the respondents from the Mexico 2006 Panel Study[1] identified with the PRI, 23 percent with the PAN, and 17 percent with the PRD; approximately one-third did not identify with any party.[2] The PRI thus remained Mexico's largest party, but a strong candidate from either the PAN or even the PRD could entertain a reasonable prospect of claiming the coveted presidential sash.

The 2006 Campaign

For the old ruling party to win a presidential race, it had to remain united at the elite level. If it did not, its political machine would not deliver enough votes to put the PRI's candidate over the top. Consequently, not only did the image of the party's nominee in the eyes of ordinary voters matter, so too did the extent to which he was able to bring together party power brokers.

Madrazo, a former governor of the state of Tabasco and the PRI's president, proved to be a weak candidate in both respects. Many voters associated him with the unreconstructed wing of his party. His 1994 gubernatorial victory (over fellow Tabasco native López Obrador) was marred by widespread electoral irregularities and subsequent revelations that his campaign had spent several dozen times the legal limit. He also suffered from personal deficits: although a practiced campaigner, he could come across as shifty—even in his own television advertisements. (Subsequent events would confirm many voters' suspicions about his character. Madrazo was a proud marathoner, and one of his earliest television spots in the 2006 campaign depicted him running. Fifteen months after the election, however, Madrazo was disqualified from the Berlin Marathon for taking a short cut in an attempt to place first in his age group.)[3] Not surprisingly, Madrazo began the campaign with by far the worst favorability ratings of the three major-party contenders; in fact, negative impressions of him actually outnumbered favorable ones in October 2005. These facts suggested that Madrazo was unlikely to appeal to independent voters.

In terms of his ability to unify the party, strains became apparent even before the primary began. In September 2005, a spat between Madrazo and the head of the powerful Teachers' Union (Sindicato Nacional de Trabajadores de la Educación, or SNTE), Elba Esther Gordillo, led to her resignation as secretary of the PRI and ultimately her separation from the party. Gordillo subsequently helped to found the New Alliance Party (Partido Nueva Alianza, or PANAL), which siphoned off a segment of the PRI's corporatist base in the general election.

During the party's presidential primary, a number of prominent governors from northern and central states openly opposed Madrazo's candidacy. Although the official name for their faction was Todos Unidos con México (everyone united with Mexico), pundits soon reinterpreted the acronym TUCOM to mean *todos unidos contra Madrazo* (everyone united against Madrazo). Madrazo won the primary after TUCOM's contender, Arturo Montiel, the former governor of the state of México, withdrew from the race following allegations of illicit enrichment. Leading figures in the PRI and elsewhere assumed the leaks had come from Madrazo's camp—in other words, that Madrazo won the primary by blackmailing his chief rival.[4] Unsurprisingly, the incident dampened enthusiasm for a Madrazo presidency among surviving figures of the old regime, whose zeal for having past corruption exposed was less than overwhelming. Madrazo's aggressiveness in placing his loyalists on the PRI's party list for the Senate and Chamber of Deputies likewise alienated powerful members of his own party.[5] (In chapter 8, Joy Langston offers a detailed account of factionalism within the PRI and its consequences for Madrazo's campaign.) All told, personal liabilities and party divisions left Madrazo a vulnerable candidate, despite the fact that he represented what was, at the time, Mexico's strongest party.

López Obrador faced almost the opposite problem; he began the race as a strong candidate from a relatively weak party. The former PRD president was a wildly popular mayor of the Federal District (from 2000 to 2005), where he drew support far beyond his party's traditional base. He had also achieved national prominence as a result of the fact that Mexico City news is rebroadcast across the country. Despite some rather serious bumps along the way—including the arrest of one of his top aides for corruption and his own impeachment by the federal Congress for violating a court order in a zoning dispute—he remained well ahead of all potential presidential rivals in the polls during 2004 and 2005. After finishing third in each of the previous three presidential elections, the PRD appeared to have found a candidate who could lead them to victory.

As the 2006 election approached, speculation persisted that Cárdenas, who had helped found the PRD in the late 1980s, might again seek his party's nomination. Indeed, Cárdenas refused to embrace López Obrador's candidacy and continued to flirt with the idea of an independent bid during the early stages of the campaign. However, polling data repeatedly indicated that even strong PRD identifiers favored López Obrador by an ample margin. In the end, he avoided being outflanked by Cárdenas and went into the general election unopposed. (Chapters 7 and 9 offer careful accounts of López Obrador's selection by acclamation.)

Calderón's candidacy evolved very differently from that of both of his main rivals. The initial favorite to win the PAN's nomination was not Calderón but rather Minister of Government Santiago Creel, who was widely regarded as Fox's preferred successor.[6] Creel's performance under Fox was not considered particularly effective, but he was seen as a centrist and a conciliator; most analysts regarded him as better able than Calderón to appeal to voters outside the party's northern, Catholic, middle-class base. Like Fox, however, Creel was viewed with skepticism by hard-core PAN partisans. For party members, Calderón was the candidate who best represented the PAN's core cultural and social values. In a hotly contested primary, they chose the conservative stalwart over a Fox protégé who, at first glance, seemed better positioned to win a general election. (David Shirk provides a more detailed account of the PAN's internal dynamics in chapter 7.)

Calderón and the president had been at odds since midway through Fox's administration, when Calderón resigned as secretary of energy after the president publicly reprimanded him for campaigning while in office. Confronted with a likely López Obrador victory in the general election, however, Fox soon threw his support behind Calderón; for his part, Creel immediately endorsed Calderón after the primary. As a result, Calderón emerged at the head of a unified, energized PAN eager to retain the presidency—or, as some PAN leaders saw matters, to truly capture it for the first time.

Calderón began the general election campaign as a relative unknown. In October 2005, only 69 percent of Mexicans felt they knew enough about him to evaluate him on a zero-to-ten scale (compared to over 85% for the other two major-party candidates). Among those who did rate him, he scored a full point below López Obrador. Mexicans also viewed Calderón as less capable of managing the economy, less competent in fighting crime, less equipped to alleviate poverty, and even less honest than López Obrador. Only 4.4 percent of Mexicans recognized his original campaign slogan, "Courage and passion for Mexico."

Optimists in his campaign saw these figures as indicating room to grow. Critics suspected that Calderón would appear too bookish and inexperienced—he was 43 when elected president—to capitalize on the opportunity. As it turned out, the optimists were right; Calderón proved to be an effective campaigner who appealed to voters initially unfamiliar with him.

From the beginning, stylistic contrasts between Calderón and López Obrador were striking. Where López Obrador was disarming and affable, Calderón came across as a policy wonk. On a talk show where the presidential candidates were subjected to a pop quiz early in the campaign, Calderón got all the answers right (though slightly mispronouncing the name of Belize's capital); López Obrador refused to take the test, saying it would trivialize the broader message of his campaign. Where López Obrador broadcast empathy, Calderón projected a command of the issues.

Calderón's initial strategy emphasized his personal honesty in the so-called clean hands advertising campaign, in which Calderón and his supporters presented their well-scrubbed palms to viewers of PAN television spots. This approach seemed to make sense, given the PAN's reputation relative to that of the PRI and the PRD, as well as the fact that Calderón himself had never been involved in a corruption scandal. He soon overtook Madrazo but remained stuck behind López Obrador in the polls. In early March, two months into the official campaign period, he abruptly changed his strategy and began portraying himself as the "jobs candidate." By the end of the race, voters still considered López

Obrador better able to reduce poverty, but they saw Calderón as more competent at tackling both corruption and unemployment. (For his part, Madrazo was judged reasonably competent in terms of combating crime, the centerpiece of his campaign, but he consistently fared poorly in the public's eyes on every other dimension.)[7]

Figure 1.1 presents a rolling average of forty publicly available polls from the time Felipe Calderón won the PAN's nomination in late October until June 23, 2006, the last day that polls could be published.[8] As it shows, Madrazo's support declined steadily throughout the race, while Calderón's rose dramatically; López Obrador suffered only a very mild decline in absolute terms but gradually lost ground relative to Calderón until about two months before election day. Four key factors lay behind these trends: candidate image, campaign strategy, evaluations of the Fox administration, and elite divisions with the PRI.

Madrazo's Fade

Given Madrazo's personal liabilities, public attention to the candidates over the course of the campaign did not improve his prospects. Almost immediately after the primary season ended in October 2005, his support began to wane. By the beginning of the official campaign season in mid-January 2006, he was firmly in third place.Continuing fallout from the PRI's divisive primary and internal conflicts over the party's list of congressional candidates exacerbated Madrazo's already poor prospects. PANAL candidate Roberto Campa readily assumed the role of Gordillo's pit bull, attacking Madrazo repeatedly and indirectly lending his support to the PAN's nominee. For instance, during the first presidential debate on April 25, 2006, Campa accused Madrazo of not having paid his federal income tax. Later in the campaign, Campa encouraged his followers to cast their presidential ballots for Calderón and support PANAL only in the congressional races. Meanwhile, Madrazo staffers began to complain publicly that governors in five of the seventeen states controlled by the PRI were not doing enough to support their party's candidate.[9] (Langston provides a detailed account of PRI factionalism in chapter 8, as noted above.)

As he fell increasingly behind his two rivals, Madrazo attempted to change course. He moved away from criticizing his opponents and, in the second presidential debate on June 6, he deplored the increasingly nasty tenor of the campaign. He also attempted to present himself more clearly as a centrist alternative to the Left and Right in a context of political polarization. These tactics helped prevent further erosion of his support, which even ticked upwards in some polls

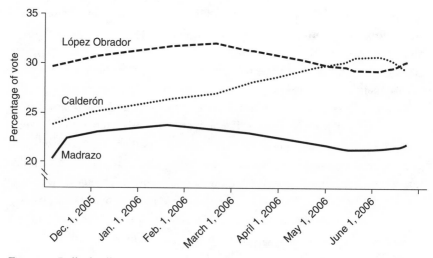

Figure 1.1 Poll of polls.

Note: Forty commercial surveys were included in the lowess regression (bandwidth = 0.5). In all instances, "undecideds," "minor candidates," and "non-responses" constitute the rest of the sample.

during the last month of the race. By that time, however, he was too far behind for a comeback.

As it became clear that Madrazo could not win, some prominent figures in the PRI openly began to shift their allegiance. In the Senate, Manuel Bartlett and Óscar Cantón announced their intention to vote for López Obrador, while TUCOM member Genaro Borrego sided with Calderón. Ten days before the election, in perhaps the cruelest blow of all, the leadership of the PRI-affiliated Revolutionary Confederation of Workers and Peasants (Confederación Revolucionaria de Obreros y Campesinos, or CROC) announced that it would urge its members to cast their ballots for López Obrador in order to prevent a Calderón victory. Finally, on election day itself, the PRI governor of the state of Tamaulipas was recorded talking on the telephone about how to turn out votes for the PAN's candidate. When the votes were counted, the party that had ruled Mexico for most of the twentieth century finished in third place in the legislative races (see table 1.1). Madrazo himself came in more than thirteen points behind his main rivals.

The Fox Inheritance

Calderón benefited from the fact that Mexico's economy, after stagnating during the first three years of the Fox administration, was finally performing well. In the first half of 2006, per capita gross domestic product grew faster than at any other point in Fox's term. On January 9, Mexico's Central Bank announced that the inflation rate for 2005 had been 3.33 percent—the lowest since 1969. Three weeks later, Standard and Poor's gave Mexico the country's lowest (i.e., best) risk rating ever: 114, down from 411 when Fox took office. As Alejandro Moreno shows in chapter 11, voters tended to sort themselves out into rival camps over the course of the campaign based on their evaluations of the president and the economy. Had the economy fared poorly, it would have been much more difficult for Calderón to convince voters that tossing out the PAN was a risky proposition.

General economic growth was accompanied by sharp increases in federal spending during the last year of the Fox administration, fueled largely by a rise in oil revenues. The Fox administration also continued to fund large-scale conditional cash transfers to very poor Mexicans (the Oportunidades program) and to expand health care coverage (with Seguro Popular). As Alberto Díaz-Cayeros, Federico Estévez, and Beatriz Magaloni argue in chapter 12, these programs helped shore up support for the incumbent party.

Although political norms forbade the president from stumping openly for his party's nominee, Fox made his preferences amply clear. At speeches around the country, the president repeatedly warned Mexicans of the dangers of "populism" and—as he put it at an April 18 appearance in Aguascalientes—called on them to "change the rider, not the horse." In case voters failed to connect the dots, the federal government launched an ad campaign trumpeting its achievements in office. On February 24, 2006, Mexico's Supreme Court issued a temporary injunction against such ads for the duration of the campaign. In the meantime, however, voters could readily make the connection between the outgoing president, his policies, and the PAN's nominee. In a country where presidents cannot run for re-election, Calderón clearly represented continuity.

The Negative Campaign

Calderón's unexpected change in strategy midway through the race was accompanied by a marked shift in the tone of his campaign. Beginning in March, the PAN unleashed a barrage of attack ads that portrayed López Obrador as a populist demagogue who would polarize and bankrupt the country. As one particularly controversial spot put it, he represented "a danger to Mexico." Another advertisement (entitled "Intolerance") compared López Obrador's campaign criticisms of Vicente Fox to comments made by Venezuela's leftist dictator, Hugo Chávez.[10] Still other advertisements called attention, albeit in highly exaggerated form, to uncomfortable aspects of López Obrador's record. For instance, after he was declared the loser in the 1994 Tabasco gubernatorial election, López Obrador had urged supporters to take over oil wells in that state; clips of these protests appeared in a PAN attack ad. A different spot showed footage from scandals two years before, in which episodes of corruption by senior Mexico City officials had been captured on videotape.[11]

The PAN and its allies struck particularly hard on the issue of macroeconomic management. One ad, "Bricks for the second story," featured the piece-by-piece construction of an edifice designed to remind viewers of the new elevated highway in Mexico City, considered a major achievement of López Obrador's tenure as mayor. The bricks bore the names of spending programs that López Obrador had proposed, and their combined weight brought the entire structure crashing down. Another ad, broadcast near the end of the race, featured a working-class family terrified about what would happen to their meager worldly possessions if López Obrador were elected. Meanwhile, private sector groups ran separate spots celebrating Mexico's recent macroeconomic stability, implicitly warning Mexicans about what they might lose.[12] Although not technically negative ads, they played to the same fears that the negative campaign attempted to elicit.

A sluggish and maladroit response by López Obrador's team contributed to the effectiveness of the negative campaign. Having enjoyed what they assumed to be an unassailable lead, they were taken off-guard by the ferocity and effectiveness of the PAN's attacks.[13] López Obrador's decision to sit out the first presidential debate on April 25 cost him an opportunity to respond directly.

Indeed, disparities in the caliber of the two campaigns were striking. As early as fall 2005, Calderón's team had prepared its response to anticipated attacks on Calderón for supporting a controversial bank bailout package;[14] the PRD did not even raise that issue in its advertisements until late spring. In contrast, López Obrador's team seemed unprepared to cope with assaults that were not difficult to anticipate. In early May, López Obrador publicly acknowledged that he had "made some mistakes" in the campaign.

The Left finally responded with an advertising blitz of its own, which included pointed attacks on Calderón and accusations of influence-peddling against his brother-in-law. López Obrador's passable performance in the second debate on June 6 also helped to reverse the damage caused by the negative campaign. (Although telephone surveys conducted by *Reforma* newspaper showed that most viewers felt Calderón had won the debate, an almost identical proportion of the sample had gone into the debate favoring the PAN.) As figure 1.1 shows, the last two months of the race saw Calderón and López Obrador jousting for the lead in public opinion polls.

As Francisco Flores-Macías explains in chapter 10, López Obrador's campaign faced certain structural weaknesses. His initial backers included a disproportionate number of independents, who presumably were more susceptible to campaign effects. Many were not natural supporters of a leftist candidate. For instance, one-third of López Obrador voters in October 2005 reported having voted for Fox in 2000; one-third gave the president high marks on his job performance; one-third thought Fox's administration had brought about "major changes" in the country; and about the same number felt the economy was performing well.

These structural weaknesses were not necessarily fatal; López Obrador enjoyed a substantial lead throughout most of the race. They became much more problematic, however, in the context of an intelligent change in strategy by Calderón and several missteps by the López Obrador campaign. The campaign ultimately left voters wondering whether López Obrador was the best candidate to bring about the sort of changes they desired—and to help them avoid the sort of economic crises that Mexico had suffered in the past. On election day, too few Mexicans were prepared to take a risk on López Obrador to push him over the top.

The 2006 Elections and Mexican Democracy

From the standpoint of democratic representation, the results of Mexico's 2006 election can be read in many ways. At the most abstract level, the contest represented a challenge for the country's constitutional order. The results of the election gave rise to tremendous controversy, stemming from allegations on the left that widespread irregularities had cost their candidate the election.[15] (Bruhn, in the penultimate section of chapter 9, places these allegations in their larger context.) As Camp points out in chapter 2, a wafer-thin victory of the PAN over the Left was one of the strongest tests of Mexico's new democratic institutions that history could have devised, and these institutions survived. Although the

Instituto Federal Electoral (IFE), or Federal Electoral Institute, an autonomous body in charge of administering elections, and the Federal Electoral Court lost some legitimacy as a result of the postelectoral controversy, especially in the eyes of PRD supporters, most Mexicans continued to hold them in high regard. Moreover, the controversy surrounding the IFE's management of the election ultimately led to further reform of the IFE and a change in its leadership. In this respect, the 2006 contest represented the continuation of Mexico's protracted process of democratization.

A second metric concerns the effect of the contest on Mexico's party system. The election confirmed a gradual secular decline in the PRI's support at the national level, a trend that dates back five decades. Among the 1,067 respondents who participated in the first and third waves of the Mexico 2006 Panel Study, identification with the PRI fell by 7 percentage points (from 28% to 21%); strength of identification among the remaining PRI partisans also declined. In addition, the campaign underscored the fact that senior PRI figures remain willing to jump ship if their party appears to be sinking, a fact which could lead to the party's unraveling at the national level.

Nevertheless, the election failed to provoke a full-fledged realignment. Of those who shed their PRI affiliation over the course of the campaign, only half took on a new one; the rest declined to identify with any party. In theory, these voters could be lured back into the fold. Indeed, recent trends confirm that the PRI remains a formidable force at the state level, with the party racking up win after win since July 2, 2006. Even if the PRI's national-level performance continues to decline at its historical rate, it will be able to claim at least 20 percent of the national vote for two more presidential cycles. Should it manage to field a strong candidate, it might even offer a serious challenge to the PAN and the PRD in the 2012 presidential race. As Camp (chapter 2) and Klesner (chapter 3) both make clear, Mexico's three-party system will not disappear anytime soon.

The 2006 election produced a modest sorting out along demographic lines, with wealthier, more educated, white Mexicans shifting toward Calderón while their poorer, darker-skinned compatriots increasingly inclined toward the Left's standard-bearer (Lawson 2006). In relative terms, however, this sorting out did not advantage either the PRD or the PAN; both gained adherents at roughly equal rates. In the third wave of the Mexico 2006 Panel Study, PAN partisans still outnumbered PRD partisans by approximately 8 percentage points (28 to 20) at the end of the race.

As these figures imply, the campaign did little to strengthen overall levels of partisan attachment. Of those respondents from the Mexico 2006 Panel Study who participated in both wave 1 and wave 3, the portion who expressed no attachment to any party fell less than 1 percentage point (from 31% to just over 30%). In other words, detachment from the PRI proceeded as fast as reattachment to the other parties. Moreover, most of those who did feel an attachment to a given party remained only weakly anchored to that party. By the end of the campaign, only one-quarter of the respondents considered themselves strong partisans—even fewer than at the beginning of the campaign (28%). Creeping realignment thus continues to leave a substantial chunk of the electorate available for persuasion in future elections.

These broad trends, however, obscure one absolutely crucial fact—the 2006 election had very different effects on the strength of each party as an institution. As both Langston (chapter 8) and Shirk (chapter 7) discuss, a divisive primary only exacerbated factionalism within the PRI. The PRD's "coronation" of López Obrador (to use Bruhn's term) also had negative repercussions for that party, which remains heavily factionalized; it now lacks either a unifying figure or a clear, established procedure for selecting its next presidential candidate. The PAN's situation could hardly be more different. Its primary demonstrated that the party's internal nominating procedures can (1) generate a fair and legitimate result, (2) mobilize the party faithful, and, perhaps most importantly, (3) produce an appealing presidential candidate. This fact gives the PAN a powerful organizational advantage over its rivals in the 2012 campaign.

To ensure representation, parties must exhibit some degree of reliability and consistency (Downs 1957). In other words, voters must be able to predict what they are going to do from their past actions and from their pledges about the future. As Kathleen Bruhn and Kenneth Greene discuss in chapter 6, leaders of Mexico's main parties do indeed hold strong, enduring views on key *positional issues* (D. Stokes 1963). There is a link between what they say in their platforms and what they try to accomplish in office. As Bruhn and Greene also make clear, however, these positions are often out of step with those of their own base, not to mention with those of the median voter. This fact, as they discuss in the introduction to their chapter, can impede democratic representation.

Moreover, voters did not seem to care, nor did the campaign lead them to do so. As Greene shows in chapter 13, candidates' positions on specific policy issues did not influence voter preferences. The 2006 election thus provided any policymakers who cared to listen with precious little guidance from the people on what they should do next with regard to trade, abortion, the role of the state in the economy, or other salient policy issues—and little sense that they would be held accountable for how they addressed those issues. In other words, reliability, consistency, and stability in the party system were insufficient to ensure policy-oriented voting.

A somewhat different way to approach this question is to ask whether the parties acted *as though* voters cared about policy issues. Although the evidence remains only suggestive, the chapters in this volume by Bruhn and Shirk indicate that the campaign itself did tend to push the candidates toward the middle of the political spectrum. López Obrador, for instance, was decidedly more moderate than his party. He did not argue for repudiating the North American Free Trade Agreement (NAFTA), as many in the PRD might have been inclined to do; rather, he limited himself to opposing the scheduled phasing out of tariffs for corn and beans. Calderón also ran a centrist campaign, studiously avoiding cultural issues in which the PAN's views were often out of step with those of the electorate. In addition, neither Calderón nor the PAN (in its party platform) came out in favor of privatization of the electricity sector, much less of the politically touchy oil-and-gas sector, despite private sympathy for the idea. Even if the campaign produced little in the way of issue voting, then, it did appear to constrain politicians from adopting positions that were wildly at variance with prevailing public opinion on key issues.

How might we reconcile such circumspection by candidates and parties with what we know of the Mexican electorate? One possibility is that politically controversial stances generate elite criticism of the candidates who adopt them, and this criticism in turn changes ordinary voters' perceptions of how competent the candidates are. For instance, a Mexican candidate who proposed abrogating NAFTA might be attacked by a range of neutral experts, leaving voters to wonder whether the candidate really had a good plan for generating economic growth. Bruhn's discussion of Luiz Inácio Lula da Silva's 2002 presidential campaign in Brazil, in which criticism of his competence in managing the economy frightened some voters, suggests the plausibility of such an argument.

Another way to reconcile these findings is that, even if voters are largely ignorant about candidates' policy positions, they may cobble together enough bits of information to form some vague summary judgment about what the parties stand for. Such an overarching assessment can then serve as a basis for vote choice. This is precisely the argument James McCann advances in chapter 14, in which he shows that voters draw on evaluations of prominent individuals who personify particular ideologies when deciding which party to support. In other words, policy-relevant considerations do influence Mexican voters, even if they know little about candidates' stances on specific issues. McCann further argues that the campaign sorted voters out along this ideological dimension, just as it did along demographic lines. If so, a policy-relevant message was buried in the signals that voters sent on July 2, 2006.

Whether or not the campaign provided any meaningful guidance to future leaders on positional issues, did it at least send a signal about *valence issues* (D. Stokes 1963)? Moreno's analysis (chapter 11) indicates that those unhappy with the country's economic performance migrated toward López Obrador in the course of the race, while those who felt satisfied moved toward Calderón. In the Mexico 2006 Panel Study, a preponderance of respondents consistently felt that the economy had gotten better rather than worse during Fox's tenure (44% to 10%), as well as that their own financial situation had improved (31% to 11%). A narrow victory for the incumbent party could thus be interpreted as an indication of public desire for continuity over (potentially radical) shifts in policy.

Moreno's analysis implies that voters reacted to assessments of national economic performance—a classic economic voting model. Díaz-Cayeros and his coauthors, by contrast, argue in chapter 12 that vote choice was primarily a product of pocketbook considerations, including the receipt of federal welfare payments and programs. These two perspectives, of course, have different implications for the signals that voters sent. The first indicates at least a primitive mandate for leaders on economic policy (continuity or change), based on sociotropic judgments. The second leaves open the possibility that citizens base their decisions on the distribution of government benefits. If so, savvy politicians should focus less energy on trumpeting their successes in economic management and more on claiming credit for specific spending programs.

One final metric for judging the campaign is whether it engaged ordinary voters. Did Mexicans pay attention to the race and, if so, did they learn anything useful from it? Here, as with the policy mandate, the evidence is mixed. Among respondents from the Mexico 2006 Panel Study who participated in both the first and third waves, campaign attention (on a scale from 0 to 3) increased from 1.13 in October 2005 to 1.46 shortly after election day in July.[16] A similar index of political interest increased by even less, from 1.21 to 1.41. At no time did more than one-sixth of the electorate express a lot of interest in either the campaign or in politics, and more than half of the respondents expressed little or no interest in these topics at the end of the race. As Camp makes clear in the following chapter, the campaign did stimulate public interest, but not nearly enough to overcome long-standing detachment from the political system.

There is some evidence that voters learned about candidates' proposals. At the end of the campaign, for instance, 63 percent of the respondents from the second and third waves of the Mexico 2006 Panel Study knew that López Obrador was the candidate who favored a pension scheme for adults over 70 years of age (up from 57% in early May 2006). Thirty-seven percent also correctly guessed that Calderón was the candidate who favored expanding the number of daycare centers for working mothers (against 16% who saw the proposal as Madrazo's and 9% who believed it was López Obrador's). In addition, voters came to perceive some differences in the candidates' positions on trade policy; by the end of the race, 57 percent felt that Calderón wanted to expand commercial ties with the United States, whereas only 27 percent felt López Obrador wanted to do so.[17] These figures represented an improvement from October 2005, when voters perceived almost no difference between the candidates. But given the vast amount of information showered on voters over the course of the campaign, as well as the prominence of trade policy in public discourse, such learning is hardly spectacular. Moreover, there remained salient issues on which the public's ignorance knew virtually no bounds. In early May 2006, for instance, only 15 percent of the respondents knew that López Obrador favored ending all imports of natural gas within three years, a key component of his proposal for managing the energy sector.[18]

What voters learned most, it appears, was information gleaned from campaign propaganda, much of which focused on the candidates. In October 2005, more than three-quarters of those who participated in the first and second waves of the Mexico 2006 Panel Study could not match any of the candidates with their principal campaign slogans. By May 2006, more than half could match at least one. (Recognition of campaign slogans were not asked in the third wave of the panel.) Likewise, in October 2005, more than one-third of the respondents who participated in both the first and third panel waves felt unable to rate at least one of the three candidates on an eleven-point scale; by the end of the campaign, only 8 percent could not rate all three. Evaluations of candidate traits (e.g., honesty) show similar changes. Moreover, judgments of the candidates tightened up over time. As one indicator, the simple correlation between feeling thermometer ratings of López Obrador between October 2005 and May 2006 was .55, but the correlation between ratings of him in May 2006 and July 2006 was .69.[19] If the campaign did one job, then, it was to help voters formulate general judgments about the candidates themselves.

To summarize, in terms of its place in Mexico's democratization, the 2006 election receives mixed reviews. It produced substantial controversy and little in the way of a policy mandate. The information conveyed in the course of the campaign—by politicians to prospective voters during the race and by the voters to their prospective leaders on election day—was sometimes of dubious quality. Messages from the candidates, including intensely negative messages, concentrated heavily on candidate image; voters considered many factors, including general impressions of where parties stood in ideological terms, but candidate traits and retrospective economic evaluations loomed largest in their decision making. The portion of the electorate that felt disconnected from political parties did not diminish, and political engagement in some segments of the population continued to coexist with large swaths of apathy. At the end of the day, however, the election performed its most basic function—it permitted citizens to form impressions about the main candidates and to act on those impressions.

The 2006 Election in Comparative Perspective

As noted above, the chapters in this volume do far more than shed light on elections in one country. They also aim to make a theoretical contribution to the comparative study of campaigns and voting behavior. We focus here on six broad findings.

First, Mexico's 2006 election calls attention to the potential magnitude of campaign effects. As in the presidential race six years before (Domínguez and Lawson 2004), many Mexican voters were open to persuasion in 2006. They changed their minds in large numbers, and these shifts in opinion altered the outcome of the race.

A second conclusion concerns the nature of these changes. At first glance, they might resemble a classic reinforcement model of campaigns derived from studies of the United States (Finkel 1993). As various contributors to this volume point out, more Mexicans identified with the PAN than with the PRD. The campaign could simply have been a matter of errant PAN voters returning to the fold. Closer inspection, however, reveals the weaknesses of this argument. Mexico's largest party, the PRI, did not reinforce its base; rather, it hemorrhaged support. In addition, Calderón's success over López Obrador did not come merely from evoking longstanding partisan sympathies among those segments of the electorate that traditionally identified with the PAN. He won by persuading independents, undecideds, and PRI defectors that he was a better man for the job.

McCann's analysis suggests that some voters did "come home" to the parties that shared their ideological worldviews; Moreno suggests that the same dynamic occurred with regard to economic evaluations; and other research indicates the same for certain demographic variables (Lawson 2006). In this sense, the campaign helped to activate underlying values, dispositions, and beliefs— that is, to sort voters into the correct camps. However, the number of ideological "leftists" and "rightists" in McCann's analysis also changed over the course of the race; so did voters' impressions of the candidates. For instance, average feeling thermometer ratings of Calderón on a scale of zero to ten rose by a full point during the race; those of López Obrador fell by a similar amount. As a result, there was still substantial room for old-fashioned persuasion over the course of the campaign.

One comparative indicator of susceptibility to campaign effects is the stability of partisan identification. In the United States, which has been the topic of most research on voting behavior, the stability of partisanship ranges from .90 to 1.0 over a period of several years once measurement error is taken into account (D. Green et al. 2002). Although partisan identification remains a reasonably stable attitude in countries like Mexico, Brazil, or Russia, it is less substantially stable than in the United States (Ames et al. 2006; McCann and Lawson 2003). As a result, campaigns in other nations should have a greater potential to persuade large numbers of voters (Domínguez and Lawson 2004). Again, we view this lesson as applicable to most new democracies, from Peru to Romania to Indonesia.

A third lesson concerns the way in which persuasion occurs. In the United States, arguments about persuasion have often relied on the notion of cross-pressures. The original studies of American elections (Berelson et al.1954; Katz and Lazarsfeld 1955; Lazarsfeld et al. 1944) conceived of cross-pressures in terms of social networks and, by extension, demographic characteristics. Thus a black physician in the United States would be more likely to switch from a Democratic candidate to a Republican one (and vice versa) than either a poor African-American (reliable Democrat) or a wealthy white doctor (reliable Republican). Exported to, say, El Salvador, this model implies that a working-class voter who was also a practicing Catholic would likely be "cross-pressured"; her friends from church might encourage her to vote for the Nationalist Republican Alliance (ARENA), while her coworkers at the textile factory might encourage her to vote for the Farabundo Martí National Liberation Front (FMLN).

More recent models have interpreted cross-pressures in terms of positional issues (Hillygus and Shields, forthcoming). In this view, Americans who held conservative views on fiscal issues but liberal views on cultural issues would be more persuadable than voters who held progressive (or conservative) positions on both dimensions. So, too, would Italian voters who both opposed immigration (a rightist position) and favored economic redistribution (a leftist position).

Chapters by both Klesner and Flores-Macías suggest only limited evidence that ideologically cross-pressured voters were more susceptible to persuasion. And as Greene's chapter makes clear, there is nothing to indicate that Mexican voters were influenced by the sort of wedge issues that Hillygus and Shields identify in the United States.

Nevertheless, large numbers of voters *were* cross-pressured in a way that had real consequences for the election. First, as Baker suggests in chapter 4, interpersonal communication exposed supporters of weaker parties to cross-pressures in some regions. Second, economic trends late in Fox's term divided López Obrador's base. A substantial chunk of the electorate began the campaign with a positive image of López Obrador, even though they believed the incumbent administration was doing a good job. In other words, they were cross-pressured on valence issues (that is, candidate traits versus economic performance). It was into this fissure that Calderón's campaign drove a powerful wedge. Calderón did not win over voters based on *how* he would tackle the country's economic problems; he won them over by convincing them that he was more competent in managing the economy than his leftist rival, offering as one piece of evidence the current state of the economy (see chapter 13).

Attitude change in the campaign thus occurred in two principal ways. First, the campaign sorted people out according to their underlying dispositions and evaluations of the incumbent administration—in particular, its economic stewardship. Second, the campaign altered voters' impressions of the personal qualities of the main candidates—especially their competence in managing the economy. Together, these two dynamics gave Calderón his come-from-behind victory.

Again, we suspect that large-scale persuasion during election campaigns is a common occurrence outside of the developed world, and that candidate image typically plays a more important role in altering voters' preferences than does ideology or issues. To take one example, Brazilian voters in the 1990s may have viewed Lula as more empathetic but seen Fernando Henrique Cardoso as more competent to manage the economy. Persuasion in favor of Cardoso would thus occur if voters who might initially have been sympathetic to Lula as a person became convinced of Cardoso's skill in generating growth and controlling inflation, with ideological and policy considerations being far less important in voters' judgments. As another example, our aforementioned Italian voter, instead of being persuadable through cross-pressuring on positional issues (immigration and redistribution), might be swayed through cross-pressuring on valence issues. For instance, he might wish to vote for the Right because of its track record in generating growth but casts his ballot for the Left because of its relatively greater success at combating corruption.

A fourth lesson from Mexico's 2006 election concerns the effectiveness of negative campaigning. Calderón's negative campaign worked reasonably well, while López Obrador's (belated) attacks on Calderón ultimately failed. As Jorge Domínguez notes in chapter 15, the opposite occurred in Mexico's 2000 presidential contest, when Fox's attacks on the incumbent party resonated, while Labastida had little to show from his criticisms of Fox.

When an incumbent administration has done very well, attacks on its performance are unlikely to prove effective; voters can simply judge the record for themselves. The representative of the incumbent party will likewise not need to "go negative"; he can simply campaign on his accomplishments. Conversely, a smart challenger will be likely to go on the attack when the incumbent's performance has been poor. All of these predictions about negative campaigning seem straightforward.

Less obvious is what should happen when the incumbent's performance on economic issues is mediocre or mixed. To the extent that voters are risk averse, they may be reluctant to cast their ballots for a challenger even if the incumbent is doing only a passable job; the more risk averse they are, the more reluctant they will be to abandon the devil they know.[20] Given that Mexican voters have experienced repeated economic crises since the late 1970s, they are likely to be deeply risk averse. In such circumstances, it is not surprising that a well-crafted negative campaign against the challenger would prove effective.

Consequently, we should expect incumbents to launch negative campaigns against challengers on economic issues when their own record is neither stellar nor disastrous and anticipate that challengers would engage in negative campaigning whenever the incumbent's performance has been poor. Under other circumstances, negative campaigning should be rare or, if it occurs, ineffectual. Thus, to take three examples in 2008, there was little negative campaigning on economic issues in presidential campaigns in Russia or the Dominican Republic (strong economic performance) but quite a bit in Taiwan's race that year (sluggish economic growth).

A fifth conclusion concerns the techniques and tactics of persuasion that the candidates employed. The chapters in this volume go a long way toward explaining attitude change in the electorate after the fact. Nevertheless, *predicting* which campaign messages in any given election will prove most effective can be a difficult task. Candidates do not always know in advance which strategies will work and which ones will flop. Even if they do, they must often change their strategy in response to those of their opponents. They must also react to events they cannot necessarily anticipate ahead of time (including gaffes), the potential impact of which is magnified by voters' higher levels of attention to politics during a campaign.

As the chapters in part II make clear, all three main candidates experimented with different strategies over the course of the race in an effort to enhance their support. Calderón abandoned the issues on which he had concentrated during the first half of the campaign, fired his original team, and refocused his message on economic concerns. The result was a ten-point rise in the polls. Eventually, López Obrador also changed course and, in so doing, reversed his decline. Around the same time, Madrazo committed himself to a more positive strategy that portrayed him as a moderate, pragmatic figure in an increasingly grubby, divisive race—with similar results. All three contenders learned more about what was effective and what was not over the course of the campaign. The strategies they adopted, and the speed with which they did so, seems to have affected their standing in the polls.

One implication is that the quality and perspicacity of campaign staffs make a difference. If campaign teams are equally competent, their impact will be invisible; measures and counter-measures will cancel each other out. Significant disparities in talent or adaptability, however, may well affect the outcome of a contest in which significant numbers of voters are cross-pressured.

So far, political scientists have generally declined to grapple with this reality, being content to either assume away any differences or to relegate their effects to the residual term of their statistical models. This approach may be plausible in a U.S. presidential election, where swarms of talented operatives buzz around the major-party candidates. Ignoring the potential impact of campaign strategy seems less reasonable in contexts where markets for consulting talent are less developed, where candidates are still familiarizing themselves with certain aspects of electoral competition, and where "professional" operatives continue to grapple with how to best exploit campaign technologies. The right approach for political scientists, therefore, would be to assume, based on existing cases studies of particular contests, that a variable like "campaign team quality" might influence electoral outcomes. Scholars could then set about devising measures of this variable that could be used to predict the outcome of future races.

A final conclusion concerns fidelity of representation—specifically, the degree to which electoral competition encourages parties and candidates to adopt the public policies favored by average voters. For five decades, the notion that parties will converge toward the center of the ideological spectrum has been a staple of electoral theory (see Downs 1957). Exactly how this process actually takes place, however, has received much less attention. The chapters in this volume both document that movement and reveal why it is likely to be incomplete.

One crucial influence on candidates' positions is the way they are chosen. The PAN's primary led it to choose a candidate who was more of a true believer than the original front-runner; presumably, this result would be similar for most primaries that are restricted to party members. By contrast, an unconstrained candidate chosen by acclamation (López Obrador) was able to adopt far more moderate positions than many in his party would have wanted. Candidate selection processes thus influenced the degree to which convergence occurred.

Another factor that works against convergence is the absence of ideological voting. If voters have only vague or changeable views on specific policy issues, even purely election-seeking parties will feel little pressure to adopt the positions of the median voter. The debate over the true extent of ideological reasoning in the mass public is alive and well, as McCann's chapter indicates; however, in Mexico's 2006 presidential election, ideological dispositions were at best only one of many ingredients in vote choice. In such a context, parties may feel obliged to avoid particularly unpopular positions, but they will still enjoy substantial room to maneuver on many issues.

Yet another limiting factor concerns the influence of valence issues (including candidates' personal traits and abilities). To the extent that voters focus on picking the right person for the job, they are far less likely to focus on ideological issues. Rather, they will concentrate on factors such as incumbent performance and perceptions of candidates' competence.

In short, we propose a model of campaigns and elections that emphasizes (1) substantial effects, whose direction depends in part on the caliber of campaign staff; (2) persuasion through cross-pressuring on valence issues, including economic performance and candidate traits; and (3) modest convergence *toward* the center but rarely *to* the center on key policy issues. This model may not be normatively attractive, but we suspect that it is applicable to a range of democracies around the world.

Part I / Cleavage Structures in a New Democracy

CHAPTER TWO

Democracy Redux?

Mexico's Voters and the 2006 Presidential Race

Roderic Ai Camp

In July 2000, Mexico elected Vicente Fox as president, taking its largest step to date in the process of a democratic transformation. Because its constitution prohibits executive re-election, all of the leading parties offered new candidates for the July 2006 elections. It is impossible to predict the outcome of any presidential race far in advance of the actual event,[1] but scholars have accumulated considerable information about Mexican voters and their behavior since 2000, and these data offer fascinating insights into why they behaved the way they did in the 2006 election.

That contest is essential for understanding Mexican politics today. The closeness of the outcome, which pushed Mexico's reformed electoral system to its limits, was the ultimate test of the rule of law and the level of maturity of Mexico's democratic structure. After more than five years of transformation and consolidation, has its institutional performance altered voter attitudes and preferences? Moreover, how has it changed their preferences for democracy itself?

The Mexican Electorate up to 2006

What are some notable characteristics of Mexican voters that might explain their political behavior since democratization? Most significantly, Mexicans generally are uninterested in politics. Even the 2000 presidential race, which provided an opportunity to fundamentally change the country's political model, did not engage them; average levels of interest in politics did not increase significantly either before or after the race. The implications are astonishing, as the 2000 election resulted in an alteration in party control over the executive branch and confirmed a basic test of functional, electoral democracy.

Citizen interest in politics is linked to broader democratic participation. In the 2003 midterm elections, abstention reached 58 percent, the highest since 1946. Two-thirds of those Mexicans who declined to cast ballots—that is, nearly half of the electorate—expressed dissatisfaction with their political system: with the way democracy works, with the parties, and with Congress (Albo 2003). That pattern did not change as the 2006 presidential race heated up. Indeed, as of October 2005, 66 percent of voters expressed little or no interest in politics.[2] Furthermore, an equal number responded with the same lack of enthusiasm for the presidential campaign. By February, well into the race, 54 percent indicated little or no interest in the campaign, and nearly two-thirds rarely or never discussed the candidates.[3] Similarly, after the election, in spite of the major controversy about the outcome, 54 percent were disinterested in politics and 51 percent in the presidential campaign.

This lack of involvement in politics deeply affects the influence that various actors, including political parties, can exercise over Mexican voters (see McCann and Lawson 2006).[4] More than half of all voters rarely or never talked about politics,[5] and this group tended to support the Institutional Revolutionary Party (PRI) rather than the National Action Party (PAN)—by 44 percent to 27 percent.[6] Better-informed voters and those who discuss political matters every day are much more likely to vote for the PAN than for the once-dominant PRI, by a sizeable margin (45% to 33%). It is clear that these two parties largely appeal to two different sets of voters, based on their level of political engagement.

A second feature of Mexican political attitudes that affect democracy is the level of disenchantment they evince toward political parties. Typically, only one out of five citizens expresses confidence in the parties, a lower level than in any other political institution in Mexico, including Congress and the courts.[7] Perhaps this is why parties, in spite of increased electoral competition, demonstrate little ability "to attract citizens to the polls" (Reyes 2004, 22). Voter dissatisfaction may be partly explained by the fact that increased party competition at the local level has not increased government responsiveness, in contrast to conclusions drawn from American politics (Cleary 2007).

Mexicans' disgruntlement with parties is a reflection, in part, of a third important quality, their disillusionment with politics. Politics is a dirty business. Of all the political institutions, only the Federal Electoral Institute (IFE) and the National Commission on Human Rights persistently attract a high level of confidence among Mexican citizens.[8] Politicians from both the PAN and the leftist Party of the Democratic Revolution (PRD) similarly give the IFE high marks.[9]

A fourth aspect of Mexican political attitudes that potentially influence how well democracy works is that Mexicans are widely divided in terms of ideological preferences. They place themselves on a centrist spectrum (33%), with large components on the left (21%) and right (19%).[10] At least until recently, Mexicans have believed that the PRI is the party of the far right; the PAN, center right; and the PRD, center left (for further discussion of ideology at the mass level, see chapters 6 and 14 in this volume.) In the 2003 election, the PRI and the PAN tied for support among centrist voters, but the PRI won handily among those on the right and the PRD among self-declared leftists.[11] The extent to which ideology exercises an influence on the appeal of certain candidates depends on how citizens see the candidates' ideological predilections in relation to their policies, the degree to which they actually understand those stated positions, and the legitimacy of various actors in conveying political preferences.[12] Current research suggests that potential voters do not always accurately identify certain public policies with the Left or Right.[13]

A fifth, and more recent, feature of most Mexican voters' views is that roughly 80 percent of them are disillusioned with their democratic system.[14] Except for South Asia and the advanced democracies, global satisfaction with democracy is generally low, and within this group, Mexican views remain comparatively toward the bottom end (Moreno and Méndez 2002). Even more significantly, 54 percent of the voters who cast their ballots for Fox in 2000 are now dissatisfied with democracy; in fact, substantial disagreement persists as to whether or not Mexico actually is one.[15] In October 2005, nearly 30 percent of Mexicans believed that it was not, and 11 percent were unsure; in May of 2006, 28 percent of Mexicans continued to believe Mexico was not a democracy. The only time this view has changed significantly since 2000 was on July 2, 2006, the day Mexicans voted. Then, a whopping 71 percent believed Mexico was a democracy (versus 21% not), the highest level ever recorded, but their opinions dropped again to 63 percent after the results for their candidates became public.[16]

Mexican attitudes toward democracy remained crucial to the 2006 electoral outcome because change, defined as an alteration in power in the executive branch, was the decisive factor in Fox's 2000 presidential victory.[17] This alteration in power is an essential component in defining democracy, so if democracy and change are linked in the mind of voters, this fact may affect voter turnout, as well as their candidate and party preferences.

The Mexico 2006 Panel Study suggests some significant patterns related to voters' concepts of Mexican democracy. For example, those Mexicans who believed Mexico was democratic were strong supporters of the PAN, and those who did not share this view were equally strong proponents of the PRD. Seventy percent of the voters who favored PAN candidate Felipe Calderón in October 2005 thought Mexico was a democracy, compared to only 54 percent of those supporting his leftist rival, Andrés Manuel López Obrador. This distribution is similar to the PRI/PAN gap in 2000, where those who were convinced Mexico already was democratic supported the PRI and those who did not favored the PAN. Thus, in the eyes of those voters who did not believe democracy existed in their country, the PAN replaced the PRI in 2000 as their party of choice, and the PRD supplanted the PAN in 2006.

An important explanation for this division among supporters of the two leading candidates, Calderón and López Obrador, can potentially be linked to their perceptions of democracy. Unlike Costa Ricans or Americans, Mexicans are divided on what democracy means. The two most common conceptualizations are that democracy means liberty and that it stands for social and economic equality. Thus, in addition to viewing their candidate as outside a political system which is preventing him from obtaining victory, it is likely that partisans of López Obrador would also see democracy as creating socioeconomic improvement and would expect this from it (Camp 2003).

A sixth general attitude influencing voter behavior in the 2006 presidential race was that Congress attracts little interest. Most voters do not know their legislative representatives. Mexico's constitutional prohibition on re-election also impedes accountability; if this barrier were removed, it would presumably increase voter interest in Congress and thus strengthen democratic institutions. The other structural variable that plays a role in decreasing support for Congress is that 40 percent of the members of the Chamber of Deputies represent no district and 25 percent of the senators do not represent a state, further limiting the linkage between citizens and their representatives.

The 2006 congressional pattern largely repeated that of 2000.[18] Mexico has evolved into a three-party system, but independents remain the largest group of voters; they included 44 percent of all voters as of April 2006 and still constituted 36 percent of the electorate immediately before the election. In contrast, the PRI boasted 23 percent partisan support, the PAN 21 percent, and the PRD only 17 percent.[19] Thus, assuming a party could actually retain the loyalty of all its supporters, it would still have to attract most of the independent voters to obtain a simple majority in Congress.

Seventh, voters are most interested in what is going on in their back yard, where, in terms of democratic consolidation, the real political action is taking place. For example, in the 2003 federal elections, when state governorships were being contested, 54 percent of the voters turned out, and where races for local deputies or city councils were taking place, 49 percent participated. Only in those elections where the challenges were for congressional districts alone was the turnout—at 38%—alarmingly low (Albo 2003). This pattern was repeated in 2006, with turnout rates as high as 68 percent in some states with contemporaneous elections.

The importance of local politics is significantly decreasing the potential influence of some traditional political groups while defining the political base of the parties more clearly and consistently. Even more importantly, recent scholarship in many countries has shown that state and local settings produce significant variations in voter participation and in support for democratic models (Hiskey and Bowler 2005). What is apparent from examining election data from 1991 through 2003 is the slow decline of the PRI and the rise of the PAN, as well as the fact that all three parties are converging toward roughly equal levels of support among the electorate. In spite of this overall trend, the PRI continues to demonstrate its ability to maintain a stronger presence at the local level than the PAN or the PRD, and it is this presence that served as a foundation for its national ambitions in 2006. The PRI controlled over half of all governorships in Mexico. Its electoral performance in defeating the PAN in 2004 in the northern state of Chihuahua (a traditional PAN stronghold and the origin of the democratization movement in the 1980s) showed that strong candidates with local roots are more important than party labels. If one thinks of growing local electoral competition—and the alteration in power in state governments—as a healthy indicator of robust federalism, then these patterns can be viewed as contributors to grassroots democratic consolidation.

The caliber of local leadership also has an important effect on the presidential race, as revealed in data from the March 2006 Consulta Mitofsky poll, which breaks down candidate preferences according to the governorships controlled by the parties (see table 2.2). The distribution of voter preferences, measured by this variable, was more exaggerated than with any other demographic factor at this stage of the campaign. The PRI appeared to have reclaimed the North from the PAN through good governance, with 51 percent of the voters in those seven PRI-controlled states preferring Madrazo. Similarly, the nine states controlled by the PAN and the five states controlled by the PRD favored Calderón and Ló-pez Obrador by 53 and 60 percent, respectively. In the actual balloting in July, Calderón received 36 percent of the vote nationally, but he actually polled 53 percent in the nine PAN-controlled states, and in seven of them he received the most votes of any candidate. López Obrador won all five of the PRD-controlled states with 46 percent of the vote, compared to 35 percent nationally. Interestingly, however, in an election this close, López Obrador lost a sizable percentage of his original support from these PRD states, which benefited both Calderón and Madrazo. Equally enlightening, support in the ten PRI-controlled states in the Center-South of Mexico, although more evenly distributed among the three candidates, consistently favored López Obrador and Calderón over Madrazo, and that same distribution was maintained throughout the campaign.

Some of these preferences by state changed dramatically only weeks before voters went to the polls, when it became apparent that Madrazo had no chance to win the election. Thus Calderón became the primary beneficiary of the shift in support away from Madrazo, declining from an initial 51 percent to 35 and then to only 27 percent after the election, in the PRI-controlled northern states. Calderón simultaneously increased his support in those same states from 26 to 42 to 49 percent from March to June to July 2—a dramatic and electorally pivotal increase.

In the last five years, results from state and federal elections demonstrate several additional consistent patterns linked to Mexican voter attitudes and behavior. Perhaps the clearest trend revealed during this period is that little long-term party loyalty exists among voters in Mexico. Voters want practical results, and especially since 2000, they have shown that they will repudiate any party that does not deliver what they seek from government. Local elections are highly competitive, and vote totals tend to be close. The party winning these local elections typically does so with approximately 44 percent of the vote. Since parties are winning with pluralities, it makes it easier each time for the incumbent to lose, and voters have consistently demonstrated loyalty to outcomes and performance rather than to parties. From 1988 through 2002, incumbent parties holding mayoralty posts wielded a tremendous advantage over their opponents, winning 90 percent of the elections in 1988. By 2003, this figure declined to 48 percent (Varela 2004b).

At the state level, it is the PAN, not the PRI, that has shown the largest increase in votes since 1991. The results in local legislatures during this period show that the PAN won 139 seats, compared to 138 for the PRI. Again, no party holds the majority of these seats, mirroring the distribution in Congress nationally (Albo 2003).[20] The congressional results in 2006, noted above, followed this same pattern. Interestingly, this three-party division can be found in Korea and Taiwan, which also recently evolved from a dominant one-party system to consolidating democracies (Solinger 2001). Earlier in the Mexican campaign, those who expressed a particular intent indicated that they would cast their votes for PAN, PRI, and PRD deputies at the rate of 27, 28, and 20 percent, respectively. As the campaign progressed, potential voters divided their support evenly at 32 percent for each party in February 2006, a preference which remained essentially the same through June.[21]

As these facts suggest, party loyalty remains fluid. In 2005, 42 percent of the PAN, PRD, and PRI partisans became supporters only since 2000. Just slightly more than a third of all voters have been party loyalists since the 1994 presidential election. The party that has held on to its adherents from the 2000 presidential election most strongly was the PRD, with 91 percent of them continuing to support its candidate going into the election six years later. In contrast, the PRI retained only 69 percent of its voters, and the PAN merely 56 percent.[22]

As Joy Langston (chapter 8 in this volume) and others discuss, the most dramatic change in party identity during the 2006 campaign was the decline in PRI loyalists. Essentially, the number of PAN and PRD supporters remained static through June (with 17%–21% and 13%–17%, respectively), but the PRI, which always sustained the largest group of partisan voters, declined from 27 percent to 21–23 percent. This pattern raised the crucial question as to which party, the PRD or the PAN, would be the beneficiary of these former PRI partisans.[23] The results of the July 2 election demonstrated that the PRI candidate, who obtained 22 percent of the vote, received 74 percent of his votes from the party's supporters; the remaining PRI partisans split down the middle for the PAN and the PRD. Both Calderón and López Obrador were able to retain 89 and 93 percent of their party's partisan voters in the polling stations. However, in spite of the significant increase in support for the PRD and the PAN in Congress in 2006, these data, obtained both before and after the election, are not suggestive of any party dominating the electorate in the foreseeable future.

Images, Capabilities, and Expectations in the 2006 Campaign

As is often the case in the United States, Mexico's 2006 presidential election appears to have been about the economy and the personal economic situation of voters. When asked what mandate they would give to a new president, a whopping 36 percent said fighting poverty and improving economic conditions. Of all the individual issues mentioned in 2006, voters considered poverty to be the most urgent. Yet despite López Obrador's heavy concentration on this single issue, after six months of campaigning voters did not consider it any more important than before (see table 2.1). The only other topic receiving significant interest, as it has in the last two presidential races, was public safety. Crime remained the single most important issue in both the 2000 and 2006 races. In fact, among residents of the Federal District, an incredible 42 percent considered it the most important problem facing the country.[24] As Kenneth Greene postulates in chapter 13 in this volume, despite strongly opposing positions between the two leading candidates, voters typically were drawn to candidate competence, not their policy positions.

As Jorge Domínguez (2004) has argued, several variables appear to contribute to altering voter preferences for their candidates by the time an election occurs. Of these, I believe four played a role in 2006. First, voter perceptions of presidential candidates have an impact. Fox, for example, was seen as the candidate of change, which significantly determined the outcome in 2000. In 2006, López Obrador was considered to be the candidate of change, but in an entirely different way, and that drew large numbers of voters in support of his candidacy. Second, issues shape the behavior of voters. In the 2000 presidential election, the desire for change affected the outcome even though that issue was not perceived as important early on in the campaign. The desire for change, and especially the extent of that change, polarized the electorate in 2006, evenly dividing those voters between the two leading candidates representing the incumbent party (the PAN) and the challenger (the PRD). Third, judgments about the economy's future also shape voter behavior. This is traditionally an important issue, but it did not exert a significant impact in 2000 or 2003. In 2006 it became a major determinant of voter preferences, linked not only to personal economic expectations but to how voters perceived the incumbent administration's economic policies. Fourth, major public events can modify voter preferences. In 2000, there is no question that the televised presidential debates

Table 2.1   Voter attitudes toward presidential candidates and campaign issues
(in percentages)

1994 (1 mo. prior)		2000 (4 mos. prior)		2006 (8 mos. & 2 mos. prior)		
Campaign issues						
What is the most important problem facing the country today?						
Unemployment	24	Public safety	21	Public safety	29	34
Economy	16	Economy	19	Unemployment	13	17
Poverty	15	Poverty	12	Poverty	12	10
Public Safety	9	Unemployment	9	Economy	11	10
Corruption	8	Corruption	8	Corruption	7	6
Presidential candidates						
How would you rate the candidates on their honesty? (very/somewhat)						
Zedillo	39	Labastida	40	López Obrador	48	40
Fernández	19	Fox	39	Calderón	35	49
Who is the most capable of governing?						
Zedillo	50	Labastida	48[a] 46[b]	López Obrador	52[a] 44[a] 47[b] 41[b]	
Fernández	23	Fox	45[a] 44[b]	Calderón	41[a] 57[a] 35[b] 48[b]	

Sources: 1994 data are from Belden and Russonello, "Mexico 1994, summary of a survey of electoral preferences in Mexico" (unpublished ms, 1994), from a national random sample of 1,526 respondents, July 23–August 10, 1994. The 2000 data are taken from the Mexico 2000 Panel Survey, first wave. The 2006 data are taken from the Mexico 2006 Panel Survey, national sample, first and second waves.

[a]economy
[b]crime

significantly helped shift voter interest to Fox, who was viewed as a clear winner of the debates. In 2006, several events were crucial to the outcome of the election, including both López Obrador's blunt, public criticism of then president Fox and his denunciation of Calderón for allegedly using his cabinet post to allow his brother-in-law to benefit financially.

Surprisingly, when voters were asked to identify specific attributes of individual parties in 2006, they made no distinctions among the three parties in terms of good government or improving the future. However, they did express significant differences in their responses to a party's image in relation to the issue of corruption. Half of the respondents identified the PRI with corruption, the highest single response to a campaign issue associated with any party in Mexico. On the other hand, since the average voter perceives all politics as corrupt and all political parties as part of this tainted process, this issue may not have been translated into a significant variable in determining electoral outcomes.[25]

Of all the groups of voters, most likely it was the independents who influenced the outcome of the 2006 election, as was the case in 2000. In 2003, when voting for federal deputies, they markedly shifted their support from the PAN to the PRI.[26] Early in the campaign, when asked similar questions, independents gave decidedly different answers from partisan voters as to their images of the three parties. The independents ranked the PRI significantly below the other two parties in providing good government, and they rated it equally low on providing a better future in 2006. Especially interesting is that fact that independents, by a huge margin (32%), believed the PRD was interested in people like them, compared to 16 and 12 percent for the PAN and the PRI, respectively.

These differences are reflected in the data, which suggest that as of November 15, 2005, voters favored the PRD presidential candidate by a margin of 36 percent, versus 29 and 27 percent for the PRI and PAN candidates, respectively. Among independent voters, however, the responses were 32 percent for the PRD, followed by 10 and 14 percent for the PRI and PAN candidates, a completely different distribution of preferences.[27] The pattern among independents remained similar through February, with 32 percent still opting for the PRD candidate, and 12 and 19 percent for the PRI and PAN candidates.[28] However, by April their preferences had shifted significantly, to only 29 percent for the PRD candidate compared to 25 percent for the PAN candidate. Madrazo continued with the same low level of support, at 10 percent.[29] In May, independents favored Calderón over López Obrador for the first time, 42 to 36 percent.[30] These significant differences suggest why this group played a major role in the outcome.[31] Yet in the actual voting, López Obrador performed better, obtaining 43 percent of the independents' votes, as compared to 34 percent for Calderón.

The general voters' perceptions of the three leading parties, on the other hand, do not seem to correspond to their evaluations of the individual candidates. If we look specifically at the qualities associated with the three candidates, they gave much higher marks to the PRD candidate, López Obrador, regarding his ability to reduce crime and poverty and manage the economy, all of which would provide a better future in Mexico. According to Dan Lund, who conducts polls for the PRD, López Obrador defined his economic/poverty capabilities in terms of jobs, specifically, in creating new jobs. Simple language, therefore, was critical to how prospective voters actually understood the issues.[32] Even more surprising, Calderón scored higher than Madrazo on every personal perception by voters early in the campaign, especially his honesty and ability to manage the economy, yet voters favored Madrazo by a small margin at the end of 2005. Interestingly, in May Madrazo was viewed as nearly equal to López Obrador in terms of his abilities to manage the economy and reduce crime, yet he never came close to the support obtained by the PRD candidate. In 2006, López Obrador continued to maintain a huge lead in voter perceptions of his capabilities to solve controversial issues such as lower energy prices and immigration, typically by a two-to-one margin over his two leading opponents.[33] In May, however, Calderón caught up with or surpassed López Obrador in three of the four categories voters were asked to rank: honesty (49%), ability to reduce crime (49%), and ability to manage the economy (57%). Voters' views of Calderón's ability in this last category helped him the most in achieving parity with López Obrador and eventually edging him out in the final balloting.

If a candidate's capabilities to address specific policy issues do not necessarily translate directly into determining voter preferences, perhaps it is the candidate's personal qualities and image which exert a greater influence. For example, Madrazo continued to have the highest negative image, twice that of the next candidate, throughout the campaign.[34] In April, after López Obrador publicly told President Fox to "stop squawking and shut up," voters responded strongly and turned away from the PRD standard-bearer. This and other actions help explain why he was seen as the most aggressive of the candidates by 53 percent of the voters. Consequently, for the first time in the race, Felipe Calderón was viewed more positively than the PRD candidate, witnessed by the dramatic shift in favorable opinions from fall 2005 to spring 2006.[35] Immediately following the election, Calderón retained his low negative image, while López Obrador increased his significantly, almost to the level of Madrazo.

Less direct opinions appeared to reinforce the overall unfavorable ratings voters assigned to Madrazo (even though this declined somewhat in April). When asked a series of adverse questions, such as who was most likely to commit corrupt acts, or abuse power, or move Mexico backwards, Madrazo again scored far above his competitors, with over 40 percent of the voters identifying him in these terms. Despite such strong negative perceptions, Madrazo remained in a statistical dead heat with Calderón, and not all that far behind the front-runner, when this poll was taken.[36] Since then, the candidates drew firmly apart in most polls, and from January until May 2006, Calderón remained ahead of Madrazo by an average of 6–10 percentage points among potential voters.

One can only conclude that in the 2006 presidential race, positive views of a candidate's party were not translated into significant support for the candidate; otherwise, Calderón should have been looked upon much more favorably than Madrazo by those who expressed a voting preference. Second, opinions regarding a candidate's capabilities showed Calderón scoring more positively than Madrazo in every category, yet these perceptions were not translated into significant voter preferences for the PAN candidate until late in the campaign. In 2000, no significant distinctions existed among the candidates. In 2006 they did exist, but until April they exerted a stronger influence on preferences for the PRD candidate than they did between the two runners-up.

In 2000, Fox was able to use his own polling to determine what specific groups of voters wanted. He responded to those constituencies by reinforcing their views of him as fulfilling such expectations. Most significantly, Fox encouraged voters to consider him as the candidate of change, while praising an alternation in power as a means to promote good government and accountability. These qualities appealed strongly to educated, younger voters, who increasingly shifted their support in favor of Fox's candidacy (Rottinghaus and Alberro 2005). In addition, younger voters exercised an inordinate influence in 2006, since according to the Federal Electoral Institute, voters between the ages of 18 and 34 accounted for 44.4 percent of the electorate.[37] Furthermore, 12.7 million of the individuals eligible to vote were first time voters (3.1 million aged 18–19 and 9.6 million aged 20–24).[38] Voters under age 35 initially favored López Obrador.[39] However, unlike 2000, when Fox captured 17 percent more of these voters than Labastida, this age group favored López Obrador over Calderón by a much smaller margin. Thus Calderón was able to catch up to López Obrador and surpass his popularity among younger voters by June, improving again on his appeal with this group when voters cast their ballots. In fact, he outperformed López Obrador among all voters under the age of 49, who accounted for 79 percent of the electorate.

Finally, demographic preferences were distributed unevenly among the three leading candidates, with important changes from 2000. These can make a substantial difference in the outcome if actual participation is skewed in favor of one demographic group versus another. A party's performance at the state level and voters' ages both had a potential impact on candidate preferences. Income differences, as demonstrated in table 2.2, were also significant, with lower- and middle-income groups preferring López Obrador, while Calderón appealed strongly to high-income voters.

What is noteworthy, however, is that Mexican voters, when categorized by standard demographic variables, demonstrate few extreme disparities on the basis of age, gender, income, education, and place of residence. In other words, even though López Obrador fared better among older voters, Calderón was only 3 percentage points behind in support from that same group, similar to the divide favoring Calderón among younger voters. Among the variables measured in table 2.2, the most distinctive in terms of percentage differences are based on prior support for presidential candidates in 2000 and the existing partisan preferences found in certain states and regions.

A critical variable in the 2000 presidential election, according to the Mexico 2000 Panel Survey, is that one out of three voters changed their intended vote within 5 months of the election. The first wave showed that only two-thirds of the voters expressed firm support for one of the main parties, while the remaining third indicated that they either could change their minds or were uncertain which candidate they supported. In February, the figure for those who had a party choice increased to 80 percent, but dropped in March.[40] In April, fully 18 percent still remained unsure.[41] This number is remarkable because in the United States, presidential campaigns typically do not matter significantly—that is, only a tiny percentage of the voters change their mind as a result of the campaign (Morris 2005). The pattern in Mexico suggests that if groups or institutions can influence voter perceptions, the potential exists for them to significantly affect the outcome.

However, the 2000 election itself may well be unique, as the 2006 election does not represent change in the same way the previous one did. Forty-three percent of the voters were motivated to participate in the 2000 election because they perceived it as involving a change in the political model and the type of leadership for their country; this figure was twice that of any other reason given for voting for a candidate.[42] Because Fox was able to persuade two-thirds of all voters that he alone represented this change in 2000, many independents and PRD members voted for him.[43] The 2006 race suggests a similar level of change, but based on a different set of premises. For example, change in 2006 was not equated with altering the political model, but with changing the ideological direction and party. Nearly half of the respondents in the Mexico 2006 Panel Study altered their views of their candidates between October 2005 and May 2006, making it difficult to assess the effect of this premise on the outcome.

Finally, in 2000, the only other significant variable which determined the amount of voter participation was the candidate's proposals, the reason given by

Table 2.2   Voter preferences before and during the 2006 election

Variable	Calderón			Madrazo			López Obrador		
	March	June	July	March	June	July	March	June	July
Gender									
Male	31	34	36	21	25	22	39	37	37
Female	30	31	38	30	30	23	36	32	32
Age									
18–29	28	36	38	31	31	21	35	31	34
30–49	34	33	38	27	28	21	37	35	35
50+	28	28	34	27	32	26	42	37	37
Income[a]									
0–3 times min. wage	29	—		33	—		36	—	
3–7 times min. wage	30	—		20	—		42	—	
7+ times min. wage	41	—		23	—		32	—	
Education									
Primary	—	26	34	—	36	29	—	35	33
Secondary	—	29	37	—	34	21	—	33	35
Preparatory	—	35	—	—	18	—	—	40	—
University	—	51	42	—	12	14	—	28	38
Region[b]									
North	31	42	—	47	35	—	20	22	—
Center	36	33	—	24	31	—	36	30	—
South	19	14	—	40	37	—	39	47	—
Federal District	26	25	—	11	8	—	60	57	—
Residence									
Urban	33	34	40	24	25	20	39	36	35
Rural	21	25	31	47	41	28	31	30	36

slightly more than a fifth of all voters. Interestingly, although 34 percent of the voters in 2006 indicated a candidate's ideas were the most important reason for supporting him, they seemed unable to make significant distinctions among the candidates' proposals or, at the very least, to accurately characterize their stated positions. For example, typically two-thirds of the voters could not even express what topics or issues drew them to a presidential candidate.[44] However, after the election, voters thematically identified López Obrador with poverty, Roberto Madrazo with security, and Felipe Calderón with employment. Naturally, these pre-election position-identification percentages increased for all candidates as the campaign continued, but López Obrador was the person most understood on the issues. By speaking in a language that potential voters could understand, rather than in a politician's vocabulary, López Obrador was able to capture voter interest in a series of simple but clear promises, focusing on such pragmatic

	Calderón			Madrazo			López Obrador		
Variable	March	June	July	March	June	July	March	June	July
2000 election									
Vicente Fox	56	—	57	10	—	8	30	—	29
Francisco Labastida	7	—	13	69	—	64	22	—	19
Cuauhtémoc Cárdenas	7	—	7	2	—	4	91	—	88
New voters	—	—	36	—	—	19	—	—	37
Governorships[c]									
7 PRI states in North	26	42	49	51	35	27	21	21	24
10 PRI states in South	29	27	32	26	30	26	42	37	42
9 PAN states	53	40	53	25	30	23	20	26	24
5 PRD states	24	23	27	11	13	27	60	54	46

Sources: March and June: Consulta Mitofsky, "Así van . . . la carrera por la presidencia de México," national survey, March 17–23, 2006, 1,000 respondents, ±3 margin of error, and June 8–11, 2006, 1,400 respondents, ±2.6 margin of error. The question asked was "If the elections were held today, for which candidate and party would you vote?" July: *Reforma*, exit poll, 5,803 voters, July 2, 2006, ±1.3 margin of error. For the *Reforma* poll, the question was "For whom did you vote?"

  [a]The exit poll on July 2 used different income measurements by pesos. Calderón obtained the votes of 43% and 50%, respectively, of the two highest income groups, and López Obrador received 34% and 39% of the two lowest income groups. The two candidates were essentially tied at 36%–37% for the middle income group.

  [b]The regional divisions in the July 2 poll were different. Calderón obtained 43% in the North, 47% in the Center-West, 34% in the Center, and 27% in the South. López Obrador obtained 24%, 27%, 44%, and 40% from each region, respectively.

  [c]Governorships were calculated on the basis of the percentage of votes each candidate received among the votes cast for only the three leading candidates. All other votes were excluded. The PRI-controlled northern states during the presidential campaign were Chihuahua, Coahuila, Durango, Nuevo León, Sinaloa, Sonora, and Tamaulipas; the PAN-controlled states were Aguascalientes, Baja California, Guanajuato, Jalisco, Morelos, Querétaro, San Luis Potosí, Tlaxcala, and Yucatán; and the PRD-controlled states were Baja California del Sur, Chiapas, Guerrero, Michoacán, and Zacatecas. All other states were PRI-controlled south-central states; the Federal District is excluded from these calculations.

concerns as potable water, sewage, cheap electricity and gasoline, free education, and health.[45] These are the issues that resonate with the largest numbers of Mexicans.

The race tightened up at the end of April, and support wavered for López Obrador, improving Calderón's chances of overcoming his opponent as the two front-runners found themselves in a statistical tie. By May, most polls showed Calderón leading López Obrador by several percentage points. The candidates' personal behavior, and the personality qualities reflected by that behavior, appeared to be affecting the potential outcome, perhaps even dramatically.[46] López Obrador maintained support throughout the campaign because he had been viewed as an ordinary Mexican who lived like most other citizens, was the most disposed to listen to voters, and could communicate effectively with a typical voter. As a result of Calderón's public statements, however, voters began viewing him as having equal credibility and honesty in what he said as López Obrador, as well as demonstrating greater tolerance and the temperament to be president.[47]

López Obrador was especially appealing to independent voters who, as of the beginning of June, still accounted for more than two-fifths of all voters. But because of his public statements toward the president, support for López Obrador among independent voters then declined significantly—to only 28%, its lowest level in 2006—while simultaneously increasing 13 percent for Calderón.[48] These alterations in the independents' views of the candidates' personal qualities began to affect all voters' perceptions of their professional characteristics; nevertheless, López Obrador remained ahead in most of those professional categories. The sharp changes in voter impressions of the two candidates' personal attributes did not translate into equally significant declines in their perceived capabilities, as voters expressed similar preferences for both López Obrador and Calderón in this area.[49] Immediately before the election, voter perceptions once again began to slightly favor López Obrador, but the differences were not statistically significant.

The other influential variable altering voters' attitudes was negative advertising. Calderon initiated this strategy, painting López Obrador's policy postures as risky and his prior achievements in the Federal District as questionable.[50] Specifically, the negative spots suggested that López Obrador was a coward and arrogant for not participating in the April 25 debate, that he was intolerant for telling the president to shut up, and that his programs in the Federal District produced a huge deficit.[51] It is important to distinguish personal attacks from aggressive, discrediting, policy-oriented accusations. It was the latter that wore away at the PRD candidate's support among independent and nonpartisan PRD voters, while Calderón's new strategy led voters to then begin viewing the campaign process as one of attacks on the candidates themselves.[52] Taking a lesson from Calderón, López Obrador pursued a negative ad campaign in May–June and especially focused on the issue of Calderón's integrity, which produced a dramatic change in voter perceptions.[53]

Aside from the issue of negative advertising, what does the composition of the voters who cast their ballots for these candidates tell us about other attitudes and their consequences for the outcome of the presidential election? If we assess some of the prominent demographic variables found among voters for each candidate, they reveal some useful insights that are linked to our established characteristics of Mexican voters.

Incumbency, in direct and indirect ways, was a defining influence on support for the two leading candidates. First, approval of Fox's performance as president differentiated the partisans of both candidates. Fifty-one percent of those who voted for Calderón approved of Fox's administration; an almost equal percentage (56%) who voted for López Obrador found Fox's performance lacking. It is worth noting, however, that 43 percent of the voters who agreed that Fox performed well still voted for the PRI or PRD candidates (see table 2.3.) A second measure of the importance of incumbency was the degree to which voters identified themselves as beneficiaries of government social programs. Although more than half of the beneficiaries voted for the PRD and PRI candidates in nearly equal percentages, it was Calderón alone who was the clear leader in this category, obtaining two-fifths of these votes.[54]

A third indicator of the valuable role incumbency plays stemmed from how a voter viewed his or her personal future economic situation, a traditionally important campaign variable that became crucial in this campaign. Their opinions were strongly linked to Fox's and the PAN's economic performance in the presidency. Again, a sharp divide existed between those voters who thought their situation would improve, 60 percent of whom voted for Calderón, and those who believed their economic position would deteriorate, 52 percent of whom voted for López Obrador. What is crucial about the distribution of this variable, however, is the percentage of voters overall who believed Mexico was on the right track, another reflection of the incumbent administration's positive image. Two important achievements under Fox contributed to this favorable economic outlook: a significant effort by the government to provide support for mortgages that allowed working-class Mexicans to buy homes, sparking what one newspaper termed "a building frenzy," and a sizeable increase in the creation of jobs in May 2006.[55] As Zogby International reported in mid-June 2006, "Calderón may well be benefiting from a sense of optimism across the nation—almost half (49%) of all voters polled said they think Mexico is headed in the right direction, with only 33% saying things are off on the wrong track."[56] The Zogby poll found that 52 percent of respondents who thought Mexico was headed in the right direction planned to vote for Calderón, compared to only 22 percent for López Obrador.

Most Mexicans (57% versus 30%) believed it was the individual's—not the

Table 2.3   Demographic variables and the presidential vote in 2006 (in percentages)

	Calderón	Madrazo	López Obrador
Gender			
Male (52% of sample)	36	22	**37**
Female (48% of sample)	**38**	23	32
Age			
18–29 (30% of sample)	**38**	21	34
30–49 (49% of sample)	**38**	21	35
50+ (21% of sample)	34	26	**37**
Education			
Basic	**34**	29	33
Middle	**37**	21	35
Higher (22% of sample)	**42**	14	38
Income			
<2,000 pesos	31	30	**34**
2,000–3,999 pesos	32	24	**39**
4,000–6,499 pesos	36	21	**37**
6,500–9,199 pesos	**43**	16	36
9,200+ pesos	**50**	14	30
Residence			
Urban	**40**	20	35
Rural	31	28	**36**
Presidential approval			
Approved	**51**	17	26
Disapproved	8	31	**56**

government's—responsibility to improve the country's economic situation, and that in addressing poverty, private investment was preferable to redistributive strategies. Calderón supported these positions.[57] Despite the fact that more voters endorsed Calderón's strategies for solving Mexico's economic problems, however, López Obrador helped raise the issues of poverty and social inequality to a degree that had never been witnessed previously. The significance of this issue as a long-term theme in Mexican politics is illustrated by the facts that half of all Mexicans feel that people are not treated equally under the law, 52 percent believe that the only difference that counts in politics is between the wealthy and the poor, and 62 percent believe that the rich in Mexico have everything and the poor nothing.

Ideological divisions were also clearly represented in candidate support (see table 2.3). Although each candidate attracted backers from the Right, Center, and Left, López Obrador captured nearly two-thirds of the voters who identi-

	Calderón	Madrazo	López Obrador
Ideology			
Left	18	16	**62**
Center	**37**	24	31
Right	**48**	25	24
Partisan supporters			
PRI	11	**74**	12
PAN	**89**	4	5
PRD	3	3	**93**
None (35% of sample)	34	10	**43**
Region			
North	**43**	27	24
Center-West	**47**	20	27
Center	34	15	**44**
South	27	29	**40**
Beneficiaries of social programs			
Oportunidades	**41**	26	29
Seguro Popular	**44**	25	26
View of future economic situation			
Improve	**60**	15	20
Same	30	24	**40**
Worse	12	31	**52**
Vote in 2000			
Fox	**57**	8	29
Labastida	13	**64**	19
Cárdenas	7	4	**88**
New voters	36	19	**37**

Source: Reforma, exit poll, 5,803 voters, July 2, 2006, ±1.3 margin of error.

fied themselves as left-leaning, while Calderón received the votes of nearly half of all voters on the right. Calderón did much better among the Right than had Fox, suggesting a major shift since 2000 (Moreno 2006). Calderón was also able to attract more of the crucial centrist voters, who make up the largest proportion of the electorate.

In addition, party loyalties proved influential in the 2006 campaign. As expected, Madrazo lost the most partisan voters, but they divided their support evenly among the other two leading candidates. Both Calderón and López Obrador retained extraordinary high percentages of their supporters at the ballot box (89% and 93%, respectively). The fight was thus over independents. As one exit poll demonstrated, only 40 percent of Calderón's and López Obrador's support came from those who indicated that they always voted for the same party. More importantly, a third of Calderon's voters were drawn to him during the campaign, while only a fourth made the same decision about López Obrador.[58]

The fluidity of the electorate is suggested by the historic record of voters' past performance in the 2000 election. Half of Fox's support came from people who were not PAN partisans; Calderón was not able to keep these voters, two-fifths of whom cast their ballots for someone else. Madrazo, given the larger PRI base, was able to retain a higher percentage of voters who supported Labastida in 2000; nevertheless, he lost a third of them. Finally, although Cárdenas ran a distant third in 2000, 88 percent of his voters stuck with López Obrador to the balloting box in the 2006 campaign, giving him a solid partisan base with greater continuity than PAN or PRI voters. Among new voters, the percentages supporting each party's candidate were much more evenly distributed, with slightly more than a third each to the PAN and the PRD, and a fifth to the PRI. These findings reinforce the argument that all three parties will remain competitive in the future. Nevertheless, the PAN's victory provided it with a powerful boost. Four months after the election, Mexicans assigned many more positive attributes to the PAN, and more than half said they were likely to vote for it in the future.[59]

As chapters 3 and 4 in this volume make clear, regional patterns in partisan support remain. The results in 2006 along regional lines are even more skewed than in the 2000 race. The PRI's losses in states and localities where it had traditionally remained strong provides a potentially new regional base for the PRD, notably in states in the South and Center, where two-fifths or more of the voters supported López Obrador. By contrast, the PAN and Calderón, in slightly higher percentages, drew equally strong support from states in the North and Center-West. These patterns are not just determined by regional rural-urban, income, and educational distributions. As table 2.3 illustrates, other variables contribute to this geographic bias; local candidate performance may be one such factor. Lawson's preliminary analysis concurs with this general argument, suggesting that not only are the regional differences striking and more influential than all other traditional demographic variables combined, but they are "even more pronounced when we descend below the level of region to that of particular states" (Lawson 2006, 10; see also chapter 4 in this volume and Klesner 2006).

Finally, and most importantly, what does voter behavior in 2006 say about the performance of Mexican democracy? It can be argued that the closeness of the election, and the legal process by which claims were adjudicated, was the ultimate test of a functioning democracy.[60] In spite of López Obrador's demonstrations and media attention focusing on the alleged fraud, what is remarkable is not that the favorable image of the IFE had declined somewhat after the election, but that confidence remains strong in both it and in the Federal Electoral Court. The IFE regained its earlier level of integrity by September, when 59 percent of Mexicans expressed trust in both the people who counted the votes and the court, which later certified the election results.[61] In this sense, the 2006 presidential election, and the behavior of voters, can be seen as strongly reinforcing democratic consolidation in Mexico.

On the other hand, however, six years of experience after 2000 has not altered Mexicans' perceptions of whether or not a democracy is functioning in their country. In November 2000, shortly before Fox took office, 28 percent of Mexicans felt their country was not a democracy (Moreno 2003a). In 2006, after the election, they gave precisely the same response. Mexican views of democracy—especially the electoral process—continued to be tenuous, determined by partisan preferences and electoral outcomes. PRD supporters and self-described leftists remained skeptical, while PAN supporters overwhelmingly considered Mexico a democracy. Thus, 93 percent of those who voted for Calderón thought the election was clean, compared to 60 percent for Madrazo, and only 16 percent for López Obrador.[62]

Yet immediately after the election, more than four-fifths of all Mexicans agreed that living in a democracy was very important to them; three-quarters believed that it was the best system of government, that it resolved disputes through discussion, and that it was the only system which could reach an advanced stage. These findings accord with comparative research in Latin America, suggesting that people still value democracy despite the vicissitudes of government (Encarnación 2003–4). However, Mexicans' confidence in these statements declined significantly from June to September. The percentage who believed that a democratic government was not important if autocracy could boost their standard of living increased by 27 percent, to nearly half of the respondents.[63] Thus support for democracy among many Mexicans, beyond the confines of the electoral process itself, remains tepid and is strongly linked to its perceived or real individual economic benefits.

CHAPTER THREE

A Sociological Analysis of the 2006 Elections

Joseph L. Klesner

The extent and persistence of postelectoral conflict imply that Mexican society was deeply divided in 2006. Certainly the rhetoric of the failed contender, Andrés Manuel López Obrador, suggests a profound cleavage between the haves and the have-nots. If indeed there are deep cleavages dividing Mexicans, they may be the result of social class or other demographic differences, such as ethnicity, gender, generation, or region. Alternatively, they may reflect preferences about regime principles or fundamental policy positions that do not map neatly onto social differences.

In the pivotal 2000 presidential election in which Vicente Fox of the National Action Party (PAN) brought an end to the long rule of the Institutional Revolutionary Party (PRI), regime-based differences predominated over social class, ethnicity, region, or other sociological categories (Domínguez and Lawson 2004; Klesner 2005; Magaloni and Poiré 2004a; Moreno 2003a). However, with the end of the PRI's rule, the reasons for the regime-based cleavage in Mexican politics have dissipated. In this chapter I adopt the perspective that attitudes to the old regime no longer structure Mexican electoral behavior in the way they did in the dozen years before 2000 (Domínguez and McCann 1996; Klesner 2005; Molinar Horcasitas 1991; Moreno 1998). Instead of focusing on that traditional division, I explore the sociological bases of partisan choice in 2006 (several other chapters in this volume explore the attitudinal and political factors driving voter decisions more extensively). Can we find major social differences among the voter bases of López Obrador, President Felipe Calderón, and the failed PRI nominee, Roberto Madrazo? Did voters' social class, ethnicity, gender, age, religion, or region determine their choices in 2006?

Who Voted for Whom?

Using the exit poll conducted by the newspaper *Reforma*,[1] table 3.1 reports simple cross-tabulations between respondents' self-reported vote choice in the presidential election and several basic socioeconomic and demographic variables.

From these figures, Mexico appears to have a gender gap. López Obrador polled much more strongly among men than women, although the differences are small; Calderón received less than 2 percent more votes from women than men while López Obrador's gender gap was about 5 percent. In the recent past, Mexican men have been notably more willing to vote against the president's party than Mexican women. In 2000, for instance, males were more likely to vote for Fox, while females opted disproportionately for the PRI's nominee, Francisco Labastida (Klesner 2001, 110 [table]). As elsewhere, women in Mexico have also been less likely to vote for the Left.

In terms of the age profile of his supporters, Calderón continued Vicente Fox's trend of performing well in age groups other than the elderly. PRI candidate Roberto Madrazo, not surprisingly, performed best among voters over 50, suggesting that the PRI base continues to age and that its decline may have as much to do with the generational replacement of PRI stalwarts as anything else. Among respondents in the national sample of wave 3 of the Mexico 2006 Panel Study,[2] the average Madrazo voter was nearly four years older than the mean Calderón supporter ($t = 2.57$, $p = .01$) and about three years older than the average López Obrador voter ($t = 1.92$, $p = .06$). In contrast to his rivals, López Obrador did no better and no worse among the young than the old. This widespread support across age groups mirrors his relative success across different categories on the various socioeconomic variables explored here.

Moving to these factors, as we ascend the income brackets, Calderón's vote share rises steadily; he clearly polled better among higher-income groups than with poorer voters, gaining less than a third of the votes of those making under 4,000 pesos (US$400) monthly but almost half of the ballots of those earning more than 9,200 pesos (almost US$1,000) a month. In contrast, Madrazo's gains were disproportionately from impoverished voters, as has been the case for PRI candidates for many years (Klesner 2005). Despite his special campaign appeals to the poor, López Obrador gathered votes at similar rates across all income groups, with the possible exception of the very richest Mexicans. These findings mirror those for education: a strong positive relationship emerges between education and voting for Calderón, while the reverse is clear with Madrazo. Again,

Table 3.1 Socioeconomic characteristics and the presidential vote in 2006 (in percentages)

	Distribution of the popular vote			Percent of sample	PRI Congress and		
	Calderón	Madrazo	López Obrador		López Obrador	Calderón	Madrazo
Sex							
Male	36.4	21.5	37.3	53.2	58.7	50.3	52.8
Female	38.2	22.5	32.3	46.8	41.3	49.7	47.2
Age							
18–29	37.7	21.2	33.5	30.8	35.5	41.4	28.0
30–49	38.3	20.7	35.2	48.7	49.2	42.0	46.9
50+	33.8	26.1	36.5	20.5	15.2	16.7	25.2
Rural/Urban							
Urban	39.6	19.5	34.8	71.4	74.0	77.5	63.8
Rural/mixed	31.4	28.2	35.5	28.6	26.0	22.5	36.2
Monthly income (10 pesos ≈ US$1)							
<2,000 pesos	30.5	30.4	34.2	20.1	17.9	12.7	28.6
2,000–3,999 pesos	32.1	23.9	38.6	25.5	25.4	23.6	27.3
4,000–9,200 pesos	37.7	19.0	36.7	36.6	40.5	42.0	32.4
9,200+ pesos	49.8	13.9	29.9	17.8	16.2	21.7	11.6

Education level							
None	29.1	32.0	35.5	4.0	0.5	1.7	5.6
Primary	34.8	28.6	32.2	29.4	15.3	19.7	39.4
Secondary	35.9	23.6	34.4	25.9	29.6	28.9	27.5
Preparatory	38.9	16.1	36.6	18.2	22.4	22.5	12.3
University	42.4	14.1	37.8	22.4	31.6	27.2	14.6
Union member in family?							
Yes	33.1	22.2	36.8	11.6	15.8	11.6	11.7
No	37.8	21.9	34.8	87.4	84.2	87.9	87.0
Religion and religiosity							
Catholic	39.0	21.6	33.5	84.2	80.6	89.1	82.9
Protestant	31.4	26.7	37.8	7.6	8.7	6.3	9.5
Non-believer	23.3	17.5	51.4	5.0	5.1	2.8	3.8
Weekly church attendance	38.8	24.8	31.2	45.2	39.1	48.0	51.6
Never attend services	31.1	17.0	45.0	10.1	14.2	12.7	7.8
Total	37.2	22.0	35.9	100.0			

Source: Reforma, exit poll, July 2, 2006.

Note: Cells of the first three columns show row percentages. Rows do not sum to 100% because respondents who voted for other candidates and those who refused to answer are not reported. Cells of the final four columns show column percentages within variables.

López Obrador polled well across all levels of learning. In terms of educational background, Calderón and López Obrador voters do not differ significantly ($p = .78$).

The PRI has had a long relationship with organized labor (Middlebrook 1995); the PAN has not. However, in the *Reforma* exit poll, the number of votes for either Calderón or Madrazo were not distinguishably different among the small segment of unionized families than among those with no union affiliation.[3] Despite his populist rhetoric, López Obrador, too, received votes in almost the same proportions from union and nonunion families. Of course, as organized labor has withered, this population segment is growing smaller and smaller.

Although religious issues have been at the root of much violent conflict in postindependence Mexico, in recent decades religion has not been central in shaping the major issues on the public agenda. As Bruhn and Greene (chapter 6 in this volume) argue, although the party elites for the PAN and the leftist Party of the Democratic Revolution (PRD) are quite divided on moral issues such as abortion, these topics did not mobilize public opinion in the campaign. That said, the PAN has clearly identified itself as pro-Catholic ever since its founding (Loaeza 1999; Mabry 1974). Bishops have become increasingly willing to speak out on political positions over the past two decades, mainly in promoting participation and democratization (Chand 2001), but only to a lesser extent in favor of particular parties.[4] In 2006, church-going Catholics were more likely to vote for Calderón than were Protestants, those with no religion, or those who rarely attended religious services. López Obrador, meanwhile, did especially well among the nonreligious, although again this is a small segment of the population.

The *Reforma* exit poll does not include data on respondents' ethnicities, so to explore the effects of skin color, I relied on the Mexico 2006 Panel Study.[5] Among respondents in the postelection wave of the panel study, 48 percent of those classified by the interviewer as white supported Calderón, whereas white Mexicans showed considerably less enthusiasm for either of his main opponents—14 percent chose Madrazo and 27 percent opted for López Obrador. Notably, Madrazo did well among darker-skinned Mexicans, indicating that the PRI continues to pull a disproportionate amount of its votes from the millions of Mexicans of indigenous heritage. Again, these figures suggest that a large part of Calderón's support comes from upper social strata, a substantial amount of the PRI's from lower social echelons, and López Obrador's in roughly equal amounts across social groups.

In short, Calderón drew a greater segment of votes from the "new" Mexico—

younger, better educated, and wealthier; the PRI vote remains concentrated among the less educated, the poor, the old, and those living in rural areas. Both the PRD and the PAN are urban-based parties. Observant Catholics tend to vote for the PAN; that party does poorly among the nonreligious, who support the PRD. One important difference is that women apparently felt more comfortable voting for Calderón than for López Obrador. So although there was some evidence of socioeconomic status and religion shaping vote decisions, particularly for the PAN and the PRI, the part of the electorate supporting López Obrador's PRD cannot be clearly understood in class terms.

Social Context

If individual characteristics of voters do not yield many significant differences between those who chose Calderón and those who supported López Obrador, could their social contexts have provided the cues that led to their decisions? The Mexico 2006 Panel Study includes a series of demographic and socioeconomic indicators for the *municipios* (counties) and *localidades* (localities) in which the respondents reside. Those indicators show that López Obrador drew voters from more densely populated areas than either Calderón and Madrazo. The mean population density of counties in which respondents in the Mexico 2006 Panel Study who reported voting for López Obrador lived was 3,787 people per square kilometer, as opposed to 1,772 for Calderón ($t = 5.00, p = .00$) and 1,333 for Madrazo ($t = 4.67, p = .00$). In part, this result is an artifact of López Obrador's strength in Mexico City, but the PRD vote is also concentrated in urban areas elsewhere in the country. PRI support is primarily in the least densely populated counties, which confirms the "green" (rural) vote noted in table 3.1. Madrazo's voters came more from in townships with a higher share of the workforce in the primary sector (26.0%, compared to 19.9% for López Obrador and 16.7% for Calderón) and a lower share in the services sector (45.1%, compared to 53.4% for López Obrador and 52.3% for Calderón). Calderón did significantly better in localities where the workforce was more heavily employed in manufacturing and construction (the secondary sector) than did López Obrador (27.1% compared to 22.7%; $t = 4.554, p = .00$). Average years of schooling in areas where PAN voters live is not significantly different from that for López Obrador's supporters, although PRI voters tend to reside in locales where the amount of education completed is somewhat lower (7.07 years, on average, compared to 7.46 and 7.54 for the PAN and the PRD, respectively).

An important indicator of the greater material security in the communities where Calderón voters were found is the higher percentage of residents who were covered by health insurance—state-provided or privately acquired—in those localities. Respondents who reported voting for Calderón lived in townships where 45.1 percent of the population had health insurance, compared to 39.2 percent for each of his rivals ($t = 3.74$, $p = .00$). Also, of the three main candidates, supporters of López Obrador resided in the localities with the lowest percentage of households receiving remittances from abroad, mostly the United States; the panel data indicate that Calderón did best among those with relatives living in the United States.

Overall, then, this analysis of socioeconomic context reinforces what we know of voters at the individual level. Important patterns of both difference and similarity emerge between Calderón and López Obrador, with the former's voters residing in more materially secure communities in which the workforce is more engaged in the secondary sector. The latter drew votes more successfully from panel respondents who lived in localities with more speakers of indigenous languages, an indicator of ethnicity. The PRI, or at least Madrazo,[6] remains relatively successful in more backward parts of Mexico—that is, less densely populated, heavily agricultural areas with lower levels of education.

Regionalism

A prevalent line of analysis posits a blue/yellow divide that geographically divides Mexico, much akin to the red state/blue state division popular in media accounts of recent U.S. elections.[7] In this view, the nation separates into a northern, "blue" Mexico, where Calderón won most states, and a southern, "yellow" Mexico where López Obrador carried most states (see map on p. xiv).[8] The central problem with this perspective is that it allows no place for the green of the PRI. These congressional candidates performed much better than their standard-bearer, with the PRI and its coalition partner taking 28.2 percent of the popular vote nationally (compared to 29.0% for the PRD-led coalition's candidates and 33.4% for the PAN). At the time of the 2006 election, the PRI governed a majority (17) of Mexican states, including every border state except Baja California; it also dominated the South, other than Morelos and Yucatán (governed by the PAN until 2007, but since reclaimed by the PRI) and Guerrero, Chiapas, and Michoacán (PRD).[9]

Figure 3.1 offers a more complex vision of regionalism in the 2006 election,

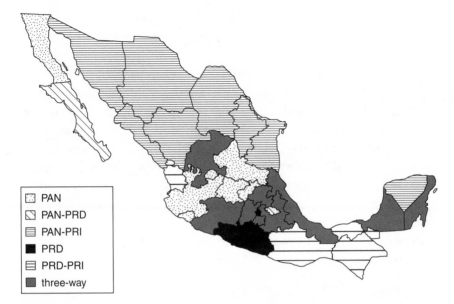

Figure 3.1 Patterns of party competition in the 2006 election for the Chamber of Deputies.

using results for the Chamber of Deputies races to chart patterns of party competition. Where a party won by a margin of greater than 15 percent, I placed the state in a one-party dominance category. Where no more than 15 points separated the first and the third parties, I treated it as a zone of three-party competition. Otherwise, I categorized the states by the two parties that competed for first and second place. Here we still see regionalism, but a much more variegated version.[10] The PAN owns the center-west region, Mexico's Bible Belt, but it must compete on roughly equal terms against the PRI in the northern states; in 2006, many races in that region remained very close, even with a weak PRI presidential candidate. The PRD dominates the Federal District and Michoacán, and it vigorously challenges the PRI in the southern states of Guerrero, Chiapas, and Tabasco (the home state of both Madrazo and López Obrador). Most of the other states now see three-party competition. In gubernatorial elections held since July 2006, the PRD beat the PRI by a whisker in Chiapas but lost Tabasco to the PRI; the PAN lost Yucatán to the PRI. In other words, all three parties remain serious electoral competitors.

At the state and local level, then, the division of Mexico into "blue" and "yellow" is misleading. PAN and PRD activists are not struggling primarily against each other, but often against their old nemesis, the PRI. Consequently, more complex patterns of cooperation and competition may emerge. Before 2000, for instance, the PRD and the PAN often cooperated to support candidates in the state and local elections to oust the PRI; even today, they belong to the same anti-PRI electoral coalition in Oaxaca. Meanwhile, in the immediate aftermath of the 2006 election, the PAN courted the PRI as a national governing partner by supporting its candidates in the Chiapas and Tabasco gubernatorial elections. To be sure, the PRI is losing position everywhere compared to its glorious past and even to its performance in state-level elections during the middle years of Fox's term. The only major regions that are not competitive today are not those where the PRI still dominates, but rather where the PRD and the PAN have established a new hegemony. In national races, however, Mexican voters everywhere still have more than two choices.

Ticket Splitters and Converts

Voters sometimes take advantage of those choices by splitting their ballots—about one in five voters split their ballot between presidential and Chamber of Deputies votes, and about one in four did so between presidential and Senate votes. These voters offer insight into which segments of the electorate are most electorally mobile.[11] The last three columns of table 3.1 summarize the results of the sociological analysis described above when it is applied only to those who voted for the PRI in the Chamber of Deputies races in 2006. These columns show ticket splitters (those who voted for the PRI for the lower house but not for its presidential candidate) and standpatters (those for Madrazo and the PRI congressional candidate). We see some revealing evidence about which PRI voters can be lured away from the party by stronger candidacies and, among them, which are more likely to move toward the PAN rather than the PRD.

PRI stalwarts are older than those who divide their votes, and Calderón drew more of the younger ticket splitters than did López Obrador, mirroring the differences among these candidates in the general electorate. Ticket splitters are more likely to live in urban areas than those PRI voters who did not split their ballots. Straight-ticket PRI voters are poorer and less educated than those who chose PRI congressional candidates but abandoned Madrazo. Wealthier ticket splitters were more likely to opt for Calderón than López Obrador, although educational differences among them were not significant. Those PRI congressional voters who chose Calderón were also more likely to be Catholic than straight-ticket PRI voters or those splitters who chose López Obrador. In other words, differences between straight-ticket PRI supporters and those who divided their ballots parallel the overall sociological bases of partisan support shown in the first three columns of table 3.1. They suggest that PRI stalwarts are older, poorer, less educated, and more rural than those who chose Calderón and López Obrador. Younger, more affluent, better-educated, more urban Mexicans who find the PRI to be an attractive electoral option are also more likely to abandon it if they dislike its particular candidates. Splitters' choices between the PAN and the PRD likewise reflect the different social bases of these two parties.

Another way to explore flux in the Mexican electorate is to examine the social characteristics of voters who chose the candidate of one party in 2000 but did not cast ballots for its nominee six years later.[12] Loyalists are those who stayed with the candidate of the same party in both 2000 and 2006, while those who changed parties I term "defectors." The two most significant groups of defectors are Fox voters who moved to López Obrador in 2006—fully one-tenth of all respondents in *Reforma*'s exit poll—and Labastida voters who moved to either the PAN or the PRD candidate—about one in twenty voters.

Those who voted for Fox in 2000 but for López Obrador in 2006 were overwhelmingly male (61%). Those who stayed loyal to the PAN were wealthier and more religious. Madrazo lost erstwhile PRI voters in the 30–49 age group to both of his rivals. In contrast, older voters remained loyal to him. Those leaving the PRI for Calderón enjoyed higher incomes than PRI loyalists or those who defected to López Obrador; those moving from the PRI to either of its main rivals were among the most highly educated. PRI defectors to the PAN were more likely to be Catholic than either PRI loyalists or those changing from Labastida in 2000 to López Obrador in 2006.

This analysis of ticket splitting and switching thus has the strongest implications for the PRI. Younger, better-educated, and higher-income Mexicans who were PRI voters even in recent pivotal elections are now willing to defect to the PAN and the PRD. Many of the same voters will cast their ballots for the PRI's congressional slate, but they no longer feel obliged to vote straight ticket. Of course, Madrazo was an unusually unattractive candidate who ran an especially bad campaign (see chapters 7 and 8 in this volume), as perhaps was Labastida before him (Klesner 2001). But the PRI no longer has the critical mass of stalwarts to allow it to make those mistakes and remain competitive in presidential politics.

A Sociological Model of Voting

So far, we have focused on simple bivariate relationships—that is, the relationship between any one demographic category and partisan support. What we do not know yet is how these factors operate in a multivariate context. Do northerners disproportionately support the PAN because they are wealthier than southerners, or is there something else about living in the North that inclines them toward the PAN? Do women avoid the Left because they are females, or because women are, on average, less well-educated and more religious than men?

An analysis of municipal-level electoral results indicates that the regional concentration of support for the PAN and the PRD has actually intensified.[13] Regression coefficients for the 2006 presidential election are remarkably similar to those of the midterm elections of 1997 (Klesner 2005). In other words, the cleavage structures that manifested themselves in 2006 are not new, but rather constitute the re-emergence of divisions that had been developing as the PAN and the PRD grew in strength in the 1990s; the 2000 election was an anomaly related to the pivotal nature of that election and to Vicente Fox's effectiveness in priming the issue of change.

An analysis of aggregate returns also reveals the same demographic patterns of partisan support described above. Calderón performed better in more urban municipalities where the percentage of Catholics and literates was higher, and where a greater share of the labor force worked in the secondary sector. This has been the standard PAN profile for a long time (Barraza and Bizberg 1991; Klesner 1993, 2005; Magaloni and Moreno 2003; Mizrahi 2003). López Obrador, in contrast, did better in counties that are somewhat less urban, where the population is not concentrated in manufacturing and construction, and where there are relatively fewer self-professed Catholics. He, too, won higher vote shares where the population has a higher literacy rate, if other factors are held constant. Finally, in keeping with the PRI's recent experience (Moreno and Méndez 2007), Madrazo did better in rural municipalities, those with a relatively low proportion of self-professed Catholics, and those where more people were unable to read. The PRI, too, does relatively well in areas where more people are employed in the secondary sector.

In counties where only 70 percent of the population professes to be Catholic, the model predicts that Calderón would have won 33.1 percent of the popular vote, compared to 37.7 percent for López Obrador and 22.4 percent for Madrazo. In contrast, in more heavily Catholic counties, where 90 percent adhere to that faith, the PAN standard-bearer's predicted vote rises to 40.4 percent, in contrast to 35.5 percent and 17.2 percent for the PRD and PRI candidates.[14] In terms of literacy, the model shows only Madrazo losing vote share as literacy levels rise; although López Obrador gains more rapidly than Calderón, the predicted differences are very small—on the order of 1 percentage point.

If we predict values for the PAN, PRD, and PRI candidates by region, based on the same aggregate data analysis, we find that Calderón would do markedly better in the North and the Center-West, even after controlling for the other demographic variables. This model—taking into account levels of urbanization, industrialization, and literacy as well as the share of the population that is Catholic—predicts that the PAN candidate would win 42.3 percent of the vote in the North and 43.6 percent in the Center-West. In the actual election, he took 45.4 percent and 48.1 percent in those regions, respectively. In other words, the power of region as an explanatory variable overwhelms these other important demographic predictors; it is not just that the North is more modern, or the Center-West more Catholic, that accounts for these regionalized voting effects. Meanwhile, López Obrador received a vote share much lower in the North and in the Center-West than that which he received in the South or the Center regions, but his greater Mexico City result was considerably higher, again controlling for the effects of the other variables. In the Federal District and the state of México, the model suggests López Obrador would take 53.2 percent of the vote, whereas he actually won 55.7 percent. Region has much less of an influence on support for Madrazo, especially after taking other factors into account. Aggregate data, then, largely supports what we have already discovered in our bivariate analysis of individual and contextual variables, as reported in table 3.1.

Municipal-level analyses are potentially vulnerable to the ecological fallacy, in which aggregate trends are inaccurately applied to individuals. For instance, it may be that support for English as an official language in U.S. counties increases as the percentage of Latinos rises; that result would not necessarily mean Latinos favored adopting English as the official language, but rather that Anglos in regions with large numbers of immigrants would be much more likely to endorse such a measure than Anglos who never encounter immigrants from another ethnic group.

To address this issue, I estimated two versions of a multinominal logit regression model on vote choice for respondents from the national sample of the

Mexico 2006 Panel Study. The first model uses only individual-level variables, such as those reported in table 3.1, while the second adds contextual factors.[15] Here, for ease of presentation, I summarize the results of the latter model in table 3.2 using CLARIFY.[16] Probabilities are derived by varying the characteristics listed in the first column, while holding the values of all other variables in the list at their means.

Other than region, where the same pronounced distinctions among the candidates emerge, two differences in support for Calderón and López Obrador stand out: Calderón voters are more likely to be female and wealthy than López Obrador voters.[17] The logit model predicts that the PRD standard-bearer would win among men, 41.2 percent to Calderón's 37.7 percent, but among women the PAN candidate is predicted to take 50.6 percent to López Obrador's 31.7 percent. In addition, those residing in localities where a higher percentage of the population is covered by health insurance (a proxy measure for affluence and/or security) would be more likely to support the new president, but Calderón would do more poorly than his PRD rival among those living in localities with higher levels of education (although the individual-level education measure did not provide a statistically significant contrast). These results yield predicted vote shares that mirror the bivariate relationships illustrated in table 3.1 in most respects. After controlling for the effects of other factors, voters for the top two contenders do not differ significantly in terms of their age profile, their level of education,[18] or their religion or religiosity. Figure 3.2 shows the pronounced differences in the income profiles of Calderón voters, on the one hand, and López Obrador and Madrazo supporters on the other, using simulated probabilities from the same analysis summarized in table 3.2. As income rises, Mexican voters moved toward Calderón.

Figure 3.3, based on the same analysis, shows the relatively similar education profiles of those casting ballots for López Obrador and Calderón, as well as the stark contrast between their followers and those of Madrazo. These findings thus reinforce those from the aggregate data analysis that suggest that Calderón and López Obrador voters did not differ significantly in their educational profile.

Again, regionalism emerges as a key explanatory variable—just as it did in the ecological analysis. Predicted results from the logit model indicate Calderón and Madrazo did significantly better in the Center, Center-West, and especially the North than López Obrador, even after controlling for a host of individual-level characteristics of the respondents. His rivals from the PAN and the PRI performed significantly worse in the Mexico City metropolitan area.

Table 3.2 Predicted vote shares in 2006 presidential election based on multinomial logit analysis

	Calderón	Madrazo	López Obrador
All variables set to mean	44.5	19.4	36.2
Sex			
Male	37.7	21.0	41.2
Female	50.6	17.8	31.7
Age			
Under 30	45.6	21.6	32.8
30–49	46.4	16.0	37.6
50+	39.7	23.8	36.5
Rural/urban			
Rural	30.9	33.6	35.4
Urban	48.7	16.0	35.3
Skin color			
White	49.5	18.5	32.0
Brown	39.6	18.9	41.6
Dark brown	50.2	20.2	29.7
Religion and religiosity			
Catholic	45.5	19.2	35.4
Non-Catholic	39.2	20.5	40.2
Weekly church attendance	45.6	21.9	32.5
Less-frequent church attendance	43.0	17.2	39.8
Union member in family?			
Yes	38.1	23.8	38.1
No	45.3	18.8	35.8
Region			
North	51.8	27.4	20.8
Center-West	55.1	15.9	29.0
South	34.5	24.7	40.8
Mexico City area	28.6	8.7	62.6
Center	51.5	20.8	27.6

Note: Simulations using CLARIFY (Tomz et al. 2001), based on the model reported in the Mexico 2006 Panel Study's supplemental materials for chapter 3, table 3.E (http://web.mit.edu/polisci/research/mexico06/book.html). In addition to the variables listed above, the model controls for income, education, the percentage of households in the locality with health insurance, average years of education in the locality, the percentage of the population in the locality that speaks an indigenous language, the percentage of the workforce in the secondary sector, and the percentage of households in the municipality receiving remittances from family members living in the United States. The sample includes only those respondents who were surveyed in all three waves of the panel study, who were also in the national sample, and for whom there was no missing data ($n = 545$). Results for the relevant demographic variables are similar when contextual factors are excluded, with the exception of regional variables; Calderon performed better among southerners and worse among residents of the North and Center-West when contextual factors are included. Results from the model without these contextual factors are discussed in the text.

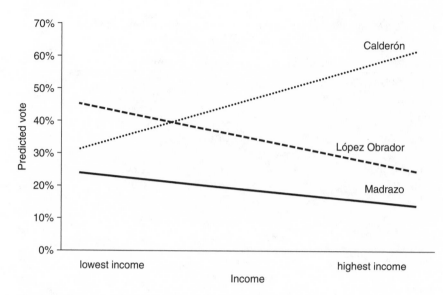

Figure 3.2 Income and vote choice, with predicted values based on multinomial logit analysis.

Note: Simulations are based on multinomial logit analysis of vote choice, as described in table 3.2.

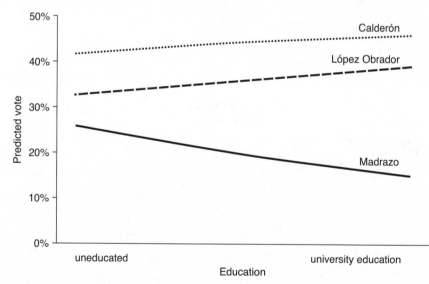

Figure 3.3 Education and vote share, with the predicted vote based on multinomial logit analysis.

Note: Simulations are based on multinomial logit analysis of vote choice, as described in table 3.2.

To give a sense of the power of region, consider the simulations from the model that includes only individual-level demographic factors: age, gender, education, income, rural residency, skin color, church attendance, union affiliation, and region. This model predicts that a typical PAN voter—a white-complexioned, Catholic woman under 30 years of age living in an urban area—would have a 49.5 percent probability of voting for Calderón if she lived in the North, 51.5 percent if she made her home in the Center-West, 41.9 percent in the South, but only 29.1 percent in the Mexico City area.[19] A female with the same attributes, but who lived in the metro area, would have a 30.4 percent probability of voting for López Obrador. In contrast, a man aged 50 or above would have a 34.6 percent chance of voting for the PAN nominee in the North, 33.3 percent in the Center-West, 22.2 percent in the South, and 14.3 percent in Mexico City. A man with the same characteristics would only have a 13.3 percent probability of choosing López Obrador if he lived in the North but a 57.6 percent likelihood of voting PRD if greater Mexico City were his home.

The Meaning of Region

If region is so central to electoral behavior, even controlling for so many other demographic factors, what exactly does region signify? First, we could be tapping deep historical and cultural differences across different parts of the country. Second, regional voting patterns could reflect the differential impact of socioeconomic modernization and economic integration. Third, regionalism could be an artifact of the emergence of opposition to the former ruling party, which conferred advantages to first movers (see Lawson 2006). Finally, it is important to underscore the central argument about regionalism in chapter 4 in this volume—once regional divisions are established, quotidian social intercourse will tend to reinforce patterns of partisan support.

According to the first line of argument, for over a century a distinct northern regionalist way of thinking has stressed that the North has a frontier mentality, a can-do spirit, and a much more individualist orientation, similar to attitudes prevalent on the other side of the northern border. Its work ethic, the argument goes, is not shared by the Mexico City-dominated Center (which serves a grasping central government) or the South (in this view, often expressed by northerners, the domain of lazy Indians).[20] The Center-West region, the heart of which is the Bajío, Mexico's breadbasket and its most orthodox Catholic region, has been associated with the nation's *charro* or ranch culture—which some identify as *the* uniquely Mexican culture. Yet other observers regard the South as the heart of "deep Mexico" (Bonfíl Batalla 1996)—a region where most of the country's culturally indigenous people still live, but also where poverty rates are by far the highest, people are the most tied to their villages, and *caciques* (local bosses) associated with the former ruling party exercise the most sway.

To the extent that the PAN has adhered to a more individualist philosophy, it may be especially attractive to voters in the North; to the degree to which López Obrador's campaign appealed to voters with statist philosophies, it would draw support from the greater Mexico City area (D. Davis 1994). Evidence from the Mexico 2006 Panel Study indicates that when given a choice between promoting private investment or depending on the state to provide resources to address poverty, those living in the North and the Center-West are far more likely to prefer encouraging private investment, while those in the Center, the South, and the Mexico City metropolitan area are more inclined to tax the rich to give to the poor.

In addition to its long-standing focus on political reform and good governance, the PAN has also long flirted with Christian Democracy (Mabry 1974; Magaloni and Moreno 2003; Middlebrook 2001), which may be especially appealing to the Catholics who dominate in the Center-West. The heritage of the bloody Cristero rebellion of the 1920s—in which Catholic peasants took up arms against a rabidly secular state—has left the Bajío region with a stronger religious identity than other parts of the country.[21] This intense identification with Catholicism cannot be measured simply by the percentage of voters who claim this as their faith to census takers. The legacy of the Cristero rebellion may lead voters in this region to disdain both the PRI and the PRD, whose predecessors persecuted them in that war.

Second, the regional variable may tap differential impacts of modernization and economic assimilation. Mexicans living in northern states have benefited more from economic integration with the United States than those living in other regions, especially the South, where competition with large grain growers from the Midwestern states of the United States have pushed many peasant producers off the land or into penury.[22] Those from the northern states also tend to have been migrants from other parts of Mexico. They travel much more frequently to the United States than those from other parts of the country.[23] The Center-West has also been well served by globalization, as multinational firms have extended their production chains more deeply into Mexico, particularly to regional cities such as León, in the state of Guanajuato (Rothstein 2005). The

Center—which includes the nation's capital, the surrounding state of México, and the nearby state of Puebla—is the most densely populated zone in Mexico. These regions benefited the most from the capital's centralist control of the development process during import-substituting industrialization (D. Davis 1994). Heavy manufacturing in the Center may be the sector most threatened by economic integration. Moreover, Mexico has been ruled from this region for centuries, and the officials most directly associated with the national government live in greater Mexico City.

At least in terms of preferences about trade relations with the United States, which in part may reflect voters' evaluations of the impact of trade on their pocketbooks and on the national economy, those from the North and the Center-West rather more enthusiastically support improving such relations with the United States. In the second wave of the Mexico 2006 Panel Study, 60 percent of northerners and 55 percent of those from the Center-West reported that they would prefer increased trade with the United States, compared to 38 percent of southerners and 42 percent of those from greater Mexico City. Those in the North and Center-West were also far more likely to evaluate the economy's performance positively, in terms of both sociotropic and pocketbook assessments, a more favorable judgment than those from the Mexico City area or the South. Indeed, those from the North and the Center-West are considerably more optimistic about the economic future than residents of other regions. In the postelection wave of the Mexico 2006 Panel Study, 47 percent of northerners and 43 percent of those from the Center-West expected the nation's economy to improve over the next year, while 43 percent and 39 percent from, respectively, those two regions saw their household's prospects in brighter terms. In contrast, only 24 percent of greater Mexico City residents and 26 percent of southerners were optimistic about Mexico's economic future. The region variable, then, is probably capturing this aspect of contemporary Mexican reality.

Third, contemporary regional patterns of party competition are built on past patterns of opposition-party development. According to this path-dependent argument, outside of Mexico City, in those places where electoral opposition emerged early on, the PAN established a presence that makes it difficult to dislodge. Since 1988, when the PRD came onto the scene, it has gained the advantage, especially where competition developed from the defection of local PRI organizations.[24]

Opposition has certainly emerged in different regions at different times. Outside of Mexico City, strong challenges first appeared in several northern states (e.g., Baja California), some center-west states (e.g., San Luis Potosí), and the state of Yucatán as early as the late 1950s, but they arose especially during the 1982–86 economic downturn. The PAN established party organizations and won control of local governments in those areas first (see the cases analyzed in Rodríguez and Ward 1995). In contrast, electoral opposition made little headway in the Center and South until well into the 1990s. When it did, the PRD was already on the scene and prepared to compete for office, sometimes by opportunistically absorbing the PRI's local machines (Bruhn 1997; Wuhs 2008). Because the PRI did not easily yield to its rivals, the pattern that emerged tended to be two-party competition—the PRI versus either the PAN or the PRD—depending on which opposition bloc first emerged as a viable challenger. Political contests thus assumed an "ins-versus-outs" character, rather than an ideological struggle.[25]

This conflict also played out within each region. In the smaller states of Baja California Sur, Nayarit, and Zacatecas, the PAN made little headway during the 1980s, but the PRD successfully challenged the PRI in the late 1990s (Klesner 1999). The PRD continues to have a strong presence in those three states, and López Obrador won them all in 2006. In contrast, by the time the opposition was able to compete electorally in the South—only after 1988—the PRD already existed, and in many cases it accepted into its ranks former *priístas* (PRI partisans) who had failed to win party nominations for important state-level offices. These defectors often brought along their portion of the PRI party machinery. The PAN has been less effective at breaking into the South.

The foregoing paragraph begs a final question: Why was the earlier-existing PAN able to get a foot in the door in the North and Center-West in the 1980s and before, but not in the South? To a considerable extent, the answer is due to the first two factors discussed above: disparate regional political cultures and the differential impact of economic integration. The PAN's ideology was more appealing to religious Mexicans; it also drew strong support in those areas that were sufficiently well developed to have an independent business sector and a larger middle class.

The bottom line is that those factors began operating two decades and more ago. In much of the country, the PAN and the PRI kept the PRD out of the contest for state and local positions and still do so today. This fact undoubtedly allowed Calderón to win the 2006 presidential election. Unless the PRI collapses, allowing the PRD to pick up its pieces in the North and Center, the current pattern of regional division will continue. In fact, if economic integration maintains its differential impact on northern and southern Mexico, these regional bases of partisan competition may even strengthen.

In their seminal study on the emergence of partisan cleavages, Seymour Martin Lipset and Stein Rokkan (1967) argued that the party systems in place in postwar Europe had their origins in profound conflicts that had taken place much earlier in those nations' histories. The sequence of these conflicts and the way they were resolved determined the partisan preferences of social groups. Parties proved able to reproduce these loyalties over subsequent generations, long after the conflicts from which those cleavages emerged had subsided.

The PRI's dominance prevented the appearance of such cleavages in post-revolutionary Mexico. Nevertheless, resentment of the PRI smoldered among the descendents of the Cristeros and business groups that grew to find the PRI's statist economic policies objectionable in the 1970s and 1980s. The PAN exploited this opposition, and in so doing helped to create the current partisan divisions.

Are we seeing the emergence in Mexico of true cleavage structures, like those described by Lipset and Rokkan? Probably not. The country's protracted transition to democracy meant that opposition activists spent a decade and a half focused on ousting the PRI from Los Pinos (Mexico's presidential compound). Today, electoral pressures to act as catch-all coalitions militate against defining their social bases of support too narrowly (Klesner 2005). The demographic indicators used in this chapter, including region, collectively explain only about 20 percent of the individual-level variation in the vote. Clearly other factors—political values, evaluations of the incumbent president and the economy, candidate qualities, and campaign messages—still shape voters' decisions to a greater extent than do their social and demographic characteristics. Nevertheless, we may be witnessing the emergence of a partisan cleavage that revolves around the nation's response to globalization, including economic integration into the larger North American economy. Elsewhere in the hemisphere, voters have responded to the impact of globalization in a classic economic retrospective fashion—for example, in Brazil's 2006 presidential election (Hunter and Power 2007)—but without the distinct regional pattern we see in Mexico. Those in the North and the Center-West have more successfully met the economic challenges of globalization; the wealthy and the educated have the resources and skills to benefit from it. Finally, younger Mexicans can more effectively adapt to globalization's demands than their elders. Because the PAN is the party most supportive of Mexico's integration into the global economy on liberal terms, that party has grown disproportionately in the North and Center-West, with the Mexican middle and upper-middle classes, and among the younger generations. In contrast, López Obrador's message clearly resonates better among older Mexicans. The PRI, which has not yet found a clear programmatic position after falling from power, has relied on the votes of the old, the economically vulnerable, and the ignorant—those least able to choose a new partisan preference. If the PRI continues to do so, it will gradually fade from the electoral scene as its social base passes away. Whether the PRD succeeds in López Obrador's strategy of appealing to the PRI base may determine whether these social divisions come to dominate the electoral landscape.

CHAPTER FOUR

Regionalized Voting Behavior and Political Discussion in Mexico

Andy Baker

Mexico's political landscape is dominated by a regional cleavage. During and after the 2006 election campaign, "blue" and "yellow" became pundits' shorthand for expressing the divide between the mostly conservative North with its blue National Action Party (PAN) states and the more left-leaning South awash in yellow Party of the Democratic Revolution (PRD) states.[1] The stark regional concentration of each party's support base was actually not new in 2006; such a division has existed ever since Mexican elections became competitive in the late 1980s and early 1990s. With the gradual decline of the PRI, however, the regional cleavage has captured analysts' attention.

To date, scholars have attributed Mexico's regional cleavage to individual-level traits, such as differences in wealth and issue attitudes that correlate with region, or they have left it entirely unexplained. I argue that the reasons for Mexico's most salient political cleavage remain poorly understood. Furthermore, I introduce political discussion to the study of Mexican voting behavior, contending that politically colored conversations among citizens reinforce and sustain Mexico's regionalized politics, because such exchanges expose citizens to the political biases of their immediate social environments. In other words, voters' social milieus shape the availability of candidate preferences among their potential discussion partners. For example, northerners were more likely than southerners to have conversations with committed PAN partisans during the 2006 campaign, whereas southerners were more likely to encounter and discuss politics with PRD supporters. These interactions were often persuasive enough to shape voting behavior.

In the following section, I discuss the nature and individual-level sources of Mexico's regional political cleavage and place it in a comparative perspective.

The third section proposes immediate social environments and political discussion as an additional reason behind the high degree of voter-preference regionalization in Mexico, laying out the theoretical foundations for how such factors might play this explanatory role. The remainder of the chapter conducts two types of statistical analyses with data from the Mexico 2006 Panel Study.[2] One is descriptive and conveys the nature of political discussion networks in Mexico's 2006 campaign to see if their overall makeup is compatible with the theory and to place them in comparative perspective. The second is explanatory and links the supply of political preferences in voters' immediate social environments to their eventual voting behavior. It also illustrates how this helps to account for the regionalization of political preferences in Mexico.

Regionalism in Mexican Voting Behavior

As the hegemony of the Institutional Revolutionary Party (PRI) began to crack in 1988, opposition parties rushed to fill the void. They did so, however, in a geographically uneven manner. Throughout the 1990s, the PAN was a capable challenger to the PRI in elections that occurred in the North, while the PRD was the primary challenger in the South. Neither of the two main opposition parties, however, had any meaningful presence in the other's stronghold. This arrangement led some analysts to speak of an electoral "bifurcation" or of "two separate two-party systems" instead of a three-party system (Klesner 1995, 143). Many northern states featured competition between only the PRI and the PAN, while only the PRI and the PRD competed in southern states.

The momentous presidential election of 2000 marked a change in the political landscape. PAN candidate and eventual winner Vicente Fox had enough of a national following that he actually out-polled the PRD candidate, Cuauhtémoc Cárdenas, in many southern states. However, this result reflected the overall weakness of Cárdenas's candidacy more than it did any fundamental shift in Mexico's political geography; Fox's best draw was still in the North and Cárdenas's was in the South. The PRI, for its part, remained a "national" party, albeit a losing one, as its vote was much more evenly distributed across Mexico's different regions.

The 2006 presidential election saw a further decline for the PRI, as it gave way to the PRD and the PAN as the front-running challenger in numerous states. PAN candidate Felipe Calderón had much greater success in the North than the South, while leftist candidate Andrés Manuel López Obrador (AMLO) outran Calderón in the South. Calderón won all but three of the eighteen states lying to the north of Michoacán's and Hidalgo's northern borders, and López Obrador won all but two of the fourteen states (including the Federal District) lying to the south of this obvious political fault line.

Scholars of Mexican voting behavior have thus stressed region as a primary, if not *the* primary, "cause" of vote choice (Dominguez and McCann 1996; Klesner 1993, 1995; Magaloni 1999; Poiré 1999). "Region, not class, remained the dominant cleavage in electoral politics [in 2006]. Our findings thus support the conventional wisdom that Mexico has increasingly become a nation of 'blue states' and 'yellow states'" (Lawson 2006, 2, 4; see also Klesner 2007). Indeed, comparative data do tend to suggest that preferences in Mexico are highly regionalized and grew more so in 2006. Table 4.1 documents both of these facts, showing political regionalization in each of the Western Hemisphere's three most populous countries: Mexico, the United States, and Brazil. Regionalism is measured by the standard deviation of each presidential candidate's vote share across all states. A variable was created for each candidate that recorded his percentage of the vote in each of his country's states (each case is thus a state). Candidates with support bases that were highly regionalized—i.e., much higher in some states than in others—have a large standard deviation on this variable. Those with support bases that were more evenly spread across the country have a small standard deviation. As standard deviations, the numbers are in the original units (percentage of state vote), but these results are best understood in comparison with each other.

The first two columns depict geographical concentration in Mexico's 2000 and 2006 elections. In 2000, PRI candidate Francisco Labastida had the most evenly distributed vote base, whereas those of the two opposition candidates, Fox and Cárdenas, were less evenly spread across the Mexican states. By 2006 this distinction sharpened; the PRI's vote base became more evenly distributed, while that of the PRD and the PAN grew all the more concentrated.

Cross-national comparisons indicate the extent to which the Mexican vote was regionalized in these two presidential contests. The 2000 election in the United States introduced the world to the red state/blue state distinction, a now-famous shorthand for the political and cultural differences between the Democratic coastal and Great Lakes states and the Republican southern and central states. Fox's vote base in Mexico's transformative 2000 election, which occurred 5 months before the U.S. election, was just regionally concentrated as were Bush's and Gore's; by 2006, the degree of regionalization in Mexico

Table 4.1   Degree of political regionalization in three democracies

Mexico 2000		Mexico 2006		US 2000		Brazil 2002	
Fox	10.3	Calderón	12.4	Bush	10.4	Lula	5.5
Labastida	7.1	Madrazo	6.3	Gore	10.2	Serra	7.6
Cárdenas	9.3	López Obrador	12.2	*N* = 51		Garotinho	7.1
N = 32		*N* = 32				Gomes	7.3
						N = 27	

Note: Entries are the standard deviations of each candidate's vote share across states.

had surpassed that in the red-and-blue-obsessed United States. The substantial amount of regionalization in Mexico is even more striking when compared to Brazil, where *all* candidates in 2002 had, at least by Mexican standards, relatively national degrees of support. Brazil's most regionally concentrated parties resembled the PRI in 2000 more than they did Mexico's opposition parties. In short, analysts were clearly correct in identifying region as a powerful force in Mexican politics.

There are many reasons for the regionalization of voting behavior, but in general scholars have mentioned the following four (see chapter 3 in this volume). The one most frequently cited is the disparity in living standards and in overall levels of economic development in different parts of Mexico (Magaloni 2006). Northern states are more economically developed, featuring higher living standards and greater rates of industrialization, literacy, and education (Klesner 1995). Since wealthier, middle-class voters tend to be more attracted to the market-oriented policy proposals of the center-right PAN, the more highly developed North leans toward its candidates, while the less-developed South favors the PRD. Moreover, NAFTA and the rise of the *maquiladora* (export-oriented, in-bond processing) sector have been partially responsible for the North's relative prosperity and its thriving middle class. As such, pro-market rhetoric no doubt resonates more favorably among middle-class northerners than among poor southerners, who see few benefits from integration with the United States.

Second, the PAN is a culturally conservative party—opposing capital punishment, abortion, and the inclusion of the morning-after pill in the government health insurance plan—with historically tight bonds to the Roman Catholic Church. Numerous northern and central states and cities, especially Guadalajara and Monterrey, feature higher-than-average levels of church attendance and more conservative dispositions on religious, moral, and cultural issues. For example, residents of Mexico's central region launched the 1927 Cristero rebellion in reaction to the government's anticlerical policies. In contrast, the secularist PRI and the PRD tend to pull their support from voters with less-traditional beliefs who disproportionately reside in the Federal District and the South, and in the rule-proving exception of the heavily Catholic state of Yucatán.

Third, Mexico's urban/rural divide is an important political cleavage that could have regional consequences. Even at the height of its hegemony in the 1960s, the PRI polled more strongly in rural areas, while the PAN enjoyed greater relative success in Mexico's urban centers (Klesner 1993). After the late 1980s, the Left crept into the PAN's urban redoubt by competing with it for opposition voters, eventually establishing a stronghold in the Federal District (Distrito Federal, or DF), where much of Mexico City is located. As such, urbanization has sharply stratified PRI versus non-PRI voters since the late 1980s. Despite the Left's incursion onto the PAN's territory, the PAN remained the strongest urban party throughout the 1990s and 2000s, especially outside the Federal District (Klesner 1993, 1995, 2004). The urban/rural divide may thus induce a regional effect, since the South is more rural than the North.

A final factor relates to the brief history of democratic contestation in Mexico (Lawson 2006). As elections became more free and fair, Mexico's plurality-rule contests for governors, mayors, and most federal deputies encouraged two-party competition at the state and local levels. Most voters also tended to approach multiparty elections with "regime cleavage" foremost in their mind, asking themselves above all whether they wanted to prolong the hegemonic rule of the party of the state (Dominguez and McCann 1995, 1996). For the PRI's opponents, *which* opposition party won was often secondary, so voters merely chose between the PRI and the strongest opposition party. This fact gave tremendous first-mover advantages to whichever opposition party established an organizational presence in each state and emerged as the PRI's most viable challenger in the early 1990s (Greene 2007; Hiskey and Canache 2005; Lawson 2006). A positive byproduct of achieving this early front-running-challenger status was the emergence, down the road, of a much larger pool of partisan sympathizers in the state. This explanation, by itself, cannot clarify why preferences initially clustered so much in contiguous states, but it can provide reasons for the persistence of the divide.[3]

What Are Regional Effects?

Scholarly work on Mexican voting behavior has demonstrated that these four factors certainly help to account for Mexico's regional divide, yet they only explain a small part of Mexico's regional effects. After all, statistical models of Mexican voting behavior tend to control for these factors, yet they often still reveal statistically significant regional effects (typically measured with dummy variables). These lingering effects can be thought of in two useful ways.

From one perspective, they exist because scholars find that respondents with identical individual-level traits but varying regional locations have vastly different probabilities of voting for each candidate. To find statistically significant regional effects simply means that, for example, a college-educated, middle-class, economically liberal, religiously observant, culturally conservative, urban woman enjoying increased real income and residing in a northern state has a much higher probability of voting for the PAN than a woman in the South with equivalent traits. Both voters share prototypically pro-PAN traits, but the voter from the North ends up having a greater likelihood of choosing the PAN than the voter from the South. The precise reasons for and causal mechanisms behind this lingering differential, however, remain unclear—and even unexplored—when regional variables remain statistically significant.

In more technical terms, regional dummy variables fail to drop out of multiple regression models—that is, they remain statistically significant and explain residual variance that the individual-level demographic and ideational factors cannot. Regional dummy variables are thus acting as atheoretical fixed effects variables, or proper nouns, that are merely identifying important unexplained group-level behavioral differences (Przeworski and Teune 1970). Regional effects variables merely indicate that these remaining differences exist; they do not explain *why* they exist.

I claim that social context (i.e., the arena in which one engages in interpersonal interaction) explains why individuals with identical traits and beliefs exhibit different voting behavior patterns that correspond to their region of residence. Voters do not decide which party to favor in a social vacuum. They reach political decisions amidst ongoing conversations. They discuss politics and openly deliberate over their choices with family and friends, accepting advice and information from others while at times attempting to persuade. In short, citizens are embedded in social networks that sustain politically relevant interpersonal exchanges. These interactions have the ability to induce disparities between individual-level patterns and aggregate outcomes (Huckfeldt et al. 2004).

Consider yet again the two prototypical PAN voters with identical individual-level traits. A crucial but largely overlooked distinction between the northerner and the southerner is that the former lives in an environment in which she is far more likely than the southerner to encounter other PAN supporters. The supply of PAN discussants that may persuade her to convert away from a non-PAN option or, alternatively, reinforce her partisan predispositions is relatively high in her blue state. In contrast, the southerner would find far fewer pro-PAN interlocutors to reinforce her "natural" pro-PAN predispositions. Even though inclined to favor the PAN, she may often find herself in the uncomfortable position of supporting a minority viewpoint when discussing politics. Since the "socially heroic partisan is a rare event" (Huckfeldt et al. 2004, 43), she is more likely than her blue-state counterpart to cave in to the majority position (see also Asch 1951; Lazarsfeld et al. 1944; Noelle-Neumann 1984). In sum, the lingering effects that make region in Mexico more than the sum of its individual parts may be due to differences in the relative supply of reinforcing versus countervailing discussants.

Political Discussion and Social Networks in Mexico: Descriptive Evidence

If this network approach can help explain regional effects, then the evidence should, at the very least, indicate that (1) Mexicans discuss politics, and (2) they tend to do so with people with whom they agree politically. This section describes how frequently and with whom Mexicans talk about politics by reporting discussion frequency, average network size, and attitudinal homogeneity among discussion partners. It also places Mexicans in a comparative perspective on these dimensions. To gauge political discussion frequency, the Mexico 2006 Panel Study contained a straightforward question, asking respondents if they discussed politics with other people "daily," "a few times each week," "a few times each month," "rarely," or "never." To gauge network size, the final two waves of the panel each contained a political discussant "name generator." The battery read as follows: "Could you tell me the names of the three people with whom you most discuss politics? If you would like, you may tell me their complete names or just their first names and last initials."[4] These name-generator data are the first of their kind for the Mexican case.

The median response in both waves was "a few times each month." A relatively small number of Mexicans—less than 10 percent—discussed politics daily. Moreover, a plurality said they "rarely" talked about politics. At the same time, however, the vast majority of citizens *did* discuss politics at some point. Only about 15 percent claimed they "never" did so, and about 35 percent broached the subject of politics more than just a few times per month. It is worth adding that the overall rate of political conversations did not change substantially during the campaign. In short, wide variation in discussion frequency existed around a rather low—but still positive—mean response.

Network size, or the number of political discussants that respondents named, also varied substantially; the two most frequent categories were the two extremes, "three" and "zero." In the second wave, 38 percent of respondents named three discussants, while 40 percent mentioned none. The number of named discussants increased between May and election day, as the percentage of individuals reporting no discussants fell to 28 percent in the third wave. The overall mean reflects this shift: the mean respondent reported 1.47 political discussants in wave 2 and 1.76 in wave 3. In sum, the campaign did not increase the perceived frequency of political conversations, but it did encourage Mexicans to broaden their contacts and increase the number of different people with whom they talked about politics.

Taken together, these results appear to be generally consistent with standard characterizations of citizens living in most democracies; average citizens are clearly not preoccupied with politics to such a degree that it permeates their daily conversations (Lippmann 1922). However, multi-country data do reveal that the frequency of political discussion and network size in Mexico were both low by international standards. In particular, according to the seventy-nation 2000 World Values Survey (www.worldvaluessurvey.org), Mexicans were in the 20th percentile in their self-reported rate of political discussion. They were also tied for last (with the United States and Russia) in an eight-nation comparison of network size.[5]

Do these findings about a relative dearth of discussion in Mexico portend that politicized conversations may not matter and, in particular, may not be a mechanism for Mexico's regionalization? Three reasons suggest that the answer is no. First, and of primary importance, most individuals engaged in some politically relevant conversations, even if only occasionally. Only a minority of citizens mentioned no discussants or reported never discussing politics. Second, Mexico's urban majority does talk about politics with impressive frequency.

The panel data reveal a meaningful divide between Mexico's politically "mute" rural residents, who constitute a minority of the population, and its politically "chatty" urban majority. Urban residents reported, on average, two discussants—60 percent more than the number reported by rural respondents, and a number that is much closer to the international mean. In other words, urban settings in Mexico *do* feature rich networks of interpersonal exchange, but the nation's overall mean is pulled down by rural dwellers.

Third, the political nature of social networks is just as important as their size in determining the extent to which conversations can reinforce political biases in one's surroundings. In particular, the level of network political heterogeneity is a crucial characteristic of discussion networks that is particularly relevant for understanding how such dialogs can strengthen regionalized voting. Network heterogeneity reflects the extent to which individuals in a network disagree—that is, hold politically divergent viewpoints. Networks are homogenous when people are prone to talk only with like-minded individuals, and they are heterogeneous, or diverse, when people tend to engage in conversations with those holding dissimilar political opinions. Individuals embedded in heterogeneous networks hear countervailing viewpoints, while those in homogenous networks are more insulated from differently-minded beliefs (Granovetter 1973; Huckfeldt et al. 2004; Mutz 2006).

If voters are not more likely than random chance would dictate to talk about politics with like-minded individuals—that is, if they do not tend to cluster together with discussants that share their candidate preferences—then such conversations cannot possibly explain regionalized voting in Mexico. In contrast, if discussion is responsible for the regionalization of voting behavior in the country, then, at a minimum, discussion networks should feature reasonably high levels of political agreement among their members. When preferences are highly regionalized, the supply of discussants in one's immediate social environment is more highly skewed in favor of one candidate within particular states and municipalities than it is nationwide. Thus the number of differently-minded conversationalists in one's immediate social environment will tend to be much smaller in such a context. High rates of agreement are therefore a necessary—but not sufficient—condition for establishing the link between discussion and regionalization.

The panel study followed each discussant name-generator battery by asking for whom each named discussant was voting in the presidential race. Using these results, table 4.2 indicates the extent to which Mexican discussion dyads were

Table 4.2   Prevalence of political agreement in Mexico, Brazil, and the United States

		(1) Share of dyads in which both partners agreed	(2) Probability two randomly chosen people agreed (based on election results)	(3) Observed agreement given random probability of agreement: (1)/(2)
Mexico 2006	Wave 2	.67	.32	2.11
	Wave 3	.70	.32	2.19
Brazil (2-city) 2002		.69	.41	1.68
United States 2000		.74	.50	1.48

characterized by political agreement. A discussion dyad is any pairwise combination of a panel respondent and one of her or his named discussants.[6] Political agreement exists in a dyad when the discussant's presidential candidate preference (at least as perceived by the respondent) was the same as that of the respondent. Disagreement exists when they preferred two different candidates.[7]

Agreement was clearly the rule in Mexico. Column 1 shows that in both waves, a large majority (about 70%) of dyads featured agreement; only 30 percent of them were characterized by disagreement. Also, only about 40 percent of all respondents had at least one disagreeing discussant. That citizens tended to cluster with like-minded individuals is not at all surprising or rare; crossnational evidence shows rates of agreement in discussion networks to be much higher than sheer chance would dictate (Huckfeldt et al. 2005). But do a greater-than-typical number of Mexicans shy away from conversations with those who disagree with them? Table 4.2 provides two points of comparison: Brazil and the United States. Column 1 suggests that the rate of agreement in American and Brazilian dyads was essentially equivalent to that observed in Mexico, but these raw rates of agreement are misleading. After all, the nature of party competition, and in particular the number of party or candidate options, establishes different cross-national probabilities in the overall potential for disagreement. Two randomly chosen people in a system where votes are divided evenly between eight parties have a much higher probability of disagreeing ($p = .875$) than do two such people in a two-party system ($p = .5$). Therefore, any international comparison of how amenable citizens are to engage in conversations with those holding competing political opinions must adjust for these differences.

Column 2 thus reports the probability—based on the actual election results— that two randomly chosen voters would agree. Americans and Brazilians had more opportunities for agreement than did Mexicans,[8] which casts the equivalent raw rates of agreement from column 1 in a new light. Mexicans, despite having a more limited supply—at least at the national level—of like-minded discussants, were just as likely to find them as were Americans and Brazilians. Column 3 illustrates these cross-national differences most effectively: Mexicans were more than twice as likely to have agreeing discussants than we would expect them to have purely by chance, whereas Brazilians were just 1.7 times as likely and Americans just 1.5 times as likely.[9] In short, Mexicans have a comparatively higher propensity to discuss politics with like-minded individuals, suggesting a mechanism by which regionalism is propagated.

Can Discussion Account for Regional Effects?

If these discussion networks help explain the regionalization of Mexican politics, two more conditions must hold. First, the distribution of preferences in one's broader social environment must influence the makeup of one's discussant network. Second, discussion itself must affect vote choice. If it does not, then the distribution of preferences in one's immediate social environment is irrelevant to regional variation in partisan support.

Does social environment condition the political leaning of each respondent's discussant network? The distribution of preferences in one's social environment establishes the supply, or relative availability, of each political preference among potential discussants. Therefore, even if voters choose discussants randomly from their social environment, supply will shape the distribution of the political preferences they encounter in conversation (Huckfeldt and Sprague 1988). For example, PRI supporters living in the DF, where only 9 percent of its residents voted for Madrazo, are likely to end up discussing politics with differently-minded persons, because they would have a hard time finding fellow PRI discussants. If so, then aggregate factors such as region hold the potential to influence individual-level political choice, because they constrain the availability of viewpoints to which citizens are exposed in everyday conversations.

It is unlikely, however, that citizens choose their discussion partners in a random fashion. Rather, voters probably exercise discretion in choosing discussants from among the available supply. As a result, citizen demand for discussants may also play a role, and it may even cancel out supply effects. Citizens could be so politicized that they seek out like-minded discussants even in contexts where they may be hard to find, preferring pleasant conversation with those of similar opinions to conflictual discourse with differently minded ones (Huckfeldt and Sprague 1988; Mutz and Martin 2001). For example, PRI partisans in the DF may still seek out sympathetic conversation partners and avoid political conversation with citizens who adhere to their environment's majority opinion (Finifter 1974). If so, then the aggregate distribution of political preferences in their social environment may be irrelevant.

To distinguish among these explanations, I modeled three separate dependent variables with the 2006 panel data: the number of pro-Calderón discussants a respondent had, the number of pro-AMLO discussants, and the number of pro-Madrazo discussants. Each of these variables ranges from 0 to 3. For example, a respondent with two pro-Calderón discussants, one pro-AMLO discussant, and (by virtue of having capped the number of discussants at three) zero pro-Madrazo discussants received scores of 2, 1, and 0, respectively. Respondents reporting no discussants, or not knowing any of their discussants' preferences, received a score of 0 on all three.

To measure the supply of each type of discussant in a respondent's social environment, I used local-level election results—each candidate's vote share in the respondent's county—as the key independent variables.[10] If the aggregate distribution of vote preferences matters, then these county-level variables will have an important impact on the types of political preferences that the respondents encountered in their political conversations. To measure demand-side factors, I included various measures of respondent political preferences, such as partisanship, past vote choice, and candidate evaluations. All such variables, the statistical model, hypotheses tests, and a more thorough discussion of the results are reported in the Mexico 2006 Panel Study's supplemental materials for chapter 4.[11] To stay focused on the concept of region, here I discuss in detail only the impacts of supply-side factors and depict them graphically.

Respondents' social environments, as measured by the distribution of preferences in their county, were statistically and substantively significant predictors of the types of individuals whom respondents mentioned as political discussants. Figure 4.1 illustrates the effects of these environmental constraints on supply by showing predicted values from the statistical models for the average Mexican across three different counties. Similar to the running examples discussed in the second section of this chapter, I considered the impact that county of residence would have on three hypothetical citizens with equivalent individual-level traits. These three citizens are exceedingly typical Mexicans, ones with average values on all individual-level political and demographic variables. They also have an equivalent number (the average) of discussants. Figure 4.1 quantifies the iso-

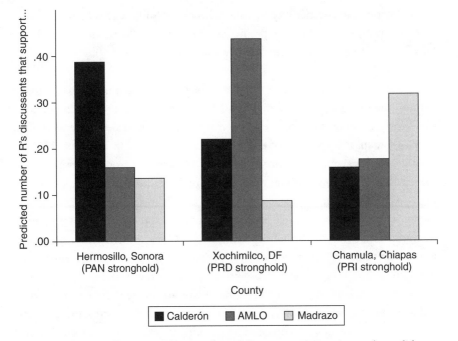

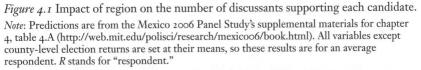

Figure 4.1 Impact of region on the number of discussants supporting each candidate.
Note: Predictions are from the Mexico 2006 Panel Study's supplemental materials for chapter 4, table 4.A (http://web.mit.edu/polisci/research/mexico06/book.html). All variables except county-level election returns are set at their means, so these results are for an average respondent. *R* stands for "respondent."

lated impact of social environment by taking these hypothetical citizens with identical individual-level traits and varying only their county of residence.

The first such individual resides in Hermosillo, a mid-sized city of about 700,000 people that serves as the capital of the state of Sonora (in Mexico's northern region). Sixty-two percent of Hermosillo's residents voted for Calderón.[12] The predicted number of pro-Calderón discussants for this individual is almost .40, as the leftmost black bar indicates. The adjacent grey bar shows that this would have about .16 pro-AMLO discussants, and the white bar, .14 pro-Madrazo discussants. As the middle set of bars indicates, an equivalent individual residing in historic Xochimilco (part of Mexico City) would have a completely different predicted array of discussants. For a person in this PRD bailiwick (where 66% of the voters chose López Obrador), the model predicts just .20 pro-Calderón discussants, almost .45 pro-AMLO discussants, and less than .10 pro-Madrazo discussants. Of course, citizens do not speak with fractions of people, so another way of thinking about the differences between these two contexts is to note that the predicted ratio of pro-Calderón to pro-AMLO falls from more than 2:1 to less than 1:2 with this move from "blue" Sonora to "yellow" DF.

A similarly sized shift occurs when considering the third individual, a resident of one of Mexico's few remaining PRI redoubts. In San Juan Chamula, a small town of about 35,000, five miles from San Cristóbal de las Casas in the state of Chiapas, 65 percent of the voters chose Madrazo in 2006. In this environment, the average citizen would have .16 pro-Calderón discussants, .18 pro-AMLO discussants, and more than .30 pro-Madrazo discussants. The ratio of pro-Calderón to pro-Madrazo discussants falls from 3:1 in Hermosillo to 1:2 in San Juan Chamula. In short, social environments and the supply of potential discussants mattered above and beyond individual-level traits. These aggregate-level factors clearly determined the kind of politically colored information that Mexicans heard in their conversations during the 2006 campaign.

The following question remains: Did these politically relevant conversations influence voting behavior? To answer this, I estimated a second set of statistical models to explain vote choice. The dependent variable is the respondent's vote choice on election day (i.e., from wave 3 of the panel), so the models are multinomial logits. The set of models accounts for potential discussant effects while also controlling for many of the individual-level factors—such as wealth, religiosity, urbanization, and partisanship—that might help explain the sharp regionalization of preferences in Mexico. I reported the full model results in the Mexico 2006 Panel's Study's supplemental materials for chapter 4, rather than here, because many of the results are redundant with those given by other authors in this volume. Moreover, the goal of this chapter is not to construct and support a comprehensive analysis of Mexican voting behavior in 2006, but rather to assess whether discussant effects help account for regional differences in voting behavior. Thus, my focus remains on regional measures and discussant effects and, in particular, on how the latter conditions the impact of the former. The main substantive points are presented in figure 4.2.

I estimated three different voter choice models. "Model 1: Regional Effects Only" contains just two independent variables, Calderon's and AMLO's vote share in the respondent's county (only two variables are needed to specify the full distribution of preferences, at least across the three main parties, in each respondent's social environment). These are the same measures of social environment profiled as the key independent variables in figure 4.1. "Model 2:

Regional and Individual-Level Effects" contains as independent variables these two regional effects variables *plus* about fifteen different independent variables that measure the individual-level factors (such as wealth, religiosity, urbanization, and partisanship) that previous scholars have reputed to be determinants of regionalism in Mexico. "Model 3: Regional, Individual-Level, and Discussant Effects" is the most fully specified model. It contains the regional effects variables and all of the individual-level factors of model 2, but it also includes discussant effects. These discussant effects are measured using six independent variables: the number of pro-Calderón discussants in panel waves 2 and 3, the number of pro-AMLO discussants in waves 2 and 3, and the number of pro-Madrazo discussants in waves 2 and 3. Measuring the preferences of discussion partners at t and $t - 1$ captures both short-term and medium-term influences from discussions.

The purpose of proceeding iteratively, or building up, to the most fully specified model is to observe the extent to which successively adding in individual-level factors, and then discussion measures, eliminates lingering regional effects (i.e., replaces the proper nouns with theoretical variables). In other words, if these two sets of factors—individual-level characteristics and discussant networks—are the reasons behind the sharp regionalization of political preferences in Mexico, then the regional effects should attenuate (i.e., the coefficients on the county vote share variables should fall toward zero) as each set is added.

Figure 4.2 illustrates this process. The figure plots the multinomial logit coefficients for the two regional effects variables—"AMLO's vote in R's county" and "Calderon's vote in R's county"—in each of the three models. For each of these two independent variables, the individual models produce three coefficients—that is, one for each candidate. The size of each coefficient is designated by its horizontal placement on the *x*-axis. As a result, the further right a candidate's name is, the stronger the positive impact of the corresponding regional effect variable (labeled on the *y*-axis) on the probability that a respondent voted for that candidate.

For example, row 1 (model 1) plots the three coefficients that quantify the impact of AMLO's vote share in the respondent's county when controlling only for the county's vote share for Calderón. The logit coefficient for Madrazo is about −.09, that for Calderón is about −.05, and that for AMLO is zero. The relative, not the absolute, size of these coefficients is what matters, because one of the coefficients is arbitrarily chosen to be anchored at zero. In other words, the zero coefficient does *not* mean that region has no relationship to a respon-

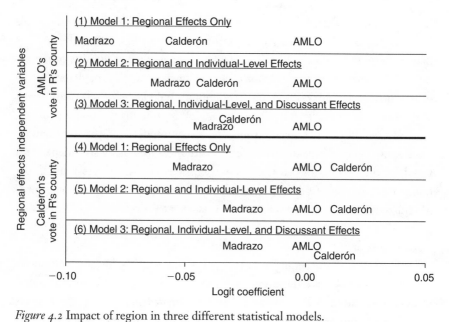

Figure 4.2 Impact of region in three different statistical models.

Note: Each candidate name represents a "regional effect" logit coefficient generated from the three multinomial logit models reported in the Mexico 2006 Panel Study's supplemental materials for chapter 4, table 4.B (http://web.mit.edu/polisci/research/mexico06/book.html).

dent's chances of voting for AMLO. On the contrary, the large (horizontal) distance between the AMLO coefficient and the other two coefficients indicates that AMLO's county-level vote is negatively related to the probability that the respondent voted for Madrazo and Calderón and thus positively related to the probability that the respondent voted for AMLO. It is neither surprising nor important that the statistical analysis reveals this regional effect; it merely indicates that the survey sample was more likely to find AMLO voters in counties where AMLO polled well than in counties where he did poorly. Quite obviously, the goal should be to explain or reduce the relative differences in these coefficients (or the size of the horizontal gaps) rather than assign substantive meaning to them.

The model 2 results in row 2 are a first attempt at doing so. Recall that model 2 contains these two county-level factors along with all potentially relevant individual-level political factors, such as partisanship and issue attitudes. A comparison between this row and the top row shows how accounting for these individual-level factors results in a convergence among the three coefficients. The horizontal spread of the names shrinks dramatically between the model

1 and model 2 results, a sign that the coefficients are converging toward zero. Substantively, the so-called regional effect is weakened by the inclusion of these theoretically sharper variables. In other words, model 2 attributes less of the cross-individual differences in voting behavior to county-level political preferences, because it accounts for variation in the individual-level differences that previous scholars of Mexican regionalism have highlighted.

The model 3 results in row 3 reflect the size of regional effects when controlling for individual-level factors *and* discussant effects. Again, the coefficients have converged even further horizontally (toward zero); controlling for discussant effects reduces lingering regional differences all the more (the vertical distances are irrelevant, established only to ensure readability). Given a northerner and a southerner with identical individual-level traits, model 3 more satisfactorily explains why the former would be less likely to vote for AMLO than would the latter—the northerner is less likely to have pro-Calderón discussants. Discussant effects were particularly important for nearly eliminating the residual aggregate-level variance between Madrazo and Calderón voters. Still, model 3 does not completely eliminate regional effects, because the unexplained regional gap between Calderón and AMLO remains quite large.

The lower half of figure 4.2, rows 4 through 6, walks through the same exercise for the other regional effect variable, Calderon's share of the vote in each respondent's county. The introduction of individual-level factors reduces the horizontal spread among the three coefficients considerably (compare rows 4 and 5). Discussant effects (added in row 6) close the gap between AMLO and Calderón voters entirely, although they do little to bring the conditional mean of Madrazo voters closer to that among AMLO and Calderón voters.

One interesting commonality across the two independent variables (comparing the top half of the figure to the bottom half) is that individual-level and discussant-level factors fail to completely explain the gap between Madrazo and AMLO voters. For example, given a resident of the Federal District and a rural resident of Chiapas with identical individual-level traits and identical discussant networks (i.e., in terms of the political preferences they encounter), the one in Chiapas is still more likely to vote for Madrazo. The potential omitted factor might be clientelism and local political machines, which are particularly important for the PRI, but I leave to future research the goal of getting regional effects to completely drop out of statistical models. Regardless, discussion networks are clearly an important aspect of the theoretical infrastructure that explains voting behavior and regional effects in Mexico.

According to advocates of deliberative democracy, the quality of citizenship and democracy is enhanced when citizens seek out a diverse array of political viewpoints and deliberate in polite but reasoned exchange with differently minded associates (Gutmann and Thompson 2004). Citizens are alleged to be more tolerant, more knowledgeable, and more politically engaged when thinking about and discussing issues across lines of political difference. In reality, however, citizens rarely have the motivation to seek out political information in such a purposive and open-minded manner. Moreover, even if they did have such an inclination, the supply of diverse and differently minded perspectives in their immediate social milieus would circumscribe their ability to find them.

The constraints imposed by the supply of competing viewpoints in one's social environment can thus have a variety of consequences. One important effect is that they reinforce the regionalization of mass political preferences. In Mexico, the impact of region is greater than the sum of its individual parts, because citizens are embedded in political communication networks that vary greatly by their place of residence. Many Mexicans with similar or identical individual-level political predispositions nonetheless cast different ballots on election day. They have been exposed to a set of politically colored arguments through their interpersonal conversations, and these points of view vary with the relative supply of beliefs upheld in their social environments.

The findings from this chapter should urge scholars of voting behavior to treat the existence of statistically significant regional effects (which are often in the form of dummy variables) not as a substantive conclusion, but rather as a starting point for further inquiry into why regional differences remain unexplained. In the Mexican case, much work has in fact already been accomplished on this front. This chapter thus builds on, rather than refutes, previous interpretations of Mexican voting behavior, as it confirms that individual-level factors such as wealth and partisanship are partially responsible for Mexico's deepening blue state/yellow state divide. The findings go a step further, however, to point out that political discussion reinforces this division. Many individuals do not necessarily fit the dominant political profile of their regional context, as plenty of northerners are poor, a large number of southerners are pro-NAFTA, and not all inhabitants of Mexico City are PRD partisans. Many such individuals, however, vote with the prevailing opinion of their surroundings, by virtue of having absorbed it through political conversations.

CHAPTER FIVE

Absentee Voting and Transnational Civic Engagement among Mexican Expatriates

James A. McCann, Wayne A. Cornelius, and David L. Leal

In the 2006 presidential election, Felipe Calderón, the candidate of then president Vicente Fox's National Action Party (PAN), outpolled all of his competitors among the small number of Mexican expatriates who voted absentee. A clear majority of the ballots—58 percent—went to Calderón. Andrés Manuel López Obrador of the Party of the Democratic Revolution (PRD) received 34 percent, and Roberto Madrazo of the Institutional Revolutionary Party (PRI) was credited with just 4 percent. In the following section, we discuss the legislative history of this *voto remoto* (absentee voting) reform and some possible explanations for its failure to induce large numbers of expatriate voters to participate. We then present findings from the 2006 Mexican Expatriate Study, a large-scale survey of Mexican nationals in three very different regions of the country: Dallas, San Diego, and north-central Indiana.

Our analysis shows that presidential preferences among U.S.-based Mexicans were strikingly similar to those of Mexicans living in Mexico, both in the levels of support given to the candidates and in the attitudinal underpinnings of these preferences. In addition, there was an ample reservoir of informal civic engagement in the 2006 election, even for the Mexican-born residents of midwestern cities hundreds of miles away from the border. Such findings should be reassuring to reform-minded Mexican officials wishing to expand upon the 2006 absentee-voting experiment in future contests. Although many Mexican nationals living in the United States appear to be little interested in Mexican politics, a sizeable number appear ready, willing, and able to become transnational political participants if more user-friendly mechanisms can be devised to facilitate their involvement.

Absentee Voting: Political and Administrative Background

Since 1990, the United States has seen a historically unprecedented "great wave" of Mexican migration. This, the latest of four waves since the late nineteenth century, is adding approximately 400,000 Mexican nationals to the United States each year. This immigrant population is expected to grow from 9.9 million in 2004 to 18 million in 2030.[1] Mexican migrants are increasingly the objects of political mobilization efforts by political parties and candidates from south of the border. In the run-up to the 2000 Mexican presidential election, for example, there was a significant amount of campaigning in the United States, especially in areas where Mexicans could conceivably travel south to vote in special polling stations set up for Mexicans who found themselves outside their electoral districts on election day. In 2004, a number of Mexican nationals living in the United States ran successfully for mayoral and state legislative office in their places of origin, after changes in Mexican state law made it possible for expatriates to hold such offices (Bakker and Smith 2003).[2] More generally, the period following the North American Free Trade Agreement (NAFTA) has seen an explosion of cross-border organizing activity by nongovernmental organizations—based on nationality, ethnicity, religion, and economic interests—and much of this activity seeks to tap the human and financial capital of Mexican immigrants in the United States (Bada et al. 2006; Brooks and Fox 2002; Fitzgerald 2002; Fox and Rivera-Salgado 2004; Hondagneu-Sotelo et al. 2004).

As Mexico has struggled with profound economic issues (a devastating devaluation crisis in 1994–95, inadequate job creation, stresses on its middle class, shaky investor confidence, and so forth), its leaders have sought closer ties to U.S.-based expatriate communities. Vicente Fox himself visited selected immigrant neighborhoods in the United States during his term as president, and he praised expatriates as "heroes," "cultural ambassadors," and "Mexico's gift to the world." The proliferation of hometown associations linking expatriate Mexicans in U.S. cities with their places of origin in Mexico has also provided new vehicles for stimulating development efforts in these places that tap the human and financial capital accumulated by expatriates. Moreover, these associations encourage their members to see themselves as stakeholders in hometown development.

In various ways over the last decade, on a formal-legal level, Mexico has attempted to extend political rights to its expatriates in the United States. Until recently, however, these rights were incomplete. A constitutional reform approved by Mexico's Congress in 1996 allowed Mexicans living abroad to be dual nationals and granted them suffrage in Mexican elections.[3] But the implementing legislation for absentee voting was blocked by partisan wrangling, grounded in expectations of differential electoral advantages among Mexico's three major parties if expatriates were allowed to vote from abroad. Disputes raged over the mode of absentee voting (electronic via the Internet, regular mail, voting at Mexican consulates), ballot security measures, updating voter identification cards, whether absentee voting should be allowed only for presidential races, whether Mexican parties should be allowed to raise money from expatriate groups or fund campaign activities abroad, and the level of government spending needed to organize and count the expatriate vote. The stalemate in Congress was finally broken in mid-2005, barely in time to implement absentee voting in the next national election.

On July 2, 2006, for the first time, Mexicans living abroad had the opportunity to cast an absentee ballot in a Mexican presidential election. However, only 33,131 actually voted absentee, which represents 0.06 percent of Mexico's registered voter population and 0.46 percent of the Mexicans of voting age who are believed to be living in the United States. Mexican election authorities had predicted a 10 percent turnout of those who were eligible to vote and had a voter credential—about 400,000. Based on 2001 survey data gathered from Mexicans living in Los Angeles County who had voted in the 2000 Mexican presidential election, Marcelli and Cornelius (2005) had estimated a participation rate of 1.5–4.2 percent (125,000–360,000 voters).

Why so few takers? Much of the explanation undoubtedly lies in the highly restrictive system for absentee voting that the Mexican Congress approved.

- The six million expatriates who did not already have a *credencial* (voter identification card) issued by the Federal Electoral Institute (IFE) were excluded; they could not apply for an absentee ballot unless they returned to Mexico and applied for an identification card.
- Even if one possessed a voter identification card, the procedure for obtaining an absentee ballot was cumbersome, time consuming, and expensive. People without Internet access had to physically go to a Mexican consulate to pick up a registration form. They then had to

get photocopies of their voter identification card and of a utility bill or some other proof of U.S. residency, go to a post office, and send the whole application package back via international registered mail (costing approximately $8). Applicants had to wait several months to find out whether their request for a ballot had been approved. Once they received a ballot, it had to be returned to Mexico City, again by registered mail.

- Registration for absentee ballots did not even open until October 1, 2005, and the application deadline was January 15, 2006—for a first-ever absentee registration process! The publicity effort was minimal, as the Mexican Congress had not approved a budget for promotional advertising in the United States. Consequently, many Mexican immigrants were not even aware of the opportunity to cast an absentee ballot.

- Voting by expatriates was limited to a mail-in ballot; no polling places were established on U.S. soil. Opponents of this restriction argued that turnout would be boosted by allowing multiple voting mechanisms, including voting in person at Mexican consulates and electronic voting via the Internet (if vote security issues could be resolved). But the Mexican Congress was willing to approve only a single mode of absentee voting.

- Absentee voting in 2006 was limited to the presidential race, despite the fact that most congressional seats, several state governorships, and hundreds of mayoral posts were also being filled that year.

- The implementing legislation prohibited political parties and candidates from campaigning in the United States. Generating expatriate interest in an election with no paid media advertising on the U.S. side is a formidable challenge. In 2006, if voters wanted to know the presidential candidates' positions on specific issues from the IFE, they had to go its website—and have the correct software to download the files.

Why such a restrictive process? Or, put differently, why did Mexico's three main parties even bother to implement absentee balloting? The numerous restrictions reflect the three major parties' uncertainty about the impact of a more open process on the 2006 election (Escobar 2007). Pre-election academic analyses suggested that no one party could be guaranteed a commanding advantage in competing for the expatriate vote. Using records from the 2000 Mexican presidential election, Marcelli and Cornelius (2005) estimated that the PAN would likely be the most attractive party for expatriates in 2006 but that the PRD and PRI might also draw a considerable portion of the expatriate vote. Lawson (2003) came to a similar conclusion regarding the PAN and the PRD in advance of the 2006 campaign, although he expressed skepticism about the PRI's prospects. Such forecasts notwithstanding, no party really wanted to take a chance on unfettered absentee voting. Even if turnout were minimal, expatriates could determine the outcome in an extremely close presidential contest. This prospect troubled many reformers (Calderón Chelius 2004; Escobar 2007).[4] Even more problematic was the possibility that specific constituencies in Mexico might be angered by expanding the franchise abroad.

Why, then, did the implementing legislation finally pass, and by an almost unanimous vote? First, there was broad public support for it within Mexico. Polling data over a three-year period had shown that well over half of the Mexican population favored granting suffrage to U.S.-based migrants; only one-third opposed it. On the U.S. side, there had been sustained grassroots mobilization on this issue by expatriate organizations, especially in big cities like Chicago and Los Angeles. The migrant organizations greatly ratcheted up their lobbying effort in spring 2005 and began threatening all three parties with retribution if they failed to approve the legislation in time to permit absentee voting in 2006. This was not an entirely empty threat. More than three out of every five Mexicans living in Mexico have at least one relative living in the United States, and expatriate organizations vowed to influence their choice of a presidential candidate in 2006. No political party wanted to be blamed for the failure to give effective suffrage to the 14 percent of the Mexican electorate that lives abroad. Fear of voter retaliation outweighed concerns that one party or another would benefit disproportionately from expatriate balloting. The result was legislation that allowed expatriates to vote but made it practically difficult for them to do so. In other words, the implementing legislation was hedged so much that the risks of electoral reform were minimal.

But the vanishingly low participation of expatriate voters in 2006 implies that there was more at work than less-than-user-friendly absentee voting procedures and legal restrictions on campaigning within the United States. Even if these constraints had not been present, inducing U.S.-based Mexican migrants to participate in home-country elections would still have been an uphill battle. The most recent wave of Mexican immigrants in the United States is much less transient than previous cohorts. These migrants are more likely to settle in the United States and develop strong attachments to American society—partly as a consequence of tighter border enforcement, which has not deterred Mexicans from migrating illegally but *has* made it more costly and risky to come and go across the border (Cornelius and Lewis 2006). How much untapped potential was there for effective transnational electoral involvement in 2006?

Transnational Political Engagement: Hypotheses

Political scientists generally recognize two dominant factors that promote civic engagement in democracies around the world: resources and mobilization. All things being equal, individuals with more formal education and with greater social status, economic affluence, cognitive abilities, and life experience are incorporated more readily into politics (Dalton 2002; Domínguez and Lawson 2004; Domínguez and McCann 1996; Domínguez and Poiré 1999; McCann 1998; Rosenstone and Hansen 1993; Verba et al. 1978). To be sure, correlations between socioeconomic resources and participation vary considerably across countries and over time. Yet it appears to be axiomatic that those at the upper rungs of society pay greater attention to election campaigns, engage in discussions about candidates and issues more frequently, become better informed, and are more eager to vote. It is quite likely that this generalization extends to Mexicans in the United States; immigrants with more resources would be expected to follow electoral politics south of the border more closely, even if only a select few actually requested an absentee ballot.

Even more significant than resources, however, are the various mobilizing forces that emerge or are reinforced during an election. As noted above, political parties and candidates from Mexico were formally barred from contacting absentee voters and canvassing Mexican neighborhoods in the United States. This policy eliminated what could have been a major—if not the principal—conduit for transnational political engagement (D. Green and Gerber 2004). But even without the active mobilization efforts of partisan and candidate organizations, partisanship may still play an important role in shaping orientations towards electoral politics in Mexico. Prior research on Mexicans in the United States has found that many immigrants continue to see themselves as supporters of one of the three major parties—the PRI, the PAN, and the PRD—long after they have left Mexico (Camp 2001; Lawson 2003; Moreno 2005; see also Portes et al. 2007 on Colombia, the Dominican Republic, and El Salvador).[5] Sizeable numbers also take ideological stands on the left or right. Such residual party identifications might well have prompted expatriates to follow the campaigns from a distance in 2006 and choose sides. The Mexican president—by far the dominant figure in that country's politics—could play a comparable mobilizing role. Expatriates with strong feelings toward Vicente Fox should have been pulled more easily into Mexican electoral politics, much like their counterparts south of the border.

We would also expect that the immigrants' more personal self-identifications and assessments could serve as a basis for transnational mobilization during the campaign. After relocating to the United States, does an expatriate continue to identify first and foremost as a *Mexican*? Does the immigrant desire to return to Mexico one day to live? And does he or she hold fellow Mexicans in high esteem? As Michael Jones-Correa (1998) describes in his study of Latino immigrants in New York City, a considerable number of people who migrate to the United States long to return to their country of origin, even if they have lived in the United States for many years. Mexican immigrants who felt this way would likely be more attentive to the campaigns in 2006, inasmuch as elections are not solely about selecting leaders for the next term but also about displaying cultural pride and celebrating national identity (Edelman 1964). On the other hand, immigrants who identify themselves as Mexican-*Americans* or simply as *Americans* would feel less pull toward Mexico as the campaign progressed; this would be a signal that they had found a niche in their adopted country.

Research on electoral mobilization further suggests that ostensibly nonpolitical organizations, such as churches and social clubs, can foster turnout and deepen civic engagement (Putnam 2001). For Mexican immigrants, these types of social attachments might be especially important for transmitting information about the elections, given the absence of Mexican party organizations and overt campaigning north of the border. Those who stay in close touch with family and friends who are still in Mexico, or have their Mexican identity reinforced through regular contact with other Mexicans in their neighborhood, would also have greater access to information and presumably feel pulled more strongly toward transnational engagement.

Beyond self-identification and organizational attachments, we must take into account other aspects of an immigrant's experience in the United States when considering mobilizing factors that condition cross-border civic engagement: length of residence in the host country, immigration status (legal resident or unauthorized), the strength of his or her social network within the United States, and attitudes toward Americans who are not of Mexican descent. Immigrants who have deeper roots in the United States and are legally eligible to vote in American elections may find the demands of U.S. politics to be sufficiently challenging so as to leave them with little time and energy for following public affairs in Mexico. But those who feel marginalized in American society, who have few friends and family members in the United States, who lack the proper legal authorization to reside in the country, or who hold Americans in low regard may strive to maintain ties to Mexico.

Survey Design and Findings

We explored the contours of cross-border political engagement through the 2006 Mexican Expatriate Study, a survey of Mexican immigrants residing in Dallas, San Diego, and north-central Indiana. The three sampling sites were selected to obtain as representative a picture as possible of the current Mexico-born population in the United States. Dallas and San Diego are, of course, traditional immigrant destinations. Since the early 1990s, north-central Indiana, like many areas in the Midwest and Southeast, has become an increasingly popular destination for Mexican migrants. Initial sampling work for the 2006 Mexican Expatriate Study took place in Indiana between February and May. During this period, 151 randomly chosen Mexican immigrants participated in face-to-face interviews conducted in public places where Mexicans often congregate: laundromats, parks, Mexican-oriented shopping malls, and the area adjacent to the Mexican consulate in Indianapolis. In June, an additional 953 Mexicans were surveyed in the three regions, 200 in person and 753 by telephone. In total, the survey encompassed 1,104 respondents.[6]

Since the July 2 election, various news commentators have posited that expatriate turnout was so low because the typical immigrant had little interest in taking part in Mexican electoral politics. According to this argument, transnational activists lobbied long and hard for the right to vote, but their enthusiasm was not matched at the grassroots level. Is this, in fact, the case? In our survey, immigrants were asked how attentive they were to the campaigns, how often they talked about Mexican politics with family and friends, and whether they had a preference in the presidential race. The questionnaire wordings paralleled those used in the second wave of the Mexico 2006 Panel Study,[7] which was fielded at roughly the same time as the expatriate surveys. Table 5.1 shows the responses

Table 5.1 Political engagement among Mexican expatriates and
Mexicans in Mexico (in percentages)

	Dallas	San Diego	Indiana	Mexico
How closely are you following the Mexican presidential campaigns?				
Great deal	8	12	10	11
Somewhat	19	10	16	27
Only a little	33	38	32	37
Not at all	41	39	42	25
How often do you talk about Mexican politics with friends and family?				
Daily	3	6	3	8
Few times a week	12	14	15	28
Few times a month	16	17	20	15
Rarely	42	40	40	36
Never	27	23	22	13
If you were able to vote right now in the Mexican presidential election, for whom would you vote?				
Stated a clear preference	56	64	67	91
Not sure or would abstain	44	36	33	8

Sources: Mexico 2006 Panel Survey, national sample, wave 2 (April/May, lowest n = 1,165); 2006 Mexican Expatriate Study (lowest n = 1,092).

to these three items, disaggregated by region—Dallas, San Diego, and Indiana versus a nationally representative sample from Mexico.

Contrary to conventional wisdom among postelection commentators, we find that a relatively large bloc of immigrants claimed to follow the campaigns quite closely—approximately the same percentage as in Mexico—and that there was very little region-to-region variation. In Dallas, 8 percent followed the election "a great deal," while the percentage was higher in Indiana (10%) and San Diego (12%). On the low side of the scale, however, we see a larger distinction between U.S.-based Mexicans and Mexicans interviewed in Mexico. Approximately four out of ten respondents in the United States declared no interest at all in the presidential campaigns, but only about one-quarter of the sample from Mexico were likewise disengaged.

Responses to the latter two survey items in table 5.1 reinforce this impression. Between 15 and 20 percent of the expatriates reported discussing politics with friends and family at least a few times a week; in Mexico the corresponding figure was 35 percent. At the bottom end of the scale, fewer Mexicans in Mexico stated that they rarely or never talk about Mexican politics.

Respondents in Mexico were also more inclined to state a preference in the presidential contest; only 8 percent were unsure, indicated they would abstain, or intended to spoil their ballot.[8] Among Mexicans in the United States, one-third or more of the survey participants had not formed a preference.

No electoral reform could have attracted all Mexican expatriates to the political process. A large portion—perhaps close to half—would have preferred to keep their distance regardless of the rules for absentee balloting. However, the data in table 5.1 point to considerably greater civic potential than the miniscule number of expatriates who cast ballots would suggest.

Correlates of Transnational Political Involvement

What factors prompted expatriates to follow electoral politics in their home country? Several survey items touched on the key socioeconomic resources and mobilizing forces mentioned earlier.[9]

Demographics and resources

- household affluence, determined by a count of the number of items that respondents had in their residence (computer, television, stove with an oven, personal car or truck)
- level of formal education, ranging from none to university graduate
- age (in years)
- gender
- language used at home, on a three-point scale (3 = Spanish, 2 = both Spanish and English, 1 = English)

Political dispositions

- whether the respondent identified with one of the Mexican political parties
- whether the respondent described him- or herself as on the ideological right or left
- intensity of evaluations of then president Vicente Fox, based on an eleven-point feeling thermometer (this thermometer was folded, so that high scores reflect strongly positive or strongly negative evaluations, and low scores denote more neutral assessments)

Personal identification with Mexico and Mexicans

- describing oneself solely as Mexican, and not American, Mexican-American, Hispanic, or Latino
- evaluation of Mexicans on an eleven-point feeling thermometer
- desire to live in Mexico again someday, rather than remain in the United States

Social networks

- church attendance (on a five-point scale, ranging from "never" to "more than once a week")
- contacts with Mexican social or sports clubs
- ethnic composition of one's neighborhood (3 = mostly Mexican, 2 = mixed, 1 = mostly non-Mexican)
- whether the respondent had visited Mexico over the last three years
- frequency of discussions with family and friends in Mexico
- sending remittances to Mexico

Personal, social, and legal ties to the United States

- evaluation of Americans on an eleven-point feeling thermometer
- describing oneself as Mexican-American or American
- number of family and friends living in the United States
- whether the respondent had felt mistreated for being an immigrant
- length of stay in the United States
- whether the respondent was a naturalized citizen

The correlations between these predictors and the three measures of transnational political engagement appear in table 5.2. In keeping with the vast literature on socioeconomic resources and civic involvement, we find many significant relationships at the top of this table. One's level of education stands out as particularly important. The more highly educated the immigrant, the greater the tendency to follow the campaigns, talk about politics south of the border, and state a clear preference in the election. Older immigrants were somewhat more likely to have paid attention to the campaign than younger ones were. A gender gap also surfaced for political discussions, with men being more talkative about home-country politics than women. Moreover, immigrants who spoke Spanish at home were somewhat more inclined to have a preference in the 2006 election (see also Portes et al. 2007).[10]

Table 5.2 Correlates of political engagement among Mexican expatriates

	Campaign attentiveness	Political discussion	Stated a vote preference
Resources			
Household affluence	.01	−.01	−.03
Education level	.16**	.16***	.11***
Age (years)	.06*	.01	−.02
Gender (female)	−.04	−.07**	−.05
Use Spanish at home	−.01	−.01	.07**
Political dispositions			
Identify with a Mexican party	.18***	.19***	.35***
Take an ideological position	.11***	.09***	.14***
Intensity of Vicente Fox evaluation	−.01	.03	.12***
Personal identification with Mexico and Mexicans			
Identify oneself only as Mexican	−.01	−.01	.09**
Affective evaluation of Mexicans	.04	.06*	.08***
Desire to live in Mexico again	.02	.03	.06*
Social network activity, local and transnational			
Church attendance	.14***	.14***	.01
Involvement in Mexican clubs	.14***	.10***	.05
Live in Mexican neighborhood	−.01	−.03	.05
Visited Mexico in last three years	.08***	.05*	.01
Talk with family/friends in Mexico	.15***	.18***	.07**
Send funds to Mexico	.07**	.14***	.12***
Personal, social, legal connections to the United States			
Affective evaluation of Americans	.09***	.14***	.06**
Identify oneself as American/Mexican-American	.05	.01	−.04
Number of family/friends in the United States	.04	.06*	.08*
Perceived discrimination	.11***	.11***	−.02
Length of stay in the United States	−.01	−.04	−.12***
U.S. citizen	.03	−.04	−.06**
Have working papers	.03	−.05*	−.02

Source: 2006 Mexican Expatriate Study.

Note: Attention to the Mexican campaign measured on a four-point scale (1 = none, 4 = much); discussions of Mexican politics coded on a five-point scale (1 = never, 5 = daily); stating a preference measured dichotomously (1 = had a preference, 0 = was not sure or would not vote if given the chance). See the Mexico 2006 Panel Study's supplemental materials for chapter 5 (http://web.mit.edu/polisci/research/mexico06/book.html) for the wording and distributions of the variables listed here.

Pearson correlation coefficients: * = $p < .10$; ** = $p < .05$; *** = $p < .01$.

Even more relevant are the respondents' basic political dispositions. Mexicans in the United States who retained a party identification were much more likely to follow politics in Mexico. The same held true for ideological position-taking; describing oneself as on the right or left of the ideological spectrum is strongly and significantly linked to campaign attentiveness and political discussions and, to a lesser extent, to voicing a preference for one of the contenders. Expatriates with strong feelings toward Vicente Fox were likewise more inclined to favor one of the candidates to be his successor. Turning to more personal identifications and evaluations, immigrants who thought of themselves principally as Mexicans, held Mexicans in high esteem, and expressed a desire to live in Mexico again were significantly more likely to back a candidate. Rating Mexicans highly on the feeling thermometer is significantly linked to talking frequently about Mexican politics.

Social networks further conditioned transnational political engagement. Involvement in religion significantly spilled over into politics, as did participation in social clubs for Mexicans, and more personal ties to family and friends still in Mexico. Immigrants whose neighbors were mostly from Mexico, however, were not any more likely than individuals living in ethnically diverse areas to either pay attention to the elections south of the border or voice a preference for president.

At the bottom of table 5.2, we see that the immigrants' experiences and legal status in the United States shaped attentiveness to Mexican politics as well, though these effects do not always operate consistently in the same direction. Those who had lived north of the border for a longer time were less likely to mention a preference in the 2006 election, as were Mexicans who had become citizens of the United States. Respondents who believed that they had been mistreated in some way because they were foreign-born were more inclined to follow Mexican politics, perhaps out of a desire to maintain their connection with a society in which they are fully accepted. Yet we observed positive relationships between evaluations of Americans and transnational political engagement. Consequently, it would be wrong to regard political engagement as a zero-sum game in which individuals must trade allegiance to one society for another.

The principal lesson from table 5.2 is that the factors that cause Mexicans in Mexico to follow national campaigns operate in a comparable fashion within expatriate communities. Socioeconomic resources, social networks, partisanship, ideological positioning, and related attitudes favor participation.

The Meaning of Expatriate Voting Preferences

Were candidate preferences among expatriates also derived in ways that are comparable to models of voting choice in Mexico? Or was the structure of partisan cleavages different? Was there a greater tendency for immigrants to offer "top of the head" responses that were not meaningfully connected to partisanship and other major determinants of candidate preferences (Zaller and Feldman 1992)?

As shown in table 5.3, those expatriates who voiced a preference in the Mexican presidential contest were not markedly different from Mexicans in Mexico. Roberto Madrazo of the PRI was less popular in all three U.S. sampling sites than in Mexico, a finding consistent with earlier survey research on expatriate partisanship (Lawson 2003). Yet the similarities between Mexicans residing in Dallas, San Diego, or Indiana and those living in Mexico proper outweigh the differences.

Judging from the breakdown of preferences in this table, Mexico's three major parties would have little reason to fear an expanded absentee balloting system in future elections. Each of the three main parties—even the PRI, preferred by more than one-fifth of the respondents in our survey—could be competitive in the United States. This finding contrasts with the official expatriate voting count, where the PAN's Felipe Calderón outpolled his opponents by substantial margins. Presumably, the Mexicans best able to overcome the hurdles to participation more closely resembled the profile of a PAN voter—again, a finding that echoes past research on turnout in Mexico (Lawson and Klesner 2001).

Without any active campaigning to crystallize and solidify the attitudes of expatriates, we might expect their voting preferences to be only loosely linked to partisanship, ideological self-positioning, and evaluations of the incumbent Mexican president—three core political dispositions in the Mexican context. For some immigrants, it is entirely possible that preferences in the 2006 election took the form of Philip Converse's "non-attitudes" (1964). If this were so, expatriate voting would largely be a symbolic gesture, with little rhyme or reason behind decisions. To assess the roots of candidate choice, we regressed voting preferences on these three predictors.[11] We also controlled for several social and demographic factors (gender, age, education, household affluence, church attendance, and, for the expatriates, place of residence in the United States) to sharpen inferences about attitude linkages. Since the dependent vari-

Table 5.3   Support for presidential candidates among Mexicans in the United States
and Mexicans in Mexico (in percentages)

	Dallas	San Diego	Indiana	Mexico
Felipe Calderón (PAN)	41	44	33	34
Roberto Madrazo (PRI)	22	20	20	27
Andrés Manuel López Obrador (PRD)	28	26	41	34
Another candidate	9	10	7	5

Sources: Mexico 2006 Panel Study, national sample, wave 2 (N = 1,345); 2006 Mexican
Expatriate Study (n = 278 in Dallas, n = 80 in San Diego, and n = 321 in Indiana).
    Note: Respondents who would abstain or did not have a clear preference were excluded.

able is a choice with three options (preference for Calderón, Madrazo, or López
Obrador), multinomial logistic regression models were fit.

Table 5.4, based on these models, lists the expected probabilities of backing
each of the candidates, depending on the values of the independent variables.[12]
With respect to political ideology, we find that in Mexico and the United States,
self-described leftists were more likely to support López Obrador to approximately the same degree, whereas those on the right leaned toward Calderón.
Given the positioning of the PRD and the PAN along the ideological spectrum,
these tendencies are quite reasonable. When 95 percent confidence intervals are
taken into account, however, we find that self-reported ideology did not shape
voting preferences in either country to any marked degree.[13]

In contrast, a strong "Vicente Fox" effect is apparent in both samples. Respondents on each side of the border who had a negative impression of the
president were much more likely to favor López Obrador over Calderón or
Madrazo. Among those who gave Fox a very warm "10" on this scale, Calderón
was the most preferred candidate. For expatriates, this probability is .47, with a
confidence interval ranging from .38 to .56; for Mexicans in Mexico, we observe
a slightly higher range of .50 to .69.

We also find strong evidence for partisan conditioning of candidate preferences. Identification with one of the major parties is by far the most powerful
predictor in the model, with the forecasted probabilities being nearly the same
in both countries. The only exception to this is the connection between PRI
identification and a show of support for Roberto Madrazo within the immigrant
sample. In this case, PRI identifiers had a 66 percent chance of backing the PRI
nominee, appreciably lower than the 81 percent chance of supporting Madrazo
for PRI identifiers in Mexico.[14] In keeping with the data from Mexico, however,

Table 5.4 Predicted probabilities of candidate support among expatriates

	Felipe Calderón	Roberto Madrazo	Andrés Manuel López Obrador
Left-right self-placement			
Expatriates			
Left	.38 [.23–.55]	.19 [.09–.32]	.44 [.28–.59]
Right	.42 [.30–.53]	.29 [.19–.41]	.29 [.19–.41]
Neither left nor right	.37 [.30–.44]	.23 [.18–.29]	.40 [.33–.47]
Mexico			
Left	.30 [.18–.44]	.21 [.12–.32]	.49 [.36–.63]
Right	.43 [.30–.57]	.25 [.15–.39]	.31 [.19–.46]
Neither left nor right	.43 [.35–.51]	.21 [.15–.28]	.36 [.29–.44]
Evaluation of Vicente Fox (0–10 scale)			
Expatriates			
0	.21 [.12–.33]	.23 [.14–.35]	.55 [.42–.69]
5	.33 [.26–.40]	.24 [.19–.30]	.43 [.36–.50]
10	.47 [.38–.56]	.22 [.16–.29]	.31 [.23–.38]
Mexico			
0	.11 [.06–.20]	.28 [.16–.43]	.61 [.46–.75]
5	.30 [.22–.38]	.24 [.18–.32]	.45 [.38–.53]
10	.60 [.50–.69]	.16 [.11–.23]	.24 [.18–.33]
Party identification			
Expatriates			
PAN	.81 [.74–.87]	.10 [.06–.16]	.09 [.05–.15]
PRI	.18 [.10–.28]	.66 [.54–.76]	.16 [.10–.25]
PRD	.03 [.01–.08]	.07 [.03–.15]	.90 [.80–.95]
Other/none	.40 [.34–.46]	.19 [.15–.25]	.41 [.35–.47]
Mexico			
PAN	.85 [.79–.90]	.07 [.04–.11]	.08 [.04–.11]
PRI	.10 [.06–.15]	.81 [.75–.87]	.09 [.05–.14]
PRD	.09 [.05–.14]	.02 [.01–.05]	.93 [.88–.97]
Other/none	.44 [.36–.53]	.19 [.14–.26]	.37 [.29–.44]

Sources: Mexico 2006 Panel Study, national sample, wave 2; 2006 Mexican Expatriate Study.
Note: Cell entries indicate predicted probabilities, with 95% confidence intervals in brackets. Voting preference probabilities are based on multinomial logistic regression models, where several social and economic background variables (gender, age, education, household affluence, and church attendance) have been controlled. In the expatriate sample, place of residence (Dallas, San Diego, or Indiana) was also controlled, although these fixed dummy effects are not statistically significant. Respondents who did not prefer one of the three top candidates were omitted from the analysis. Predictions and confidence intervals were calculated using CLARIFY (Tomz et al. 2001), with all other predictors that were not being evaluated set to mean values. The logistic regression coefficients, standard errors, and measures of model fit appear in the Mexico 2006 Panel Study's supplemental materials for chapter 5 (http://web.mit.edu/polisci/research/mexico06/book.html).

PRI identification does not dispose voters more toward one of the two other parties than toward the other, once additional factors are taken into account.

Assessed collectively, the findings in table 5.4 tell us that among expatriates who kept up with Mexican politics enough to state a preference, choices were grounded in terrain that would be quite familiar to students of voting behavior in Mexico. Partisanship, presidential appraisals, and, to a much lesser extent, left-right ideological placement provided meaningful templates for decision making. Regrettably, for the vast majority of respondents in the 2006 Mexican Expatriate Study, this would be only a hypothetical rather than an actual choice.

As with other democratic reforms in Mexico's recent history, absentee voting by Mexican expatriates, deemed a failure in many quarters because of the low turnout in 2006, may evolve into a genuine political force. Many of the activists on both sides of the border who lobbied for absentee balloting in 2006 have resolved to push even harder to expand these rights in future elections. They will urge the next Congress to accept a wider array of mechanisms for expatriate voting, including via the Internet, at Mexican consulates across the United States, or in neighborhood absentee-voting centers.

Contrary to the more celebratory assessments of Mexican migrants' home-country political involvement, our survey evidence underscores that as many as four or five out of ten Mexican-born residents of the United States would likely be out of reach, regardless of the procedures established for future absentee voting. This would be true not because they live in out-of-the-way locations such as north-central Indiana, but because they pay practically no attention to public affairs south of the border. However, that still leaves a considerable reservoir of transnational civic potential. As political theorist E. E. Schattschneider (1975) wrote long ago, democracy is an inherently expansive and forward-looking enterprise. Candidates, parties, and political groups are constantly on the lookout for new markets to enter and new issues that can energize citizens. We expect this dynamic to operate in Mexico's fledgling democracy, both within its national borders and transnationally. The three major parties can all be competitive players north of the border. The lopsided expatriate vote in favor of Felipe Calderón in 2006—and the low absentee turnout overall—are not necessarily indicative of how Mexican immigrants will position themselves in future electoral contests.

The survey results further suggest that open-air rallies, door-to-door canvassing and fundraising, and the other accoutrements of traditional campaigning may matter less in shaping electoral preferences than simple word-of-mouth (as discussed in chapter 4 in this volume) and involvement in ostensibly nonpolitical organizations (such as local churches and social clubs). After all, the Mexican government prohibited formal partisan campaigning north of the border, and the parties complied. Indeed, since so few Mexicans in the United States solicited an absentee ballot before the January 15 deadline, the political parties in Mexico had little reason to mobilize the vote from abroad. Yet in the weeks leading up to the July 2 election, the key elements of candidate choice were largely in place for those respondents—more than half of all expatriates—who voiced a preference.

Part II / Parties, Candidates, and Campaign Strategy

CHAPTER SIX

The Absence of Common Ground between Candidates and Voters

Kathleen Bruhn and Kenneth F. Greene

Campaigns in competitive party systems can be viewed as exercises in retail politics, in which candidates try to sell their policy proposals and voters signal which proposals they are willing to buy. In long-established democracies like the United States, the effectiveness of retail politics is muted by voters' standing decisions to support a particular party as a result of the internalization of a partisan identity, the parties' reputations, and the parties' positions on specific issues. In new democracies such as Mexico's, however, the parties' limited track records in office means that voters can infer less about the candidates' likely behavior in office from their party affiliations. Furthermore, Mexico's constitutional prohibition on re-election means that voters are constantly choosing among nonincumbents, about whom they may know very little. As a result, in Mexico electoral campaigns represent much more important periods for voters to learn about parties and candidates, and for parties and candidates to signal their responsiveness to certain constituencies. Campaigns can thus play a significant role in the process of political representation.

There are four reasons why understanding political representation through similarities in points of view on salient issues between those running for office (the elites) and the general electorate is important. First, if democracy is the process of translating citizens' will into public policy, then candidate-voter alignments are, by definition, correlated with the quality of democracy (Luna and Zechmeister 2005).[1] Second, tighter links between the preferences of the governors and the governed enhance the probability that representatives will be responsive to their constituents and thus pursue substantive policies that serve the public (Kitschelt et al. 1999). Third, scholars of Latin American politics have raised alarm bells about the "crisis of democratic representation" throughout the region (see Domínguez 1997; Mainwaring et al. 2006; O'Donnell 1994). Although multiple factors affect popular perceptions of government, having more accountable and responsive leaders will likely diminish citizen disenchantment with politicians specifically and democracy in general.

Fourth, beyond these long-term concerns, the question of policy representation is particularly salient following Mexico's polarized 2006 presidential campaign that pitted Felipe Calderón of the National Action Party (PAN) on the right against Andrés Manuel López Obrador of the Coalition for the Good of All, led by his Party of the Democratic Revolution (PRD), on the left. This polarization, combined with the virtual tie in the election, contributed to postelectoral battles that ranged from demonstrations and street blockades to fistfights in Mexico's Congress. But the chain of events unleashed by the protagonists in this drama may not accurately reflect the extent to which ideological polarization in Mexico extends to the broader political elite, much less to the voters themselves. To what degree do parties reflect deeper cleavages among voters? And, in policy terms, how connected are political elites to their supporters?

In this chapter, we assess the degree of elite-voter correspondence on some prominent issues. We are particularly interested in whether candidates from the leading political parties were disposed to *stand for* their constituents with a mandate that implies tight agreement between the two or whether, alternatively, candidates *act for* the voters as trustees who attempt to lead voters on the issues (Kitschelt et al. 1999; Pitkin 1967). Following a long tradition among scholars of American (Achen 1978; Miller and Stokes 1963) and comparative politics (Barnes 1977; Converse and Pierce 1986; L. Powell 1982), we examine the level of mandate versus trustee representation in Mexico's new democracy.

In the first section of this chapter, we draw upon data from electoral platforms to show that Mexico's three main parties have been ideologically polarized since at least 1979, two years after electoral reforms helped intensify partisan competition. In the second section, we extend this analysis using new survey data on congressional candidates. We find that during the run-up to the 2006 elections, the PAN and PRD candidates for these offices were polarized on the issues along the same dimensions as their respective presidential candidates, and that these differences were crucial in informing their decisions to run under the label of one party or the other. In the third and fourth sections, we compare the issue preferences of the candidates and the voters. We show that the elites are much more polarized than voters, both collectively and dyadically in their individual electoral districts.

We conclude by arguing that the candidates lack popular mandates for their issue positions. Even partisan voters did not strongly identify with the specific issue positions of candidates in their own parties. Not only does this imply that Mexico has not undergone a deep partisan realignment since the onset of fully competitive elections, but it also indicates that, to the extent candidates act on their own (and often extreme) positions in the legislature, governance will become more difficult. Voters may then grow even more frustrated with deadlock and polarization in a Congress that is both unresponsive to their real, urgent concerns and unrepresentative of their priorities and preferences. Although we view these representational failures as significant, we recognize that candidate-voter alignments in Mexico's structured party system create more efficacious relationships between governors and the governed than in other countries in Latin America, where dramatic partisan dealignments and even party-system collapse have severely weakened representational linkages. Mexico's party elites and the voters that identify with them are at least on the same side of the political spectrum as each other, even if the former stake out much more radical positions.

Polarized Parties: The Historical Picture

Ideological differences have long divided the PAN from the parties of the independent Left, including the PRD after it was formed in 1989. The long-term differences in party platforms imply that the current level of polarization among candidates in the 2006 election is nothing new. In fact, there has been something of a convergence between the two blocs when viewed in historical perspective (see also Greene 2007).

To demonstrate these ideological differences, we offer evidence from a content analysis of the parties' electoral platforms from 1979 to 2006. Each platform was coded using the methodology developed by the Comparative Manifestos Project to analyze parties' ideological placement over time in advanced industrial democracies.[2] In accordance with their approach, we assigned each sentence in a given platform to one of 56 common categories.[3] We summarize these categories according to "left" and "right" orientations. *Leftism*, as defined here, is associated with public ownership of the economy, economic redistribution, and welfarism (discussed below); labor rights; curbs on international capital flows; and opposition to the military in domestic and international affairs. In contrast, *rightism* is associated with support for markets, business, and investment; limits on redistribution and social safety nets; sympathy for traditional values (including patriotism and the family); and support for the military. In this coding, ideological orientations capture distinct worldviews that include—but extend far beyond—the sphere of economic policy.

Figure 6.1 expresses the relative level of left-right orientations for the major parties in every presidential and midterm election since 1979; the scores along the vertical axis indicate the percentage of the platform emphasizing right issues minus the percentage of the platform emphasizing left issues.[4] Three findings stand out. First, the parties of the independent left and, after 1989, the PRD are indeed clearly leftist during the entire period under study. Second, the PAN and Institutional Revolutionary Party (PRI) occupied similar positions during the 1990s, but most often the PAN was on the right and the PRI was in the center. Some of the bumpiness in the parties' positions, most evident for the PRI, comes from the differences between presidential-year platforms (1982, 1988, 1994, 2000, 2006) and midterm-election platforms (1979, 1985, 1991, 1997, 2003). Third, the level of polarization between the PAN on the right and the PRD on the left decreased dramatically from the late 1970s to the early 1990s. However, we also see a slight increase in polarization, beginning in 2000, with the transition to fully competitive elections. We attribute the PRD's leftward drift to the PRI's defeat in 2000 and the concomitant decrease in the salience of the regime cleavage that divided authoritarians from democrats. With this cleavage diminished, the PRD refocused its appeal on economic policy and social justice concerns. The PRD's 2006 platform is, in fact, significantly leftist in the Latin American context. For instance, it is further to the left than the Brazilian Workers' Party platform in 2002, the Chilean Socialist Party in 2001, or Argentina's Justicialist (Peronist) Party under Nestor Kirchner in 2003.[5]

Although the three parties' ideological differences span multiple-issue areas, one of the clearest contrasts concerns the classic question of economic policy. To draw out these differences, we created two additional indices: an economic investment index that includes platform mentions of infrastructure investment, incentives to business,[6] and technology acquisition; and an index of welfarism that combines mentions of social transfers, welfare programs, and basic public education.[7] Parties of the left score higher than the PAN on welfarism, with an average of 11.1 percent of their platform dedicated to these themes versus 8.5 percent for the PAN. In contrast, the PAN devotes almost twice as much space to economic investment (10.3% of its platform compared to 5.5% for the PRD). One particularly striking indication of the increasing differences between the

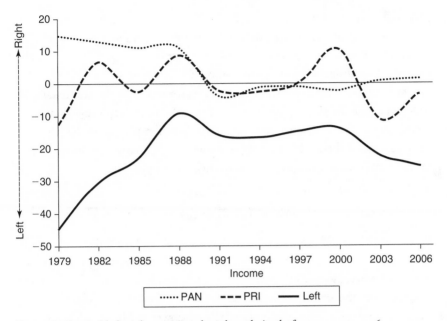

Figure 6.1 Parties' left-right positions based on their platforms, 1979–2006.

PAN and the PRD comes from the degree of welfarism in their 2006 platforms. The PAN's emphasis on welfarism and economic investment is roughly balanced, with just a 0.4 percent advantage to welfare transfers, but the PRD's document focuses on welfarism a whopping 13.2 percent more than investment. These differences account for the lion's share of the divergence between the two parties on the general left-right scale presented in figure 6.1. This figure also shows that the PRI has occupied the middle ground on economic policy. In the 1970s and mid-1980s, it emphasized welfarism, like the Left; since the late 1980s, it has highlighted investment.

Our analysis of party platforms shows that the Mexican Left and Right have held clearly distinct positions from one another over time. Unlike parties in many other competitive systems that converge toward the center as a strategy for maximizing the vote,[8] the PAN and the PRD staked out starkly different positions on the issues. Greene (2007) demonstrates that these differences resulted from the process of opposition-party-building in a one-party-dominant regime. Given the widespread (and accurate) belief that the PRI was the only game in town, most prospective candidates and activists joined the incumbent party as their best chance for pursuing a successful career in politics. Joining a different party not only ensured a lower likelihood of winning office, it also invited the sort of physical coercion often deployed against opposition activists and their families. The opposition parties' lack of resources meant that they were unable to offset these disincentives to participation with material side-payments. Thus the only citizens willing to pay the high costs (or settle for the scanty tangible benefits) of joining the opposition were those who held deeply anti-status-quo policy beliefs. These relative radicals built opposition parties on the right and left and imbued them with a strong sense of identity that emphasized sacrifice for the cause and prioritized moral authority over popularity.

Polarized Congressional Candidates in the 2006 Elections

Party platforms offer strong evidence that the PAN and the PRD have histori-cally been polarized on the issues, and that their differences have even increased somewhat since the transition to fully competitive democracy in 2000. These platforms are important, as they reflect the will of the national parties. Central party committees (CENs) wield extraordinary power in Mexico, through their control over 200 party-list seats in the 500-member lower house of Congress as well as over the gargantuan public resources allotted to them for campaigns.

Nevertheless, the national platforms may not represent the positions of con-gressional candidates for Mexico's 300 plurality districts. Although the prohibi-tion on consecutive re-election may make these candidates more dependent on CENs than are legislators elected by plurality in other political systems, they have stronger incentives than party-list candidates to campaign actively in their districts, develop a personal profile, and respond to the interests of their local constituents (at least during the campaign). Moreover, because many of them have come up through local party and government service, they may be more aware of and focused on local issues than their counterparts on the regional party lists. Thus, if an electoral connection between candidates and voters is emerging anywhere in Mexico, we would expect it to emerge among plurality-district candidates.

To measure their attitudes, we draw on data from the Mexico 2006 Candidate and Party Leader Survey, conducted in the three weeks prior to that year's fed-eral election.[9] These more detailed data from district-level competitions reveal striking differences between the PAN and PRD candidates over ideology and salient political issues in 2006, paralleling the broader trends evident in the par-ties' historical platforms.

Our original intent was to include all three major parties in the candidate survey; however, the PRI declined to provide us with the necessary contact information. The survey therefore includes only candidates from the PAN and from the PRD-dominated progressive Coalition For the Good of All.[10] Yet since the dataset contains responses from Mexico's two largest and most ideologically distinct political groupings, it gives us a good picture of the extent of polarization at the elite level. Furthermore, because the legislative candidates in the survey are, it turns out, mostly drawn from local political elites who had resided in their districts for an average of thirty years and had more often served as municipal or state party leaders than national ones, the differences we document are not limited to a narrow Mexico City elite; rather, they represent real, substantive, and widespread ideological differences between these two parties, both nationally and locally.

Congressional candidates from the PAN and the PRD agreed on the key problems facing Mexico. When we asked them to name the most important problem, they spontaneously identified "jobs and unemployment" most frequently, followed by "crime and public security." PRD candidates were more likely than their PAN rivals to name poverty first, but poverty was still the fourth most frequently cited problem among PAN candidates. Another open-ended question asked candidates to identify the theme they personally emphasized in their congressional campaigns. Again, candidates from both parties named jobs and employment as their principal focus, followed by education, health, and social spending.

Consensus about Mexico's major problems is where this agreement ends. The candidates disagreed so substantially about solutions that they can be fairly said to represent distinct world views. When we asked whether the government or individuals should be responsible for citizens' personal economic welfare, 75 percent of the PAN candidates opted for personal responsibility, while 68 percent of the PRD candidates stated that the government should be partly or even fully responsible.[11]

A question about the appropriate size of government generated fascinating responses. Specifically, we asked if candidates preferred a government with fewer services and lower taxes or one with more services and higher taxes. Fifty-six percent of the PAN candidates opted for a smaller government, compared to just 11.7 percent of the PRD candidates. However, only 40 percent of the PRD candidates openly chose the greater services/more taxes option. Instead, a plurality (48.1%) apparently insisted to interviewers that they wanted both lower taxes *and* more services. In part, their position may simply reflect the official position of their presidential candidate, who stated that he could pay for all his new social programs by cutting government waste. Yet the spontaneous refusal to recognize a tradeoff between spending and taxing, despite question wording designed to straightjacket their answers, gives us strong evidence of their economic policy leanings. It is also, of course, precisely what had the PAN and many investors so worried about a López Obrador presidency.

On the critical question of commercial relations with the United States, differences were less stark. Virtually all PAN candidates (95%) preferred expanding commercial ties. Despite rhetoric from the PRD leadership that elements of NAFTA should be renegotiated, only 22 percent of the party's congressional candidates wanted to either maintain commercial ties at current levels or reduce them. Although that figure is significantly different from the PAN's view,[12] it highlights the limits of the PRD's leftism, especially when compared to leftist parties and candidates in Venezuela, Peru, Bolivia, and Argentina that more vehemently criticize free trade. Of course, the position of the PRD's candidates may simply reflect the recognition that, unlike its South American counterparts, Mexico sends over 85 percent of its exports to the United States, and thus its economic performance depends heavily on continued integration.

For two questions—abortion and privatization of the electricity sector—we asked respondents to locate not only their own personal position but also that of their rival. These views suggest some projection of polarization beyond what actually exists. As we would expect, the average preferences of the PRD candidates are pro-choice and opposed to privatization of the electricity sector, whereas the PAN candidates line up on the opposite side of these issues. Yet PRD candidates view their PAN counterparts as being 14.1 percent more pro-life and 24.3 percent more in favor of privatization than they actually are. PAN candidates similarly view those in the PRD as 23.2 percent more in favor legalized abortion under all circumstances and 8.4 percent more in favor of prohibiting any private investment in the electricity sector than they really are.[13] This perceived polarization may add some fuel to the ideological fire.

The differences between candidates of the two leading parties on individual issues are packaged into dissimilar world views. We used factor analysis of issue questions in the surveys to uncover the latent dimensions of party competition, as seen from the candidates' perspective. This space, shown in figure 6.2, can be thought of as the canvas upon which partisan differences are drawn. Its content is virtually identical to the underlying perceptions of the major issues of the

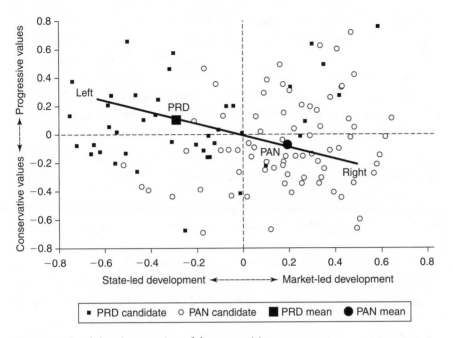

Figure 6.2 Candidates' perception of the competition space.

day, captured in open-ended questions. One major line of division concerned economic development policy, ranging from pro-market positions that included selling off public enterprises and downsizing social safety nets to pro-state positions that involves expanding public enterprises and welfare programs. A second major (though somewhat less salient) line of cleavage involved moral issues and ran from pro-life positions on abortion and the death penalty to pro-choice and pro-capital-punishment positions.

Ideological and issue differences were so important to each party's slate of candidates that they were an almost perfect predictor of whether a given candidate ran under the PAN or the PRD label. A logistic regression model of the candidates' party-affiliation choice correctly predicts 95.8 percent of the choices, using just ideology on the left-right scale and personal preferences on the abortion issue, the privatization of electricity, and the extent of social safety nets as predictors. If we set the values for all variables to their leftmost position, a candidate has a predicted probability of 99.8 percent of joining the PRD instead of the PAN. When a putative candidate's issue profile is shifted all the way to the right, he or she has a 99.3 percent probability of running as a representative of the PAN.[14] We cannot know the causal story from these data alone: whether issue preferences lead individuals into the parties to begin with, whether ideologues are more likely to try to seek office, whether the parties tend to select ideologues as their candidates (but see Greene 2007), or some combination of the above. Under any of these scenarios, however, it is abundantly clear that different world views are deeply ingrained in the meaning of running for office under the PAN or the PRD label.

Collective Representation: National Candidate-Voter Differences

Elites were clearly polarized on the issues. This is an interesting finding in and of itself, not least because it raises important questions about the viability of legislative negotiations. However, a crucial underlying question is whether these differences were reflective of divisions within the electorate. In comparing elite and mass opinion, our analysis has one significant advantage over some of the most prominent studies (Miller and Stokes 1963). Since we participated in the design of both voter and candidate surveys, we were able to use the same wording on questions for both types of respondents and to apply the surveys at roughly the same time. Although certain terms may not always have the same conceptual significance to both the candidates and the voters (G. Powell 2004), the correspondence between the elite and mass surveys enhances the validity of our comparisons.

In examining candidate-voter alignments, we analyzed both national, or *collective*, representation and district, or *dyadic*, representation. The strength of central party committees (CENs) in Mexico means that party discipline is closer to that found in European countries with parliamentary systems than it is to most presidential systems. Thus we followed techniques used in prior work on these systems (see Barnes 1977; Converse and Pierce 1986; Dalton 1985; Weissberg 1978) and compared the mean preferences of candidates to those of voters, with the idea that proximity in policy preferences underpins citizen influence in democratic politics. At the same time, because we interviewed candidates from single-member districts (who have the greatest incentives to respond to the preferences of their constituents), we also looked at dyadic representation between individual candidates and the mean preference of voters in their districts (based on data from the Mexico 2006 Panel Study[15]).

Mexico's voters are, in general, more moderate on the issues than the candidates. As we would expect, the smallest differences appeared between candidates and voters who identified with the same party; however, even in this case, the candidates were more extreme than their own core voters on the issues of privatization, abortion, and social welfare. When it came to independents and the electorate as a whole, the candidates were badly out of step.

On the question of privatization of the electricity sector, the PAN and PRD candidates endorsed very different positions, but voters were clustered fairly closely toward the center and against privatization (see figure 6.3.) These data indicate the striking isolation of the PAN candidates, who appeared as radical privatizers, out of tune with a tepid base. On this issue, the PRD candidates hold beliefs much closer to those of the average voter, as well as to those of their own constituency.

A similar pattern emerged on the legality of abortion in the case of rape. The PAN was closer to the voters in general, but found itself on the "wrong" side of the issue. Perhaps the biggest surprise was that the PRD candidates were much more in favor of abortion rights than their own core voters. Though important for policy, these differences probably did not matter much in the election; the abortion question has never been as politically mobilized in Mexico as it has in the United States.

On the question of social welfare, the PAN candidates were much more in favor of individual responsibility for citizens' social welfare than were their own constituents, who desired some level of government assistance. The bigger surprise, however, was that the PRD candidates were more in favor of government assistance than their core voters. We would typically expect voters to place more demands on government, whereas prospective legislators who know the real constraints on government spending might be expected to hold back somewhat. Not only did this not appear to be the case, but the rightward skew in preferences suggested that Calderón's emphasis on job creation may have resonated more broadly—even among PRD voters—than López Obrador's call for poverty alleviation programs.

A different pattern emerged over the question of commercial relations with the United States. The PRD candidates were much less opposed to expanding economic ties with the United States than their national-level campaign rhetoric suggested. Unsurprisingly, the PAN candidates were uniformly in favor. What we find more interesting is the much lower level of support on this issue by the voters. Even among PAN voters, often thought to come from those who benefit from free trade, there was skepticism. PRD voters were the least sup-

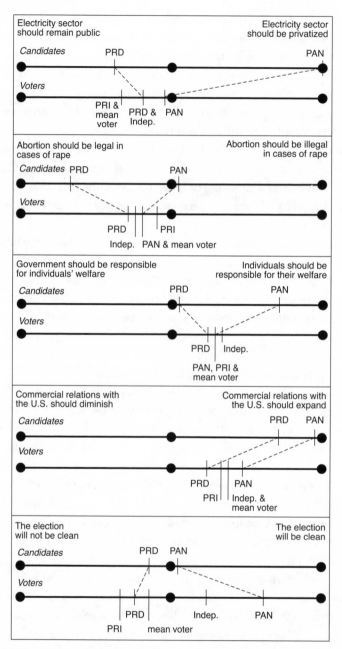

Figure 6.3 Candidate and voter preferences on five major issues.

Note: *n* = 84 for PAN candidates; 77 for PRD candidates; 303 for PAN identifiers; 214 for PRD identifiers; 310 for independents; 1,049 for all voters.

portive, as we would expect, since the PRD draws more voters from the ranks of the poor and those in the South who have benefited less from free trade. But it is notable that even these voters were more in favor of than opposed to expanding economic ties with the United States. These findings appear to cast doubt on the productiveness of López Obrador's campaign rhetoric, which was somewhat further to the left on this question.

We also explored prospective opinions about how clean respondents thought the July election would be. As shown in figure 6.3, candidates were much closer to each other than were their parties' voters. PRI and PRD voters were the most skeptical that the elections would be clean, while PAN voters apparently trusted in the elections much more than the candidates they supported. The level of skepticism about clean elections needs to be underscored here, given that prior to 2006, analysts roundly applauded the nonpartisan Federal Electoral Institute (IFE) and Mexico as a shining example of how new democracies should run elections. Apparently, as chapter 2 in this volume suggests, substantial segments of the political class and voters did not agree. After the election, Calderón used this skepticism to lure segments of the PRD legislative bench into supporting at least some of his fiscal reforms, in exchange for electoral reforms that López Obrador publicly opposed.

Finally, elite polarization and mass moderation was also reflected in self-placements on a more abstract left-right scale, as shown in figure 6.4. As they did on the issues, candidates from the PRD placed themselves on the left and those from the PAN placed themselves on the right; they were not self-identified "centrists." In contrast, voter placements were more diffuse and spread across the left-right dimension. We make no claims about the particular meaning of "left" and "right" in these data and want to draw attention to the fact that 27.5 percent of the voters either could not place themselves on the scale or responded that they had no position. Nevertheless, those who did identify a position were far less polarized than were the candidates.

Before moving on, we must address the possibility that the observed centrism among voters reported above results from measurement error in the survey instrument, rather than the respondents' true attitudes. For such an error to affect the mean scores on which we based our analysis, it would have to be systematic in nature. A plausible source of such error would be levels of political knowledge. If measurement error biased self-reported positions toward the mean, then poorly informed respondents would more often choose the middle option in tradeoff questions, simply because they lacked firm issue preferences. In ef-

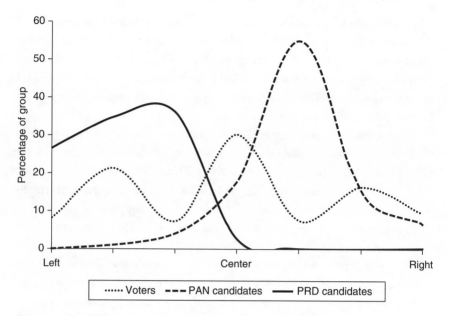

Figure 6.4 Candidate and voter positions on the left-right dimension.

Note: *n* = 84 for PAN candidates; 77 for PRD candidates; 1,049 for all voters. Difference in means test for PAN vs. PRD candidates: *t* = 18.9, *p* < 0.001.

fect, the middle option would substitute for "don't know" answers. To test for this possibility, we compared mean issue preferences for the respondents with different levels of political knowledge.[16] On three of the five questions employed for this analysis (privatization, the social safety net, and level of democracy), high-knowledge respondents were in fact closer to the center than low-knowledge respondents. This relationship held for each group of party identifiers and for independent voters.

On the questions of abortion and commercial relations with the United States, high-information respondents were further from the center than low-information ones. Regarding abortion, this pattern probably does not result from measurement error, as abortion is a high-impact question that is easily understood and about which nearly all respondents have readily accessible attitudes. Even if the statistically significant deviations did result from measurement error, such error would have been minor, since the average rightward shift among low-knowledge respondents was just 6 percent over the range for abortion attitudes. The question of commercial relations with the United States provided more opportunities for measurement error. Unlike prior questions, which began with dichotomous response categories, this question started with three possible answers (increase, decrease, or stay the same), thus giving respondents a greater opportunity for misinterpretation. Difference-in-means tests show that low-knowledge voters were closer to the center overall, as well as when parsed by party identification.[17] Although these differences were generally statistically significant, they were substantively small and averaged just 9 percent of the theoretical range.

Thus, although a minor amount of measurement error may have affected responses on one of the five questions we analyzed, it cannot account for the voters' observed centrism. Voters' preference for the middle of the road, and the contrast between their positions and those of the congressional candidates, are a faithful representation of polarizing collective representation in Mexico.

Dyadic Representation: Candidate-Voter Differences by District

The collective differences between candidates and voter groups in the prior section may not accurately reflect the correspondence between individual representatives and their constituents in each district. In particular, large cross-district differences among the voters might produce the appearance of centrism on average, even if individual candidates are highly responsive to their constituents' preferences. In this section, we examine dyadic representation and show similar results to those above; candidates are, on average, more extreme on the issues than the voters in their districts.

To construct candidate-voter dyads, we matched mean voter issue preferences by district from the Mexico 2006 Panel Study to elite responses from the candidate survey. As the respondents in the panel study were selected in clusters, we ended up with many candidate responses from districts that were not represented in the voter survey. Unfortunately, these data were simply lost for this analysis. Nevertheless, the available data still yield insights into the relationship between candidates and their constituencies.[18]

We examined dyadic representation on the issues of abortion and privatization of the electricity sector. We are persuaded by Hill and Hurley's (1999) argument that elite-mass congruence should only emerge over "easy" positional issues that clearly divide party elites and over which voters have real preferences. When issues are too complex, mass surveys may yield garbage-can answers that reflect non-attitudes. We therefore selected two issues from very different domains that should have been easy for voters to identify. The abortion question, though not highly politicized, clearly divides the PAN and PRD candidates and constituencies, and it strikes such a personal chord that it would be difficult for voters not to have clear preferences. The question of electricity sector privatization is also salient and clearly divides the parties and the voters. Public ownership of the energy sector is genetically linked to the modern Mexican state and to Mexicans' sense of national self-determination. In addition, the recent round of privatizations throughout Latin America has crystallized voters' preferences on this issue (see Baker 2003).

We examined the relationship between candidates and the mean voter preference across districts through simple bivariate regression models, as suggested by Achen (1978). In models where district-level voter preferences form the dependent variable, perfect dyadic representation would exist if the coefficient on the variable representing the candidates' preferences was one and the intercept was zero. We used such models to generate the mean level of over-representation of the voters' district preferences. On the question of privatization, the PAN candidates were, on average, 32.7 percent further to the right than were the voters. The PRD candidates were significantly closer to the voters and skewed an average of just 3.2 percent to the left of the mean preferences. On the question of abortion, the two parties flanked the voters almost evenly, with the PAN 15.2 percent to the right and the PRD 13.7 percent to the left of the voters' mean preferences.[19] Thus, just as we saw with our analysis of collective representation, the congressional candidates were systematically polarized, to one degree or another, around the districts they sought to represent.

Candidates also consistently underestimated their own distance from voters, though the PRD did so to a lesser degree than the PAN. For the abortion and privatization questions, we asked the candidates to place both themselves and the "majority of voters in their district" on an eleven-point scale (0–10). On abortion, the PRD candidates placed themselves 1.2 points away from the voters in their district—about 11 percent of the total issue space—whereas the true distance, as noted above, is 13.7 percent. On privatization, the PRD candidates thought of themselves as being just 0.08 points away from the voters they sought to represent, or a scant 0.7 percent of the issue space, compared to the actual distance of 3.2 percent. The PAN candidates placed themselves less than one point (0.8) away from the voters in their districts on this issue, just 7.3 percent of the total issue space, when they were, in fact, badly out of touch (at 37.2% away from the mean). On abortion, the PAN candidates also placed themselves at a tiny distance from the voters (0.6), representing 5.4 percent of the issue space, about one-third of the true distance (15.2%).

Even more remarkably, the candidates expressed extraordinary confidence in their ability to move the voters toward their own position. On the abortion question, for example, 84 percent of the PAN candidates and 58.3 percent of the PRD candidates thought they could influence voters "a lot" or "some." They may be doomed to disappointment. Asked whether they were "sure" of their opinion about abortion or whether they "might change" it, 82 percent of the voters indicated that they were sure—hardly a surprising result for that issue. We can scarcely imagine a more problematic situation for political representation; not only do candidates not stand for voters' demands, they also seem oblivious to that fact.

This chapter demonstrates that ideological differences structure divisions within Mexico's political class. Not only were the presidential candidates in 2006 polarized on the issues, but the party platforms of the left and right have been far from one another since at least 1979, and the respective parties' congressional candidates were highly polarized in the run-up to the most recent elections. Candidates from the PAN combined fiscal and social conservatism, much like Christian Democrats in Europe (with which the PAN is affiliated).[20] They were pro-life, favored privatization of the electricity sector and an expansion of commercial relations with the United States, and believed in private investment and individual responsibility as the best way to reduce poverty. The PRD candidates sharply disagreed on most of these issues. They were pro-choice, wished to maintain public ownership over the strategic electricity sector, and endorsed an expanded social safety net. They were also somewhat more skeptical about the benefits of commercial ties with the United States, although not as much as we originally anticipated and not nearly as much as leftist parties in some South American countries, including Venezuela, Bolivia, and Peru. In contrast to Smyth's findings that in Russia's new party system "there is tremendous variance within party organizations, rendering [issue positions] statistically indistinguishable" (2006, 166), we found a clear ideological structure at the elite level that gives voters the opportunity to evaluate candidates on the issues.

This obvious ideological polarization among political elites did not reflect sentiments at the mass level, either in general or among PAN and PRD identifiers (who typically clustered quite closely around the mean voter). The candidates were out of step with the voters when viewed at both the national and district levels, and they did not seem to realize just how distant they were. In fact, our research shows that the candidates had the hubris to believe that mass opinions which contradicted their own could be changed through "issue leadership," even when such claims were—at the very least—highly dubious.

We draw three main conclusions from this examination. First, polarization does not spring from deep divisions in the electorate. The issues that occupied the national political agenda during the 2006 campaign were similar across party elites and among voters, including jobs, public security, and poverty. Yet the positions that candidates took on these issues did not accurately represent the positions of their own partisan supporters, much less those of the independent voters. Thus, despite the transition from authoritarian dominant party rule under the PRI to fully competitive democratic politics by 2000, Mexico has not undergone a major partisan realignment along ideological lines. To the extent that voters have developed partisan attachments, these may be structured more by social networks than by ideological preferences (see chapter 4 in this volume).

Second, there is a significant representation gap between voters and their congressional representatives. Whether out of ignorance or arrogance, the PAN and the PRD engage in what Kitschelt et al. (1999) refer to as "polarized trusteeship," fostering legislation that leads rather than follows public opinion on the issues. Such representatives are out of step with the electorate and, in some sense, seek to contravene the public will. This representation gap may help explain the relatively low level of party identification that voters expressed, a general lack of trust in the government, and the declines in normative support for democracy since the disputed 2006 presidential election[21] (for a more detailed discussion of attitudes toward the political system, see chapter 2 in this volume).

Although the representational failures we document are real and significant, they should not be overstated. Mexico's comparatively structured party system yields far more positive representational outcomes that the weakened or collapsed party systems of Venezuela, Bolivia, and Peru, where dramatic partisan dealignment has left major groups without representation and has deeply compromised policy linkages between political elites and voters (see Mainwaring et al. 2006). In addition, Mexico's three strong parties give voters much clearer choices than they would have if the major parties campaigned on virtually the same policy promises. Thus, while we view reducing Mexico's representation gap as an important task for its fledgling democracy, we recognize that some other new democracies are in a far more precarious condition.

Finally, given the extent of their policy differences, the prospects for legislative collaboration between the PRD and the PAN were limited, even without López Obrador's intransigence. Not only do we see difficulties in forging coalitions on economic policy issues, but we also note that events surrounding the 2006 elections raised a new type of division. Where the PRD and the PAN once agreed on the types of electoral reform required for democracy, they have now diverged. The PAN candidates are largely content with the state of democracy in Mexico, but López Obrador's loss has only encouraged the PRD candidates' critical stance on questions of electoral fairness. In the 2007 electoral reforms, the PRD won PAN (and PRI) support for important restrictions on privately funded advertising, intended to prevent the kind of negative advertising that marred the 2006 election (see chapter 9 in this volume), but it failed to secure changes in the IFE's procedures and had to settle for a housecleaning of personnel. Divisions over the extent to which these recent reforms have addressed weaknesses in the electoral system continue to fuel a growing split between López Obrador and more moderate segments of the PRD leadership. This new debate has the potential to become a deeper division among Mexico's political class.

The legislative impasse that may emerge from polarization between Mexico's two largest parties leaves a potentially important role for the discouraged and largely discredited PRI. The correlation of forces in Congress and the PRI's weakened position imply that we may see PAN-PRI alliances to construct legislative majorities. On many issues, the PRI occupies the middle position between its rivals. The PRI's relatively large legislative delegation in the 2000–3 and 2003–6 legislatures raised hopes that the party's candidate could capture the presidency in 2006 and discouraged cooperation with then president Vicente Fox (see chapter 8 in this volume); its much lower seat count in the 2006–9 legislature left the party much weaker, but it retained a pivotal position. It could use its middle stance in one of two ways. First, it could extract concessions by voting with the PAN and the president, thus helping it make a comeback at the expense of its two main rivals. In following this path, the PRI would do well by doing good. Its pivotal centrist votes would help avoid the perils of legislative gridlock that have immobilized so many Latin American democracies and would create compromise legislation that is, in fact, closer to the average voter's preferences than the policies favored by the PAN legislators alone. An early example of this path was the PRI's September 2007 decision to vote with the PAN to approve Mexico's first major fiscal reform in ten years, including increased gasoline taxes and taxes on bank deposits.

The second and more ominous possibility is that the PRI could allow the PAN and the PRD caucuses to reach deadlock and wait for voters to return it to office as the responsible centrist option it has tried to become in recent elections. An example of action in this direction involves the PAN's proposals to allow foreign investors to provide capital for further oil exploration. In March 2008, the PRI signaled its reluctance to support these measures, but it did not pledge to join the PRD in opposing them. Deadlock was only avoided because Calderón submitted an amended proposal that was passed by all three parties. Nevertheless, the process of negotiation included mass protests and a prolonged sit-in by PRD deputies in the Mexican Congress that disrupted all legislative activities.

In following either path, the former ruling party stands to gain. Paradoxically, the smooth operation of Mexico's new democracy may yet depend on the role of its one-time nemesis, the PRI. Unfortunately, polarization between the PAN and the PRD also seems likely to continue.

CHAPTER SEVEN

Choosing Mexico's 2006 Presidential Candidates

David A. Shirk

Mexico's presidential sash had barely been laid across Vicente Fox's chest on December 1, 2001 before political observers began speculating about who would replace him at the end of his term. Over the course of his 2000–6 presidential administration, the long list of potential nominees, or pre-candidates, included high-ranking members of Fox's cabinet, several state governors, and even an ambitious first lady. Uncertainty prevailed less than one year before the July 2006 elections, when the ultimate winner was then just another dark-horse candidate trailing the front-runner for his party's nomination; the former ruling party seemed poised to make a major comeback after a series of encouraging state-level electoral victories; and the Left was still considering a three-time loser as its presidential candidate. Obviously many things changed during the nomination process (pre-campaign), contributing to a very different kind of contest than many anticipated. Hence, understanding the 2006 Mexican presidential elections requires knowing how the political parties chose their candidates and, in so doing, lined up on the electoral playing field.

The 2006 election presented numerous firsts in Mexican presidential candidate selection. It was the first election in which the Institutional Revolutionary Party (PRI) lacked the firm hand and watchful eye of its own sitting president to guide the nomination process. For the Party of the Democratic Revolution (PRD), it was the first election where the party ran a different candidate than its principal founder, Cuauhtémoc Cárdenas, as well as the first presidential race in which that party also appeared likely to win. Finally, 2006 was the first time in which a relatively unknown National Action Party (PAN) contender with limited electoral experience defeated better-known rivals for his party's nomination and ultimately captured the presidency.

Each of these new developments illustrates the important role that candidate selection procedures play in shaping the political arena. Ample research in the United States and elsewhere demonstrates that political parties' internal nomination processes influence not only the candidates who are selected to run for public office, but also what interests and constituencies the candidates represent, the support that a candidate receives from his or her party in the general election, the relative positions of the candidates at the outset of the campaign, and the emphasis that party programs receive during and after the contest (Aldrich 1980; Cronin 1982; Galderisi et al. 2001; Lengle 1981; Marshall 1981; Meinke et al. 2006; Walters 1988). On the one hand, a party's candidate selection procedures can bolster its chances of success, because the timing and the methods used can help a party identify more electable candidates (i.e., candidates with greater popular appeal). In addition, media coverage of a primary can attract increase exposure for the party's nominee. On the other hand, if competition for the nomination proves highly divisive, the resulting bad blood may alienate the losing aspirants and—more importantly—their supporters; overambitious nominees may expose the dirty laundry of their opponent, or of the party itself; and the financial drain of protracted campaigns for the nomination can hobble the ultimate nominee (Atkeson 2000; Bernstein 1977; Lengle 1980; Lengle et al. 1995). In short, candidate selection procedures significantly influence each candidate's prospects at the start of the general election, as well as the fate of his or her party over the longer term.

In the grand scheme, the development of internal party candidate selection procedures impacts the processes of party institutionalization and democratic consolidation in a number of fundamental ways. First, whatever system of candidate selection a party employs, there needs to be relative acceptance of the rules of the game and the way that it is played within the organization, in order to prevent individuals who are passed over for the nomination either from withholding their support from the party's eventual nominee or from defecting and running under another party label or as independents in the general election. Candidate selection mechanisms ideally establish an internal democratic bargain, even in parties that are not especially democratic; that is, they establish the willingness of competing individuals and factions to accept uncertainty and potentially accept defeat as part of the larger organizational enterprise. When such a bargain is strengthened by widely accepted rules or norms for candidate selection, it helps to ensure the organization's longer-term survival and institutionalization. Second, to the extent that a party's candidate selection procedures facilitate choice between competing alternatives and involve citizens in the decision-making process, they strengthen the degree of contestation and participation in a democratic system. In Latin America, where scholars often express concern that many parties are weakly institutionalized, there is a surprising lack of attention to the evolution and impact of candidate selection procedures as part of the democratic process.

This chapter offers insights on how Mexico's political parties chose their 2006 presidential candidates, how these choices influenced the general election, and what they implied for politics after the election. Considering the dynamics of candidate selection in general, and especially at each of the party's respective nomination processes in 2006, two questions are of particular interest. What political dynamics led to the specific candidate selection procedures and outcomes followed by the three major parties? And what advantages (or liabilities) did more open and competitive candidate selection methods confer? Mexico provides a unique context in which to examine these questions, because the prohibition on executive re-election ensures that no presidential candidate has a direct incumbency advantage, and because the three main parties each experienced a distinctive nomination process in 2006.[1] Their varied experiences enable us to evaluate different hypotheses about the methods of candidate selection, as well as their relevance to comparative debates about political parties.

The 2006 nomination process offered at least three lessons. First, though the campaign affected voters' choices among the presidential candidates (as discussed in the following section of this volume), the different nomination procedures employed by all three parties were also crucial in determining the actual choices available to voters. Perhaps most significantly, the PRI's internal dilemmas seriously compromised the former ruling party's prospects in the general election (see chapter 8 in this volume) and effectively made the PAN's candidate the default alternative to front-runner Andres Manuel López Obrador. Second, party leaders must balance programmatic and strategic objectives as they determine whether their parties opt for an open competition, select a candidate of unity, or choose a doctrinaire candidate more representative of the party than the electorate at large. The experiences of both the PRI and the PRD illustrate how pressure from a strong "preordained" candidate creates serious dilemmas for party leaders, while the emergence of Calderón as the PAN candidate illustrates how the use of a relatively closed primary can favor a nominee with strong ties to the party. Finally, as all three major parties adapt to Mexico's new democratic context, candidate selection procedures have begun to evolve in response to—and with significant implications for—the process of democratic consolidation in Mexico. In spite of significant tensions in selecting their presidential candidates, all three parties managed to avoid a damaging rupture; however, both the PRI and the PRD exhibited worrying signs of institutional vulnerability. Meanwhile, the fact that all three parties also made significant attempts to open their candidate selection procedures to public scrutiny and mass participation suggests a general direction that bodes well for Mexican democratic consolidation.

Candidate Selection in Mexico

With Mexico's gradual democratization over the 1980s and 1990s, candidate selection processes became more decentralized; internal primaries and the preferences of party members became much more important in choosing and electing candidates. Certainly, the whim of the outgoing president and the smoke-filled offices of party leaders are not entirely inconsequential today. However, unlike previous presidential elections in Mexico, where executives handpicked their successors and elections were marred by fraud, the participation of rank-and-file members in relatively inclusive party primaries are now what ultimately determine the choices available to the electorate at large. The current reality presents a stark contrast to the past, and party leaders, candidates, and organizations are still adjusting to Mexico's new political context: learning what kinds of internal decision-making rules produce the most favorable results, adapting to the influences of a media-saturated political environment, and becoming accustomed to the still-evolving procedures and regulations of Mexico's autonomous electoral authorities.

Candidate selection mechanisms have thus become the focus of considerable concern for party leaders and candidates. As Wuhs (2006) demonstrated, Mexican party leaders strategically manipulate candidate selection procedures at the national, state, and local level as they attempt to balance their power, programmatic agendas, and electoral ambitions. At the same time, candidates vie to improve their chances of obtaining the party's nomination. Using media-savvy campaigning and independent fundraising, Vicente Fox outmaneuvered party leaders and would-be opponents to capture the PAN's nomination in 2000 (Shirk 2000). As the party's unopposed "candidate of unity," Fox trounced the PRI and PRD candidates, who were hobbled by divisive internal contests (especially in the case of the PRI). However, once in office, the costs of Fox's highly independent campaign—which relied less on his party than on his own personalized political action committee (i.e., Friends of Fox)—could be found in his administration's relatively low level of partisanship in political recruitment to the executive bureaucracy and even in certain tensions between Fox and key PAN party leaders (Shirk 2005). Presidential selection procedures thus have important implications not only for the outcome of the nomination process and the election, but for governance as well.

Like the country's democratic system itself, scholarly research on Mexico's presidential selection mechanisms is still emerging. Fortunately, this literature builds on a strong foundation of research on Mexican party organizations, especially those of the political opposition (Arriola 1994; Bruhn 1997; Chand 2001; Hernández Vicencio 2001; Loaeza 1999; Lujambio 2000, 2001; Mabry 1974; Magaloni 2006; Mizrahi 2003; Reveles Vázquez 2003, 2004; Von Sauer 1974; Wuhs 2002). Pioneering research in this area has generated valuable and broadly generalizable insights into the dynamics of candidate selection and the process of party institutionalization in democratizing countries. In particular, the emerging consensus among many observers of Mexican candidate selection is that external competitive pressures resulting from democratization have impelled leaders in each party to open their organization's procedures to greater internal competition and mass participation (Langston 1997, 2003; McCann 2004a; Reveles Vázquez 2003; Wuhs 2006). Doing so provides an important test of their candidates' electoral viability in the political marketplace, but it also poses the risk of electing candidates who are relatively independent from the party and possibly less representative of its programmatic agenda. The PAN's central dilemma in nominating its 2006 presidential candidate reflected this pragmatic-programmatic dilemma, since it pitted a better-known, less staunchly partisan candidate against a longtime party stalwart.

Yet, in addition to weighing the potential benefits and risks of different candidate selection mechanisms, party leaders must also take into consideration other competing interests and pressures within the organization.[2] Indeed, in making their decisions on candidate selection procedures, the PRI and PRD leaders struggled over how to minimize infighting and the possibility that prominent contenders for the nomination would exit the process. Each of the parties made decisions based partly on enhancing their electoral competitiveness and partly on factors that had less to do with winning elections and more to do with addressing pressures and tensions within their organizations. In doing so, the parties determined who emerged to compete for the Mexican presidency in 2006 and thus helped shape the course of Mexican democratic development.

Choosing the PAN's Candidate: The Disobedient Son

For various reasons, the PAN's long list of potential presidential candidates gradually narrowed to three nominees who registered and competed formally in the party primary for the 2006 election: former energy secretary Felipe Calderón, former Jalisco governor Alberto Cárdenas Jiménez, and former minister of government Santiago Creel.[3] The shadow of Vicente Fox loomed over two of these candidates. On the one hand, Creel was the clear front-runner according to polls of the general electorate, primarily because his position as Fox's minister of government made him a highly visible figure and automatic presidential candidate.[4] Tacit signals of support from the Fox administration also gave Creel the status of natural successor.[5] Cárdenas Jiménez, also a Fox ally,[6] began his gubernatorial term in Jalisco in 1995, the same year Fox took office as governor of Guanajuato; both were important industrial and agricultural states in Mexico's heartland.[7] Without the benefit of hindsight, Felipe Calderón was perhaps the least obvious choice among the three candidates running for the PAN nomination. Although Calderón had been elected on the party list to the Assembly of the Federal District (1988–91) and the Chamber of Deputies (2000–3), his only experience as a candidate in a direct election came from a failed gubernatorial bid in his home state of Michoacán in 1995.[8] Moreover, Calderón's experience in executive government was limited to two very brief stints during the Fox administration (first as the director of the Mexican credit agency BanObras and later as energy secretary). Hence, Calderón's emergence as the victor in the contest between these three men seemed somewhat improbable; indeed, given the strong role of self-proclaimed candidates in the PRD and the PRI, it constituted the biggest surprise of the major parties' nominations.

Understanding Calderón's victory requires a closer look at candidate selection processes in the PAN. As Mexico's longest surviving opposition party, the PAN has had a long history of adherence to internally democratic procedures.[9] At the same time, the number of citizens eligible to participate in the PAN's democratic process has historically been very limited because of the party's relatively small membership base. Indeed, in state and local conventions—even in some megacities and party strongholds like Guadalajara, León, Monterrey, and

Tijuana—as few as 1,000 or 2,000 people may qualify as active members of the PAN. Thus, even if all eligible members participate, only a handful of citizens may actually determine the nominee and, in places where the PAN faces little competition, who will ultimately govern. During the era of PRI hegemony, the PAN's active membership was limited by a lack of interest in supporting an opposition party (Greene 2007). Today, the party's base still remains relatively low because membership criteria remain rather exclusive. Indeed, the bulk of the party's supporters fit into the category of *miembros adherentes* (affiliate members), who have fewer privileges and responsibilities than do the PAN's *miembros activos* (active members).[10] The PAN adopted this special category of affiliate membership in 1997, when Felipe Calderón was its president, in an effort to strengthen the leadership's control of the party during a period of unprecedented growth. Only active members of the party were guaranteed the right to vote in all the party's internal elections; the participation of affiliate members was contingent on approval of the party's national council.

For the selection of the party's presidential candidates in 2000 and 2006, the PAN opted to hold a closed primary that permitted both sorts of members to participate but required formal enrollment months before the primary. This decision restricted participation to about 600,000 people in 2000 and one million in 2006, or about 1.1 percent and 1.4 percent of Mexico's registered voters, respectively.[11] By comparison, roughly 13.2 percent out of 130 million registered U.S. voters voted in the open contest for the Republican nomination in 2000, and roughly 10 percent of the 122 million registered U.S. voters participated in the open contest for the 2004 Democratic primary.[12] In the nomination procedures for the 2008 presidential election, the proportion of Republican and Democratic primary voters increased, respectively, to 14.3 and 25.6 percent of all 136.6 million voters.[13] In the U.S. case, the use of relatively open primaries lends itself to very participatory candidate selection processes and helps choose candidates with strong national appeal, but it also gives party leaders and staunch partisans less control over the outcome. This difference factors heavily into the PAN's nomination processes, which give much greater control to party leaders and members. In 2000, for example, Vicente Fox—a relative newcomer to the PAN and unrepresentative of its traditional candidates—recognized that without extraordinary measures, his appeal as a candidate might be weak inside the party. Equally important, he saw that targeting his primary campaign to the restricted audience of PAN's primary voters would not allow him to gain enough support to win the general election. Hence, well in advance of the primary,

Fox deliberately circumvented the party leadership by launching a nationwide campaign that discouraged competition from potential rivals, leading to an uncontested PAN presidential nomination for the first time in decades.

In the 2006 pre-campaign, none of the PAN candidates had an overwhelming advantage when the party leadership began defining the final rules of the candidate selection process. According to party statute, the method of selecting a presidential candidate was determined by the party's National Council and overseen by the party's Election Commission.[14] As outlined in the party's regulations, competition between formally registered candidates was to take place over a series of three staggered regional primaries, held in September and October 2005 (see figure 7.1).[15] Two procedural aspects of the process deserve mention. First, the fact that only party members and affiliates were allowed to participate in the primary strongly favored Calderón, who had a long history within the party organization and, as a former party president, had close ties to PAN partisans on the internal Election Commission and in party strongholds throughout the country. Creel, in contrast, was seen more as Vicente Fox's candidate. This perception was somewhat of a liability; many activists within the PAN had lukewarm feelings toward Fox and his presidency.[16]

A second important aspect was the decision to stagger the primaries in three sequential rounds over the course of several weeks, rather hold a simultaneous one-day primary, as Creel preferred. Staggered presidential nomination contests, like those in U.S. presidential elections, allow voters more time to evaluate the candidates and draw inferences from decisions made by voters in earlier contests. In 2006, the PAN's staggered primary contributed to a significant bandwagon effect for Calderón, as his support grew from 45.9 percent in the first round, to 49.9 percent in the second, and to 57.9 percent in the final round (see table 7.1). This momentum grew despite the fact that Calderón's opponents appeared to have stronger bases of support in states where the primary rounds came later in the process, Creel in the Federal District and Cárdenas Jiménez in Jalisco.[17]

Another interesting effect of the staggered primary was that, as the tide steadily shifted in Calderón's favor, competition became more intense and the contest potentially more divisive. In a brief bout of electoral intrigue, Creel questioned the results of the second round in certain southern states, notably raising accusations of irregularities in Yucatán, the PAN's southern stronghold.[18] Then, in the third round, further accusations came from Cárdenas Jiménez, who alleged that PAN members in Jalisco were under pressure from the na-

Figure 7.1 Regional results of the PAN primary rounds for the 2006 presidential election.

Source: www.pan.org.mx. Map prepared by Michael Myers.

Table 7.1   PAN primary results by round and candidate

	Round 1	Round 2	Round 3	Total
Alberto Cárdenas	17,049 (19.27%)	14,810 (13.08%)	19,015 (17.42%)	50,874 (16.36%)
Santiago Creel	30,790 (34.80%)	41,934 (37.02%)	26,935 (24.67%)	99,659 (32.05%)
Felipe Calderón	40,646 (45.94%)	56,516 (49.90%)	63,214 (57.91%)	160,376 (51.58%)
No. of states	10	8	14	32
Null votes	973	2,485	801	4,259
Total valid votes	88,485	113,260	109,164	310,909

Source: PAN Comisión de Elecciones, www.pan.org.mx.

tional party leadership to vote for Calderón.[19] Although these accusations were unsubstantiated, they demonstrated an uncharacteristically high degree of contentiousness for a PAN presidential primary. Such accusations of fraud were potentially damaging to the PAN's clean-government reputation.

In the end, Calderón's victory marked a sharp shift from 2000 and had major implications for the kind of candidate the PAN supported in the general election. PAN scholar Yemile Mizrahi has described the entrepreneurial businessmen who flocked to the PAN in the 1980s and 1990s as "rebels without a cause," in reference to the pragmatic and relatively nonideological orientation of these newcomers (1993, 1997, 2003). Felipe Calderón's self-proclaimed moniker as the PAN's "disobedient son"—the title of the biographical book prepared for his campaign—gave the intended impression that he was a rebel *with* a cause, a breed apart from Fox and his protégé Santiago Creel.[20] Calderón intended to serve as a more loyal standard-bearer for his party both in the electorate and in the presidency. Indeed, in PAN lore, Calderón's title as the "disobedient son" had a deeper meaning. His father, Luis Calderón Vega, was a venerable party leader, best known for his work as the PAN's official historian in the 1970s.[21] Following in his father's footsteps, Calderón obtained a religiously influenced education and later amassed vast experience within the party organization. However, Calderón Vega and a handful of other members left the party in 1981, feeling that their vision of the PAN, which emphasized post-Vatican II principles of Catholic social justice, was being corrupted and the party being pushed to the right. Calderón Vega's sons and a daughter remained in the PAN.[22]

Thereafter, Felipe Calderón found a mentor in Carlos Castillo Peraza, an intellectual who, like Calderón Vega, had joined the PAN in the late 1960s at the height of its early Catholic social justice orientation.[23] Although he never won a direct election, Castillo Peraza made enormous contributions to the PAN organization, particularly during his tenure as party president (1993–96), when the party achieved many of its most important state and local victories. At a time when the PAN seemed to be becoming a more secular and pro-business organization, Castillo Peraza steadily championed an alternative vision of the PAN that emphasized the humanistic ideals of social justice that were derived from its Catholic roots. Calderón and Castillo Peraza worked closely together when both obtained party-list seats in the Mexican legislature (1988–91), and again when Calderón served under Castillo Peraza as the party's secretary general (1993–95). Ultimately, Calderón succeeded Castillo Peraza as party president (1996–99) in the run-up to the 2000 elections.

This background provides insights into the source of Calderón's appeal and eventual success in the PAN primary. His experience in the party established him as an ideologically committed PAN leader; his skills at political brinksmanship were extremely well honed; and his ties to staunch partisans remained much stronger than those of his competitors. At the same time, Calderón also demonstrated competence as the party's chief legislator in the lower house of the legislature, working closely with the Fox administration while maintaining a critical perspective that undermined some of the president's most important initiatives. Later, Calderón's abrupt departure from Fox's cabinet provided him with an opportunity to further develop his profile as a "disobedient son." After Fox indicated that Calderón should avoid a premature campaign (or other interference with Creel's ascent to the presidency), Calderón could appear to stand up against the discredited tradition of a president handpicking his successor.

Although Calderón appealed to PAN partisans, nominating a candidate who fits the ideological preferences of partisans carries a possible political risk. Specifically, that candidate's appeal may not translate into widespread popular support among the broader electorate. Indeed, while such candidates may fare well in a party primary, they may be too unfamiliar to voters or may be perceived as ideologically extreme. In the PAN's case, it appears that the perceived liabilities of running a candidate with greater external recognition and popularity, but a weaker affiliation with the party (like Creel), was undesirable to many within the party. Calderón's well-developed reputation as a party man, his political connections to state and local party leaders around the country, and his general appeal among PAN partisans all played to his favor in the primary. In the general election, Calderón's team was ultimately able to develop a successful campaign by deemphasizing their candidate's profile as a partisan candidate and emphasizing the weaknesses of his most visible opponents.

Choosing the PRI's Candidate: A Divisive Primary

Traditionally, the selection of the PRI presidential candidate was virtually synonymous with Mexico's unique brand of authoritarianism. From 1929 to 1994, each outgoing president handpicked his successor. The party's formal candidate selection procedures—and, indeed, the general election itself—merely provided the rubber stamp to make his decision official. The first major change in presidential selection came after the last presidential candidate chosen in this fashion, Luis Donaldo Colosio, was assassinated and ultimately replaced by his campaign chief, Ernesto Zedillo. This twist of fate had significant consequences for the 2000 presidential election. In that groundbreaking contest, Zedillo became the first president to renounce the old practice and to allow a genuine party primary for the PRI's presidential nomination (see McCann 2004b). The fact that Zedillo went even further—by recognizing the PAN's victory—ensured that nomination processes in Mexico would never be the same.

Without the president's *dedazo* (big finger) to guide them, the PRI's leaders were left to their own devices. The result was a significant degree of decentralization and variation in the PRI's candidate selection process for subnational offices. In some states, even before 2000, the PRI had already begun moving toward competitive primary elections for gubernatorial and municipal candidates. As a result of growing pressure from competitive elections in the 1990s, the PRI badly needed to identify candidates with popular appeal who could, in turn, win elections. Hence in some states, the PRI opened itself to internal competition and often managed to produce candidates (like Chihuahua governor Patricio Martínez) who could win without resorting to fraud or illicit government assistance. Meanwhile, with a view toward a comeback in the 2006 presidential elections, the PRI's national party leaders were working steadily to rebuild the party machine and shape its state and local candidate selection processes. The PRI made impressive gains in Mexico's federal midterm elections in 2003; it also proved enormously successful in its efforts to place candidates in state and local office in 2004–5, even recapturing long-lost prizes in PAN strongholds in northern Mexico.[24] In 2005, the PRI won three of five gubernatorial elections, whether as a result of competitive internal primaries (as in Chihuahua) or old-style tactics (as in Oaxaca). Midway through the Fox administration, pundits were astonished to find that the PRI was not only alive and well, but poised to retake the presidency in 2006.

The apparent mastermind behind the PRI's brilliant comeback was Roberto Madrazo, the former governor of Tabasco. After Madrazo's failed bid for the PRI's presidential nomination in 2000, he secured the post of PRI party president that his father, Carlos Madrazo Becerra, had occupied in the early 1960s.[25] The PRI's internal election for party leaders in February 2002 had proved a contentious affair, pitting Madrazo against former PRI legislative leader and governor Beatriz Paredes.

In the lead-up to that confrontation, the PRI's major players—including the outgoing party chairwoman and former governor of the state of Yucatán, Dulce María Sauri, and the party's remaining 17 governors—tried to determine who could best lead the party toward recovery after its unprecedented defeat in 2000. This was a delicate proposition. Although the party's major players had a common interest in identifying a strong, viable leader, they also recognized that a powerful national party leader could seriously jeopardize their newfound autonomy.[26]

The PRI's eighteenth national convention, in November 2001, was the party's opportunity to reinvent itself.[27] In January 2002, as they announced their campaigns to replace Dulce María Sauri, both Madrazo and Paredes approached the contest with proclamations of their desire to have a cordial competition that would preserve the unity of the party.[28] This desire for harmony was evidently widely shared, but it proved elusive. At the start of the new year, key party leaders and governors from around the country gathered in a private meeting to try to identify a "unity candidate." This initiative failed, however, as party leaders appeared evenly split between Madrazo and Paredes.[29] Lacking a candidate of unity, the prospect of a nationwide contest for control of the party threatened to split the PRI, particularly if the outcome was extremely close. Ultimately, in an open election that mobilized three million voters nationwide, including independents and members of other parties, exit polls placed Madrazo and Paredes within a few percentage points of each other. The close election was considered a "technical tie" that provoked a full recount of all ballots and acrimonious accusations in both directions.[30] In the weeks that followed, irregularities were found in nearly three dozen polling places, resulting in the nullification of 10,000 votes; the final margin of victory had Madrazo winning by over 50,000 votes.[31]

The 2002 PRI party leadership election highlighted significant tensions and fissures within the party, and the later sources of support and opposition in relation to Madrazo. It is particularly notable that Madrazo and Paredes appeared to split the party on both regional and sectoral lines. Madrazo enjoyed strong support in certain states, particularly Oaxaca, Sinaloa, and Tabasco. Also, Madrazo was favored by the Revolutionary Confederation of Workers and Peasants (CROC) and the Mexican Oil Workers' Union (Sindicato de Trabajadores Petroleros de la República Mexicana, or STPRM). In contrast, Paredes seemed to garner the most of her regional support in the Federal District and in the states of México, Veracruz, and Tlaxcala (where she previously served as governor). Her sectoral support came from the Worker's Confederation of Mexico (Confederación de Trabajadores de México, or CTM), the National Agrarian Confederation (Confederación Nacional Campesina, or CNC), and the National Workers' Union (Unión Nacional de Trabajadores, or UNT).[32] Divisions among the PRI's sectoral organizations called attention to long-suppressed rivalries within the party's traditionally cohesive and dutiful corporatist apparatus.

Most important, the 2002 party leadership elections demonstrated how divisive Madrazo could be within his own party. To some degree, Madrazo sought to smooth over these tensions once he took over the party leadership. Responding to cantankerous PRI legislators who balked at his initial efforts to move the party in a moderate direction, Madrazo switched from his initial overtures to the Fox administration (on such key policy issues as fiscal reform) and adopted the more confrontational approach that Paredes had advocated during the race for the party presidency. Moreover, in his efforts to appeal to these critics, Madrazo went so far as to betray his erstwhile partner, Elba Esther Gordillo. Referred to uncharitably as "Jimmy Hoffa in a dress," Gordillo held sway over the country's gargantuan National Teachers' Union (SNTE).[33]

Madrazo had initially recruited Gordillo to serve as his secretary general during his bid for the party presidency in 2002 and later managed to impose her as the party's leader in the Chamber of Deputies. However, Gordillo's heavy-handed approach provoked consternation among PRI legislators, and she was ousted (with Madrazo's support) from the congressional leadership in 2003. Roiling at her former ally's seemingly inexplicable betrayal, Gordillo withdrew from politics for several months before returning as one of Madrazo's most vociferous critics.[34]

The height of the internecine conflict came as Madrazo neared his ultimate goal, the party's nomination for the 2006 presidential election. Beginning in early 2005, his growing list of enemies within the party—who also believed that victory would be unlikely with Madrazo as the party's presidential nominee—began colluding to find a way to prevent his candidacy. This loosely affiliated network of anti-Madrazo allies slyly dubbed their movement Todos Unidos con México (Everyone United with Mexico), with an acronym—TUCOM—that was more widely interpreted as *todos unidos contra Madrazo* (everyone united against Madrazo). In addition to leaders who sparred with Madrazo in the aftermath of the 2002 contest for the party leadership (including Dulce María Sauri and Beatriz Paredes), other enemies emerged as part of TUCOM. Among the most notable figures that joined the movement were Coahuila governor Enrique Martínez, Hidalgo governor Miguel Angel Nuñez, state of México governor Arturo Montiel, Nuevo León governor Natividad González, Sonora governor Eduardo Bours, federal deputy Roberto Campa, Senator Emilio Gamboa, Senator Enrique Jackson, former presidential candidate Francisco Labastida, and former Tamaulipas governor Tomás Yarrington.

Montiel emerged as TUCOM's best hope to win the PRI's presidential nomination. In the state of México's gubernatorial elections in 2005, Montiel had succeeded not only in nominating his protégé (Enrique Peña Nieto) over Madrazo's choice (Carlos Hank Rhon), but also in engineering a decisive

PRI victory in the general election. Montiel reached into his suspiciously deep pockets to finance an expensive national advertising campaign to boost his own presidential aspirations. According to one pundit, "in Peña Nieto's election, Montiel demonstrated that he could tap the old resources available to the PRI and engage in old-style Mexican politics."[35] Other potential contenders from TUCOM (including the two other major possibilities, Jackson and Nuñez) declined to run and closed ranks behind Montiel.[36]

Thanks to the PRI's electoral advances under his leadership, Madrazo had assembled a posse of congressmen, governors, and mayors who now owed their allegiance to his efforts to place them in state and local offices. However, growing support for Montiel appeared to be turning the tide against him. In addition, Madrazo confronted another internal problem. Before he could formally launch his candidacy, party rules required that he step down from his position as PRI party president. Because Elba Esther Gordillo still technically retained her elected position as secretary general of the party, however, Madrazo's departure would automatically trigger Gordillo's ascendancy to the PRI party presidency.[37] Madrazo's nomination to the PRI presidential candidacy was therefore hardly a sure thing, though he ultimately succeeded in outmaneuvering Gordillo by electing his supporter, Mariano Palacios Alcocer, as PRI party president, in a significant deviation from party rules.

Madrazo's nomination now hinged entirely on his race against Montiel. Yet on the eve of the party's formal vote to determine its candidate, scheduled for mid-November 2005, the heated contest between Madrazo and Montiel came to an abrupt end. Reports of financial scandals involving the governor and his family, as well as revelations that he held title to several inexplicably luxurious properties, led Montiel to withdrawal from the race. Montiel's public remarks on the matter were brief, limited to oblique references that he was the victim of a carefully orchestrated smear campaign. With PRI party statutes strictly limiting the possibilities for the last-minute registration of substitute candidates, Montiel's withdrawal was fatal to the TUCOM movement. Madrazo's only remaining registered contender for the nomination was a virtually unknown former assistant attorney general, Everardo Moreno Cruz, who drew limited support. On November 13, 2005, Madrazo won by a 10-to-1 margin.

In the general election, the impact of the PRI's candidate selection process was perhaps even more significant than in either of the other two political parties. It is hard to imagine a more divisive primary. Moreover, both Calderón and López Obrador appeared relieved by Montiel's withdrawal from the race, indicating that they saw Madrazo as the easier candidate to beat. Data from the first wave of the Mexico 2006 Panel Study[38] confirm this assessment: 33 percent of respondents nationwide expressed negative opinions of Madrazo, roughly double the negative ratings for López Obrador (16%) or Calderón (18%) and five points above those for Montiel (28%). As chapter 8 in this volume shows, disaffected Montiel supporters and TUCOM leaders withheld their support for Madrazo in the general election, and the PRI finished in third place for the first time in its history.

Choosing the PRD Candidate: The Candidate of Unity?

The PRD's internal selection process was the most anticipated contest; it was also the most important, in terms of setting the electoral agenda. Its early coronation of Andrés Manuel López Obrador as its candidate confirmed his status as front-runner in the general election. His nomination was also a major milestone for the PRD in that, for the first time in its history, the party supported someone other than three-time presidential candidate and party founder Cuauhtémoc Cárdenas. The manner in which López Obrador usurped Cárdenas's claim to the party's mantle was illustrative not only of the power of a popular, electorally viable candidate in Mexico's new party politics, but also of the perilous tensions such a candidate can create within a party organization.

The PRD's particular origins contributed to significant dilemmas in terms of the party's internal party leadership and candidate selection processes (see chapter 9 in this volume), including a tendency toward excessive dominance of the organization by Cárdenas and the challenges of managing a ragtag collection of PRI defectors, Marxists, and social movement leaders. Over time, though, ambitious middle-level and second-generation PRD leaders began to assert themselves, successfully recasting the PRD. As they did, contests for party leadership positions and nominations gradually grew more contentious, in certain cases producing highly divisive and controversial results. The election for new party leadership in March 1999, for example, was marred by irregularities and allegations that Cárdenas favored former Communist Party leader Amalia García. In 2000, Porfirio Muñoz Ledo, one of the PRD's most prominent figures, renounced his ties with the party and made harsh allegations about Cárdenas's control of it.[39]

Among the second-tier leaders that scuffled for influence under Cárdenas was Andrés Manuel López Obrador, a one-time protégé of the party's founder.

Like his mentor, López Obrador was a PRI defector and a victim of electoral fraud in his first bid for elected office outside the ruling party; he had lost the gubernatorial race in his home state of Tabasco to Madrazo in 1995. In the demonstrations he led in the aftermath of that election, López Obrador evinced a talent for popular mobilization to protest electoral fraud.[40] After later serving as PRD state party leader in Tabasco, López Obrador went on to become national party president in 1996, with the support of René Bejarano, a former independent teachers' union leader and civic organizer.[41] In that role, López Obrador strengthened the party's grassroots apparatus (the so-called Sun Brigades). These efforts helped put the PRD into second place in the 1997 midterm elections and won the party its first governorship in Baja California Sur in 1999.

Thereafter, thanks to the backing of Bejarano's Democratic Left Current within the party, López Obrador won the party's nomination to run for mayor of Mexico City in 2000. That election proved a telling precursor to the 2006 presidential race, in the sense that López Obrador survived fierce opposition and a series of underhanded efforts to destroy his campaign.[42] Indeed, when López Obrador overcame the initial lead of PRI candidate and former ambassador Jesús Silva Herzog, his opponents registered legal objections, charging that the PRD candidate did not meet the residency requirement to run for mayor and should be disqualified. Denouncing these claims as "just another dirty trick," López Obrador organized a massive rally in Mexico City's main plaza to pressure local electoral authorities and later, in protest, boycotted the campaign's first televised debate.[43] In the end, evidence that members of the PRI had forged the documents that raised questions about López Obrador's eligibility cleared the path for his victory in the mayoral race.[44]

By this point, López Obrador was the PRD's rapidly rising star, well positioned for a presidential bid in 2006. Increasingly referred to colloquially and in the press by his iconic initials—AMLO—the new mayor set out to implement an ambitious political agenda that included constructing monumental public works projects, doling out payments to the poor and elderly, providing subsidies for needy students, fighting crime, and building a second level on Mexico City's notoriously congested inner beltway. All the while, he worked actively to set the political agenda with daily press briefings, to call attention to the needs of the poor and the disadvantaged, and to emphasize his own modest lifestyle. (In contrast to many flashy and well-heeled Mexican politicians, López Obrador, who became a widower midway through his term, lived alone in a simple apartment and drove a late-model Nissan Tsuru; see Trelles and Zagal 2004). López

Obrador achieved remarkably high approval ratings (over 60%) in the world's largest city, gaining national and international recognition.

His administration was not without its rocky periods: a series of scandals that included accusations of nepotism and favoritism;[45] videotapes featuring Bejarano and members of his administration on the take;[46] a highly publicized conflict with tens of thousands of peaceful demonstrators marching for improved public safety;[47] the removal of his police chief by the federal government;[48] his own *desafuero* (impeachment) by the Mexican Congress; and an abortive attempt by the Fox government to bring criminal charges against him for violating a court injunction.[49] As in past controversies, López Obrador's general response discounted these incidents as part of a conspiracy to undermine his presidential candidacy. Whether such allegations were true or not, López Obrador's remarkable ability to overcome these hurdles and maintain his position as front-runner in national polls lent credibility his self-proclaimed "indestructibility." For most of the three years prior to the election, López Obrador enjoyed a lead of between five and fifteen points over his presidential rivals from other parties.

Although López Obrador's viability as an alternative presidential candidate was recognized and cultivated early in his administration, convincing Cárdenas to step aside was a major challenge. Cárdenas repeatedly hinted at his own desire to carry the party's banner for a fourth time. Later, when tensions between López Obrador and the PRD became evident due to the scandals of 2004, Cárdenas voiced serious concerns about whether the Mexico City mayor was fit to serve as the PRD's presidential candidate. Still, despite significant displeasure within the party over recent events in López Obrador's administration, PRD leaders maintained that the selection of its presidential candidate would—as in the past—be conducted by a "universal, free, and direct vote."[50] An open primary strongly favored López Obrador, who many speculated could easily eclipse Cárdenas in such a race. The decision to maintain an open primary therefore not only reflected party tradition, but also signaled an important shift in the PRD party leadership, thanks to a gradual takeover by López Obrador loyalists, which prevented Cárdenas from bending the party to his will. Protesting the party's tacit rejection of his leadership, Cárdenas resigned from the PRD's National Council, and by mid-April 2004, some speculated that he might bolt the party he had created.[51]

Instead, soon after the PRD decided on its calendar for selecting the candidate in mid-2005, Cárdenas declared that he would indeed run for the nomination.[52] Party leaders warily considered the risks of yet another possible rupture as a result of Cárdenas's interest in the candidacy.[53] By this point, however, with the major scandals of his administration well behind him, López Obrador was at the apex of his postimpeachment bounce in public opinion polls and in party support.[54] More importantly, López Obrador benefited from the support of well-positioned allies within the party leadership, including former governor of Baja California Sur and new PRD president Leonel Cota.[55] Evidently reconsidering his options after meeting with party leaders, Cárdenas suddenly unleashed a barrage of anti-AMLO criticism, declaring that the PRD had failed to open adequate space for a real contest. Days later, he removed himself from the race, explaining his decision in a public letter and hinting that he might construct a fourth alternative with other opposition parties.[56] Following Cárdenas' withdrawal, no one was willing to run against López Obrador; the PRD opted to cancel the nationwide open primary it had planned for September.

As other parties wrestled with their own primary contests, López Obrador emerged as a unity candidate and the front-runner in the presidential race. His candidacy drew support from two minor leftist parties, the Labor Party (Partido del Trabajo, or PT) and the *Convergencia* (Convergence for Democracy) Party, which negotiated formal electoral alliances with the PRD in November and December 2005, respectively. Despite López Obrador's public statements that these alliances were born from shared political objectives—forging a "center-left" coalition—they created significant internal frictions in the PRD because of the high price extracted by the smaller parties under the terms of the alliance. At issue in both cases was the proportion of seats to be allocated to the smaller partners in the alliance. The PRD spent three months bargaining with the PT, which vacillated on whether to support López Obrador or join forces with the PRI. Leaders of Convergence, which flirted with an alliance with the PAN, were evidently particularly concerned with ensuring that their party would obtain sufficient representation to have *caucus* status (especially in the Senate), which would require a minimum of five seats. Some PRD leaders were reluctant to cede such a large share of seats to their junior partners. In the July 2003 midterm elections, the PT's and Convergence's estimated share of the national vote approached 4 percent and 3 percent, respectively, meaning that the terms of the alliance significantly overrepresented both minor parties in the legislature.[57] In the end, however, the PRD, PT, and Convergence joined forces in the Coalition For the Good of All.

Implications of the 2006 Mexican Presidential Candidate Selection Processes

What are the larger practical and theoretical implications of the candidate selection processes employed for Mexico's 2006 presidential elections? First, while much of the emerging literature on Mexican candidate selection procedures has emphasized how external competitive pressures are driving parties toward more open primaries, the 2006 Mexican presidential nominations illustrate the role that internal party politics play in shaping the nomination process. In the preliminaries to 2006, intraparty wrangling among divergent factions proved to be an important influence on party leaders and activists, who had to weigh the benefits of external competitiveness against their programmatic and political agendas.[58] Indeed, supporting Poiré's (2003) interpretation of post-2000 Mexican primaries, the PRI's internal contest leading up to the 2006 presidential elections was conducted less with an eye toward ensuring the party's competitiveness in the general election than toward the delicate challenge of managing internal competition in the absence of an overarching authority. In this sense, political parties may gravitate toward the use of primaries as much to address "potentially vexing problems of organizational coordination and maintenance" (McCann 2004a, 267) as to increase their competitiveness. Unfortunately, primaries themselves may lead to new problems, due to the reduced influence of elites and core activists on the party organization.

Second, the 2006 election underscored the important role that political parties (and nomination processes) have begun to play as agenda-setters in Mexico's emerging democracy. Until recently, the low level of competitiveness of Mexican elections made the discretion of the sitting executive the key determinant in candidate selection. Although more democratic nominating procedures prevailed in opposition parties, especially the PAN, these procedures mattered little in the overall scheme of Mexican politics, because opposition candidate could not win in the general election. As uncertainty in the outcome of general elections has increased, the emerging mechanisms for candidate selection have grown correspondingly more important. Indeed, the divisiveness of the PRI primary explains both its own third-rate performance and the PAN's ascendancy in this election. Without the hand (or finger) of an all-powerful president to guide it, the new PRI faced a significant challenge in trying to recapture the presidency. In this sense, the PRI was at a significant disadvantage relative to the PAN and the PRD, both of which had greater experience and more established

Table 7.2   PRI, PAN, and PRD presidential candidate selection procedures,
1970–2006

	PRI	PAN	PRD
1970	presidential designation	convention[a]	n.a.
1976	presidential designation	convention[b]	n.a.
1982	presidential designation	convention	n.a.
1988	presidential designation	convention	independent coalition candidacy
1994	presidential designation	convention	semi-open primary[c]
2000	open primary	closed primary	semi-open primary[c]
2006	open primary	closed primary	open primary[d]

[a]Until 1970, PAN conventions required a solid consensus for the presidential nominee.
[b]In 1976, the party failed to produce a candidate after multiple rounds of voting.
[c]In 1994 and 2000, the PRD primary was open only to party members, but individuals were allowed to register as party members on the same day as the primary.
[d]In 2006, the PRD's efforts to hold a competitive open primary were undermined by the withdrawal of Cuauhtémoc Cárdenas, one of only two contenders.
n.a. = Not applicable.

institutions for managing competition for the presidential nomination (see table 7.2).

Moreover, in terms of agenda-setting, the nomination process seems to have had significant ramifications for the candidates' relationships with their parties, with implications that go well beyond the election. Benefiting from a closed-party primary, Calderón won precisely because of close ties to his party's inner circle. This presented a sharp contrast to Fox, who had a much more distant relationship with his party while in office. Indeed, when naming members of his cabinet and developing his policies, Calderón drew much more heavily on his party than Fox did. In turn, he appeared likely to benefit from a more loyal and cohesive governmental team and greater PAN legislative support for his programs than did Fox.

Third, with the democratization of many presidential systems over the past two decades, especially in Latin America, there has been significant scholarly interest as to whether the evolution of presidential candidate selection procedures in newly emerging democracies will follow in the direction of the United States, and as to what new insights regarding the candidate selection processes will emerge from different comparative contexts. In some ways, presidential nomination processes in Mexico are sure to exhibit some similarities with those found in the United States and other developed democracies. As McCann observes, an increasing number of countries have adopted primaries that "often resemble American contests, complete with live televised debates, prodigious fundraising, attack ads, photo ops, horserace-style news coverage, and the involvement of hundreds of thousands, if not millions, of citizens" (2004a, 266).

In some ways, this trend toward the Americanization of party politics is heartening, because candidate selection procedures in the United States have arguably become more democratic over time, and in many ways they have contributed to the stability and longevity of the U.S. party system (Aldrich 1980; Gray 1980; Mayer 2004; Reynolds 2006; Ware 2002). In Latin America, the phenomenon of Americanization has included a wholesale trend toward more open candidate selection procedures throughout the region, with at least some parties in most countries moving toward relatively open, competitive primaries. According to Carey and Polga-Hecimovich (2006), this has yielded significant benefits for both the parties that use them—by way of increased electoral support—and the democratic consolidation of these political systems.[59] In Mexico, the trend toward more competitive and sophisticated nomination procedures is also likely to yield important benefits: increasing the amount of information available to voters, producing more effective candidates, and strengthening party identification among voters who might otherwise drift in the electoral sea (or abstain from political participation altogether).

On the other hand, some scholars view the Americanization of candidate selection procedures, and party politics in general, as being laden with potentially harmful effects for new democracies (Brown et al. 1995; R. Butler 2004; Wattenberg 1990; White and Mileur 1992). In particular, the U.S. party system has come under intense criticism because of its tendency to overemphasize seemingly superficial candidate attributes, weaken voters' ties to political parties, privilege "big money" candidates and interests, and generally reduce parties' programmatic orientations—all of which could prove damaging to the institutionalization of political parties. Looking at party organizations in comparative perspective helps to sort through these positive and negative effects and sheds light on some of the major conclusions found in the literature on presidential candidate selection.

In the U.S. experience, in particular, conventional wisdom suggests that open primaries produce more successful candidates; front-runners typically win their party's nomination; and uncontested candidacies are believed to have major advantages in the general election. In the 2006 Mexican presidential election, the PAN held a relatively closed and moderately divisive primary in which a dark horse candidate went on to win both the nomination and the general election.

This suggests that, for all its warts, the PAN's primary offered some important benefits: helping to bring attention to and build momentum for its candidate, strengthening the democratic bargain between rivals for the nomination, and possibly even yielding better performance in the general election. However, the PRD and PRI experiences also imply that, when the rules for candidate selection are poorly institutionalized or otherwise manipulated, they may lead to greater internal conflict and become damaging to the party.

Meanwhile, another lesson from the 2006 Mexican election is that, in contrast to the U.S. experience, candidates of "unity" are not always unifying. In the U.S. context, unopposed candidates often have significant advantages as the candidate of unity. However, in part this unity reflects a huge incumbency advantage for sitting presidents or vice presidents, who can serve for more than one term in office—unlike their Mexican and other Latin American counterparts, who have prohibitions on executive re-election. Indeed, Mexico's was one of nine Latin American presidential elections between November 2005 and December 2006 where there was no incumbent, which in many cases led to considerably more internal competition for the nomination.[60]

Above all, the 2006 election illustrated that Mexico's major parties are still adapting to the country's new competitive political context, and their candidate selection procedures are continuing to evolve. Unlike the situation in the United States, these parties hold separate nomination processes that have very different calendars and procedures. Each of the major parties is still learning and experimenting with the internal rules used to select candidates and leaders, sanction pre-candidate conduct, promote unity after divisive internal elections, and deal with other challenges of internal party democracy in a newly competitive political context. Undoubtedly this process of party adaptation and institutionalization holds important benefits for the larger process of democratic consolidation in Mexico and illustrates an important trend among democratizing countries throughout the region.

CHAPTER EIGHT

The PRI's 2006 Presidential Campaign

Joy Langston

The Institutional Revolutionary Party (PRI) had high hopes of retaking Los Pinos[1] in the 2006 presidential elections, after its dramatic loss of the presidency six years before. The governing party between 2000 and 2006, the National Action Party (PAN), was perceived as weak and ineffective. President Vicente Fox and his delegation in Congress were unable to deliver on several campaign promises, failing to win passage of crucial bills on energy-sector reform, taxes, and labor relations. The economy grew sluggishly, especially in the first three years, and immigration to the United States surged to record numbers. While the PAN floundered in office, the future candidate for the leftist Party of the Democratic Revolution (PRD) came under attack when his closest allies were charged with corruption in 2004; in 2005, he faced an attempt by the PAN and the PRI to disqualify him from the presidential race.

Under the leadership of Roberto Madrazo, who had won the party presidency in 2002, the PRI performed remarkably well in state and municipal races. It recaptured the economically important state of Nuevo León and the smaller state of Nayarit, while losing only Guerrero.[2] It also managed to hold onto or recapture seventeen of the nation's thirty-two state governorships, despite the increasing fairness of elections. As party leader, Madrazo took much of the credit for these electoral successes. Nor, as a majority of analysts had predicted, had the PRI fallen apart after losing the presidency, in part because most PRI leaders believed Madrazo could win it back. In the 2003 midterm elections for the Chamber of Deputies, in what was seen as a referendum vote against the PAN's administration, the PRI gained seats while the PAN's legislative delegation was dramatically reduced. Taken together, all these developments gave the PRI great possibilities for winning the 2006 race. Yet, as the results streamed in on election night, the worst had occurred. The PRI not only posted a miserable third place finish in the presidential race, but its candidate's poor showing also cost the PRI over half of its congressional delegation. Madrazo's personal unpopularity, together with a poor communications strategy and internal party divisions, lay at the root of this devastating electoral performance.

This chapter elucidates the relationship between party organization and the PRI's presidential campaign—specifically, how the party elite's willingness to support or abandon the presidential candidate affected his campaign—and explains how Madrazo's reputation for betraying close allies and his declining electoral prospects provoked party leaders into changing their posture toward their supposed leader. With Madrazo's campaign floundering in spring 2006, many party elites took advantage of his weakness, publicly criticizing him and openly questioning his ability to win the race. These actions were designed to weaken him further, and they succeeded.

As Madrazo's chances of winning the presidential contest declined, other leaders in the party had less to fear from him. Losers in the fight over the distribution of candidacies for the party's legislative list criticized the enfeebled candidate, who could no longer retaliate. This breakdown of internal party unity further undermined Madrazo. If the PRI's leadership base had supported the candidate, campaign events would have been better attended, and the press, both electronic and written, would have reported on these successes; there would have been far fewer reports of party desertions, and voters would not have been subjected to the specter of a party in crisis. In the end, these factors might have led to a far less devastating defeat for the candidate and a better showing in the legislative elections.

Groups and individuals within the PRI faced different incentives. Some anti-Madrazo politicians ran the risk that by sabotaging Madrazo they would also jeopardize the party's legislative seat count, especially in the nation's 300 plurality-winner contests. Most of the party's seventeen governors were extremely circumspect in their criticisms. Even those who did not support Madrazo (although some did) attempted to shore up support for the party's legislative candidates in their states, even as they refused to appear with the presidential candidate at campaign events. Many of the other PRI elites who did openly criticize Madrazo were either not running for office or were near the top of the lists of representation seats, and so did not have to be so concerned with a drop in votes for either the Senate or the Chamber of Deputies.[3]

There are many ways one could examine the relation between party organization and presidential campaigning, such as measuring changes in the number of party activists (Scarrow 1997) or noting the activation of different organizational bases within the party (Koelble 1992). This chapter relies on the publicly expressed opinions of 132 national party leaders of the PRI toward their party's presidential candidate across a fourteen-month period. It draws on comments in newspaper reports by national leaders who have been active during the past ten years, in order to track these leaders' strategies during the electoral process. The protracted campaign is divided into four periods. The first stage extends from spring 2005, when PRI leaders began to mobilize support for the nomination battle, through October 2005, with the destruction of a strong rival in Madrazo's nomination battle. The second period spans the months between October 2005 and the beginning of the official campaign in January 2006, when Madrazo won the nomination. The third phase covers the start of the official campaign in January through early April 2006, when legislative candidates were chosen. The last period covers the final months of the campaign.

We should expect leaders to follow different types of strategies, depending both on their odds of winning a legislative candidacy and on the presidential candidate's electoral chances. If party leaders believe the presidential candidate can win the race, then they are more likely to support his bid no matter whether they individually win a candidacy or not, because with more members of the PRI in power, all PRI politicians would have a greater probability of finding a government post. And if members of the party believe there is no hope of retaking Los Pinos, they will probably still continue to back their presidential candidate in the hopes of winning a nomination for an office of their own. But if the candidate is seen as having no chance, and if a leader is not awarded a spot on the party list, he or she will be far more likely to criticize the party's official standard-bearer. As early as November 2005, few leaders in the PRI believed Madrazo could win the election, but most supported him in hopes of garnering a nomination themselves. But once candidacies had been handed out, those who had not received a spot were free to pillory the presidential candidate. Madrazo blamed his party's governors, along with other factional leaders, for his terrible performance in 2006, calling them traitors (Madrazo and Garrido 2007).

All of the PRI national leaders included in this analysis were identified before the campaign began in January 2006, to help guard against selection bias. Those who were considered national party leaders included current and recent PRI governors, senators whose terms ended in July 2006, and a randomly selected subset of those who left the Senate in 2000. Committee leaders from the Chamber of Deputies in 2003–6 were part of this group, as were members of the National Executive Committee (CEN) during Madrazo's term as party president and the 2000–2 term, and leaders of the party's three main corporatist sectors.[4] Thus members of many PRI factions are on the list—both those tied to Madrazo and those who had fought against him.[5]

Many other Latin American presidential democracies face these same sorts of internal party pressures, especially those with directly elected state executives who control campaign resources. Presidential candidates often need strong local leaders to aid them in winning votes; however, the deals that must be struck to obtain this support are often difficult to negotiate and maintain, as Mexico's case demonstrates. Comparative work in this area could be fruitful to understand how electoral rules and party organization affect the ability of local party bosses to use their local electoral strength to force the national party and the presidential candidate to yield to their demands, especially over candidate selection.

Madrazo and the PRI

The story of the PRI's disastrous 2006 campaign begins with the presidential nomination, and how the winning candidate won the right to represent his party on the ballot. Madrazo's rise to power within the PRI (and in politics more broadly) was one of perceived treachery, marred by accusations of fraud, corruption, and the willful destruction of party rivals. Madrazo acquired as many enemies inside the party as outside of it, and his image as inconstant and untrustworthy would harm him with both voters and party brethren.

His fame as an efficient political operator was first tarnished when he was accused of having bought his 1994 gubernatorial victory in the state of Tabasco, running through almost as much as was spent on the U.S. *presidential* election that year (Eisenstadt 1999). When his nonrenewable, six-year term was almost up in 2000, he decimated the state's party affiliate by imposing his personal choice for the PRI candidate for governor on the party's local leaders, thereby prompting several of his close allies to leave the party and join the PRD. The Federal Electoral Court ultimately annulled the results of the 2000 gubernatorial election in Tabasco because of irregularities committed by the state government and the state party organization (although the PRI went on to win the electoral rematch).

Despite the political scandals in Tabasco in 1994 and 2000, after the PRI's presidential defeat, Madrazo became a natural leader within the party and plotted to win its presidency.[6] In a turn of events that soured many members of the PRI toward him, Madrazo was accused of perpetrating massive fraud against his own party brethren to win the 2002 CEN elections. Once ensconced in the party presidency, Madrazo began to make promises to the Fox administration and business leaders on structural reforms that many believed were required to make Mexico competitive with other emerging economies, despite opposition from left-leaning politicians and many in the public-sector unions. However, after the PRI's strong showing in the 2003 midterm elections, he adopted a blocking strategy against the Fox government to paralyze the legislature on important policy measures (labor reform, restructuring of the energy sector, and taxation). Madrazo used this strategy both to weaken the PAN heading into the 2006 elections and to strengthen his position to win the party's presidential nomination.

During this period, Madrazo made a fateful decision to attempt to destroy his erstwhile ally, Elba Esther Gordillo, who ran with Madrazo to capture the party leadership in 2002. During her tenure as secretary general of the CEN (the second highest post in the party), Gordillo was elected to the Chamber of Deputies in the 2003 midterm elections and had openly campaigned to become the leader of the PRI's delegation in the lower house, promising to use her close personal relationship with President Fox to push through structural reforms. Madrazo then took advantage of a rebellion by the PRI's backbenchers against a fiscal reform bill to oust Gordillo from her leadership post in the Chamber in late 2003. Gordillo initially remained in the PRI, but she also helped form the New Alliance Party (PANAL) that was based on the powerful National Teachers' Union (SNTE), which she controlled.

By 2005, Madrazo, speaking as party president, stated that he preferred not to hold an expensive and potentially divisive party primary to choose the PRI's presidential candidate. But other leaders within the party mobilized against his candidacy and formed a group within the PRI known as Democratic Unity or, more informally, TUCOM (Todos Unidos con México, which was also interpreted as *todos unidos contra Madrazo*, or all united against Madrazo). TUCOM was made up of modernizing PRI governors who had just left or were about to vacate their governorships, as well as the PRI's leader in the Senate.[7] Using a complicated method, TUCOM planned to forward a single candidate to run against Madrazo in the open primary, with the losing TUCOM presidential competitors supporting the winner against Madrazo.

Madrazo consolidated his reputation for crushing his rivals during the nomination struggle. Arturo Montiel, former governor of the state of México, won TUCOM's internal selection process in summer 2005. Between July and September, preferences among PRI supporters for Montiel had climbed from 40 percent to 48 percent, while Madrazo's numbers had fallen from 45 percent to 38 percent.[8] Yet Montiel's nomination hopes were dashed when evidence of the immense fortune he had suspiciously amassed was leaked to the press in October 2005. The episode opened the way for an almost uncontested Madrazo victory in the primary, but it also reinforced the image of corruption that many voters already held regarding the PRI.[9]

The scholarly debate over primaries and their effects on campaigns revolves around whether a primary harms a party's chances in the general election (Aldrich 1980; Atkeson 1998; Boyd 1989) or brings out the troops to work in the general campaign (Carey and Polga-Hecimovich 2006; McCann 2004b). Clearly, although primaries can be used to work out differences among a party's factions (Jones et al. 2002), if they are not carried out correctly, they can damage a party's performance in its campaigning and harm its chances on election day. This was manifestly the case for the PRI in 2006.

Figure 8.1 presents evidence of changes in elite strategies across the four periods of the overall campaign. During the first period, which lasted from May to October 2005, Madrazo did not enjoy overwhelming support from his party colleagues. Pro- and anti-Madrazo forces were evenly split, with about 10 percent of the party's leaders refusing to weigh in publicly. During the period between the end of Montiel's run for the nomination and the beginning of the official presidential campaign in January 2006, Madrazo enjoyed his highest levels of support. When Montiel was carried from the field, many PRI leaders who had initially supported TUCOM shifted to the pro-Madrazo camp.

Most members of the PRI—and political analysts—expected Madrazo to simply cancel the primary and call a party convention to validate what appeared to be a foregone conclusion, his candidacy in November.[10] However, a political unknown won the right to compete in the primary, forcing the party to organize an expensive nationwide election, one which brought no political rewards in terms of energizing the party's base or showing voters that the PRI was an internally democratic party.

Despite Madrazo's jump in support within his party after he won the nomination in November, his history of treachery came back to haunt him. Gordillo used her union's ample resources to organize an anti-Madrazo drive, even before the beginning of the official campaign period. Billboards and flyers appeared in

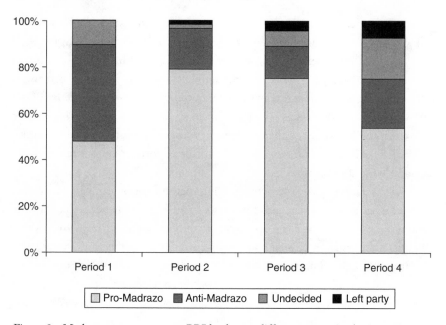

Figure 8.1 Madrazo support among PRI leaders at different stages in the campaign.

November and December 2005, asking "Do you believe Madrazo? Me neither." Her supporters showed up at early campaign events, heckling the candidate.

The PRI candidate and his team made another decision in December that turned out to be a mistake. Intent on winning independent voters, the PRI's team decided it would run in a coalition with the small, opportunistic Green Ecologist Party of Mexico (PVEM), whose candidate, Bernardo de la Garza, had spent hundreds of thousands of dollars on television spots during the second half of 2005 in a bid to win public support. With de la Garza's popularity around 8 percent, the PVEM sold its support at a high cost. To enter into an electoral coalition with the Greens—under its terms de la Garza would give up his candidacy and campaign on behalf of Madrazo—the PRI gave away roughly 12 percent of its legislative slots to the PVEM. Unfortunately for the PRI, popular support for the PVEM's candidate vanished when his party made its alliance with the PRI. De la Garza himself later quit the alliance and refused to campaign with Madrazo.

Madrazo's campaign was off to a rocky start. He had fought with the leader of the largest union in Latin America, with his political allies in Tabasco, and with the former governor of the most populous state in Mexico. He had been tied to three electoral scandals. His negative ratings stood at 40 percent, and his primary was an expensive disaster. What awaited him next was the strategic behavior of his own party's leaders as the official campaign progressed.

The Early Campaign

During its decades of hegemony, the PRI's presidential campaigns followed the "national tour" model of Lázaro Cárdenas's 1934 campaign. As a candidate, Cárdenas had spent months crisscrossing the still-rural nation, visiting small cities, towns, and villages by car, bus, and horse in an attempt to show Mexican citizens—often for the first time and in a world without television—the face of the federal government. Even into the 1980s, the typical PRI presidential campaign continued to center on candidate visits to different municipalities to deliver speeches to hundreds of *acarreados* (spectators trucked in for the event), who were then given food and a campaign souvenir for their time. In one typical campaign, that of 1970, PRI candidate Luis Echeverría visited 1,238 localities, traveled over 50,000 kilometers, and delivered 885 speeches, interviews, and declarations.[11]

Paid television advertising as such was unknown during the hegemonic period. The sole private television network, Televisa, simply covered the PRI candidate's campaign in its nightly newscasts and largely ignored opposition rivals. This pattern of campaign events and blanket television coverage of the PRI began to change in the 1994 presidential campaign, and by 2000 it had been drastically transformed by federally funded advertising for all registered parties, opinion polling, and professional campaign management (Lawson 2004a). Mexico's modernized presidential campaigns, however, are not solely run on the air, through mass-media appeals by the national party; they also continue to focus a substantial amount resources on the ground, that is, for campaign events and voter mobilization drives.

In 2006, the PRI's media strategy was run by members of the CEN who were also close allies of Madrazo, and during the first half of the campaign, the messages were largely made up of attacks on Andrés Manuel López Obrador (AMLO) and the Fox administration.[12] The appeals in the first part of the six-month campaign centered on the phrase *Qué las cosas se hagan* (So things get done) and *Yo sí puedo* (I can do it). The problem for the PRI candidate was that no one could know exactly *what* things would get done, as many questioned Madrazo's credibility and political expediency alone seemed to determine his economic positions. Madrazo and his team of advisors made a concerted effort to burnish his tarnished personal image in the advertising campaign, for example, by not using his last name (slang for "hit" or "slug"). The team also used his wife, who is handicapped, in television ads to convince voters to trust her husband. By the end of 2005, however, reports surfaced of Madrazo's extensive real estate holdings, which—given his salary as a public servant—he was unable to explain.

Madrazo's criticism of Fox centered on two issues: crime and economic growth. Yet the PRI candidate had to walk a fine line in his economic platform. He criticized the "neoliberal" policies of the PAN and Calderón, while also accusing López Obrador of populist tendencies. At the same time, Madrazo's campaign team found it difficult to produce a recognizably different development plan. The candidate's platform to improve public safety centered on harsher penalties for several major crimes, but he did not appear to have a serious strategy for attacking the enormous problems of corruption, drug trafficking, and rings of kidnappers and car thieves active in several major cities, many of which are tied to former or active police units.

The first half of the national media campaign culminated in the April 25 debate. Because the PRD candidate chose not to participate, Madrazo was left to joust with Calderón and the two minor-party candidates. The nationally televised debate turned into a failure for Madrazo when he was unable to criticize Calderón successfully or forcefully propose a serious economic platform; it proved a clear victory for Calderón, clinching his position in the polls and underscoring Madrazo's increasing irrelevance in the presidential race.[13]

During February and March, the territorial campaign began in earnest. The PRI has always followed a two-pronged strategy in this form of campaigning. The first is made up of visits and campaign speeches given by the presidential candidate in front of large crowds of prospective voters and smaller groups of local leaders; the second entails grassroots canvassing and voter mobilization drives by party activists. Both parts of the territorial campaign depend on support from the PRI governors and mayors, as well as local PRI leaders and mayors in those areas governed by other parties. If these two sets of elected executives choose to, they can aid the presidential electioneering effort in many ways, such as mobilizing voter drives, organizing campaign events, and paying for local media ads. Almost 40 percent of Mexico's population lives in states governed by the PRI, so if the party's governors had placed their electoral machinery at Madrazo's disposal, the PRI could have captured a large percentage of these voters.[14] Furthermore, once the Deputy and Senate races are underway, forces can be combined: legislative hopefuls can appear with the presidential candidate, and they can use his flyers and posters. Alternatively, they can ignore his electioneering efforts. Thus if the presidential candidate's relationship with his party is weak, it can affect his ability to win territorial support. Events will be half empty; governors will not push his campaign with state economic leaders; fundraising efforts will be frustrated; and voters, even if they do not attend campaign events themselves, will eventually hear of the candidate's inability to win support among his own party members.

Madrazo reportedly visited more than 200 municipalities over the course of the campaign—mostly large cities, state capitals, and Mexico City's sprawling bedroom communities, such as Ecatepec.[15] However, the candidate ran into several problems; he was heckled, and the campaign stops were badly attended, which began to be reported in the press.[16] Stump speeches were and are used in Mexico as a demonstration of the candidate's popularity with voters and of the ability or willingness of the local PRI apparatus to mobilize support for the candidate. These events are also an important element in the coverage of the campaign on the nightly news and in press reports. The problem of low attendance at Madrazo's campaign stops would become far more pronounced in the last period of the campaign.

Legislative candidates are chosen in late March and early April, so one might expect that most PRI leaders would *not* abandon ship during the first three months of the campaign, no matter how badly the campaign is going; they would instead wait to see if they appeared on the final lists of candidates. As figure 8.1 indicates, there was little difference between the pro-Madrazo figures between the second and third periods; his support fell by only 5% (from 80% to 75%) among the 132 national leaders we analyzed.

By the end of these first three months in 2006, it was clear that Madrazo had permanently relinquished second place to Calderón, who had meanwhile surmounted the ten-point gap that originally separated himself from the front-runner, López Obrador. According to Consulta Mitofsky, Madrazo dropped from his high of 33 percent in December to 27 percent in April, while Calderón rose to lead the race at 35 percent, with AMLO trailing by one point.[17] Falling to a distant third by April was extremely problematic, as voters would naturally begin to see the election as a two-person race, and even if the PRI were some people's first choice, they might vote for their second preference in order to avoid their least desirable alternative.

Over three million people had voted in the PRI's internal primary in November 2005, but Madrazo was not attracting new voters among independents or undecideds. From the Mexico 2006 Panel Study data,[18] we find that independents and undecideds together made up close to 33 percent of the nation's voters, higher than any group of party identifiers. Among independent voters in the panel study's October 2005 wave, 19 percent supported Madrazo and 47 percent supported AMLO. In the April/May 2006 phase, Madrazo continued to claim 19 percent of the independents, but Calderón had risen to 32 percent of this group, while AMLO dropped to 36 percent.[19] The campaign strategy was not working. To Madrazo's credit, he changed it by mid-May, after the debate debacle.

The Madrazo Camp Tries to Regroup

As his campaign refused to lift itself out of third place, Madrazo changed his strategies on both the media and the territorial sides. In the media campaign, Madrazo dropped the attacks on AMLO, and instead followed a two-pronged strategy: attack the Fox administration and make programmatic appeals on economic and social issues. As the race developed into a two-sided contest and the candidates' appeals began to polarize between the "rightist" option of Calderón and the "populist" offer of AMLO, Madrazo moved to claim the ideological center and moral high ground as a moderate. By mid-May, the PRI candidate scrapped his media team and brought on board his old marketing adviser, Carlos Alazraki, who promptly came out with a new spot that showed a criminal wetting his pants when faced with the prospect of a Madrazo presidency. Other ads presented Madrazo's economic program, and he attempted to transform himself into a center-progressive candidate, offering tax exemptions for the poor, programs with salary increases for workers in order to prime the domestic market for consumer goods and thus increase employment, and, if elected, the creation of nine million new jobs during his six-year term.[20]

In a May spot, he claimed: "I am Roberto Madrazo and I guarantee you more safety, more jobs, and less poverty." But voters did not believe him. For promises to be taken seriously, the candidate himself must be credible, and Madrazo simply was not. Data from the Mexico 2006 Panel Study show that the PRI candidate began the campaign in October 2005 under a dark cloud, as very few potential voters believed he was honest—24 percent, versus 62 percent who thought he was not. After six months of campaigning, his honesty score had only risen to 27 percent, and the number of those who saw him as dishonest also rose by one percentage point.[21] Madrazo's attempt to position himself as the moderate between two extreme options that were harming the nation was a good idea, but it could not prosper, because voters had taken into account the background of the candidate and the scandals surrounding his rise to power and decided that he was not suited for the presidency.

But if the media side of the campaign was not working, the party could depend on its territorial structure—at least in theory. In early May, César Augusto Santiago, the CEN's secretary of organization, announced another territorial strategy, the "20 with Madrazo" drive, in which over a million vote promoters would capture at least 20 voters each. PRI candidates in the single-member districts would work alongside these vote promoters, using Madrazo's videos, flyers, and advertisements in their individual races to reinforce the national campaign.[22] Between June 13 and June 26, the last day of the campaign, the candidate reportedly visited 140 *municipios* (counties), which collectively comprised 75 percent of the nation's population, to deliver his final addresses.

However, Madrazo's relations with governors and other party leaders weakened his territorial strategy. According to some analysts, many governors were not willing to activate their party's bases in their respective states because of the campaign's stagnation in third place;[23] furthermore, because the PRI's candidate had fought with the leader of the SNTE, teachers all over the nation were more inclined to campaign for other candidates.

Special mention must be made of the political role taken on by some opinion polls published throughout the campaign. Although other outlets were reporting approximately 24 to 25 percent support for Madrazo by April and May, at least one polling agency rated Madrazo as virtually tied with Calderón and only a few points behind AMLO. The purpose of these polls was to convince enough voters that Madrazo was still in the race[24] (despite numerous press accounts to the contrary) so that they would not abandon him. Poll results were also used to convince leaders and members of the PRI in the various states that Madrazo was still viable and that they should continue working for his campaign. Some supporters argued throughout the campaign that survey respondents were ashamed to admit they would vote for Madrazo, and that on the day of the election, he would win more votes than predicted.

Many PRI leaders had not only distanced themselves from their party's presidential candidate, they also criticized him openly in the press, as will be discussed below. Thus Madrazo had a difficult time moving beyond his party's base.

In fact, in wave 3 of the panel study, only 77 percent of PRI identifiers stated they had voted for Madrazo, even though the number of PRI identifiers itself had fallen from 26 percent to 19.5 percent over the course of the campaign. By contrast, 94 percent of the PRD identifiers and 88 percent of the PAN identifiers voted for their respective candidates. Despite his modified media strategy and renewed territorial efforts in the second half of the campaign, Madrazo not only came in eight points behind his main rivals, but he also dragged down his party's legislative vote to historically low levels.

With the prospects of a Madrazo victory becoming increasingly remote, legislative candidacies became more crucial in cementing the PRI leaders' loyalty to the Madrazo campaign. Yet Madrazo had no qualms about imposing his own favored candidates and scrapping the nascent primary system that had been partially implemented in the 2003 legislative midterm elections.[25] Under the conditions of the Alliance for Mexico (a coalition of the PRI and the PVEM), the governing body of the Alliance was empowered to generate a single list of Deputy and Senate candidates for each type of electoral formula (i.e., plurality winner and proportional representation).[26] The PRI's National Political Council, a larger body than the CEN, was confined to delivering an up-down vote on the lists. Its members could not change the order of the names on the closed-party lists, nor could they add or remove names.

Winning the right to represent the party in the legislative elections was a way to survive politically, regardless of Madrazo's eventual electoral fate; therefore, the incentives to compete for a candidacy were extremely high. This helps to explain Madrazo's loss of only 5 percent of his party leaders' support (from 80% to 75%) between the second and third segments of the campaign. Only a few PRI politicians criticized Madrazo *before* the party's lists were drawn up, primarily as a way to threaten the candidate into including them. Carlos Flores Rico and Heladio Ramírez are two examples of this strategy; they questioned and criticized Madrazo publicly in the third period, won candidacies for themselves, and then supported Madrazo throughout the fourth phase of the campaign. But if one did not win a spot on the ballot, there would be few reasons to support the presidential candidate to the end. Thus once the lists were finalized, the contingent nature of Madrazo's support among PRI leaders became apparent. As shown in figure 8.1, Madrazo's supporters fell from 75 percent of all leaders to 54 percent between periods three and four, a loss of a quarter of his allies. Most of the PRI leaders who switched strategies did so because they did not win candidacies, and they used the months of May and June to weaken the presidential candidate through attacks in the press.

These public manifestations of discontent took many forms. Some questioned Madrazo's ability to win the election.[27] Others, such as Senator Manuel Bartlett, recommended that PRI supporters vote for the PRD candidate to head off a PAN victory. A third group started to discuss openly how to reorganize the party's executive committee once Madrazo had lost,[28] while still others began to call for a substitute candidate to take Madrazo's place on the ticket, even as late as May 2006.[29] Support for the presidential candidate during the third and fourth periods also came in several guises, with a number of PRI leaders variously claiming Madrazo could win the election, appearing with him at campaign events, mobilizing grassroots voter drives, and, finally, calling all those who criticized him traitors.

Although party stalwarts involved in democratic elections around the world probably have the same concerns as the PRI leaders did, and voice them privately, few do so in their respective nations' media. What did the PRI leaders hope to gain through attacking their party's presidential candidate once the lists had been drawn up and their names excluded? The sheer numbers could not have made a difference in the final vote tally. According to many polls, Madrazo was already so far behind, their efforts to weaken him were probably redundant. Furthermore, the coattail effect between the presidential race and its legislative counterparts is quite strong; many PRI leaders were, in effect, driving down the party's vote and seat totals for both the Chamber and the Senate. Yet because of the party's low poll numbers, PRI leaders no longer feared Madrazo, and weakening him further would ensure the partial or total destruction of his political group within the PRI after the elections, thus opening up positions on the CEN in the postelection period.

The party's governors were far more circumspect in their criticisms than other types of party elites, because they were concerned about the possibility of negative presidential coattail effects on the legislative races in their respective states (which in fact occurred). It behooves governors to win as many of their state's seats as possible, to give their loyalists political posts. However, those individuals who did not have to worry about winning competed single-district-member races (i.e., those who were not running or who were on the PRI lists) were free to voice their criticisms in the newspapers. One credible explanation of Madrazo's weak gubernatorial support is that the party's governors had successfully negotiated many majority legislative candidacies, but the list of these names was modified by Madrazo's team shortly before being sent to the IFE (at which point it became official). The governors therefore had little reason to support the presidential campaign, even given its negative coattail effects on the congressional races, because their allies were not the candidates.

It is important to note another major finding regarding the party leaders' strategies: only nine of out the pool of 132 national PRI leaders we studied left the party, but many of their state-level counterparts did jump ship. (State leaders are those whose posts are or have been primarily in state politics or at the municipal level.) During the course of the campaign, important party leaders at this level began to desert the PRI's ranks, including former state party leaders in Guerrero, a former home minister in the state of Coahuila, and several leaders of the state SNTE in Nuevo León, Querétaro, and Coahuila.[30] The reason many local leaders were willing to leave the PRI, while their national counterparts were reluctant to do so, lies in the benefits each group hoped to gain from their PRI affiliation. The PRI's national leaders had fewer options open to them if they joined either the PAN or PRD, because of their history or political experience, but if they could weaken Madrazo within the PRI, they could take over the party. State leaders did not have this opportunity to influence the party nationally. On the other hand, they were better positioned to win direct elections in their state, and they could do so using other party labels.

In the aggregate, 39 percent of the national party leaders stayed loyal to Madrazo throughout the four periods, 14 percent were openly anti-Madrazo throughout, while 46 percent switched their strategies in one of the four periods. This "switcher" group can be disaggregated into two types: those who shifted from the anti-Madrazo group to the pro-Madrazo faction (31%), and those who were pro-Madrazo in one of the first two periods and then began to criticize him publicly in a later period (69%). In other words, a decisive majority of the total universe of switchers ended up in the anti-Madrazo camp.

Data on electoral success illustrate the strong relationship between candidacies and the loss of support for Madrazo. The two groups that supported Madrazo into the fourth period were by far the most successful at winning a place on the ballot, at 63 and 68 percent, respectively. Of those who were consistently anti-Madrazo across the four periods, only 5 percent won the right to compete for another post. The average success rate of all those eventually ending up in the anti-Madrazo group was 15 percent.

If one examines the timing of the shifts in support between periods 3 and

4, the importance of legislative nominations in Madrazo's falling leadership support becomes clearer. Of the 132 national PRI leaders, forty had at one point been pro-Madrazo and then switched to an anti-Madrazo strategy. Almost three-quarters of these pro- to anti-Madrazo switchers changed their strategies between periods three and four, after the candidacies were announced, lending credence to the argument that their desertion of Madrazo was due to being excluded from the candidate lists, not from major ideological differences with the presidential candidate.

Of the twenty-one national PRI leaders who had been in the anti-Madrazo camp and later supported him, 86 percent of them made their decisions to change their stances toward Madrazo when it became apparent that he would be the PRI's presidential candidate, that is, between periods one and two. Very few of these leaders used an attack strategy to win a candidacy of their own. Rather, many supporters of a TUCOM candidate went over to Madrazo after Montiel's fall and supported him throughout the rest of the campaign, and 68 percent of this group went on to win a candidacy.

Party organization and unity had an effect on the presidential campaign in Mexico, just as the faltering PRI campaign influenced its party leaders and their strategies. Because Madrazo was unpopular and mistrusted within his own party, much of his early support from party leaders was contingent on two possibilities: on Madrazo winning the presidential election, and on whether the particular national leader in question would win a legislative candidacy. If the party's presidential hopeful had been a serious contender, then most likely even those PRI leaders who did not win a spot on the lists would have stayed loyal and not come out publicly against him as the campaign wore on, mostly because they would have feared that if he won the election and they had been critical during the campaign, he would have ruined them politically.

The open criticisms from members of his party, and the fact that many of the PRI governors and mayors were unwilling to work for the Madrazo campaign, weakened his territorial efforts: events were poorly attended, which was then reported in the press; business leaders in the states did not feel obligated to donate resources; and grassroots mobilizing was hampered. As state-level desertions from the PRI won nationwide coverage, voters and PRI identifiers withheld their support from the party's candidate, which was reflected in the polls.

Many party elites were willing to openly criticize their standard-bearer, even though this would most likely harm the PRI in the legislative races. The politicians who would be most closely affected—both those who had won legislative candidacies and the party's governors—either supported Madrazo or were far more circumspect in their attacks, because their interests would be directly affected by a sharp downturn in the party's overall electoral success. But if there were no personal interests at stake, Madrazo was seen as such a negative force in the PRI that some party leaders were willing to harm the entire organization to weaken the presidential candidate and his group.

Even when the candidate changed his media appeals to offer himself as a moderate option between two extremes, he was not able to connect with voters. Of course, it is impossible to know what would have happened under different circumstances. If Madrazo had not destroyed so many of his rivals within the party and committed fraud in two gubernatorial elections in the state of Tabasco, perhaps his image would have been more neutral, encouraging both party leaders and voters to support him in greater numbers. But that would have made him a different candidate, and the PRI a different party.

López Obrador, Calderón, and the 2006 Presidential Campaign

Kathleen Bruhn

July 2, 2006, was supposed to be a day of vindication for the Party of the Democratic Revolution (PRD). Shut out of Los Pinos (the Mexican presidential compound) since fraud cost their founding leader Cuauhtémoc Cárdenas the presidency in 1988, PRD partisans expected their presidential candidate to win. Andrés Manuel López Obrador was the most popular ex-mayor of Mexico City in living memory. He had survived an attempt by the National Action Party (PAN) and the Institutional Revolutionary Party (PRI) to disqualify him as a candidate. He had even managed to emerge unscathed from a corruption scandal involving two of his closest collaborators. He sailed through the pre-campaign season with a stable and commanding lead over potential opponents from the PAN, which held the presidency, and the PRI. More than two months into the formal campaign, López Obrador held a double-digit lead in the polls. People began to talk about whom he would put in his cabinet, rather than whether he would win. Advisors dispatched to reassure foreign investors fretted only about whether his margin of victory would give him a sufficient mandate to effect the sort of fundamental change he sought.

Yet somehow, it all turned out quite differently. On December 1, 2006, President Vicente Fox passed the presidential sash not to López Obrador, but to a fellow PAN member, Felipe Calderón. And he did so not in the atmosphere of popular jubilation that López Obrador predicted with his campaign slogan—"smile, happiness is coming"—but in a tense and confrontational climate. In order to sidestep threats by the PRD to stop the president-elect from taking his oath of office, the new president was officially sworn in a few minutes after midnight in a private ceremony held in the presidential residence, instead of the floor of the Chamber of Deputies, as was traditional. His later appearance there sparked a physical brawl between PRD and PAN representatives. After only a few minutes, Calderón left the Congress to give his inaugural address in the quieter (and PRD-free) sanctuary of the National Auditorium.

The melee of December 1 was the culmination of months of growing frustration and escalating protest on the part of López Obrador's followers. A few days after the July 2 election, the Federal Electoral Institute (IFE) declared Calderón the official winner, albeit by the narrowest of margins (0.58%). López Obrador took to the streets. For more than a month, thousands of López Obrador supporters occupied the major thoroughfare connecting the city's financial district to the ceremonial presidential offices in the National Palace, protesting that the PAN had stolen the election. López Obrador himself slept in a tent outside the National Palace, holding press conferences to denounce irregularities in the elections and plebiscitary meetings to determine the next protest actions. On September 16, a large crowd proclaimed him "legitimate president of Mexico." The consolidation of Mexico's infant democratic institutions seemed to take a step backwards.

If the 2006 presidential election—and the one that preceded it six years before—made anything clear, it is that campaigns profoundly affect electoral outcomes in Mexico. Other chapters in this volume draw upon the Mexico 2006 Panel Study to discuss voter responses to the campaign. The purpose of this chapter is to analyze the campaign itself and, in particular, the decisions that gave PAN supporters a chance to turn the tide. Did López Obrador's team make strategic errors that cost him the election, and if so, why? What did the PAN do to pull victory out of the jaws of defeat—and what made it possible?

Episode One: Prelude to a Coronation

For Andrés Manuel López Obrador, popularly known as AMLO, the 2006 presidential campaign began in earnest the day after his election as mayor of Mexico City on July 2, 2000. Much of what he did over the next five years was calculated to enhance his presidential prospects. By means of a combination of populist programs for the poor and ambitious public works projects for the middle class, he built a cross-class coalition in Mexico City that was intended not only to give him a solid electoral base, but also to serve as the showcase for his future administration as president. Though some observers criticized his methods as a sort of new corporatism, Mexico City residents generally approved. When he resigned as mayor in 2005 to run for president, he had an 80 percent approval rating in the Federal District.[1]

The lowest point in his popularity came in February 2004, when two separate corruption scandals broke, one involving his finance minister, Gustavo Ponce, and the other involving his chief political operative, René Bejarano.[2] López Obrador briefly fell to third place in public preferences for the presidency, while preferences for the PAN soared.[3] One month later, however, López Obrador was back in first place, after insisting that he was the innocent victim of a PAN conspiracy to discredit him.

Another fruitless effort to disqualify him as a presidential candidate was an April 2005 accusation that López Obrador violated a court injunction in a zoning dispute (the *desafuero* incident, which led to his impeachment as mayor).[4] Again, he portrayed himself as the victim of a conspiracy. The government backed down in the face of growing public demonstrations defending López Obrador's right to compete in the election. Meanwhile, his popularity soared. By the time the government threw in the towel, 43 percent of Mexicans said they would vote for López Obrador for president.[5]

López Obrador seemed to have overcome everything his opponents could throw at him. It appeared especially inconceivable that he could lose to either a bland politician like Felipe Calderón or a shady character like Roberto Madrazo, the PRI's candidate. Most observers at the time shared López Obrador's confidence in an inevitable PRD victory.

In the end, this overconfidence would betray him, leading him into a series of mistakes. From his victories in the corruption scandals and the impeachment controversy, he took away the impression that he was invulnerable to negative attacks, a belief that would encourage him to discount mounting evidence that his ratings were slipping and to delay any reaction until it was too late to recover.

In January of 2006, however, few people anticipated this turn of events. And so, as López Obrador began his formal campaign, he ran in his own mind as the future president of all Mexicans rather than as the representative of a particular party. López Obrador initially distanced himself from the more leftist platform submitted by his electoral alliance, the PRD-led Coalition for the Good of All. He did not participate in assemblies held by the PRD to debate the content of the coalition platform, reportedly responding "that is your business, not mine" when asked to do so.[6] Instead, he produced a platform of his own, the "Fifty Commitments."

I coded both of these platforms (as well as those of the PRI, the PAN, and Madrazo) according to the Comparative Manifestos Project method, based on content analysis.[7] According to the left-right scale developed by Budge and Robertson (1987), "right" issues include support for traditional morality, law and order, patriotism, and social harmony, as well as support for free markets. "Left" issues include support for state intervention in the economy, protectionism, the expansion of social services, and support for labor. The left-right scale then adds together the percentage of platform sentences emphasizing "right" issues and subtracts the percentage of platform sentences emphasizing "left" issues. Thus, positive scores indicate more conservative ideological placements, while negative scores indicate a more leftist stance.

The results demonstrate that the positions set forth by López Obrador in "Fifty Commitments" put him squarely in the center of the political spectrum and substantially to the right of the PRD platform.[8] With respect to economic issues, López Obrador moved even further to the right. Issue items in the index for "market-state balance" included support for free enterprise and property rights (right), support for protectionism (left), the need for incentives to private enterprise (right), the need for long-term government economic planning (left), and the need to regulate capitalism (left). López Obrador's preference for markets over state intervention in the economy places him well to the right of not only his own party, but also Madrazo and the PRI. Only the PAN platform showed a stronger preference for market mechanisms versus state regulation and controls. Ironically, given later charges that he would spend the country into a debt crisis, his personal platform discussed economic orthodoxy eighteen times as often as his party's platform, though still less than the PAN's. Government efficiency was his platform's top priority; it ranked fourth in the PAN's platform emphases. The only concessions López Obrador made to the PRD base were a rejection of privatization of the electricity sector and support for suspending the provision of the North American Free Trade Agreement that would eliminate tariffs on corn and beans—a far cry from turning back the clock on two decades of neoliberal reform.

As López Obrador was preparing his run for the presidency, his eventual nemesis was still a dark-horse candidate for his own party's nomination. In July 2000, Calderón had just returned from a year-long stay at Harvard University, where he earned a masters' degree in public administration. When Fox won the presidential race, Calderón won election to the Chamber of Deputies and became the head of the PAN's party bench. Later, he was appointed head of the government development bank, BanObras, and then secretary of energy. He resigned in 2004, when Fox criticized his presidential ambitions. However, Calderón made the most of his party connections, developed when he was president of the PAN (1996–99), to beat rivals in the PAN's October 2005 primary election. This win gave Calderón a boost in the national polls, but he was still relatively unknown to most Mexicans. When the official campaign season began on January 19, López Obrador held a nearly ten-point lead over his rivals.[9] More importantly, he had a substantial edge among independents—34 percent versus 17 percent for Calderón, according to the first (October) wave of the Mexico 2006 Panel Study.[10]

Calderón's team believed that, as the campaign made their candidate better known, these tendencies could be reversed, yet in the first months of the campaign, nothing seemed to work. Fox actively endorsed Calderón's candidacy and sponsored television ads promoting the social programs of his administration; complaints to the IFE by opposition parties led nowhere, but on February 24, the Supreme Court ordered the government to pull all such ads during the presidential campaign.

Calderón also sought outside endorsements to raise his profile. On February 21, the PAN invited José María Aznar, the conservative former prime minister of Spain, to speak at a public forum. Aznar denounced the dangers of "revolutionary, demagogic populism," a thinly veiled reference to López Obrador. In the press conference that followed, Aznar expressed his hope that Felipe Calderón would be the next president of Mexico, "for the good of Mexicans."[11] Aznar's visit backfired when the PRD denounced the interference of foreigners. As March began, with one-third of the campaign behind them, López Obrador maintained a double-digit lead over Calderón.[12]

The Aznar incident nevertheless had important implications. Shortly afterward, on March 5, the head of image and marketing for the Calderón campaign was unceremoniously fired. Calderón hired Aznar's own media expert, Antonio Sola, as his new chief media consultant. He also reportedly sought the advice—informally, his team insists—of American political consultants Dick Morris and Rob Allyn. Little noticed at the time, this personnel change presaged a major shift in Calderón's advertising tactics that would transform the dynamics of the campaign.

Episode Two: The Ides of March

On March 18, 2006, the PAN launched a new media campaign attacking López Obrador as a dangerous radical and linking him to controversial Venezuelan president Hugo Chávez. In fact, the two had never met. López Obrador deliberately kept his distance from Chávez, fearing just this blowback effect. Indeed, he joined Calderón in denouncing Chávez's blunt characterization of President Fox as "the puppy of the empire" (i.e., the United States) in November 2005.[13] Nevertheless, in the rhetoric of Latin American politics in the twenty-first century, to be equated with Chávez is to be associated with authoritarianism, populism, anti-Americanism, anti-neoliberalism, and all manner of radical policies. These were the first of many commercials that would portray López Obrador as an extremist.

The PRD, of course, protested to the IFE. Mexico's electoral law orders that parties must "abstain from any expression that implies diatribe, calumny, infamy, insult, or defamation that denigrates other political parties and their candidates, particularly during electoral campaigns and the political propaganda that is used."[14] The IFE has the legal authority (and presumably the duty) to order parties to stop airing ads that violate these rules. On March 26, four days after the PRD lodged its protest with the IFE, the president of the PAN announced that the party would withdraw the ad "because the IFE has already made a statement to that respect."[15] But the next day, the party decided to keep the spot after all, based on the evaluation of Calderón's campaign team that "the spot has been very successful."[16] The Chávez ad was eventually withdrawn, but in the meantime other ads were prepared accusing López Obrador of paying for his public works with massive debt, reminding voters of the corruption scandals, and claiming that "López Obrador permitted these crimes," a reference to a notorious case in which two police officers were lynched by a Mexico City mob. The number and frequency of anti-AMLO ads increased exponentially throughout April.

López Obrador did little to counter the image projected by the PAN. Indeed, he inadvertently provided the PAN with additional footage when—frustrated at Fox's open support for Calderón—he warned the president to "stop squawking and shut up." The Spanish phrase used, *cállate chachalaca*, refers to a noisy tropical bird. The comment was accompanied by physically producing the bird in question, and López Obrador repeated this tactic in PRD rallies, to the great amusement of his audience. In all probability, López Obrador was simply catering to his base; while projecting a more moderate image to the nation in his ad campaign and website, he performed for the party faithful using the colorful rhetoric he had effectively deployed through much of his political career. In this case, however, media coverage of the campaign led to video clips of the *chachalaca* performance, which the PAN then used in ads as contemporaneous evidence demonstrating AMLO's wild streak. As chapter 10 in this volume suggests, voters who saw this remark as cause for concern were more likely to switch their preference from López Obrador to Calderón over the course of the campaign.

At this point, AMLO might have initiated an ad campaign of his own, either countering the PAN's portrayal of him by talking about his moderate and pragmatic performance as mayor or going negative against the PAN. He did neither. Through early April, his only public response was a series of ads in which Mexican intellectual Elena Poniatowska defended AMLO against the PAN's attacks.

Meanwhile, the IFE did little to respond to the PRD's complaints. Not until April 19—a month after the attack ads first appeared—did the IFE take up the question. The bureaucrats who make up the Junta General Ejecutiva (Executive Council) of the IFE declared unanimously that the ads comparing López Obrador to Chávez violated electoral law. Two days later, the congressionally appointed General Council rejected this resolution.[17] The General Council specifically permitted ads that called López Obrador a danger to Mexico and requested the withdrawal of only one ad (the one saying that López Obrador had allowed the lynching of police officers). The PAN announced that it would withdraw all ads critical of López Obrador, but it did not. Polls began to show Calderón catching up to López Obrador, with a gap of less than 5 percent.[18]

In tandem with the public media campaign, the PAN launched a stealthier internet campaign aimed at the media-savvy young and middle-class professionals. The source of the messages (and their sponsorship) was rarely explicit, but the content focused on sullying López Obrador's reputation. One message purported to come from a middle-class Venezuelan who had "lost everything" when Chávez took power. Others claimed that López Obrador would seize private property, including homes, and redistribute them to the poor. One (which my university students find especially horrifying) posted AMLO's college transcript in a slickly designed sequence of images that was intended to highlight his shortcomings as a student, including the fact that he once failed economics and took fourteen years to finish his degree. López Obrador had to ask the National

University to release a statement confirming that he had completed his college degree when the PAN's representative in the IFE—perhaps having misunderstood his e-mail—said that López Obrador never finished his senior thesis.

López Obrador appeared unfazed. Negative ads, he said, were just another dirty campaign against him: "We have seen this in other situations, as in the *desafuero* [impeachment controversy], where there was also a strong media campaign," but *"no me han quitado ni una pluma a nuestro gallo* [they have not touched me].["19] On April 23, in Quintana Roo, he dismissed his critics: "Since we are way ahead in the polls, they will continue to attack us on radio and television, but don't worry; that means we are doing very well. When they do not criticize us any more, then you should worry."[20] As he had done before, during the corruption scandal and then the impeachment effort, his first instinct was to stay quiet and allow the furor to die down, rather than feed the fire. In other situations, ignoring criticism had allowed him to cruise through brewing storms without altering his course. In these two instances, he was eventually forced to respond publicly, because staying silent did not work. When he did speak out, his strategy was to attack his accusers for conspiring against him. In both cases, his game plan ultimately succeeded; in the impeachment controversy, his response even escalated into mass protests.

This time, the same strategy failed, at least in part. Although López Obrador did recover some lost ground once he began his own counterattack, he did not regain his early advantage over Calderón. His approach was less successful in turning public perceptions around, even though the accusation made in 2006—that he was a radical—seemed, on the face of it, less serious than either the corruption or impeachment charges, both of which could have landed him in jail. The problem was not that the strategy itself was bad, but that the context had changed. Given Mexicans' limited interest in politics, it is likely that relatively few voters paid attention to the earlier scandals. During the presidential campaign, even people who were uninterested in politics and did not watch the news were treated to a daily barrage of ads on the subject of López Obrador's incompetence. In addition, the earlier stories principally affected the residents of Mexico City, where López Obrador remained popular. There was little reason for residents of Monterrey to spend time finding out about López Obrador until he ran for president. Vaguely positive feelings would then come under much more scrutiny, and the PAN's natural credibility advantage in the North could play a role as voters were deciding whom to believe.

Most importantly, however, the PAN's negative campaign in 2006 focused on an issue of greater significance to voters than corruption or rule of law—namely, López Obrador's competence to manage the economy. In all three waves of the panel survey, voters consistently ranked the economy and jobs as the most important problems facing Mexico. In questioning López Obrador's future ability to handle the economy, the PAN made charges that were almost impossible to refute. López Obrador could and did deny that he was another Chávez who would steer Mexico into economic collapse, but his denials did little to prove that the PAN's predictions were false. Indeed, many of them had a kernel of truth, although wildly exaggerated. For example, López Obrador borrowed money as mayor of Mexico City (albeit only with the permission of the federal Congress and less than his predecessors); thus, it was argued, he would drive Mexico into a debt crisis.

The PAN, in contrast, could point to a clear record of macroeconomic stability under Fox. Fox's role in the campaign boiled down to this—at least the peso did not crash with us in charge. References to the "danger" posed by AMLO focused less on the confiscation of private property than on currency instability, a theme that, as chapter 10 in this volume persuasively argues, was of critical importance to Mexicans after a period of several years of rising personal indebtedness. At the same time, Calderón sharpened the contrast between himself and López Obrador by shifting the focus of his own ads from "clean hands" to "the jobs president." The ultimate effect, as chapter 10 demonstrates, was a clear shift over the course of the campaign in terms of panel respondents' perceptions of which candidate would be better able to manage the economy, a change which ultimately favored Felipe Calderón.

López Obrador did have one viable response, the "Lula option." Four months before his victory in the 2002 Brazilian presidential election, Luiz Inácio Lula da Silva's rising popularity had begun to cause concern among foreign investors, leading to declines in Brazil's stock market and in the value of its currency. Nightly news reports compared graphs of Lula's standing in the polls against the "Brazil risk" calculated by foreign economists, drawing a link between Lula's election and financial instability. In response, Lula issued a June 2002 statement, the "Letter to the Brazilian people." In it, he promised to maintain a balanced budget and keep his country's international commitments to the International Monetary Fund (IMF). He also actively engaged in talks with the IMF regarding a new agreement. His actions calmed markets, reassured the middle class, and contributed to his victory in the election. López Obrador could have made a similar statement, perhaps committing himself to a balanced budget or an anti-inflationary program. He did not.

Three factors help explain López Obrador's reaction. First, the party discipline of Brazil's Workers' Party (Partido dos Trabalhadores, or PT)—and its strong identification with Lula personally—gave him more room for policy maneuvering. The party criticized his statement, but they continued to support him. López Obrador's position was more complicated. Unlike the PT, the PRD did not have strong organic ties with labor unions or popular movements (outside of Mexico City). López Obrador had reason to doubt the loyalty of his base—after all, part of it defected in 2000 to vote for Fox, even as it supported López Obrador for mayor. So, while he ran a moderate campaign in the media, he attempted to rally the party faithful with the kind of fire-breathing rhetoric they all adored, despite the risk this posed of making him look insincere. The *chachalaca* remark came out of this disjuncture.

Second, the political tide in Brazil in 2002 was running against the incumbent party. Outgoing president Fernando Henrique Cardoso was widely blamed for an economic downturn, an energy crisis, and stubbornly high unemployment. Three of the four viable candidates in the Brazilian presidential election were running from the left; the fourth, a bureaucrat from the ruling party, finished a distant second to Lula in the first round. Fox, in contrast, was a popular president in 2005 and 2006. Over half of all Mexicans thought he was doing a good job. His highest ratings came in April 2006, shortly before the election, when 66 percent approved of his job performance.[21]

Finally, López Obrador had supreme confidence in his ability to get past this negative campaign, as he had so many others. Lula knew better. The 2002 race was his fourth attempt to win a presidential election. In each of his previous tries, he came close—second place—but failed to get the swing votes he needed to win, in part due to campaigns that emphasized his radical roots. By 2002, he knew he would have to change his style, and he did: producing a softer image in his campaign materials ("Lula Light" as Brazilians put it), allying with a conservative party in his vice-presidential pick, and, finally, issuing the "Letter to the Brazilian people." López Obrador was not prepared to go that far. In public, at least, he simply denied that his popularity was dropping and declared that Mexicans were too smart to believe attack ads.

His strategy nearly worked. He got more votes than his party on July 2, and he outperformed Calderón among independent voters. But López Obrador had only two months to reverse the impressions created by the PAN's campaign of fear. He badly needed to present the Mexican people with an image to contrast with the PAN's "wild-eyed radical" version. Just such an opportunity was at hand—the first presidential debate, held April 25. Yet his position was complicated. In late February, when he still enjoyed a comfortable lead, his spokesman announced that López Obrador would participate in only one presidential debate. At the time, there seemed to be little reason for the front-runner to risk attacks by his opponents on national television. Shortly after this statement, on March 7, the National Business Chamber of the Radio and Television Industry (Cámara Nacional de la Industria de Radio y Televisión, or CIRT) announced that it would broadcast two debates instead of the originally proposed four. The PRI and PAN representatives in the IFE quickly agreed on a schedule for one debate in April and a second in June. On April 19, the PAN and the PRI made another deal; to highlight the absence of López Obrador, they would display a vacant chair for the missing candidate.

López Obrador could still have changed his mind. In the end, he felt that attending the debate would damage his reputation for keeping his word, and that it would simply offer the PAN a national forum in which to attack him. As he said the night before the debate, "we are not going as a matter of strategy. We don't want to make it easy for them by standing up there for them to throw everything at us."[22]

In retrospect, the decision to skip the debate was a mistake. Calderón appeared statesmanlike and sensible, winning the debate handily. He noted that "the candidate of the PRD did not come to this debate because he has no viable proposals . . . The right to debate is a right of the citizens, of you, not of the candidates, and even in this he prefers to turn his back on you."[23] Most Mexicans did not watch the debate; in the Mexico 2006 Panel Study, nearly 59 percent of the respondents did not watch any part of it, nor did they listen to it on the radio. However, 57 percent indicated that they had seen news reports about the debate on television or heard about it on the radio, and López Obrador's absence was widely remarked upon. The panel data show that López Obrador did not do significantly worse among those who watched the debate, but his absence did tend to confirm the PAN's portrayal of him as high-handed and autocratic. In other words, the debate did not prejudice people against AMLO, but he might have helped himself by showing up. The day after the debate, online gamblers put Calderón ahead of AMLO for the first time in the campaign.

Episode Three: López Obrador Strikes Back

Shortly after the debate, López Obrador finally decided that he had to respond to the attacks. On April 29 and 30—four days after the debate and a month and a half after the attack ads began—he met with his advisors to redefine his campaign strategy. But valuable time had been lost. During the month of April, Calderón dominated the airwaves in terms of advertising and focused on negative ads against López Obrador. Strikingly, almost 80 percent of all PAN television ads aired during the month of April, "when the campaign against the candidate López Obrador intensified and in the period when electoral trends would have shifted."[24]

As with the debate, the delay in López Obrador's advertising response probably did not doom him. Even if he had responded more quickly, the PAN ads would still have been broadcast. He could not match the PAN's ability to spend money on ads for an additional two months without real sacrifice. Though the Coalition for the Good of All qualified for more public election funds than the PAN, López Obrador did not fully control its budget, some of which was allocated to the other two parties in the coalition. Moreover, he did not have access to the kind of private money that flowed Calderón's way. Two Mexican business organizations—the Private Sector Roundtable (Consejo Coordinador Empresarial, or CCE) and the Mexican Business Owners' Association (Confederación Patronal de la República Mexicana, or Coparmex)—sponsored "public interest" ads celebrating macroeconomic stability under the PAN along with asking people to vote. Other private companies paid for the PAN's Internet campaign. Nevertheless, López Obrador's overconfident reaction to the negative campaign gave Calderón an uncontested field during a critical period.

The PRD media campaign changed immediately after AMLO's late-April strategy meeting. In May, AMLO ads during peak television hours outnumbered Calderón spots for the first time in the campaign. According to IFE records, López Obrador's campaign bought 2,736 television ads in May, compared to 1,027 purchased by Calderón. While the spending on all races increased in May, in no other category—federal deputies, senators, or general promotion of the coalition—did the Coalition for the Good of All outspend the PAN and the PRI.[25] Clearly, the media shift focused primarily on rescuing a troubled presidential campaign. Many of the new ads went on the offensive, linking Calderón to the unpopular bank bailout plan of the 1990s (known as Fobaproa).

In late May, the PRD representative in the IFE complained about a new series of ads linking López Obrador to violence and again declaring him a "danger to Mexico." The PAN, he insisted, was "pulling the leg" of electoral authorities, withdrawing previous ads judged defamatory by the IFE and then producing a series of new ads with the same intention.[26] The next day, the Executive Council of the IFE recommended ordering the PAN to pull some ads; again, the congressionally appointed General Council rejected this recommendation and agreed with the PAN, claiming that pulling the ads would curtail freedom of expression.

Finally, on May 31, the IFE took its first serious steps to regulate the campaign. Initially, the IFE ordered the removal of three specific ads, including not only the spot linking López Obrador to the police officers' lynchings, but also ads declaring him a danger to Mexico and a spot linking López Obrador to a guerrilla leader (Subcomandante Marcos). It then fined the PAN for its use of Aznar's endorsement of Calderón in ads and initiated an investigation into a "public service" DVD instructing Mexicans on how to vote, which had been paid for by a private firm.[27] Under Mexican law, only parties are allowed to spend money in an attempt to persuade voters. At the same time, the IFE ordered the PRD to withdraw ads accusing Calderón of responsibility for Fobaproa.

López Obrador had one more rabbit in his hat. During the presidential debate on June 6, he accused Calderón of having thrown lucrative oil contracts to his brother-in-law, Diego Závala, while Calderón was secretary of energy. Calderón had campaigned initially as the "candidate of clean hands," and López Obrador no doubt intended to hit Calderón at a weak point in his claims. Yet the charges fell strangely flat. Although Calderón's average rating on honesty did decline from the second wave of the panel survey to the third wave, taken after the election, the decline merely brought him down to López Obrador's level. On a scale from one to five, with five being most honest, Calderón was rated as 2.79 versus López Obrador's 2.75.[28] After months of negative campaign ads, voters saw little difference between the candidates on corruption.

On June 26, Calderón closed his national campaign with a rally in Mexico City's Aztec Stadium. In order to exclude possible hecklers, tickets were required to get into the event. The PAN then arranged to bus supporters from nearby state of México and other areas to make sure that television coverage showed a packed stadium. Calderón devoted most of his speech to urging voters to prevent the terrible calamity of a López Obrador presidency. López Obrador, for his part, waited until June 28 to hold his closing rally in a more traditional location: Mexico City's Zócalo, a large public square ringed by the national cathedral, local government offices, and the National Palace. There, beneath a steady drizzle, AMLO rallied the faithful, telling them not to worry: "We're going to win." The campaign was over. Andrés Manuel López Obrador and Felipe Calderón Hinojosa faced election day tied in the polls.

Episode Four: "To Hell with Your Corrupt Institutions"

Interviewed on TV Azteca two weeks before the campaign ended, López Obrador assured the public that he would accept a legitimate defeat by just one vote. The key, of course, was the word "legitimate." The history of the PRD conditioned party members to mistrust electoral institutions, starting with the electoral fraud of 1988 and continuing through electoral frauds suffered by the PRD (and by López Obrador personally) in subsequent years.[29] Many of its activists came out of clandestine or independent popular movements. Even during the 1990s, *perredistas* (PRD partisans) were arrested, imprisoned, and beaten in the course of their political activities. They have been spied on, investigated, and threatened. According to the PRD, hundreds of party activists have been murdered since its foundation in 1989.[30] They are, as a consequence, predisposed to expect the worst from public institutions. PRD candidates and voters were significantly more likely to doubt that the elections would be free and fair than members of other parties (see chapters 2 and 6 in this volume).

Over the years, charges of electoral fraud also became a convenient way to explain the PRD's electoral failures. On occasion, even when internal information indicated that the PRD had lost, the party would immediately cry foul and organize protests. Charges of fraud met a practical need to explain defeat, but they also responded to the deeply held convictions of many *perredistas* that even if they did not know exactly how, they must have been "done wrong." PRD politicians have frequently confused large and enthusiastic campaign rallies with broad electoral support.

More intangibly, but still importantly, protesting their defeat was a way for PRD supporters to express their frustration at political exclusion, as well as a way of whipping up enthusiasm for other causes that the party and its allies defended. When López Obrador launched his postelectoral protests, he certainly knew that PRD identifiers expected some response from him and would find it odd if he did nothing in the face of such a close result. His calls for action were met with extraordinary support and sacrifices from the party base in Mexico City. Even his rivals in the PRD leadership—with the exception of Cuauhtémoc Cárdenas—did not challenge the protest strategy publicly. His popularity among PRD members remained strong, even as it slipped badly outside the PRD base.

But the external context also mattered. Most of the tactics used by the PAN—such as open support from the incumbent president for his party's candidates, negative campaigning, and "issue ads" by private sector groups—would have been legal in the United States. Nevertheless, they were either illegal or widely considered to be improper in Mexico, and the IFE seemed unable or unwilling to enforce the law. From the PRD's point of view, the IFE's helplessness was suspicious, and from there, it was but a small step to conjecture that the count itself was flawed. In 2006, the IFE was particularly vulnerable to charges of partiality *by the PRD*. The first IFE General Council contained a balanced roster of three nominees from each party, approved by near-consensus in the Chamber of Deputies. In late 2003, when the second General Council was chosen, the PAN colluded with the PRI to exclude all of the PRD nominees.

The capture of the IFE by the PRI and the PAN followed the PRI's enormous gains in the 2003 midterm congressional elections, when the PRI ended up with 45 percent of the congressional seats, to the PAN's 31 percent. Buoyed by the hope of returning to power in 2006, PRI legislators demanded more than their three-seat quota of nominations to the IFE. As Jorge Alonso writes, "they wanted a majority because many PRI officials are convinced they lost the 2000 elections by not controlling the Electoral Institute."[31] Thus, when the PRD proposed a list of nominees which included some members of the first Council, the PRI strongly objected to "re-election" of councilors. According to reports published at the time, the PAN initially intended to support the PRD and not make re-election an issue. Learning this, the head of the PRI bench, Elba Esther Gordillo, sent for the PAN negotiators and warned them that if the PAN supported the PRD, the "situation would fall apart for the Chamber of Deputies," where the PAN and the PRI had frequently voted together to pass legislation in the first half of Fox's term.[32] The PAN therefore agreed to support the PRI instead. Together, the two parties had enough votes to push through a slate of candidates containing only PAN and PRI nominees. As requested, five of the nine positions (including the presidency of the Council) went to PRI nominees.

The PRD played into the PRI's hands with its refusal to withdraw its nominees who had served on the first Council. It is not clear why PRD negotiator Pablo Gómez would not consider changes to the slate—whether he simply thought he had the PAN's support and therefore could afford to stonewall the

PRI or whether he (and the PRD) were cynically setting up the IFE to claim fraud if López Obrador lost. The latter, of course, would be an extraordinary risk for any political party to take, and this possibility is less likely than simple miscalculation of the PRD's leverage. Whatever the PRD's motives, the outcome left even independent external critics (like the respected poll-watching organization Alianze Civica, or Civic Alliance) aghast. Not only did the process exclude one of the major parties, it also resulted in a slate of candidates that they (and others) argued were too partisan for the job.

If he expected control of the IFE to help him win, Madrazo was disappointed. But the PRI's actions affected the conduct of the campaign and the postelectoral wave of protests. The PRD went into the 2006 election with questions about the neutrality of the IFE. Before López Obrador even registered his presidential candidacy—at a time when he enjoyed a comfortable lead in the polls—the president of the PRD warned that his party would not give a "blank check" to the IFE in terms of recognizing the results of the election.[33] López Obrador himself constantly reminded supporters that despite his lead in the polls, "powerful interests" would try to stop his candidacy.[34] The climate of distrust and paranoia was pervasive from the start.

After the campaign began, suspicions were revived by the IFE's reluctance to intervene against what the PRD felt was outrageously overt interference by President Fox on behalf of Calderón. The IFE's hesitance to rein in the PAN's aggressive ad campaign further fueled concerns. Four days before the election, the editorial page of *La Jornada*, a left-leaning newspaper, published a scathing critique of the IFE's "deplorable partiality."[35] When López Obrador began to denounce Mexican institutions in late August, he did not simply say "to hell with the institutions," as was often reported in U.S. newspapers, but "to hell with your corrupt institutions."[36] Exclusion of the PRD's nominees from the IFE made it easier for the PRD to use "your" (and "corrupt") in referring to the autonomous electoral institute for which so many PRD supporters had sacrificed so much.

Ultimately, López Obrador's narrow loss made postelectoral protests inevitable, no matter who ran the IFE. Not all PRD loyalists are committed to electoral democracy. One participant in the postelectoral protests remarked to a reporter that she hoped the IFE would rule against López Obrador, because, "this is no longer a postelectoral problem, it is turning into a revolutionary process; with his little speech on Thursday, Andrés Manuel crossed the line of no return when he said that thing about 'to hell with your corrupt institutions.' Now, if the Court annuls [the election], the revolutionary moment will collapse and what a pain to have to go back again to elections, campaigns, and those things, if we can go directly to taking power."[37]

All three presidential candidates made mistakes in the course of the 2006 campaign, and all of them made some astute decisions. In the end, López Obrador did not lose the election so much as Calderón won it. Yet all of their decisions—hits and misses—occurred in a context of structural constraints that limited the opportunities they had and the choices they could make.

The first constraint was the condition of Mexico's economy. Both López Obrador and Calderón thought this factor would help their respective chances to win the election, and both had a point. Calderón recognized the need for more job growth, but he focused on the PAN's record of macroeconomic stability, framing the issue in terms of the risks associated with policy change. Current rates of job growth might be disappointing, he argued, but economic chaos would be worse. Risk-averse voters, anxious to avoid another peso collapse, agreed.

López Obrador framed his appeal in terms of neoliberalism's shortcomings, principally its failure to provide jobs and its association with a trend toward impoverishment in the countryside. This point resonated with voters in the Mexico 2006 Panel Study, who viewed such issues as immediate and pressing concerns. López Obrador's enormous sense of urgency contrasted with Calderón's argument that providing additional jobs, while important, was mainly a matter of staying the course and waiting patiently for the existing economic model to bear fruit. But urgency alone was not enough, particularly after Calderón's campaign started focusing more attention on the issue of job creation. López Obrador needed to convince voters that at least one of two alternatives was true: either his approach to job creation did *not* represent a serious risk, or continuation of the current policy *did* represent a serious risk. If the existing model of neoliberalism had no chance of delivering future improvements in jobs, but instead would further impoverish most Mexicans, then even if López Obrador's approach involved some risk, at least it had a better chance of succeeding than the status quo. Alternatively, if the risk was minimal, then it might be worth taking a chance to improve job creation and reduce poverty. López Obrador did fairly well among those who trusted his ability to handle the economy and thought the risk was minimal, as well as those who believed that economic trends were headed downward and that the status quo was unacceptable. However, it is worth noting that the PAN's negative campaign was perfectly targeted to minimize López Obrador's support among those who were disappointed in the performance of the economy—it highlighted and exaggerated the perils involved in a change of policy. López Obrador's attacks, in contrast, did nothing to minimize the PAN's advantages on economic policy.

The second constraint was the size of each party's loyal partisan base. López Obrador started off at a disadvantage. In the first wave of our panel survey, only 17 percent of the respondents identified with the PRD, slightly lower than the levels of PAN loyalty. "None of the above," in contrast, polled 22 percent—more than any political party. Clearly, much of the electorate was movable. PAN voters were also more consolidated in their loyalties than those from the PRD. Nearly a quarter of those who identified with the PRD had done so for less than two years, versus 16 percent of the PAN identifiers. The fact that López Obrador's support at the polls doubled this underlying percentage of PRD sympathizers is a remarkable performance. López Obrador succeeded in winning over more independent and moderate voters than any leftist presidential candidate before him. (After July 2, of course, he alienated many of them again.) If he had started the electoral campaign with a larger core base, he would have won easily. As it was, just mobilizing the PRD base could never have worked, because his base was too small to win.

Which brings us to the third constraint: the parties themselves. Calderón was an average rider on a strong and healthy horse. López Obrador was a strong rider on a sway-backed nag. Virtually every observer of Mexican politics agrees that the PAN and the PRD lie at opposite ends of the organizational spectrum. The PAN is seen as a model of organizational clarity, well connected to private sources of funding, relatively centralized, with more accurate membership lists, less internal factionalism, and a more careful selection of members. The PRD is seen as intensely factionalized, disorganized, unable to raise much private funding, decentralized in practice (with local committees frequently flouting central decisions), unruly, and undisciplined. Both images are something of an exaggeration, but they reflect a very real contrast between the two parties. Just as Madrazo's campaign was consumed and ultimately crippled by concerns over party unity (see chapter 8 in this volume), the options facing both Calderón and López Obrador were shaped by the party structures within which they operated.

Calderón, for example, was able to name his own campaign team and expect the support of the party organization. This small team of professionals and experts was able to shift course rapidly during the campaign. Calderón was even able to consult foreign advisors (Morris, Allyn, and Sola) on the more technical aspects of the media campaign, with no internal repercussions. López Obrador, in contrast, was forced to name a party rival with no media experience, Jesús Ortega, to head his campaign, so as to smooth over hurt feelings that resulted from López Obrador's decision not to support Ortega's attempt to become the PRD candidate for mayor of Mexico City.[38] One cannot help but wonder whether distrust in the inner circle of campaign advisors contributed to the delay in shifting López Obrador's campaign strategies.

Democratic selection of the party leadership through open elections also put López Obrador's internal opponents in a difficult position, particularly as the postelectoral protest campaign unfolded. PRD leaders have to worry about how the party's loyal base will respond to their actions or inaction. Only Cárdenas publicly questioned the wisdom of the protest strategy, and he was pilloried. As Kenneth Greene argues (2007), the process of recruiting individuals into the opposition parties during the dominance of the PRI encouraged self-selection of the more radical activists. Even if party leaders become more moderate as they get positions of power, they can only keep those positions by continuing to appeal to this radical base. López Obrador tried to move to the center in the 2006 election but kept sliding back to the left, whether out of concern for the loyalty of the bases or because he just could not help himself.

Actually winning power can mitigate these effects by attracting more pragmatic, power-seeking activists into the party. This dynamic began for the PAN in the 1990s, resulting in the departure of some of the original leaders of the PAN (including Calderón's own father), who left because they felt the party had lost touch with its ideological roots. For the PRD, this process happened somewhat later and mostly in Mexico City, where López Obrador governed as a moderate.

Last but not least, Mexican voters are relatively conservative on many issues, despite—or perhaps because of—Mexico's revolutionary past. It is no accident that López Obrador kept his distance from Hugo Chávez, Evo Morales, and other colorful characters on the Latin American left, or that he refused to endorse legal abortion even though his own party supported it (see chapter 6 in this volume).

In short, López Obrador faced a more difficult challenge than his double-digit lead in January 2006 indicated. The failure of his campaign cannot be traced exclusively to his personal shortcomings. The Mexican Left faces a problem that is inherently structural, rooted in its own intransigent past, its relatively limited base, its chaotic internal governance, and the general conservatism and apathy of Mexican voters. López Obrador's postelectoral protest campaign did nothing to repair any of these problems and even exacerbated the party's negative image among middle-class voters. The PRD, therefore, must tackle some existential questions. If it could not win with either Cárdenas or López Obrador, is it still possible for the Left to aspire to national power? How would the PRD have to change in order to win? And is the cost of change worth merely an electoral victory to those who currently support the party? López Obrador's defeat may affect the way that the Mexican Left perceives itself, and its role in democracy, for some time to come.

Part III / Ideology, Image, or Interest?

CHAPTER TEN

Electoral Volatility in 2006

Francisco Flores-Macías

The 2006 Mexican presidential campaign was a rollercoaster ride. For many months before the official campaigns started, former Mexico City mayor Andrés Manuel López Obrador enjoyed a considerable lead over all other potential opponents. For example, a poll published by *El Universal* newspaper in late November 2005—soon after Felipe Calderón had won the nomination for the National Action Party (PAN)—showed López Obrador ahead with 34 percent, versus 22 percent for Calderón and 18 percent for the Institutional Revolutionary Party's (PRI) Roberto Madrazo.[1] In mid-March, the *New York Times* published a story that echoed the conventional wisdom in Mexico: "With 108 days to go before the election," the *Times'* story read, "Mr. López Obrador . . . appears to have consolidated his position as the front-runner, and many political strategists now predict he will win unless he stumbles spectacularly."[2] By May 2006, however, the tables had turned, and Calderón led in most polls.[3] In the final weeks, López Obrador caught up with his conservative opponent and actually appeared in first place in several polls, although within the statistical margin of error. On election day, as is well known, Calderón defeated López Obrador by a hair.

The Big Picture: Large Fluctuations in the 2006 Presidential Race

Figure 1.1 in this volume presented an average of publicly available commercial polls over the course of the campaign. Four facts stand out from these polls: (1) López Obrador enjoyed a considerable lead throughout the first months of the campaign; (2) in March and April, polls began to register a slight, yet noticeable decline in voter preferences for Madrazo and López Obrador; (3) support for Calderón grew steadily until about a month prior to election day; and (4) López

Obrador bounced back somewhat toward the end, going into the July 2 balloting tied with Calderón.

In the first half of the campaign, the main question was the solidity of López Obrador's support. On the one hand, his Party of the Democratic Revolution (PRD) habitually placed a distant third in public opinion polls that asked for people's party identification, and the two minor parties in his electoral coalition, the Labor Party (PT) and *Convergencia* (Convergence), claimed only a tiny number of identifiers.[4] According to the results of the first wave of the Mexico 2006 Panel Study,[5] conducted in October 2005, 28.3 percent of the electorate considered itself *priísta* (identified with the PRI); 25.5 percent, *panista* (identified with the PAN); and 17.5 percent, *perredista* (identified with the PRD). This distribution suggests both that López Obrador's base was smaller than that of his rivals and that a large proportion of his supporters were ideological moderates and nonpartisans—arguably those with the weakest attachments and who would be the first to abandon him should something go astray. If each presidential candidate managed to capture most of its core party vote, then López Obrador faced a structural disadvantage; in order to win, he would have to persuade and retain a disproportionate number of independent voters. On the other hand, López Obrador had shown an extraordinary ability to maintain a high approval level despite the potentially damaging "video scandals" that had shaken his administration in March 2004, in which evidence of corruption among his top aides was caught on film.[6] Additionally, he had managed to turn the seemingly devastating impeachment process initiated against him in April 2005 into a successful publicity stunt both domestically and internationally.[7] To win in 2006, López Obrador needed to keep up the pace against a newly nominated PAN candidate who was still unknown to a large number of voters, but whose party was considerably more popular throughout the country. Up until the end of 2005, he had managed to do so. As 2006 began, however, López Obrador's capability to hold on to his lead was an unknown. Could a candidate who drew so much of his support from independents cruise to victory on July 2, 2006?

This chapter examines which voters switched preferences during the campaign and why. A macro-level glance at the campaign horserace offers an idea of its general patterns, but it can also conceal important information. Figure 1.1 cannot tell us whether most voters stayed loyal to their early choice (and thus most of the fluctuation was due to a small percentage of highly volatile voters) or if many more people were changing their choice of candidates. Perhaps more importantly, it offers no way to ascertain why some people switched and others did not. It is only by interviewing the same respondents several times throughout the campaign—i.e., through a panel design—that we can explore with greater precision who switched and why they did so.

The next section discusses the theoretical debate regarding which voters are more likely to switch during an electoral campaign. Section three asks who switched during the 2006 presidential campaign, presenting both descriptive statistics and multivariate regression analysis. The fourth section attempts to determine why voters switched, based on salient campaign events—such as the first debate, or the PRD's attempt to question Calderón's honesty following the second debate. Section five discusses how these findings inform scholarly understanding of the Mexico 2006 presidential race, and the final section reflects on the implications of these findings for campaigns and elections across Latin America.

As will become clear in the next few pages, the shift in preferences throughout the 2006 electoral process did not result from a spectacular collapse of López Obrador's support. Instead, Calderón's narrow victory was the product of an effective campaign that managed to bring home those PAN partisans and ideological conservatives who initially supported his main opponent, while at the same time appealing to broader sectors of society. López Obrador began the race with much to lose, a consequence of the weakness of the PRD nationally. After gradually slipping in the polls for several weeks, he closed strong, recovering some voters that he had lost earlier on in the campaign. However, running on a message targeted mainly at the "have-nots" and the party faithful proved insufficient to contain the surge in support of Calderón.

Theory Primer on Switchers and Standpatters

The theoretical debate on switching focuses on which types of voters are more likely to change their preferences. One set of authors argues that the least informed voters are the most persuadable; lacking political awareness, they do not have firm opinions on most issues. The little information that they do receive has the potential to alter their beliefs significantly, leading them to switch their choice for president. This approach originated from the studies of Lazarsfeld and his colleagues at Columbia University, which claimed that the people most likely to switch preferences were the least interested in the election; the least concerned about its outcome; the least attentive to political material in the formal media of communication; the last to settle upon a vote decision; and the most likely to be persuaded, finally, by a personal contact, not an "issue" of the election . . . The notion that the people who switch parties during the campaign are mainly the reasoned, thoughtful, conscientious people who were convinced by the issues of the election is just plain wrong. Actually, they were mainly just the opposite. (1944, 69)

This claim was later amended by Philip Converse, who observed that switching resulted from an interaction between (1) one's level of interest in the election and concern for its outcome (as the Columbia researchers argued) and (2) a minimum level of exposure to campaign information:

We can see at once, then, that the very uninvolved voters, who we have come to expect will tend to "float" politically, present us with something of a paradox in this regard. On the one hand, such voters show a high susceptibility to short-term change in partisan attitudes *provided that any new information reaches them at all.* On the other hand, when the flow of information through the society is weak, these are the individuals who are *most* likely to experience no new information intake, and hence are individuals *least likely to show changes in patterns of behavior,* if indeed they are constrained to behave at all. (1962, 586–87; italics in the original)

A contending view originates with Key (1966),[8] who argued that people who switched preferences demonstrated a higher level of rationality than many standpatters.[9] In a sort of proof by contradiction, Key reasoned that many standpatters were "party stalwarts" no matter what policies were espoused, but switchers intrinsically were not. Thus, while many nonswitchers blindly followed the party line election after election—with their issue positions shaped by their choice of party, rather than having their choice of party determined by their beliefs—switchers could be expected to show greater thoughtfulness in evaluating candidates (1966, 151).

Beyond their general argument, Lazarsfeld and his coauthors (1944) also introduced a vocabulary to refer to the different types of switchers.[10] Crystallizers were those who were undecided early on in the campaign but later selected one of the candidates; waverers were people who supported a candidate early on, then switched either to undecided or to a different party, but eventually returned to their original choice; and party changers were those who preferred one candidate initially but ultimately voted for someone else.

Two other broad approaches to switching have also been proposed. The first, which has recently been tested in the Latin American context, falls under the general rubric of a sociological theory of switching (Baker et al. 2006). It posits that the likelihood that a voter will change his or her mind is strongly dependent on the opinions of those people with whom this individual interacts regularly. When one or several of these political discussants hold views contrary to the voter's initial choice, the chances of switching increase greatly.[11] The second theory, developed recently by Hillygus and Shields (2008) in the American context, argues that voters who are cross-pressured on positional issues in relation to the party with which they customarily identify are more persuadable during the course of the campaign. Whether someone switches or not is then dependent upon whether candidates are successful in raising the salience of these issues.

In Mexico, the literature dealing with switching during electoral campaigns began in the context of single-party rule; thus, its main purpose was to understand what led voters to defect to the opposition. For instance, in analyzing the 1988 and 1991 elections, Domínguez and McCann (1995) argued that defection from the ruling party occurred in a two-step process, where voters first decided whether to support the ruling party or not and only then chose amongst the opposition parties.[12] Additionally, and more in tune with the theoretical debate on switching described above, Moreno's (1999a) study of the relationship between campaign awareness and vote choice during the 1997 congressional elections concluded that campaign effects depended on partisan attachments. Highly aware partisans were less likely to switch from one election to the next than less-aware partisans, but highly aware nonpartisans were more likely to change preferences from one election to the next than their less-aware counterparts.[13]

These studies lacked the advantage of having a rich panel dataset in which the same respondents were interviewed several times during the campaign. Magaloni and Poiré (2004b), however, analyzed data from the Mexico 2000 Panel Study[14] to understand the causes of strategic defections. In other words, they sought to explain what led many initial supporters of the PRD's presidential candidate Cuauhtémoc Cárdenas to cast their ballot in favor of the PRI's Francisco Labastida or the PAN's Vicente Fox. Lawson and McCann (2005) also used the 2000 panel study data to assess the impact of television news exposure on attitude changes throughout the campaign, finding substantial effects.

Inside Voters' Minds: Part 1

The micro-level data suggest that campaign effects were substantial during the 2006 presidential election. Of the 849 respondents in the national sample of the Mexico 2006 Panel Study who completed all three waves, a staggering 49.8 percent switched their vote preferences at least once.[15] Of these, 15.6 percent were early switchers, changing between waves 1 (October 2005) and 2 (April/May 2006); 19.4 percent were late switchers, changing between waves 2 and 3 (July 2006); 7.4 percent were returners, switching between waves 1 and 2, but afterwards coming back to their original choice; and 7.4 percent switched preferences twice, between the first and second round and then again, to a different choice, between the second and third round. Moreover, these data understate the extent of switching, as some respondents may have changed their views two or more times during the intervals between panel waves.

These same data can also be presented in the language of Lazarsfeld et al. (1944). Of those respondents who switched, 10 percent of the sample were crystallizers, who started either undecided or not intending to vote and eventually picked one of the candidates; 5 percent were waverers, showing initial support for one candidate, then switching to a different candidate or to the undecided category, but eventually returning to their initial choice; and 22 percent were true party changers, who ultimately preferred a candidate from a party different from that of their original choice.[16] The rest fall into a new category, the disenchanted, who began expressing support for one of the candidates but in the end decided not to cast their ballot at all. Of the respondents of the Mexico 2006 Panel Study, 10 percent were disenchanted and, of those, 44 percent had preferred Madrazo in wave 1. This finding suggests—in accordance with intuition—that perception of whether one's preferred candidate can win is a predictor of voter turnout.[17]

Table 10.1 divides the respondents from all three of these waves in the national sample of the Mexico 2006 Panel Study into subgroups, according to their basic demographic and political characteristics, and shows the distribution of each subgroup into the categories of those who switched and those who did not. The switchers are further separated according to the timing of their defection.[18]

Several trends stand out in the demographic characteristics. In terms of education, respondents who had completed six years or less of schooling were more likely to switch than their better-educated counterparts. Regionally, respondents

Table 10.1 Characteristics of switchers and standpatters

	N	Stand-patters (%)	Re-turners (%)	Early switchers (%)	Late switchers (%)	Switched twice (%)
Education						
Six years or less	352	45	8	20	19	7
Seven to eleven years	231	54	6	19	11	10
Twelve years or more	262	53	7	20	15	5
Age						
Younger	229	49	6	17	18	9
Middle-aged	363	53	6	22	14	6
Older	257	46	11	18	17	8
Region						
South	219	58	5	15	16	6
Center	90	46	8	29	13	4
Center-West	145	52	3	26	14	4
Mexico City area	191	57	5	19	13	7
North	204	37	14	17	20	12
Partisan affiliation						
PAN	210	61	9	13	10	8
PRI	233	42	6	24	20	7
PRD	144	69	6	8	13	3
Non-partisan	234	39	9	27	18	8
Strength of party attachment						
Strong	237	61	4	14	17	4
Weak	350	52	9	18	13	8
Ideology						
Left	153	62	5	14	9	9
Center and leaners	232	57	9	14	15	6
Right	150	46	8	19	18	9
Don't know	224	41	7	23	20	8
Attention to campaign						
Low	239	43	9	17	20	11
Medium	400	49	7	21	16	8
High	210	61	7	20	10	2
Reception of information						
Low	207	46	9	18	18	8
Medium	387	49	6	17	19	9
High	254	56	7	11	21	4
General knowledge						
Low	328	42	7	22	19	10
Medium	267	53	7	17	15	7
High	254	57	8	19	11	4

Note: Percentages may not add to 100% due to rounding. The coding of variables can be found in the Mexico 2006 Panel Study's supplemental materials for chapter 10 (http://web.mit.edu/polisci/research/mexico06/book.html).

in the northern states were least likely to support the same candidate in all three waves, although a relatively high percentage of northerners (14%) returned to their original choice between the second and third waves. In the Mexico City metropolitan area and in the South, 57 percent and 58 percent of the participants, respectively, stayed with their initial preference throughout the panel. In terms of age, no clear patterns emerge between switchers and standpatters.

Strength of partisan attachment was, unsurprisingly, negatively correlated with a propensity to switch. Regarding party affiliation, both the PRD and the PAN identifiers showed a high resistance to switching; in contrast, respondents who identified with the PRI were almost as likely to abandon their initial choice as were the independents. One likely explanation is that the PRI identifiers abandoned their party's nominee toward the end, when they figured that Madrazo's cause was lost and thus tried to defect strategically to support their second-ranked choice. The descriptive statistics show, however, that almost as many PRI identifiers left Madrazo earlier rather than later in the campaign (18% to 22%), thus suggesting that PRI defectors could have been disaffected with the process that led to Madrazo's nomination.[19] (On the PRI's contentious primary, see chapters 7 and 8 in this volume.)

An interesting trend concerns ideology. Those respondents who initially placed themselves on the left of the political spectrum switched in fewer numbers than the people in the center, who in turn switched less than people on the right. The reason is that a very high proportion (38%) of the self-identified conservatives preferred Roberto Madrazo in the first round, and an almost equal percentage chose either López Obrador or Felipe Calderón (24.5% and 25.2%, respectively). By the third wave, however, respondents on the right had massively abandoned Roberto Madrazo and López Obrador in favor of Calderón.

In terms of campaign awareness, the indicators of attention to the campaign, reception of information, and general political knowledge all show the same pattern: people with high scores on these variables were less likely to switch. Although these descriptive statistics are not enough to determine causality, they provide support in favor of the contention by Lazarsfeld et al. (1944) that the less informed citizens are, the more likely they are to switch preferences in their choice of presidential candidates.

Table 10.2 addresses the question of what percentage of each candidate's supporters in wave 1 could be counted on to support their original choice on election day. The vertical section shows the distribution of preferences in wave 1 (October 2005), and the horizontal section shows their actual choices in July

Table 10.2   Distribution of switchers and standpatters between waves 1 and 3

Candidate preference in October 2005	Vote choice in July 2006						
	Calderón	Madrazo	López Obrador	Other	Abstained/ Null	N	Percentage
Calderón	79%	3%	7%	1%	9%	202	24
Madrazo	23%	45%	13%	3%	16%	242	29
López Obrador	16%	4%	66%	2%	11%	281	33
Other	38%	13%	0%	38%	12%	8	1
Undecided	36%	18%	16%	3%	27%	116	14
N	306	148	251	24	120		
Percentage	36	17	30	3	14		

2006, as reported in the final round of the panel. The percentage of respondents who chose the same candidate in the first interview and at the end can be read from the diagonal. Thus, although 79 percent of Calderón's initial supporters stayed with him in the last round, only 45 percent of Madrazo's did the same. Not only was Calderón very successful in maintaining his original adherents, but he also beat López Obrador handily in attracting undecided voters and Madrazo defectors. Two additional conclusions can be drawn from this table: a large percentage of initial Madrazo supporters ended up not voting, probably because they were disgruntled with their candidate's chances of winning and unwilling to cast their ballot for someone else, and most of López Obrador's and Madrazo's defectors went to Calderón rather than switch to the other alternatives.

For every subgroup analyzed except one (the waverers), more voters switched to Calderón than to López Obrador or to Madrazo. In terms of education, Calderón won by the largest margin over López Obrador among the switchers (excluding the waverers, a subset of switchers) who were highly educated (46% to 14%). Similarly, Calderón performed best in drawing in the younger switchers (42% to López Obrador's 13%) and those living in the northern states (47% to 11%). In the center region, López Obrador attracted almost as many switchers as Calderón did (31% for Calderón, 29% for López Obrador), while in the Mexico City metropolitan area, Calderón won among switchers by 34 percent to 18 percent. This finding provides mixed preliminary evidence regarding sociological theories of switching, which would predict that voters would change in favor of the candidate preferred by others in their community. In the case of Mexico City, López Obrador may have reached a ceiling, so that adding new converts became increasingly difficult. In the North, on the other hand, Calderón's popularity kept growing.

How well did each candidate retain its core group of party identifiers? Calderón beat the other candidates, managing to retain 84 percent of the 146 PAN identifiers who preferred him in wave 1. López Obrador followed him closely, retaining 81 percent of the 131 PRD identifiers that chose him initially. As in other instances, Madrazo fell considerably behind, keeping 52 percent of 169 PRI identifiers who stood with him in the first round. In other words, Madrazo lost the support of a good part of the party faithful during the campaign.

The behavior of nonpartisans and ideological moderates is worth considering as well.[20] López Obrador's early lead depended heavily on nonpartisans, and their propensity to switch away from him may have decided the election. Of the 234 respondents who did not identify with any parties during the October 2005 interview, almost 37 percent preferred López Obrador, compared to 19 percent for Felipe Calderón. In July, López Obrador's support among these voters decreased to 31 percent, while Calderón's grew to 35 percent. López Obrador retained 58 percent of his nonpartisan supporters from wave 1, while Calderón held on to 70 percent of his. Of the 46 López Obrador defectors, 15 ultimately chose the PAN candidate and 13 became disenchanted (i.e., did not cast a ballot). Roberto Madrazo was only able to retain 26 percent of the 39 nonpartisan respondents who chose him in the first wave of the panel, and approximately equal numbers of Madrazo defectors joined the ranks of Calderón, López Obrador, and the disenchanted, with Calderón holding a slight edge. These figures confirm other data in showing a broad secular increase in support for the PAN's nominee and a broad erosion of support for the PRI's.

The ideological moderates exhibited behavior similar to that of the nonpartisans. This group, it should be noted, did not entirely overlap with the independents; only 32 percent of the self-identified ideological moderates in the first interview defined themselves as nonpartisans, while the PAN, the PRI, and the PRD each claimed 25 percent, 23 percent, and 20 percent of the identifiers, respectively. In the first wave, López Obrador drew 40 percent of these respondents, compared to 24 percent who chose Madrazo and 26 percent who selected Calderón. In the third round, however, Calderón was preferred by ideological moderates (38% versus 32% for López Obrador). Interestingly, the behavior of those respondents unable to place themselves on the ideological spectrum helped Calderón at the expense of Madrazo. López Obrador remained fairly stable with regard to this group, while Madrazo dropped from 34 percent to

17 percent, and support for the PAN nominee increased from 25 percent to 38 percent.

The last two groups to consider are the late deciders (i.e., those crystallizers who were undecided initially but made their choice in the final weeks of the campaign),[21] and the waverers. The sample size of late deciders is very small (n = 18), making it virtually impossible to draw inferences for the overall population. However, it is worth pointing out that a majority (n = 11) sided with Felipe Calderón. The waverers stand out for being the only group of switchers that preferred López Obrador over Calderón (33% to 25%). This finding suggests that López Obrador recovered some voters during the latter part of the campaign, a result consistent with the macro-level trend observed in figure 1.1.

Do these basic findings hold when other factors are taken into account? The results are presented in table 10.3. The dependent variable in model 1 measures whether the respondent switched preferences at least once during the campaign, including shifts to and from the undecided category. In model 2, the dependent variable indicates whether a party change occurred at any point. In other words, during the campaign, the respondent in this latter model should have expressed a preference for at least two different parties. (The coding of the independent variables is described in the Mexico 2006 Panel Study's supplemental materials for chapter 10.)[22]

In both models, the strongest effect was the number of political discussants holding a view other than that of the respondent. Talking about politics with people who preferred a different candidate greatly increased the likelihood of switching during the campaign. The second strongest variable was the strength of one's party identification. As expected, the more partisan respondents were less likely to change preferences. Also highly significant, although less powerful in magnitude, were the measures of political knowledge and attention to the campaign. These results provide evidence in favor of the theory of switching that has been advanced recently by Baker et al. (2006). Likewise, they support the early findings of Lazarsfeld et al. (1944) that the least informed and least aware respondents are the most likely to change preferences throughout the campaign. On the other hand, the sociodemographic variables were not significant predictors of switching. The regional dummy variables were also never significant, with one exception—the northern voters in model 1—which was at the 10 percent level.

A more intuitive way to present the results from nonlinear models—such as those used here—is to report the change in the predicted probability of the

Table 10.3   Multivariate analysis of the propensity to switch

	Model 1 All switchers	Model 2 Only party changers
Female	−0.140	0.068
	[0.098]	[0.130]
Age	0.005	−0.006
	[0.004]	[0.005]
Education	0.023	0.047
	[0.035]	[0.041]
Income	−0.032	0.005
	[0.021]	[0.026]
Union household	−0.008	0.058
	[0.089]	[0.115]
Church attendance	0.000	−0.010
	[0.049]	[0.058]
Party ID strength	−0.342***	−0.220**
	[0.061]	[0.082]
Ideological strength	−0.004	0.112*
	[0.049]	[0.060]
Attention to campaign	−0.074**	−0.090***
	[0.030]	[0.035]
Reception of information	0.001	0.036
	[0.028]	[0.028]
Political knowledge	−0.076***	−0.090***
	[0.023]	[0.027]
Discussants that disagree	0.365***	0.489***
	[0.055]	[0.073]
South	−0.232	−0.086
	[0.156]	[0.252]
Center-West	−0.057	−0.235
	[0.164]	[0.265]
Mexico City	−0.156	−0.088
	[0.155]	[0.253]
North	0.310*	0.230
	[0.161]	[0.265]
(Constant)	0.922***	0.199
	[0.330]	[0.454]
Log pseudo-likelihood	−395.52	−283.72
N	654	523

Note: The model is based on binary probit analysis. Robust standard errors are in brackets. The baseline for the regional dummies is the Central region.

*Significant at the 10% level **Significant at the 5% level ***Significant at the 1% level dependent variable assessed for a typical respondent, while certain independent variables are allowed to vary and the rest are kept fixed. In the sample of participants who completed all three waves of the panel, the median respondent was a forty-year-old woman from southern Mexico who had finished the ninth grade and went to church about once a month. As her partisan attachment changes from strongly partisan to nonpartisan, holding every other variable constant, her probability of switching increases from 17 percent to 39 percent.[23] Similarly, as the number of people with whom she discusses politics and who prefer a different candidate increases from zero to three, her probability of switching rises from 27 percent to 68 percent. These percentages underscore the strong explanatory power of the strength of party identification and interpersonal cues in shaping campaign effects.

Overall, for both models, cognitive factors such as party identification, political knowledge, and campaign awareness proved to be significant, while demographic ones did not. Education, income, and the frequency of church attendance, for example, were never statistically significant. Finally, it is important to mention the slight puzzle presented by the positive sign of ideological strength in model 2. The expectation was that a stronger ideological orientation would be negatively associated with switching. A possible explanation for the opposite result is that a significant number of solid conservatives changed their minds, likely being lured to the PAN's candidate by Calderón's campaign strategy.

Inside Voters' Minds: Part 2

Determining why voters decide to switch from one particular candidate to another is a complex issue, with a number of factors in play. Fortunately, the Mexico 2006 Panel Study included questions that allow us to draw reasonable hypotheses regarding why Felipe Calderón attracted voters from all persuasions in such high proportions, why López Obrador lost nonpartisans and ideological moderates, and why Roberto Madrazo's core party identifiers showed less loyalty. This analysis studies (1) the impact of particular events that may have shifted public opinion about one of the candidates drastically and (2) the effect of negative campaigns that focused on candidate traits (specifically, honesty and the ability to manage the economy).[24]

In February 2006, the newspaper *La Jornada* published transcriptions of telephone conversations between Puebla governor Mario Marín and businessman Kamel Nacif, who were plotting to illegally imprison journalist Lydia Cacho.[25]

The story soon became a scandal, infamously associated with the way in which Nacif referred to the PRI governor (*mi góber precioso*, literally, my precious governor). In the second wave of the panel, all respondents were asked if that incident changed their disposition to vote for the PRI's presidential nominee. Of the respondents who had preferred Madrazo in the first wave, 16.5 percent argued that the scandal made them reconsider their vote. Of these, a third ended up siding with Calderón and a third chose López Obrador, although their reported vote preferences indicate that a few remained loyal to Madrazo. Among those who were undecided in the first wave, the effect of the scandal was perhaps stronger, since 29 percent reported that after the incident they felt less inclined to vote for Madrazo. Of these 34 respondents, only one of them would ultimately decide to cast a ballot in favor of the PRI's nominee.[26]

In March 2006, López Obrador found himself in the middle of a controversy regarding his criticism of President Fox for weighing in on the campaign. López Obrador's now-famous *cállate chachalaca* (stop squawking and shut up) remark was mocked in PAN television commercials. When asked if the incident changed their intention to vote for López Obrador, 19 percent of those who supported him in October expressed having reservations after learning about the incident. Faring better than Madrazo, López Obrador managed to retain 38 percent of these voters, losing an additional 38 percent to Calderón and 9 percent to the PRI. Among those who were undecided in October, however, the impact on the PRD's hopeful was severe—47 percent of them reported feeling disinclined to vote for him. Of these 54 respondents, only 3 would eventually vote for López Obrador.

A third campaign event that may have significantly changed voters' minds was the first presidential debate, notorious for López Obrador's decision not to participate. Since the debate took place at a time when López Obrador was slipping in the polls, he may have missed an opportunity to communicate directly with the people and relaunch his campaign message. Yet looking at the descriptive statistics suggests that the effects of the first presidential debate were more in the form of reinforcement. Of the people who reported watching or listening to at least part of the debate (43% of the respondents), Calderón, Madrazo, and López Obrador retained similar percentages of respondents from October to July as they did for those who were not exposed to the event. Calderón did better, however, in attracting those undecideds in the first round who did watch or listen to the debate.[27] Thus the debate failed to reverse Calderón's momentum but it did not doom López Obrador's candidacy.

In terms of the impact of negative advertising, two campaign strategies are worth comparing: the PAN's effort to present López Obrador as an irresponsible populist who would mismanage the economy, and the PRD's attempt to associate Calderón with alleged wrongdoings committed by his brother-in-law's company, Hildebrando Corporation.[28] The cross-tabulations indicate that the PAN was considerably more successful in reaching voters with its message. For instance, of the respondents who preferred López Obrador in October 2005 but abandoned him between then and May 2006, the percentage of people thinking that he was "very" or "somewhat" capable of managing the economy decreased from 73 percent to 34 percent. The PRD's attacks, first launched during the second presidential debate, were considerably less successful; among those who left Calderón between May and July, the percentage that deemed him "very" or "somewhat" honest declined only slightly. In other words, those leaving Calderón toward the end of the race seem to have had reasons other than concerns about his integrity.

Finally, it is worth considering the possible effect of strategic voting in respondents' decisions to switch from one candidate to another. Strategic voters, in the context of the 2006 election, would be those who abandoned Madrazo in favor of López Obrador or Calderón primarily because they anticipated a loss by their preferred candidate and considered it best to support their second choice in a close election.[29] However, discerning a strategic voter from a persuaded voter is difficult. Moreover, strategic voting can certainly be measured in different ways. Magaloni and Poiré (2004b), in their study of the 2000 presidential election, regard strategic voters as all those who identified with the third-place party (in that case, the PRD) during the first wave and eventually voted for either of the front-runner candidates. This method, however, risks lumping strategic and persuaded voters in the same category.

In this chapter, voters are considered to have been in a "potential strategic voting situation" if they chose Madrazo in the second wave of the panel and then placed Madrazo above or equal to both Calderón and López Obrador in the feeling thermometer scales in the final wave. That is, a prerequisite for strategic voting is for respondents to still express a preference for the candidate that appears to be out of contention at the time of the election (or, in the case of the third and final wave, two weeks later), despite voting for someone else. Accordingly, actual strategic voters are those who, finding themselves in a potentially strategic situation, cast their ballots for Calderón or for López Obrador.[30]

The panel data reveal that a total of 117 respondents (approximately 14%

of the sample that completed all three waves) found themselves in such a situation. Of these, six voted for López Obrador, four voted for Calderón, and 90 stayed with Madrazo. Hence the number of strategic voters was rather miniscule compared with the total electorate (around 1%), and these voters appear to have broken fairly evenly between Calderón and López Obrador. There is, to put it mildly, little evidence that strategic voting influenced the outcome of the election.

Switchers and the 2006 Campaign

Micro-level analysis of who switched and why provides insights into macro-level trends during the 2006 presidential campaign. The *New York Times* story mentioned in the introduction to this chapter speculated that López Obrador would win unless he "stumbled spectacularly." Although López Obrador failed to win, did that actually happen?

The data presented here show a clear trend. López Obrador was able to hold on to his core party supporters, but he suffered moderate losses among nonpartisans and moderates. His decline was not spectacular. What was impressive, on the other hand, was Calderón's ability to attract voters of all ideologies, parties, and demographic characteristics.

Calderón held a structural advantage over López Obrador, since the number of PAN sympathizers far surpassed that of the PRD. As the campaign progressed, both candidates retained the support of a vast majority of their party faithful, but Calderón had a much larger pool of people from which to draw votes. The evidence at hand also suggests that Calderón's message resonated much better among undecideds, centrists, and nonpartisans than did that of his principal rival. In addition, Calderón's attempts to portray López Obrador as an authoritarian leader destined to bankrupt the country probably persuaded enough potential switchers to overcome the former's disadvantage early on in the polls.

An important question is why so many Madrazo defectors were persuaded to vote for Calderón over López Obrador. Part of the explanation, once again, is structural, determined before the campaigns began in earnest. Of all the PRI identifiers in October, nearly 30 percent placed themselves on the right of the ideological spectrum, whereas only 13 percent located themselves on the left. As PRI partisans scrambled to find an alternative to their party's nominee, it appears that many more were predisposed to choose the conservative candidate.

Other chapters in this volume speak directly to the question of why voters decided to cast their ballots for Calderón, López Obrador, or Madrazo, and why they may have switched from one choice to another. Chapter 11, for example, highlights the role that economic considerations played late in the campaign for a specific segment of the electorate; chapter 12 examines the impact of social programs in voters' decision making. Chapter 13 emphasizes the importance of a candidate's personality and image to capture votes, whereas chapter 14 argues that ideology was an important predictor of voting preferences. Each of these perspectives provides important insights on what occurred in the voters' minds, and together they offer a comprehensive explanation of the campaign dynamics of 2006 and the general trends of Mexican voting behavior.

In terms of which voters switched during the campaign, however, the pattern is fairly straightforward. Those citizens with weak partisan attachments, and those who discussed politics with people who were going to vote for a different candidate, were overwhelmingly more likely to change their minds. This result is testimony to the importance of cognitive and social factors in shaping public opinion. Perhaps most importantly, it underscores the fact that both structural factors and campaign dynamics played a role in the outcome of the election.

The 2006 Campaign and Latin American Electoral Politics

In comparative terms, the Mexican election of 2006 stood out in Latin America, due to the fact that, contrary to forecasts, the conservative candidate triumphed. However, Mexico was not the only country where the candidate who originally led in the polls was overtaken by a competitor of a different ideological persuasion. In Peru, for example, conservative candidate Lourdes Flores saw her early advantage disappear, and she was relegated to third place in the first-round election in April 2006. Similarly, only one month prior to the runoff contest in November of that same year in Ecuador, conservative candidate Álvaro Noboa lost the fifteen-point lead that he had enjoyed in public opinion surveys.

In contrast, Brazilian president Luiz Inácio Lula da Silva retained his early advantage in his 2006 re-election campaign, despite the corruption scandals that surfaced involving high-ranking members of his administration and the Workers' Party (PT), as well as the controversy surrounding his decision not to participate in the presidential debates (Nicolau 2008). In fact, Lula's ability to overcome corruption allegations was reminiscent of López Obrador's. The challenge for Lula was perhaps more difficult, since one of the scandals occurred only two weeks prior to the election. Having little time for a recovery, he still was able to contain a potential increase in support for his main opponent, Geraldo Alckmin. Unlike the circumstances in Mexico, Peru, and Ecuador, the switching that occurred in Brazil was not enough to change the outcome of the election.

In order to understand why some campaigns witnessed greater levels of switching, the differences among countries' electoral rules must be kept in mind. When a runoff election is held, opportunities for strategic voting become more salient, especially if one candidate is perceived as being particularly extremist. In this situation, strategic switching was presumably strongest in Peru, where high numbers of conservative voters are believed to have switched from Lourdes Flores to Alan García in an effort to prevent the more radical Ollanta Humala from reaching office. In Nicaragua, electoral rules also played a role, but they did so by preventing potential strategic voting. In that country, a recently approved electoral reform had made it possible for a candidate to win the presidency with less than 40 percent of the vote in the first round, allowing Daniel Ortega of the Sandinista Party to avoid facing an alliance of conservative voters in a second round (Lean 2007).

Although more detailed analyses, using panel data, are necessary to pass judgment on the dynamics of these elections, recent voting results in Latin America further suggest that switching during electoral campaigns is, indeed, the result of the interplay between partisanship and campaign events. A strong partisan base can attenuate the effects of campaign errors, as voters may be willing to give some candidates a second or even a third chance throughout the race. For candidates from weaker parties—as was the case for López Obrador—mistakes can be more costly. When facing a clever opponent who adopts the right campaign strategy, they can be lethal.

CHAPTER ELEVEN

The Activation of Economic Voting in the 2006 Campaign

Alejandro Moreno

One of the most striking developments in Mexico's 2006 presidential race was the way leftist challenger Andrés Manuel López Obrador lost his substantial lead over the incumbent party's candidate, Felipe Calderón. This decline has been attributed to tactical errors, such as not attending the first of two televised presidential debates and engaging in constant mudslinging with President Vicente Fox. It has also been attributed to attacks on López Obrador by Calderón, the National Action Party (PAN), and its allies in the business community. This chapter offers a more formal explanation that does not conflict with, but rather supports the role of many of these campaign events; specifically, I argue that campaign discourse and events linked the economy to candidate preferences. Unlike in 2000, when Vicente Fox called for political change after 70 years of Institutional Revolutionary Party (PRI) rule, the PAN candidate in 2006 offered economic stability and the continuation of current policies; he called for no change and voters answered.

The most basic evidence of economic voting in the 2006 presidential election is that the governing party's candidate benefited from favorable views about the economy, whereas his leftist challenger was heavily supported by voters who perceived Mexico's economic performance as poor. This is straightforward economic voting. My goal here is more ambitious; I attempt to link changes in voters' preferences to evaluations of economic conditions. Based on the first and third waves of the Mexico 2006 Panel Study[1] (conducted in October 2005 and July 2006), I argue that the campaign activated voters' assessments of the economy, strengthening the relationship between favorable economic views and the PAN vote. This dynamic allowed Calderón to attract enough votes to win the most closely contested presidential race in Mexico's history.

Theoretical Expectations

The literature on economic voting has successfully linked individual opinions about the economy with vote choices (Fiorina 1981; Kinder and Kiewiet 1981) and actual macroeconomic behavior with election outcomes (Lewis-Beck 1988). According to Lewis-Beck, "what gives meaning to the foregoing statistical associations between economics and elections is the underlying belief that individual citizens react systematically to economic stimuli at the ballot box" (30). As Alesina and Roubini argue, "voters like growth and dislike inflation and unemployment. They are retrospective: They vote in favor of the incumbent if the economy is doing well (low unemployment and inflation, high growth) during his term of office" (1999, 19).

This rational behavior, to use Alesina and Roubini's term, is likely to take place on two levels. First, voters tend to support an incumbent party when they perceive—or have benefited from—good economic performance. Second, politicians mobilize support on the basis of economic performance. If the economy is doing well (many times as a result of government stimulation before elections), the incumbent party's candidate would presumably seek to remind voters of recent economic achievements, such as financial stability, low inflation, low unemployment, and so on. If the economy is doing poorly, a challenger would have more incentives to mobilize support by priming the government's economic failure. This represents a "relationship between politicians' *opportunistic* behavior and rational *opportunistic* voting" (Alesina and Roubini 1999, 9; italics mine).

My main argument is that, on the one hand, the Calderón campaign mobilized political support by focusing on economic issues, and, on the other, voters who evaluated the economy positively responded favorably to Calderón's messages. The Calderón campaign worked, not because he convinced an increasing number of voters that the economy was doing well, but because he convinced voters who already thought so to cast a vote for him, not for López Obrador. If we consider the rational expectation of economic voting—that economically satisfied voters reward the incumbent party—as a theoretically expected predisposition among voters, campaigns effects related to economic reasoning are not necessarily about persuasion, but about activation. This means that voters who evaluate the economy favorably are simply asked to come out and vote for the incumbent party candidate and, as I will show later, Mexican voters under such characteristics responded accordingly.

The concept of activation dates back to studies of voting in the 1940s. As Paul Lazarsfeld and his colleagues put it, "political campaigns are important primarily because they *activate* latent predispositions" (Lazarsfeld et al. 1944, 74). Using an activation model, Finkel argued that in the American presidential elections of 1984 and 1988, "campaigns served mainly to activate existing political predispositions and make them electorally relevant" (1993, 1). Later, Finkel and Schrott reported that, in the German election of 1990, "the dominant effects of the campaign on German voters . . . were the 'reinforcement' of earlier preferences and the 'activation' of latent vote dispositions" (1995, 349). More recently, Larry Bartels has elaborated on the differentiation between persuasion and activation. "Campaigns matter," he argues, "*because* they tend to produce congruence between fundamental political conditions and predispositions on the one hand and vote intentions on the other. This supposition is supported by survey-based findings on political activation" (2006, 79–80; italics in the original).

The notion of activation presupposes that, when a predisposition or belief is activated, it follows its natural (or theoretically expected) relationship with another variable, in this case, with candidate support. One obvious example would be a liberal voter who supports a liberal candidate after he or she had previously considered voting for a conservative one. Activation, not persuasion, is what sometimes explains the discrepancies between the standings of the candidates in the early polls and the final election results (Bartels 2006; Gelman and King 1993). Following this logic, one feature of the 2006 Mexican presidential race is how voters who evaluated the economy in favorable ways increased their support for the incumbent party candidate during the campaign season, thereby reducing the early ten- to fifteen-point disadvantage that he had in the polls.

The panel data shown in this chapter provide clear evidence of the increase in support for Calderón among economically positive voters (i.e., those who held favorable evaluations of the economy), rising from 35 percent in October 2005 to 57 percent in July 2006. But that fact alone is not sufficient to make the argument for economic activation. It is also necessary to demonstrate four other conditions. First, objective economic conditions must have been favorable enough for the PAN to pursue an economically oriented campaign (otherwise, such a campaign would be neither rational nor opportunistic, to use Alesina and Roubini's terms). Second, the PAN campaign must have consciously attempted to activate economic voting (as expected in a rational opportunistic model). Third, the increase in PAN support among economically optimistic voters must not have been the result of an increase in the number of voters in that group. Fourth, this increase in support among those voters must have affected only the incumbent party candidate, rather than opposition candidates (in which case, arguing in favor of activation would be nonsensical). The following sections address these issues and provide the data and analyses that support the argument that economic voting activation took place in the 2006 presidential campaigns.

The Economy, Public Opinion, and Voting

Despite overwhelming evidence that economic voting is a predictable pattern in advanced democracies, establishing a relationship between economics and election outcomes has not been an easy task in Mexico. For example, Magaloni (2006) found a positive but rather weak relationship between support for the dominant party and economic growth from the 1940s to 2000. Moreover, she argues that individual-level data from the late 1980s and 1990s are ambiguous with respect to typical economic voting, concluding that "a theory of retrospective voting does not adequately account either for support of an incumbent during recession or mediocre economic performance, as shown by Mexican voters between 1985 and 1994, or for voters turning against the incumbent despite an objective improvement of economic conditions, as Mexicans did in 1997 and 2000" (2006, 85). The 2006 presidential election seems an exception to that ambiguous pattern. Economic voting did play a significant role in 2006 (Moreno 2006, 2007), and campaign messages are very likely to have activated voters' economic reasoning.

During the Fox administration (2000–6), Mexico's economy behaved in two very different ways. The first three years were characterized by null growth and increasing unemployment.[2] In contrast, from 2004 to 2006, economic growth resumed, formal employment rose, consumption of durable goods took off, housing development peaked, and—something new for most Mexican families—consumer credit flourished. Skyrocketing international oil prices gave the Mexican government ample and unexpected new revenues (Moreno 2007).

Public opinion surveys accurately reflect the country's economic slump and recovery from 2000 to 2006. As growth in the GDP approached zero in 2001, public opinion became increasingly pessimistic. Those who thought the economy had worsened in comparison to the previous year outnumbered those who thought it had improved (see figure 11.1). However, as the economy started to take off in 2004, public opinion became increasingly optimistic, mirroring the

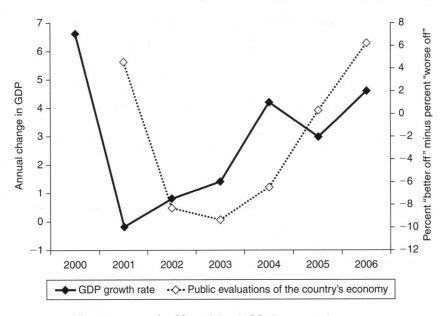

Figure 11.1 The economy and public opinion in Mexico, 2000–6.
Source: INEGI for GDP, and *Reforma*, national quarterly face-to-face polls, yearly averages.

pattern of economic recovery with correspondingly favorable evaluations about the economy.

On election day, economic evaluations were strongly related to candidate support. According to national exit poll data gathered by the newspaper *Reforma* on July 2, 2006, López Obrador carried most of the economically dissatisfied votes. About 47 percent of those who thought the national economy was somewhat worse than the previous year, and 58 percent of those who deemed it much worse, voted for the Party of the Democratic Revolution (PRD) candidate (see table 11.1). In contrast, Felipe Calderón only got 17 percent and 9 percent of the vote among those same groups. Nonetheless, the PAN candidate did superbly well among economically optimistic voters, attracting a clear majority; he garnered 74 percent of the vote among those who thought the economy was in much better shape compared to the previous year, and 58 percent among those who said it was somewhat better off. López Obrador received 12 percent and 23 percent of the votes among those two groups, respectively. Calderón's ratio of victory over López Obrador was almost 7 to 1 among the most economically optimistic voters—who represented 9 percent of the respondents in

Table 11.1   Retrospective economic evaluations and presidential vote choice in 2006 (in percentages)

	Vote choice		
	López Obrador	Madrazo	Calderón
National economy compared to previous year			
Much better	12	11	74
Somewhat better	23	16	58
About the same	41	25	30
Somewhat worse	47	29	17
Much worse	58	29	9
Personal economy compared to previous year			
Much better	14	12	70
Somewhat better	22	16	58
About the same	41	24	31
Somewhat worse	49	30	15
Much worse	55	32	8

Source: Reforma, national exit poll, July 2, 2006, $N = 5,515$.

the exit poll—and almost 3 to 1 among the moderately optimistic ones, who formed 24 percent of the sample. In total, economically optimistic voters represented 33 percent of the actual voting population in 2006, compared to 24 percent six years earlier (according to a similar national exit poll conducted by *Reforma* in 2000). Economically dissatisfied voters in 2006 stood at 17 percent, down from 28 percent in the 2000 election. Previous work has confirmed that economic evaluations were one of the most significant explanatory variables of individual vote choice in 2006, coming second only to party identification (Moreno 2006).

Economic evaluations per se did not change significantly during the months of the presidential campaigns, as evidenced by the Mexico 2006 Panel Study (see table 11.2). Positive evaluations of the national economy represented 45 and 42 percent, respectively, in the first and third rounds, or waves, of interviews (October 2005 and July 2006), whereas the proportion of positive evaluations about personal economic conditions were 31 and 30 percent.[3] This variation indicates a slight deterioration in voters' economic assessments, but it is not significant. Thus the panel data show that views about the economy remained rather stable from October 2005 to July 2006.[4] This means that the impact of the national economy on the vote cannot be attributed to changes in the proportion of voters who expressed positive views about the economy; changes in political prefer-

Table 11.2   Retrospective economic evaluations in waves 1 and 3 of the Mexico 2006 Panel Study (in percentages)

	October 2005	July 2006
National economy since Fox in office		
Much better	10	8
Somewhat better	35	34
About the same	39	45
Somewhat worse	7	5
Much worse	6	5
Don't know	3	3
Personal economy since Fox in office		
Much better	6	5
Somewhat better	25	25
About the same	53	58
Somewhat worse	8	6
Much worse	6	5
Don't know	2	1

Source: Mexico 2006 Panel Study, national sample, waves 1 (*N* = 1,600) and 3 (*N* = 1,067).

ences took place despite the stability in their perceptions about the country's economic conditions. In other words, the Calderón campaign did not convince voters that the economy was better off (although there were indeed improvements in the immediate months prior to the election); it only convinced those who thought so to vote for him (or not to vote for López Obrador).[5]

But who were the economically satisfied and dissatisfied voters? Was there any underlying socioeconomic basis for their satisfaction/dissatisfaction? The panel study shows that socioeconomic variables do not relate to economic evaluations as much as political identity variables do. For example, a composite index of socioeconomic status based on household equipment, considering eight items (television, radio, cable TV, stove with an oven, refrigerator, washing machine, automobile, and personal computer), does not show a significant relationship with the respondents' economic evaluations. Neither do indicators of income, occupation, or benefits from social programs. In a multivariate model, age is the only demographic variable that moderately relates to economic views—the older the respondent, the more negative the assessments of the economy he or she expresses—and education was statistically significant in the first round of interviews but not in the third wave. Unlike the lack of explanatory power from the sociodemographic variables, party identification was a strong predictor of the economic evaluations in the survey: PAN identifiers expressed favorable views of the economy, whereas PRD identifiers provided negative evaluations (PRI identifiers did not show any significant relationship between party affiliation and their views about the economy). This partisan bias of economic evaluations will require further research. Wlezien et al. (1997) have suggested that economic perceptions are to some extent structured by vote choice, so endogenous factors (i.e., *endogeneity*) create a significant problem. But the fact that positive and negative views of the economy showed such a strong partisan component provides further evidence of activation of prior political predispositions. It is not just economic reasoning that is activated during the course of a campaign, but partisan-based economic reasoning.

The evidence shown here supports two of the claims stated in the preceding section: claim one, that objective economic conditions were sufficiently favorable for the PAN to reasonably pursue an economically oriented campaign, and claim three, that an increase in PAN support among economically optimistic voters is not a result of an increase in the proportion of the latter during the campaign. The following section will address claim two, that the PAN campaign attempted to activate economic voting.

The PAN Campaign: From Values to Economics

From March to June 2006, the PAN presidential candidate concentrated on economic issues, calling on voters to support economic stability and the continuation of most of Fox's economic policies. Calderón asked voters not to vote for a leftist candidate who could jeopardize the economy, calling López Obrador a "danger to the country." He thus framed the election as a choice between a future of economic stability and employment, on the one hand, or a return to a past of economic crisis and debt, on the other.

However, this was not always Calderón's central message. He had won the PAN caucuses of party members by running on the issues of integrity and moral values. One of Calderón slogans in his primary campaign—"clean hands"— attempted to portray him as an honest man, as a rare Mexican politician with (as another slogan put it) "courage and passion for Mexico." In the primary, he drew on the support of conservative PAN followers to defeat President Fox's former interior minister, Santiago Creel, who, according to most polls at the time, enjoyed broader support among the electorate as a whole. In a speech delivered on October 23, 2005, after he clinched his party's presidential nomination, Calderón called his primary efforts "the campaign of principles and values, the campaign of a firm hand and passion for Mexico" (Calderón 2006, 17). In another speech given when he accepted the presidential nomination, on December 4, 2005, Calderón referred to his campaign as an alliance in defense of values and said that he would "continue basing his campaign on the strength of those values and ideas" (Calderón 2006, 39). He maintained a conservative message during the first few weeks of the general election campaign, in January and February 2006, when he was trailing López Obrador by ten to fifteen points in the polls. In a nationally televised interview with Televisa network's main news anchor, Joaquín López Dóriga, Calderón took a conservative stance on several social issues, such as abortion and contraception.

Messages based on moral issues and family values did not seem to attract additional support for the PAN candidate in the general election campaign. In a sudden shift of strategy in early March, Calderón publicly announced that his campaign messages were mistaken, and that his campaign staff was making him say and do things he did not mean. This shift made more than one political commentator think that Calderón's campaign was doomed; it seemed just a matter of time for López Obrador to be elected president. Nonetheless, driven by Calderón's new messages, the economy arose as a crucial issue in the following months, changing the campaign dynamics and, ultimately, the election result.

A journalistic account of how the Calderón campaign team chose economics over other issues illustrates this shift.

> The campaign was at a dead point in February; [Dick] Morris . . . made the suggestion to adopt the issue of crime, but others in the team fought for economic issues. As the arguments on both sides were equally passionate, they agreed to conduct a poll . . . to determine which of the two issues mattered most to citizens. It resulted in a document known as "Adjusted Strategy," which made it clear, once again, that they had to stick to the economy as their issue. That research also helped them decide that, in addition to [portraying] Calderón as the "President of employment," they also had to link Andrés Manuel López Obrador with the word "Debt," not "Crisis" as others had wanted, so the effect was stronger . . . The definitive shift toward economics as their campaign theme had the tremendous advantage that it was an area in which Calderón felt very comfortable. Moreover, that decision left behind a strategy based on attributes (clean hands). (Camarena and Zepeda Patterson 2007, 114; translation mine)

The PAN candidate's new strategy focused on economic stability and jobs. On March 14, 2006, Calderón officially launched what his team called the second phase of the campaign. The following part of his speech clearly illustrates this shift from values to economics.

> Principles and values do not change. Principles and values have to do precisely with who we are; what changes are the circumstances, the moments . . . It is important to always be willing to revise and to change strategies, and that is what we are doing . . . We Mexicans want a better standard of living . . . We can and we will have a better standard of living through employment; that is why I am going to be the president of employment in our country . . . For us to have a better standard of living we need jobs, not debt; we need employment, not economic crisis; and we need a president that knows how to lead Mexico into the future. I will lead Mexico into the future. (Calderón 2006, 150–51; translation mine)[6]

The continuation of Fox's economic policies also became a central feature of the new strategy—messages that Fox himself reinforced during the campaign. López Obrador was portrayed as a populist who would increase Mexico's debt and plunge Mexico back into economic crises. The PAN campaign framed the election in terms of the idea that Mexico had achieved financial stability and economic growth, and that voting for López Obrador was not worth the risk.

At first, the label "a danger to Mexico" seemed to have political implications; López Obrador was portrayed as an intolerant and undemocratic man. In a political rally, he told President Fox "*cállate chachalaca*" (stop squawking and shut up), an episode that was taped and aired repeatedly in PAN ads. Another PAN television ad compared the leftist candidate to Venezuela's President Hugo Chávez and asked viewers "Is this the type of authoritarian we want to elect?" As the campaigns developed, it became clearer that labeling López Obrador a "danger to the country" had more economic implications than political ones, and that economic stability, not democracy, was supposedly at stake if he won the election. The 2006 presidential race was ultimately about economic conditions and economic policies. Campaign messages helped mobilize voters, not by convincing Mexicans that the economy was better off, but by convincing those who thought it was better to vote for the PAN candidate. Hence messages appealing to economic conservatism worked for the PAN.

Let us briefly review the contents of some PAN television ads.[7] This one aired before the first presidential debate (in which, as noted above, López Obrador declined to participate):

VOICE-OVER, OFF CAMERA: López Obrador made an economic mess in the Federal District; he achieved the highest unemployment rate and last place in economic growth in the nation. No wonder he doesn't want to debate! But, how do you create better jobs and salaries? Watch the debate, Felipe Calderón will tell you.

Another ad linked López Obrador to government debt:

VOICE-OVER, OFF CAMERA: The only thing López Obrador knows how to do is increase our debt.

A YOUNG WOMAN SPEAKS: Because of him, our families in the Federal District owe more than 23 thousand pesos each.

FELIPE CALDERÓN's VOICE: We Mexicans want peaceful progress, and I know how [to get it]: creating jobs, not debt; bringing investment, not economic crisis.

Calderón's offer of economic stability was usually accompanied by direct or indirect attacks on his main opponent. This dichotomy is illustrated in the following statement, in which Calderón asked what Mexicans would pass onto their children: "Are we going to give them a stable economy where they can find jobs when they grow up, or an economy in crisis like in the past, full of debts?" (quoted in *Reforma*, May 1, 2006).

President Fox continuously joined in with the strategy, praising the state of the economy, calling for continuity, and criticizing the leftist candidate without mentioning his name. "We Mexicans will make sure," Fox said in mid-May, "that we choose a good president, the best one for things to keep going, so that everything good that there is in the country continues . . . Populism, demagoguery, is a cheat; unbalanced public finances are a cheat; corruption is a cheat" (quoted in *Reforma*, May 16, 2006). Later that same month, Fox stated that "it is indispensable to maintain budgetary discipline, to avoid spending one more cent that is not part of our income; we do not want to increase the country's debt . . . Mexico has left its difficult years, now we have solid economic growth with stability and no inflation" (quoted in *Reforma*, June 3, 2006). References to populism evoked López Obrador's policies of cash transfers to the poor and the elderly in Mexico City. On May 25, President Fox said in a public speech that "there is no better social policy than that of creating jobs, and no better way to fight poverty than generating wealth. That is why demagoguery and populism do not better people's lives" (quoted in *Reforma*, May 25, 2006). Fox delivered the paramount economic argument on June 10, 2006, reminding voters that the economy was doing well: "We have 24 or 25 days until election day, and nobody would have thought that the economy was growing, that we were creating jobs, and that this is the best moment the economy has had in the last five years" (quoted in *Reforma*, June 10, 2006).

The PAN framed the election, as Calderón succinctly put it, as a choice "between economic stability and an unstoppable spiral of economic crisis" (quoted in *El Universal*, May 3, 2006). A striking fact is that López Obrador did not react to this strategy based on economic issues. His efforts to focus on the poor (*primero los pobres*, first, the poor) throughout the campaign—even at the expense of the rich and privileged—did not help him maintain his early advantage in the polls. (This result was surprising in a country where 40 million people live in poverty, and I will return to it in the following section.) López Obrador's reactions centered on critical exchanges with President Fox and denigration of the PAN candidate, whom he called a *pelele* (nobody). During the most intense period of attacks, in May, when polls started to show the gap between the two candidates closing, López Obrador would argue that he was leading the race by ten points. López Obrador attacked Calderón directly in the second debate, calling attention to allegedly questionable contracts that the government had awarded to his brother-in-law's private company, some of which were presumably granted during Calderón's tenure as secretary of energy.

In sum, Calderon's call for stability and his attacks on the leftist candidate as a threat to it were effective, because the Mexican economy had performed relatively well in the second half of the Fox administration. Indeed, there were objective reasons to support Calderón's campaign claims of economic continuity. Importantly, economic factors were not as politically influential before the campaigns as they were on election day. This fact indicates that voters were mobilized to a great extent by economic arguments.

Apparently, López Obrador's image as a "danger to the country" resonated with Mexicans who prized economic stability. Many of them had recently used their credit to purchase durable goods, automobiles, or housing. Mortgages became a new commodity in the Mexican electoral market, and mortgage holders were likely to cast an economically conservative vote in 2006. But they were not the only ones. Calderón obtained a disproportionate share of the vote among Mexicans who expressed positive evaluations of economic conditions, both national and personal, regardless of any direct economic benefit.

Changes in Candidate Support by Economic Evaluations

Observing campaign effects is not an easy task, and it may require measuring several information-related variables, such as the level of media exposure, selective attention to messages, and an analysis of "reception gaps" on persuasion (Zaller 1996). This chapter argues that economic voting in the 2006 Mexican presidential race resembles an activation effect more than a persuasion one. Evidence provided by the Mexico 2006 Panel Study allows us to show changes in political preferences in a relatively simple way, through the respondents' positive and negative views about the economy. While the latter remained stable throughout the campaign, the political preferences linked with each economic view varied significantly. Voters who evaluated the economy favorably increased their support for Calderón and reduced it for López Obrador. In contrast, voters who rated the economy negatively increased their support for the leftist candidate.

In October 2005, when the first panel wave was conducted, there was already a positive relationship between economic assessments and support for Calderón, but it was rather moderate compared to the linkage observed by the end of the campaign. Only 6 percent of those who expressed negative views of the economy in October 2005 supported Calderón, a proportion that increased to 14 percent among those who perceived no changes in the economy, and to 35 percent among those who perceived economic improvement during the Fox administration. This positive relationship was remarkably stronger by July 2006, as shown by the postelection round of interviews. Support for Calderón among economic pessimists remained low, at 7 percent, but self-reported votes for the PAN candidate had grown substantially among the other two categories: 24 percent among those who perceived no economic change, and 57 percent among those who perceived better economic conditions (see figure 11.2). The twenty-nine-point gap between economically satisfied and economically dissatisfied voters observed in October 2005 increased to a fifty-point gap by July 2006. In addition, Calderón also gained support (a net ten-point favorable shift) among those who did not perceive any economic changes. This finding suggests that Calderón attracted mainly voters who saw economic improvement, as well as many who thought there was stasis. Although López Obrador obtained more total votes than Calderón in the no-perceived-change segment, the PRD candidate was not able to mobilize many more additional votes in his favor amongst this sector during the course of the campaign. The net gain for

Calderón, then, was observed among economically satisfied and economically indifferent voters.

Support for López Obrador behaved in an analogous way. The panel study confirms a negative relationship between the leftist vote and positive economic evaluations before the campaigns, and an even stronger negative relationship after the election (see figure 11.2). Support for López Obrador increased significantly, from 49 percent to 64 percent, among those respondents who thought the country's economy had deteriorated during the Fox administration. In contrast, support for the leftist candidate dropped moderately, from 26 percent to 20 percent, among those who perceived better economic conditions. Despite this drop, López Obrador was able to maintain about a fifth of the vote among economically satisfied voters. The support gap for López Obrador between economically satisfied and dissatisfied voters was twenty-three points in October 2005, but it increased to forty-four points by July. The net shift in this gap was twenty-one points, the same that Calderón had. These data show that the months of campaigns tilted economically dissatisfied support toward López Obrador and economically satisfied support toward Calderón at almost the same rate, as if it was a zero-sum game. But, most importantly, this shift in preferences corresponds to theoretical expectations about economic voting, and it provides evidence of the activation of voters' politically relevant predispositions.

These changes in candidate support, broken down by economic evaluations, are based on the total national sample of the panel study. As mentioned earlier, party identification is one of the main predictors of economic assessments in this study, having a much more significant effect on them than income, occupation, and even benefits from government programs—variables that, surprisingly, have little influence on economic evaluations. The activation of economic reasoning during the campaign would be expected to be particularly strong among partisans. But what about independents? Hillygus and Jackman suggest that "responsiveness to campaign events is greatest among Independents, undecided voters, and 'mismatched partisans'" (2003, 583). The panel data also show that the nonpartisan electorate actually responded to the economic framework of the campaign in a fashion similar to the electorate at large, and even economically satisfied independents swung from left to right in their voting preference. Recalculating figure 11.2, but considering only independent voters (an item not shown here for reasons of space), indicates that support for López Obrador increased by ten points (from 51% to 61% between October 2005 and July 2006) among economically dissatisfied voters; it remained stable among those who

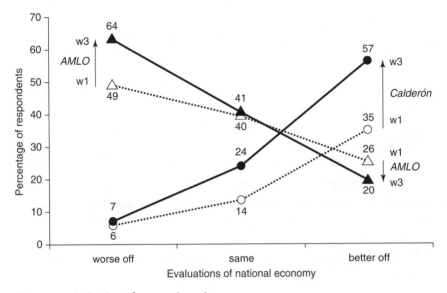

Figure 11.2 Activation of economic voting.

Note: Support for Felipe Calderón and for Andrés Manuel López Obrador (AMLO) according to economic evaluations in wave 1 (w1, during October 2005) and wave 3 (w3, during July 2006) of the Mexico 2006 Panel Study.

perceived no economic change; and it dropped nine points (from 44% to 35%) among the economically satisfied voters. In contrast, Calderón's vote increased twenty points among the latter (from 29% to 49%) and eight points among voters who perceived neither economic improvement nor deterioration (from 22% to 30%). The PAN candidate only lost two points among the economically dissatisfied independent voters (from 16% to 14%).

The most revealing finding in this analysis of independents is that Calderón was able to reverse an early disadvantage among economically satisfied, nonpartisan voters. Whereas the PAN candidate was ahead of López Obrador among the economically satisfied electorate in October 2005, he was nonetheless trailing the leftist candidate among independents who evaluated the economy favorably. That same month, the PAN candidate had a fifteen-point disadvantage among independent voters who had positive views of the economy. By July, however, there were more of the latter supporting Calderón than López Obrador, with a positive fourteen-point difference. These data show that economic reasoning was activated—and observed—even when partisan biases were removed. The other observation with respect to independent voters is that Calderón closed his disadvantage gap among those who did not perceive changes in the economic situation, from twenty-six points in October to sixteen points in July.

Candidate images also changed in significant ways from one round of survey interviews to another, providing evidence of how priming the economy played out in favor of Calderón. Holding economic evaluations constant on wave 1 (October 2005) of the panel study, feeling thermometer differentials show significant changes favorable to Felipe Calderón in general, but most notably among those who evaluated the economy in positive terms. Regardless of how voters rated the economy, López Obrador was significantly more popular than Calderón in the first round of interviews—although the economically satisfied respondents were almost indifferent toward both of them. By May and July 2006, Calderón had reduced the gap between himself and his PRD opponent among the economically dissatisfied respondents and actually led in opinion scores among those who perceived improvement or no change. The panel data show that changes in candidate image, when controlling for economic evaluations, are significant, even when holding the latter constant in the first round of interviews. In other words, these data are confirming evidence that economically satisfied individuals became increasingly supportive of Calderón (and less likely to back López Obrador) as the campaign progressed.

One final piece of evidence about economic reasoning is related to *issue ownership*—that is, how competencies on some issues were attributed to candidates throughout the campaign. López Obrador centered his campaign messages on fighting poverty, whereas Calderón emphasized economic stability and jobs. In its three waves of interviews, the panel study asked respondents which issues they thought each candidate was paying the most attention to. In October 2005 and May 2006, the percent of respondents who mentioned that López Obrador focused on poverty was only 5 percent and 10 percent, respectively, and it doubled to 21 percent on July. The relatively low percentages that resulted in the first two rounds of interviews indicate that, despite the leftist candidate's efforts to get a message across about the country's poor, only a small proportion of the voters actually said that he was focused on that particular issue. In May, a similar proportion of voters who perceived López Obrador as paying attention to poverty also thought of him as paying attention to unemployment (10%). There was no clear issue ownership in this pre-election wave of interviews. Respondents made a much clearer connection between López Obrador and the poverty issue in the postelection round, when 21 percent of them said that it was the PRD candidate's most important campaign topic.

Calderón's ties to the unemployment issue were weak when perceptions were measured in the first round of interviews (only 2% of the respondents in October 2005 said that the PAN candidate was paying the most attention to unemployment), but they grew stronger in the second and third rounds (when 23% and 29%, respectively, made that same connection). The proportion of voters who linked the PAN candidate with the poverty issue remained low, around 2 or 3 percent in all three panel waves. Calderón was simply not associated with that issue, but he held the field with respect to unemployment.

These data on issue ownership provide some evidence of what Bartels (2006) calls the "priming of economic perceptions." During the course of the campaigns, not only was Calderón increasingly associated with fighting unemployment (as a reflection of his economically oriented messages), but the attacks on López Obrador had a negative result for the leftist candidate, preventing voters from affiliating him with competence in the battle against poverty, especially before the election took place. According to Bartels, "occasionally, campaign events do seem to prime an electoral consideration where one party or the other enjoys a marked advantage in the distribution of opinion in the electorate" (91). It appears that Calderón's image of economic competence grew in importance as the campaign went on. To what extent this is a result of priming and, moreover, how this explains the election outcome, are questions that remain unsolved. Based on the American National Election Studies from 1980 to 2000, Bartels argues that, "for the most part, campaign priming seems to be a matter of academic interest to political psychologists, not a major factor in determining the outcome of a presidential election" (92). However, the fact that these findings from Mexico derive from panel data, and not from cross-section samples, provides solid evidence for economic voting activation. The results shown in this chapter indicate (1) that support for Calderón increased during the campaign, (2) that this increase was significantly higher among economically satisfied voters, and (3) that Calderón came to own the unemployment issues more clearly than Lopez Obrador did the poverty issue. The first two findings support a thesis of campaign activation, while the third points toward priming.

Economic voting mattered in the 2006 presidential election, in a way that it previously had not. In addition to straightforward economic voting, economic reasoning was activated during the presidential campaigns. Activation, not persuasion, seemed to drive the changes in candidate preferences that were observed in the Mexico 2006 Panel Study. Support for the incumbent party's candidate increased significantly among economically satisfied voters, and support for his leftist opponent rose among economically dissatisfied ones. Such changes took place despite the fact that their assessments about the country's economy remained stable during the campaigns. Calderón's messages seemed to have worked, not because he convinced voters that the economy was doing well, but because he attracted the votes of those who already thought so and thereby prevented them from supporting López Obrador. Framing the election as a choice between economic stability, on the one hand, and economic crisis and debt, on the other, was a strong cue for Mexicans who had favorable views about the economy and had benefited from low inflation, housing development, a significant increase in durable goods, and flourishing financial credits.

The panel data used in this volume provide clear evidence of increasing support for Calderón among economically satisfied voters, but additional reasons make my argument about economic activation more convincing. First, there were objective fiscal conditions in Mexico that bolstered an economically oriented PAN campaign. Second, the PAN campaign made a substantial attempt to activate economic voting by focusing on economic issues. Third, the upswing in support for the PAN among economically optimistic voters was not the result of an increase in the overall proportion of these voters during the campaign. Fourth, the growing support among economically optimistic voters pertained only to the incumbent party candidate, not to the opposition candidates.

These findings have several important implications for the study of Mexican voting behavior, only some of which can be discussed here. For a start, they indicate that an environment of increasing electoral competition in Mexico, coupled with the fading of a regime cleavage that placed economic concerns in a secondary role for many years (Moreno 1999b), have brought economic issues back to the center of political contests. In the future, Mexican voters may see more economically oriented campaigns that address fiscal and redistribution issues, as well as the development of rationally opportunistic patterns of voting behavior. Next, if Mexican voters are more economically retrospective now than they were before, this may have implications for party responsiveness to electoral choices, and we could begin observing an increasing pattern of electoral accountability based on economic results. Such behavior evokes a theory of control, which depends on retrospective voting and maintains that elections make governments responsible for the outcomes of their past actions (Lago et al. 2007). Third, some observers of Mexican politics have suggested that the campaigns are too long and too costly, but evidence over time from other democracies shows that voters are able to learn more about their country's economic conditions in longer campaigns than in shorter ones (Stevenson and Vavreck 2000). This finding poses an immediate dilemma for Mexico's young democracy. Should Mexicans reduce campaign costs, particularly at a time when voters are starting to connect their political preferences with government performance and thereby are making the party system potentially more responsive? Finally, although economic voting in Mexico would seem to focus on valence issues, it also divides parties and candidates on policy proposals. In that sense, the 2006 presidential election was significantly ideological, with the Left voting for López Obrador and the Right for Calderón. We may thus see more ideologically and programmatically oriented campaigns, a development that would, in turn, redefine hitherto existing political coalitions in Mexico.

The findings in this chapter also have some comparative implications. To what extent is economic voting—a common feature of voting behavior in established democracies—becoming important in new democracies? The European voter, for example, "is an economic voter in the sense that negative evaluations of the economy hurt the electoral fortunes of incumbent parties" (Listhaug 2005, 231). What about the Latin American voter? Despite the presence of both deep crises and substantial economic recoveries in some recently democratized Latin American societies, the role of economic considerations in their voting behaviors has been rather ambivalent. In the 2005 Chilean election, for example, short-term influences on vote choices based on economic assessments were rather weak (Gutiérrez and López 2007), and the winner, Socialist Party candidate Michelle Bachelet, did not benefit substantially from economic reasoning, despite the fact that her predecessor had had "impressive economic achievements" (Angell and Salinas 2007, 12). In contrast, the 2007 victory of Cristina Fernández de Kirchner in Argentina has been greatly attributed to that country's economic recovery during her husband's administration, providing evidence that voters rewarded good performance. There was also evidence of strong economic voting in Peru, where economic optimism translated into support for the incumbent in the early 1990s, but there was also a certain ambivalence about the effect of economic assessments on the vote in Uruguay (Echegaray 2005). These mixed results in recent Latin American elections show that economics is not always a driving force in electoral decisions, but it is not ignored, either.

To what extent do politicians mobilize support around economic achievement or underachievement? How do voters react? Mexicans showed little—as well as ambivalent—economic behavior during elections under a dominant-party system, but the 2006 election has probably reversed that. Economic voting was a strong determinant of the election results, and campaign efforts to mobilize favorable economic assessments paid off for the incumbent party. Are elections now an efficient way to punish or reward government performance, leading to more responsible governments? If so, is that a sign of more maturity in these new democracies? Moreover, have politicians and voters learned about the dynamics of performance and used it rationally in elections? The evidence in this chapter, based on the Mexican 2006 campaigns, indicates that this may actually be the case.

CHAPTER TWELVE

Welfare Benefits, Canvassing, and Campaign Handouts

Alberto Díaz-Cayeros, Federico Estévez, and Beatriz Magaloni

This chapter analyzes the effects of social assistance programs, campaign hand-outs, and canvassing on Felipe Calderón's razor-thin victory in the 2006 elections. Many interpret the close contest as the outcome of an ideological battle between two radically different visions that divided Left from Right, rich from poor, and North from South. From this perspective, the 2006 election was an exercise in determining future directions for the nation, with a clear choice between right-wing continuity and left-wing populism. In our view, the triumph of the National Action Party (PAN) would not have materialized without the support of ample sectors of the urban poor, who voted for the Right as a result of two highly effective programs aimed at them, Oportunidades and Seguro Popular. The PAN also resorted to intense canvassing and distributed some gifts to voters prior to elections. However, in contrast to the powerful effects of welfare benefits, our results show that canvassing and gifts had, at best, marginal effects on the vote. One broadly comparative implication of our findings is that, in contrast to opportunistic clientelist transfers, welfare-enhancing social policies can and do generate significant longer-term dividends, including creating partisan loyalties among the poor.

Accusations were repeatedly leveled at the Fox government regarding the manipulation of Oportunidades throughout campaign season. In particular, the Civic Alliance (Alianza Cívica), one of the most influential nongovernmental poll-watching organizations, had been warning for months that the PAN was using federal social programs to buy votes (Alianza Cívica 2006). This perception was seconded by Fundar, a nongovernmental organization providing budget information and analysis and charged with public oversight in budgetary matters (Fundar 2006). The accusations could not be taken lightly, to the extent that they came from credible sources. Civic Alliance must be credited with having created the most prominent network of poll-watchers in Mexico, vital for the transition to democracy. And Fundar played a key role in improving transparency and accountability in the federal budgetary process.

President Vicente Fox and the Social Development Ministry (Secretaría de Desarrollo Social, or SEDESOL) had the foresight to anticipate these types of accusations, and as a result engaged in a strategy of what was called *blindaje electoral*, namely, providing safeguards in advance to shield federal social programs from electoral manipulation (SEDESOL 2005). One of these measures included a prohibition against expanding the programs' coverage during a federal election year. Furthermore, in order to assess whether there was coercion or vote buying through social programs, SEDESOL reached an agreement with the United Nations Development Program (Programa de las Naciones Unidas para el Desarrollo, or PNUD) to carry out a thorough study of the way in which these programs operated during the electoral period, including a survey of beneficiaries and nonbeneficiaries of the various social programs already in place (PNUD 2006).[1]

Our position in this debate is that Oportunidades and Seguro Popular made the PAN's victory in 2006 possible, but that voters acted out of their own free choice. Vote buying and credit claiming are complementary facets of democratic politics. However, their scope is quite wide, ranging from voters responding voluntarily to programmatic appeals and entitlement programs to voters supporting a party out of fear of losing their benefits, as happens with clientelist manipulation (Kitschelt and Wilkinson 2005). The key difference between these two modes of electoral exchange lies in the implicit threats involved in clientelism. The possibility of coercion is embedded in the institutional design of any given program. However, the programs studied here differ dramatically from the discretionary policies of social transfers that prevailed in the past in Mexico in two main respects.[2] For the first time, beneficiaries are selected according to objective criteria based on poverty indicators, rather than following a strictly political logic. Second, politicians can no longer withdraw the transfers at will if beneficiaries happen to support the "wrong" political party. These features alone place the two programs closer to the programmatic end of the vote-buying spectrum.

The first section of this chapter presents an overview of the transformation of Mexican social policy under Vicente Fox. The second portion is a methodological discussion, justifying our modeling choices. The remainder focuses on empirical analyses of the effects of Oportunidades, Seguro Popular, and targeted campaign gifts and canvassing.

Social Policy under the PAN

During the autocratic era in Mexico, major social programs were designed to grant ample discretion to the government, which in turn used social transfers to reward partisan supporters and mobilize voters in elections. In a country where the incomes of more than half of the population fall below the poverty line, the ruling party's control of these programs and other state resources gave it tremendous advantages over the opposition. In 1997, the establishment of Progresa (Programa de Educación, Salud y Alimentación, or National Program for Education, Health, and Nutrition), the precursor of Oportunidades, represented a watershed in the design of social policy in Mexico (Levy 2006; Levy and Rodríguez 2004). Progresa reduced the government's discretion in the selection of beneficiaries, which is now made on the basis of poverty criteria rather than political loyalties, and in the irreversibility of benefits, which currently can be withdrawn only when beneficiaries no longer meet the income-related or behavioral requisites for retention in the program. With Progresa, Mexico witnessed the advent of social entitlements for its poorest sectors.

Progresa consisted of three complementary elements: (1) a cash transfer, intended primarily for food consumption; (2) a scholarship, to cover the opportunity cost of children's labor so they could stay in school; and (3) nutritional supplements. From September 1997 through 2000, Progresa was implemented mainly in rural areas.

After numerous international policy evaluations supported Progresa's effectiveness in reducing extreme poverty, the Fox administration opted to continue with the program. They rebaptized it with a new name, Oportunidades; greatly expanded its rural coverage program; and extended its benefits to the cities, as well. At the end of 1999, Progresa had reached approximately 2.6 million families, or about 40 percent of all rural households. By December 2005, coverage under Oportunidades had doubled, to almost 5 million families, one-third of whom resided in urban or semiurban zones. Today, more than half of all families living in poverty are recipients of these transfers.

Progresa/Oportunidades is an example of what is known as a conditional cash transfer (CCT) program, in which the government provides money to poor families, conditional upon certain verifiable actions—typically, investments in children's human capital and basic preventive health. There are various advantages of CCTs relative to other social transfer programs. First, they are highly effective at targeting the poor. Most CCT programs combine geographic and household targeting, where areas are selected first, based on poverty indexes, and then individual households are chosen, based on either microcensus information (for rural Progresa and rural Oportunidades) or on demand (for urban Oportunidades).

The second advantage of CCTs is that they have both an immediate income effect for the beneficiary household, reducing poverty and inequality, and a generational effect, as the conditional component pushes poor families to invest in the formation of human capital. Progresa originally required minimum daily school attendance and regular medical checkups. Oportunidades added bonuses for school attendance and participation in health-awareness seminars.

Third, CCTs significantly reduce discretion in allocating benefits, leaving less room for political manipulation of the funds. Monies are distributed according to technical criteria that combine geographic targeting with a household assessment mechanism called proxy means testing (using multidimensional indicators that are correlated with poverty). In addition, benefits cannot be discretionally assigned and withdrawn, which is precisely what sets these apart from clientelist transfers.

In addition to Oportunidades, the Fox administration introduced Seguro Popular, an ambitious program created to extend health coverage to the uninsured (King et al. 2007; Lakin 2005). This program was intended to remedy the truncated nature of health care delivery, which grants access only to those working in the formal sector of the economy; according to the 2000 census, some 58 percent of Mexico's population falls outside of this coverage. The Seguro Popular program began in five states in 2001, and by 2005 it had been implemented in all thirty-one states and the Federal District, covering almost 3 million families. In contrast to Oportunidades, which is centrally administered by the federal government, Seguro Popular is decentralized; coverage and spending still vary widely among states. Moreover, issues remain concerning how well it targets potential participants. Despite these shortcomings, Scott (2006) calculated the incidence of benefits distribution under Seguro Popular and concluded that the new insurance program is more pro-poor that any other health care service except for Oportunidades. He further argued that piggy-backing Seguro Popular onto the poverty relief program, thus allowing automatic enrollment for families that are already registered in Oportunidades, can only improve its efficiency in targeting the poor.

Given the unequal nature of access to primary health care services in both the public and private sectors, Seguro Popular is intended to provide coverage for households without the resources to pay for medical care, especially for emergency room treatments and protracted ailments. Registration is voluntary, but free insurance is conditional on means-testing. Subsidized contributions are required from households with incomes above the poverty line, but since the program is tied in with Oportunidades, this still results in much lower transaction costs for individual participants. Scott (2006) notes that the selection process has legal loopholes that allow uninsured Mexicans to be enrolled at the organizational level, which perhaps can contravene means-testing requirements and be conducive to particularistic politics and rent-seeking. However, there is a certain degree of protection, as federal outlays subsidizing the insurance program require formal intergovernmental agreements with and matching funds from state governments. By late 2005, all lower-level governments had entered the Seguro Popular program, but some imposed different priorities or restrictions on its implementation. For example, in the Federal District, López Obrador agreed to the program's deployment in only two of the capital's sixteen boroughs, where demand had far outstripped the local government's public health system. Notwithstanding such obstacles, the federal government mounted effective registration campaigns throughout the country, state by state, and by election day almost 3 million households were covered by Seguro Popular. The program's rapid expansion, and its emergence as a campaign issue in the spring (when López Obrador advised against voluntary enrollment), raise the obvious question of how effective, in electoral terms, it was for the governing party.

Electoral Effects of Oportunidades and Seguro Popular in 2006

Our central claim is that support for the PAN among beneficiaries of Oportunidades and Seguro Popular, concentrated within the poorest half of the electorate, was a striking component of Calderón's victory against the Left. Since its founding, the cornerstone of the PAN's programmatic reputation has been democratic reform, complemented—in the era of hyperpresidentialism under the Institutional Revolutionary Party (PRI)—by an enduring distrust of central government and its highly discretional, and thus corruption-laden, fiscal management. Anticentralism, with a strong dose of antitax militancy, is hardly conducive to building a reputation for fostering redistributive policies.[3] Thus the notion that the PAN might appeal to poorer sectors of the electorate on the basis of its social development policies and the delivery of benefits through targeted, formula-based, and means-tested programs is somehow counterintuitive. However, it is our contention that electoral incentives pushed the PAN to design social policies that would assist the poorest sectors of the electorate without increasing the tax burden on its traditional middle-class constituencies.

The political payoffs of these social transfers, which are discussed in the rest of this chapter, produced critical support for the PAN among portions of the electorate that might otherwise have voted for the Left. Our analysis provides simple descriptive statistics of the political differences between the beneficiaries and nonbeneficiaries of both programs in table 12.1. These are frequencies and averages taken from the national exit poll fielded by *Reforma* in early July, with a sample of 5,807 voters from 137 precincts around the country. Roughly 19 percent of the respondents declared themselves to be registered in Oportunidades, and 15 percent in Seguro Popular (with about 8% reporting dual registration).

If one were to examine only the average vote shares for the three main presidential candidates among nonbeneficiaries of either program, a close tie between Calderón and López Obrador emerges, with Madrazo in distant third place overall. Among beneficiaries of the programs, however, Calderón outpaced López Obrador by double digits (reaching a maximum in his twenty-point lead among dual beneficiaries). Any of these spreads would have been enough to tilt the national election in Calderón's direction. Furthermore, the recipients of social policy benefits, on average, consistently rewarded Calderón with higher feeling thermometer ratings than his two rivals, reported stronger levels of partisanship and support for the PAN, and had more positive retrospective evaluations in general than nonrecipients. To the extent that (1) pocketbook evaluations undergird poor voters' assessments of government performance and their partisan attachments and (2) these retrospective elements, in turn, influence candidate preference, the raw data from the exit poll would appear to indicate an important cushion of support for the PAN from poor voters who directly benefited from social development and poverty reduction programs.

To explore the systematic effects of these social policies on voting behavior, however, one has to address key methodological issues that stem from the fact that program participants are not selected randomly, but on the basis of certain sociodemographic characteristics that are, in turn, causally related to voting

Table 12.1 Political attitudes and vote choice by enrollment in social welfare programs

	Oportunidades beneficiary?		Seguro Popular beneficiary?		Double beneficiary
	Yes	No	Yes	No	
Vote choice					
Calderón	37.2	32.3	40.6	31.9	42.4
López Obrador	25.9	31.7	22.9	31.9	21.7
Madrazo	23.1	17.9	22.3	18.4	23.9
Rating differential (–9 to 9)					
Calderón–					
López Obrador	0.86	0.46	1.32	0.40	1.32
Calderón–Madrazo	1.44	1.13	1.53	1.12	1.66
Partisan identification					
PAN	31.2	23.9	33.7	23.8	37.7
PRD	18.3	17.5	14.5	18.2	13.4
PRI	23.5	20.3	23.4	20.4	23.9
Independent	26.9	37.9	28.4	37.1	25.1
PAN scale (–2 to 2)	–0.17	–0.23	–0.06	–0.25	0.03
Presidential					
approval (1–4)	3.16	2.77	3.17	2.8	3.27
Pocketbook					
evaluations (1–5)	3.48	3.11	3.42	3.14	3.56
N	1,117	4,690	864	4,943	486

Source: *Reforma*, exit poll, July 2, 2006.

decisions. Because of these endogenous factors, assessing the impact of Oportunidades and Seguro Popular on voting behavior is challenging. Both programs are targeted toward the poor, who generally have not supported the right-wing PAN but leaned instead toward the other two alternatives, the former ruling party and the leftist Party of the Democratic Revolution (PRD).[4]

Thinking in terms of medical research and experiments helps conceptualize some of the problems involved in studying these types of policy interventions. To estimate the effects of a drug or medical treatment, ideally one would like to have two individuals who are identical in all respects (age, diet, gender, lifestyle, ethnicity, etc.) except for the treatment (e.g., the drug). Medical research solves this issue through experimental design, where a group of people with similar characteristics are randomly selected and divided into two groups, the treated group receiving the drug and the other, or control, group receiving a placebo.

Experiments in the social sciences are harder to design. First of all, many of the outcomes we are interested in cannot be controlled within the limited framework of experimental settings.[5] Secondly, experiments always raise questions of external validity. Progresa, envisioned by a former academic well trained in economics, was originally designed to allow for experimental evaluations. Communities with similar characteristics were identified at the onset of the program, but only a randomly selected group began to receive benefits immediately, while the others were incorporated fifteen months later.

Tina Green (2005) and Ana De la O (2006) took advantage of the program's randomization and the delay in extending it to certain target areas to assess the effects of Progresa on turnout and voting choices in the 2000 presidential election, but they arrived at opposite conclusions. Green found that Progresa had no effect on voting choices, while De la O observed that it affected turnout by five percentage points and increased the incumbent's vote share by four points. One of the difficulties with reconciling these results is that in order to get leverage from the experimental design, these studies ended up comparing localities with very different characteristics.[6] Green's (2005) highly nuanced study first identified 3,739 communities (out of 105,749) where the area covered by the electoral polling stations coincided with the boundaries of the locality. Within this sample, she then compared the treated locales (i.e., those incorporated into Progresa) with the untreated ones. Green's selection strategy yielded highly atypical places where the PAN received very low levels of support (around 20%). De la O (2006) carefully crafted a randomized experimental setup utilizing 505 Progresa-affiliated localities, where 300 of them had received benefits for twenty-one months before the election, while the rest had only done so for six months. Given this design, both groups were receiving transfers before the presidential election in 2000. So the inference from her results is about the effects of the duration of the treatment on voting decisions, rather than effects of the treatment itself.

Unlike these two studies that got leverage from the Progresa randomization, we relied on national observational data coming from *Reforma's* exit poll for the 2006 elections. Cornelius (2002, 2004) also depended on similar surveys to assess the effects of Progresa on voting choices in 2000. However, the problem with the conventional parametric estimations he uses, in which dummy variables for being a beneficiary of a social program or receiving visits or gifts from a political party are used as independent variables, is that this creates a natural nonrandom selection of observations for those variables. Therefore, inferences drawn from conventional parametric estimations can be rendered unsound, because of selection bias.[7]

By using surveys to examine the electoral payoffs of social transfers, we can explicitly model the selection process to create something akin to an experimental situation. That is, we can contrast treated and untreated individuals by selecting two almost identical persons—at least in terms of the nonrandom set of characteristics that make them subject to being chosen in the policy intervention—with one receiving the treatment and the other not. Specifically, we draw upon our joint study (Díaz-Cayeros et al. 2008) that uses a nonparametric technique, propensity-score matching, to pair individuals along these lines. The treatment variable in this quasi-experiment is being an Oportunidades or Seguro Popular recipient. This nonparametric test has several advantages, including that the estimation does not depend upon specific assumptions of linearity or other aspects of model dependence (Ho et al. 2007; Imai 2005; Rosenbaum and Rubin 1983).[8]

Calculating a propensity score is straightforward; one estimates a probit or logit of the determinants for the treatment. In our study, we followed the advice of Ho et al. (2006) and chose the most parsimonious specification for covariates for the propensity score, which, while satisfying the balancing property, included all the control variables expected to influence the treatment and excluded variables that were not good predictors of the treatment, in order to retain estimation efficiency. The covariates for this propensity score calculation included individual-level indicators related to the sociodemographic characteristics of respondents, geographic variables pertaining to the physical environment they inhabit; and aggregate characteristics of the municipality.

In matching, the indicator of interest is a measure of the mean impact of the treatment. In this case we were interested in comparing the mean probability of voting for a given party between a treated group and its matched nontreated group, known as the average treatment effect on the treated (ATT). Given the assumption of unit homogeneity, the outcome for the nonparticipant can be taken as an indication of what would have happened holding all other relevant variables constant. In this sense, the hypotheses tests do not control for covariates, since they are already incorporated into the selection of observations to be compared.

Table 12.2 displays the results from our work, presenting difference-of-means tests between treated and untreated respondents matched according to the nearest neighbor and differentiated by the calculated propensity scores for inclusion in one of the two social programs. The table also contains simple means tests obtained from the raw data, which are plagued with the endogeneity problem discussed above. Thus, a comparison between pre-matched and post-matched means tests reveals the inferential virtues of the propensity-score matching technique. Not controlling for selection into the two programs, and not matching individuals on traits that enter into that selection, runs the risk of finding practically all political variables significantly associated with the one under consideration, participation in the social programs Oportunidades and Seguro Popular (see the columns labeled "Pre-matching" in table 12.2).

Once propensities are matched, beneficiaries of the poverty-relief program Oportunidades were 11 percent more likely to vote for Calderón than nonbeneficiaries with very similar propensity scores—that is, individuals with the same sociodemographic and community-level characteristics. At the same time, beneficiaries of this program were 7 percent less likely to vote for López Obrador, and indistinguishable from nonbeneficiaries in their support levels for Madrazo. These leanings among beneficiaries are reinforced by (1) marked increases in the feeling thermometer differentials between Calderón and both López Obrador and Madrazo combined, (2) stronger attachments to the PAN at the expense of other partisan ties and (especially) nonpartisan status, and (3) more positive evaluations of government performance and personal well-being. Thus the data strongly support our claim that Oportunidades gave Calderón a crucial boost at the polls among poor voters who might otherwise have supported López Obrador.

The impact of Seguro Popular was similar, in this case increasing the propensity of an individual to vote for Calderón by 7%. Coverage under this health-care program also lent itself to greater identification with the PAN and to better evaluations of government performance and personal finances, although the magnitudes of all these effects were smaller than those for the poverty alleviation program. Seguro Popular was only slightly less effective than Oportunidades in raising voters' support for Calderon and identification with the PAN, but it was substantially weaker in generating positive assessments of government performance and candidate attributes. Despite considerable overlap between the beneficiaries of both programs, Seguro Popular is much more urban than the poverty relief program, and its political geography is distinct.

Although the electoral bonus of financial redistribution through Oportunidades favored the PAN, it is notable that the party responsible for the program's

Table 12.2   Effect of receiving welfare benefits on political attitudes

Correlate	Oportunidades		Seguro Popular	
	Pre-matching	Post-matching	Pre-matching	Post-matching
Vote choice				
Calderón	.05***	.11***	.09***	.07**
López Obrador	−.06***	−.07***	−.09***	−.04
Madrazo	.05***	.00	.04***	−.00
Rating differential				
Calderón–				
López Obrador	.40***	.63**	.92***	.59*
Calderón–Madrazo	.31**	.59**	.41***	.28
Partisan identification				
PAN	.08***	.11***	.11***	.08***
PRD	.01	−.04	−.04**	−.02
PRI	.04***	−.03	.04***	−.02
Independent	−.11***	−.05**	−.09***	−.03
PAN scale	.06	.26***	.19***	.21***
Presidential approval	.39***	.40***	.39***	.18***
Pocketbook evaluation	.37***	.40***	.28***	.15***

Source: Reforma, exit poll, July 2, 2006.

Note: Cell entries represent differences in means between those who receive welfare benefits and those who do not, calculated for various indicators of partisan preferences or political attitudes.

*Significant at the 10% level **Significant at the 5% level ***Significant at the 1% level

creation and early administration, the PRI, was left untouched by the dynamics of the program's influence on voting decisions. Six years of accumulated change in the program's operation under the aegis of the PAN—the rival party that ejected the PRI from control of the federal government—affected neither the Oportunidades beneficiaries' support for the PRI's presidential candidate nor their level of partisan attachments to this party. This was especially true for the rural electorate, which monopolized Progresa transfers until 2000. Hence the 2006 campaign announcements by Madrazo and other leading PRI figures, trumpeting authorship of the original program and committing the party to its continuation. It is equally true, however, that the PRI received no reward from the program's current recipients. It is entirely possible that the program's expansion of non-urban coverage under Fox neutralized what was a strong electoral premium for the PRI from rural beneficiaries of Progresa in the 2000 presidential contest.

Canvassing and Campaign Handouts

Calderón's slim victory, we have shown, can be plausibly accredited to the social policies implemented by the Fox administration that allowed his party to attract support among the poor, a group that otherwise could have been expected to vote for the PRD candidate. Many of those receiving benefits from Oportunidades and Seguro Popular approached the elections feeling more satisfied with their personal well-being, credited the president and the PAN for these material improvements, and gave their votes to Calderón as a result. In effect, the PAN did manage to buy off segments of the poor through its social assistance programs. Nonetheless, that is not at all the same as clientelism.

Campaign handouts, however, are a different story from the well-institutionalized welfare benefits of Oportunidades and Seguro Popular. Campaign handouts are opportunistic gifts—money, foodstuffs, t-shirts, livestock—that have limited effects on voters' welfare but are given out during the election season in an attempt to influence voting decisions. This final section explores the effects of canvassing and campaign handouts in the 2006 elections. We asked two basic questions. To whom did the PAN direct its canvassing efforts and deliver its handouts? And did either of these influence voting choices?

To explore these questions, we made use of the Mexico 2006 Panel Study,[9] which allowed us to track changes in voting decisions and opinions during the course of the campaign. The selection bias problem discussed in the previous section is not limited to beneficiaries in targeted social programs, but can also be found in lesser interventions during the campaign, such as canvassing and handouts. For example, political parties might choose to canvas or reward some voters over others precisely because these individuals have characteristics that render them susceptible to switching their vote. Thus canvassing and campaign gifts are not randomly assigned to voters, but depend on traits that are plausibly correlated with their voting choices. However, any links between, say, canvassing and voting choice might only reflect the underlying socioeconomic or partisan characteristics that led party operatives to target certain voters, rather than the direct effect of the attention given to them. To deal with the problem of selection bias, we again employed propensity-score matching. We first modeled the selection procedure (i.e., what makes an individual more likely to be canvassed or given a handout). We then matched individuals with similar predicted propensity scores that differed only in the treatment (i.e., were they beneficiaries of one or both of the two social programs, or not). Lastly, through difference-of-means tests, we compared their likelihood of voting for the incumbent party.

With respect to canvassing, the panel study revealed considerable door-to-door campaigning.[10] Of the respondents from the national sample who participated in all three panel waves, 24 percent reported having been contacted by representatives of at least one party or candidate. All three parties canvassed actively, although the PAN and the PRI enjoyed a slight edge (14.2% and 14.4%, respectively) over the PRD (11%). Both the PAN and the PRD did considerably more canvassing in the cities (16% and 13%, respectively) than in rural areas (9% and 8%, respectively). The PRI, by contrast, appeared to canvass almost as intensively in each type of community (14% in rural areas and 16% in urban ones). All these facts reflect the size and traditional geographical strengths of the Mexico's main parties (see chapter 2 in this volume).

Campaign handouts were infrequent, at least as revealed by the respondents; only 8 percent reported having received gifts, money, food baskets, or some kind of help from any party during the course of the campaign. Unsurprisingly, the PRI was more prone to resort to these clientelist practices than its rivals—approximately 5 percent of those sampled received handouts from the PRI, more than from the PAN (2.7%) and the PRD (1.5%) combined.

To uncover the logic of canvassing and handouts, we modeled the probability that the PAN contacted an individual or gave him or her a campaign handout.[11] The results suggested that the PAN concentrated on reaching its own core supporters, which we identified as those who, in October 2005 (at the start of the campaigns), reported identifying strongly with that party. There is also evidence that the PAN canvassed more intensively in states governed by its representatives, again conveying the idea that canvassing was more prevalent among core supporters. Finally, the PAN concentrated its efforts among lower income groups, but not among beneficiaries of Oportunidades. This implies an urban focus for the party's canvassing, in line with its core constituencies.

In terms of handouts, the PAN attempted to buy off the support of marginally opposing voters, which we defined as those who reported weak partisan identifications with the PRD or the PRI in the first wave of the panel. This pattern reflects the expectations for swing-voter opportunism (see, for example, Dixit and Londregan 1995 and S. Stokes 2005). The model also suggested a bidding equilibrium, in which parties channeled gifts to voters who were already targeted by other parties. Indeed, the coefficients for handouts by the PRI and the PRD were both positive and statistically significant, suggesting that all parties gave handouts to swing voters rather than core supporters. In lieu of income, the handout model included dummies for ownership of various items (cable television, telephone, car, and stove with an oven), possession of which presumably differentiated the lower middle class from poorer strata. While not statistically significant, the plus signs suggested that campaign handouts from the PAN were not aimed at the poorest voters.

To assess the impacts of canvassing and handouts, we proceeded as before, using differences-in-means tests between treated and untreated respondents, differentiated by calculated propensity scores that came from the models described above. The first three columns of table 12.3 refer to the effects of canvassing. First off, canvassing had no favorable effect for Calderón in the national vote and in the urban subsample. Among rural voters, canvassing by the PAN affected Calderón's candidacy negatively, and these voters appeared to support López Obrador even after the PAN approached them. However, canvassing had a substantial impact on changes in voting decisions throughout the course of the campaign. For example, canvassing led to a more than 10 percent increase in the probability that a voter would switch his or her voting intention from López Obrador, Madrazo, or another candidate to Calderón. Again, this was not the case for rural voters, who did not switch their support to the PAN even when canvassed. Door-to-door canvassing also decreased the probability that a voter would abandon Calderón for any other candidate during the campaign, although the size of this effect was moderate. Canvassing had a marginal effect in increasing partisan loyalties over the course of the campaign in favor of the PAN, but only in the cities. By contrast, rural voters canvassed by the PAN did not switch partisan loyalties toward the PAN, but instead converted to the PRD. However, between the first and third waves of the panel, canvassing did increase the feeling thermometer differentials among rural voters, tilting them in favor of Calderón and against López Obrador. Lastly, canvassing impacted other facets of this group's voting behavior. Although it did not appear to increase turnout, canvassing seemed to increase political interest among rural voters.

With respect to campaign handouts from the PAN (column 4 of table 12.3), there was generally a negative impact from opportunistically targeting independents and marginally opposed voters. Handouts did not increase voting support, strengthen partisan sympathies, or enhance a candidate's image. Indeed, vote-buying efforts seemed to backfire. Possibly such opportunism went against the grain of the party's reputation, as with the Radical Party in Argentina (Calvo and Murillo 2004).

Table 12.3   Tracking the electoral effects of canvassing and campaign handouts

	Canvassing			Handouts
	National	Urban	Rural	National
Vote				
For Calderón	−.00	.07	−.17*	−.16
For AMLO	.06	.00	.32**	.05
For Madrazo	−.03	.02	−.11	.13
Change in choice (waves 1 to 3)				
Converted to PAN	.11***	.14***	−.13*	−.06
Converted to PRD	.00	−.01	.07	−.02
Converted to PRI	−.04*	−.05*	−.15**	−.02
Abandoned PAN	−.04**	−.02	−.04	.00
Abandoned PRD	.04	.04	−.03	.00
Abandoned PRI	−.14***	−.10***	−.06	−.11
Change in party ID				
In favor of PAN	.06	.07*	.12	−.28**
In favor of PRD	.03	.01	.17*	.13*
In favor of PRI	−.05*	.04	−.12*	.13*
Political mobilization				
Political interest	−.10	−.15	.46**	−.14
Turnout	.03	.01	.03	−.13*
Change in rating differential				
Calderón–AMLO	−.19	−.34	2.47**	−2.88***
Calderón–Madrazo	−.37	−.10	−.13	−3.12***

*Significant at the 10% level **Significant at the 5% level ***Significant at the 1% level

The delivery of welfare-enhancing benefits through targeted social programs and sustained policy innovation matters for a governing party's electoral prospects. In 2006, the urban beneficiaries of the Fox administration's two major social policy initiatives, Oportunidades and Seguro Popular, rewarded the PAN with crucial votes that very likely represented their margin of triumph at the national level.

The influence exerted by Oportunidades and Seguro Popular on voting decisions in 2006 was logically tied to a retrospective calculation by voters that partially neutralized prospective possibilities. What is ironic in 2006 is the reversal of partisan identity for these two aspects of vote-buying, with the Right delivering on policies that were not associated with its historical reputation versus the

Left's credibility in promising changes in distributive policies in the future. In the end, the average beneficiary reasoned along the lines of "Better a bird in the hand than two in the bush." The Spanish version exaggerates the discount rate of the future: *más vale pájaro en mano que cien volando* (better a bird in the hand than a hundred flying). In keeping with this folk wisdom, effective vote-buying is usually based on tangible benefits from the past rather than welcome promises in the future.

The PAN's claiming credit for social policy benefits, we believe, is what propelled poor people receiving help from Oportunidades and Seguro Popular to support that party. Beneficiaries of these social programs were significantly more satisfied with their personal finances and with the way the president was handling the economy than were similarly poor individuals who did not receive these welfare benefits. As a result, the former were more likely to support Calderón, even when his party lacked a reputation for welfarism. While electoral clientelism and vote coercion cannot be ruled out in the 2006 campaigns, the evidence presented here makes it highly improbable that voters were pressured into supporting the PAN through fear of losing these benefits. Beneficiaries' favorable reaction to the party in power may indicate successful vote-buying by the incumbents, but it is likely to be vote-buying of the positive sort.

Without these two innovations in its social policy, the PAN would have been unable to garner support among a crucial sector of the electorate who otherwise might have preferred the PRD, or even the PRI. In contrast to the effects of the welfare-enhancing Oportunidades and Seguro Popular programs, the PAN's campaign handouts had no impact on voting decisions. As the swing voter model demonstrated, the PAN disproportionately assigned campaign handouts to marginally opposed voters. However, Mexican voters were able to distinguish between the two types of benefits—welfare-enhancing and opportunistic—and rewarded the PAN only for the former.

Canvassing was a more effective way of influencing voters than campaign handouts. The PAN canvassed most heavily among its core supporters, that is, those who reported strong identification with this party at the onset of the campaign. Although canvassing had no effect on their voting decisions, it was highly effective at convincing these supporters to remain loyal to the party's candidate until the end. Overall, our results uncovered more sophistication among Mexican voters than had been conventionally assumed. They were capable of discerning good from bad vote-buying, thus responding to welfare-enhancing policies rather than to opportunistic campaign handouts.

Our findings raise some broad comparative implications about social policies and voting behavior in Latin America, where governments in several countries have instituted conditional cash transfer programs akin to Oportunidades. Our results suggest that well-designed welfare programs to alleviate poverty can produce significant electoral payoffs for incumbent parties, not only from the Left, but also from the Right.

CHAPTER THIRTEEN

Images and Issues in Mexico's 2006 Presidential Election

Kenneth F. Greene

Mexico's 2006 campaign was more polarized on the issues than any other national election in the country's history. The two leading presidential candidates, Felipe Calderón of the conservative National Action Party (PAN) and Andrés Manuel López Obrador of the left-wing Coalition For the Good of All, led by his Party of the Democratic Revolution (PRD), staked out starkly different positions on key economic issues, including the privatization of state-owned enterprises, commercial relations with the United States, and plans to diminish poverty. As the media campaigns intensified, these differences became increasingly apparent. On one side, Calderón and his allies in the business community invested massively in television spots that portrayed López Obrador as an irresponsible populist destined to run up the national debt and provoke an economic crisis. On the other side, López Obrador depicted himself as a crusader for redistributive justice against a conspiracy of domestic and international power holders aimed at smothering his candidacy and Mexico's fledgling democracy. Ideological distinctions also extended to PAN and PRD congressional candidates for plurality-district seats, who staked out polarized positions on the issues in local races throughout the country (see chapter 6 in this volume).

Mexico's tense presidential campaigns occurred against the backdrop of rising concerns over Latin America's "left turn." Populist leaders in Venezuela, Argentina, and Bolivia had come to power in part by mobilizing class antagonisms that threatened to polarize their societies over economic issues. Could something similar have occurred in Mexico? Did the virtual tie between López Obrador and Calderón spring from a public deeply divided over important national issues? If so, then the election results reflect counterposed mandates that are balanced on a razor's edge and foreshadow a presidential term marked by legislative gridlock that would leave Mexico without policy solutions to vexing problems.

Alternatively, the virtual tie may have emerged for other, less dangerous reasons. Perhaps instead of leaning toward some of its southern neighbors, Mexico's new democratic politics reflect the kind found to the north. Decades of voting-behavior studies in the United States highlight the importance of more mundane factors, such as candidate traits and the incumbents' performance in office. If Mexico's election results sprang from these forces and not from ideological differences, then the polarized campaigns were manufactured by the elites alone, with the voters being surprisingly immune to the candidates' exhortations to care about their alternative economic projects. The absence of distinct issue publics would imply that Mexico is much further from the brink than sensationalist commentary has made it out to be, and that the parties' constituencies would not stand in the way of legislative consensus. It would also imply that the PRD's advance owes more to López Obrador himself than to broader forces pushing the Left's renaissance in several Latin American countries.

This chapter shows that despite the candidates' polarizing rhetoric on economic issues, the voters' economic policy preferences played a surprisingly small role in choosing Mexico's president in 2006; rather, variables traditionally associated with voting behavior in the United States, and particularly candidate traits that were consciously manipulated by the campaigns, mattered quite a bit. Yet in contrast to the United States, where research has long shown that campaigns have minimal effects on voting behavior (Berelson et al. 1954; Finkel 1993; Lazarsfeld et al. 1944), I argue that Mexico's 2006 campaign itself played a key role in shifting votes from López Obrador to Calderón. In particular, voters were both persuaded to think of Calderón as more competent at solving key national problems than López Obrador and primed to think of competency as being more important in their vote choices. These campaign effects played a major role in the outcome of the election.

The first section of this chapter shows the size and timing of the large vote swing in favor of Calderón that ultimately helped him win the election. The second section shows the surprisingly low level of issue polarization among voters (i.e., the absence of distinct issue publics). The third discusses candidate traits, focusing on the crucial change in voters' perceptions of the candidates' competencies between October and May—a change that I argue was induced by the campaigns themselves. The fourth describes a statistical model of vote choice that demonstrates the almost negligible effect of issue preferences and the quite strong effects of candidate images. The concluding section draws out the implications of these findings for studying campaign effects, politics during the Calderón administration, and the future of the Mexican Left.

The Vote Swing

A huge chunk of the electorate was up for grabs during the 2006 presidential race (see chapter 10 in this volume). Of the 849 respondents who participated in all three survey waves of the national sample in the Mexico 2006 Panel Study,[1] half changed their minds about whom to support over the course of the campaign.[2] Calderón was the overwhelming beneficiary of their reconsiderations. By election day, he had captured nearly one-quarter of Madrazo's original supporters, one-sixth of López Obrador's, and a larger proportion of those who were initially undecided than his two main rivals combined. In all, Calderón added more than 12 percent of the total electorate to his vote share, as measured by the national panel survey (for details, see table 10.2).[3]

Almost two-thirds of the votes Calderón eventually picked up were won between October 2005 an May 2006, rather than during the hard-fought final two months of the campaigns (see chapter 10 in this volume). Even more impressive is the fact that fully specified models of vote choice (see the third section of this chapter), with all variables and each respondent's vote intention measured in October 2005, predict a wide margin of victory for López Obrador in that wave of the panel; by contrast, applying these models to the May 2006 and July 2006 waves instead predict a thin margin of victory for Calderón. Thus the events that had the largest impact on the elections occurred between the first and second waves of the Mexico 2006 Panel Study.[4] The size of the swing during the 2006 campaign dwarfs the changes measured in similar panel studies conducted in established democracies (Bartels 2006; Finkel 1993; Johnston et al. 1992).

Weakly Divided Issue Publics

If the vote shift emerged from a process of ideological alignment where right-wing and left-wing orientations were initially unrelated to vote choice but eventually affected candidate support, then by the end of the campaigns we should have observed clearly divided issue publics. Despite rhetorically distinct campaigns between the leading candidates, polarization among party elites, and the candidates' confidence that they could lead voters on the issues (see chapter 6 in this volume), most voters did not hold significantly different preferences on the issues. Although the strongest PAN and PRD partisans, who represented just 8.4 percent and 5.6 percent of the electorate, respectively, were divided over certain issues and also responded to their parties' candidates by becoming more polarized over the course of the campaign,[5] Mexico's electorate in general was not divided into distinct issue publics by election day.

Figure 13.1 reports issue preferences in May according to vote choices in July and shows that positional issues did not open a deep and abiding chasm between supporters of the leading candidates. This comparison of pre-electoral issue positions and final vote choice is perhaps the most relevant, given that two-thirds of the final vote choice changes had already occurred by May. Using July issue preferences does show a stronger differentiation between the two candidates' supporters, but it is not clear whether the issue positions that were measured after the elections propelled vote choice or whether voters simply rationalized their final vote choices by adjusting their issue preferences post hoc.

Based on even a cursory visual inspection of figure 13.1, we cannot conclude that Calderón's supporters were thoroughly right-wing while López Obrador's were completely left-wing. There are, in fact, no substantively or statistically significant differences between the two support groups on issues that played front and center in the campaign, including how to tackle poverty and whether the public social safety net should expand or contract. The question of whether or not to privatize the electricity sector and the preferred extent of commercial ties with the United States did generate statistically significant differences across the two groups; however, the substantive differences are small enough that they do not give the impression of polarized issue publics. Most importantly, on all economic issues, Calderón's and López Obrador's supporters were on the same side of the issues. If preferences sprang from a bifurcated electorate, then we would expect pronounced differences in direction, not just minor differences in magnitude that defy visual interpretation and require complex multivariate statistical models to detect.

The biggest differences between the two candidates' supporters appear on moral issues, yet they should not be overblown. López Obrador supporters were the most strongly pro-choice, but all groups of voters favored a woman's right to have an abortion in cases of rape. Supporters were on opposite sides of the electricity privatization issue, but the differences were so small that they could be attributed to measurement error. Although there were some differences on moral issues, ironically, the candidates did not highlight these topics and, fur-

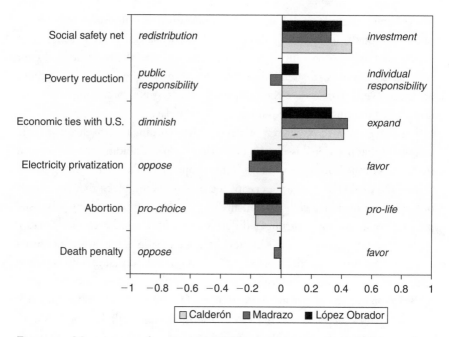

Figure 13.1 Mean issue preferences in April/May 2006 by vote choice in July 2006.

ther, sought to downplay them in their campaigns. In particular, Calderón consistently ducked questions about his antichoice position on abortion. Overall, then, even by the end of the campaign, partisans were separated far less on the issues than one would expect, given the rhetorical rancor, fiery statements, and harshly negative advertising by the candidates dedicated, in part, to stoking these divisions.

Another way to examine elite-mass alignments is to test the structure of the issue space, that is, how respondents package issues together. The more the content of elite and voter issue spaces match, the more plausible it is that the voters responded to the candidates' policy offers when casting their ballots. Parties and their candidates have incentives to reduce the complex political world into packages that are more easily digested by voters, such as left-versus-right orientations. Doing so provides a shortcut, or heuristic device, that diminishes the time and energy that voters need to invest in order to assess the candidates' issue positions. A clearer structure in the competition space can also reduce voters' perceived uncertainties over where the parties and their candidates stand on the issues, and research has shown that voters may be willing to trade some level of issue agreement with a candidate if they are more certain about his or her stance (Alvarez 1998).

We would expect that parties in Mexico's new democracy would work especially hard to provide voters with such shortcuts. The PAN's and PRD's limited record in office, and the Institutional Revolutionary Party's (PRI) attempts to shed its past record, militated against retrospective voting and provided incentives for the parties to provide hints about their likely behavior in the future. The low level of party identification since the late 1990s (noted in chapter 10 and elsewhere in this volume) also gave the parties incentives to fight over the content of such shortcuts. Winning the framing battle could be an important step both in converting more citizens into voters who identified with a particular party and in establishing stable party-voter alignments.

Congressional candidates had clearly defined mental maps of the partisan competition space, ones that involved differences over economic policy and over moral issues such as abortion and the death penalty (see chapter 6 in this volume). Ideological orientations mapped easily onto this space, dividing pro-state social progressives from pro-market social conservatives. Before the election, however, voters' mental maps were not nearly as tidy. Although voters did package issues together, they did so at such a low level of aggregation that it is difficult to speak of a single overriding heuristic (such as left versus right).

To examine how voters package issues, I conducted a factor analysis (similar to the procedure performed on the candidate data in chapter 6 in this volume), using data from the May wave of the panel study. This procedure produced three latent dimensions that might be thought of as the main arteries in the electorate's cognitive map. The first and most important dimension concerned economic redistribution, which separated those who preferred an expanded social safety net and a bigger government able to reduce poverty through resource transfers from those who opposed such redistributive measures. The second dimension included the question of privatization and commercial ties with the United States. The final (and least important) dimension concerned moral values issues, dividing pro-life and anti-death-penalty positions associated with the Catholic Church from pro-choice and pro-death penalty stances.

The existence of three complicated issue dimensions among voters makes it clear that no single electoral heuristic has emerged in Mexico.[6] Instead, voters' mental maps of politics remain complicated and in too much disarray to supply a relevant shortcut for choosing one party or candidate over another. This finding is all the more surprising given that data from the Mexico 2000 *Panel Study*[7] revealed two clear cleavages involving regime issues and economic policy ones (Greene 2007). Once the regime dimension disappeared, analysts expected the standard economic policy dimension to emerge as the primary factor. Instead, it appears that the regime dimension played an anchoring role in partisan competition under the PRI's rule, and its disappearance has led to ideological disarray among voters.[8]

This low level of structure in voters' pre-election mental maps of the issue space is further corroborated by the lack of clear meaning voters attached to left versus right orientations. The left-right scale is often considered an important heuristic that candidates use to help voters align their personal interests with voting decisions (see McCann and Lawson 2003 on the Mexico case). Zechmeister (2006) cleverly argued that left-right self-placements may have a policy component related to positional issues, a valence component tied to consensus issues (also see D. Stokes 1963), and a symbolic component linked with group affect. I followed this approach and tested the meaning of left-right self-placements in July 2006 by examining the effects of policy preferences, candidate traits, party identification, and demographic variables. The most complete model (see the Mexico 2006 Panel Survey's supplemental materials for chapter 13 at http://web.mit.edu/polisci/research/mexico06/book.html) did a relatively poor job at nailing down the meaning of self-placement on a left-right scale, accounting for just 18 percent of the variation in voters' orientations. Among the four sets of explanatory variables, symbolic and valence attachments clearly mattered most. Voters who identified with the PRD and rated López Obrador as the best candidate for dealing with pressing national problems thought of themselves as on the left; those who identified with the PAN and preferred Calderón's problem-solving abilities labeled themselves as rightist. These effects in the 2006 elections wash out all the explanatory value of positional issues (D. Stokes 1963).[9] Thus, the left-right heuristic appears not to have taken on any clear programmatic significance that is independent of the particular political actors themselves in 2006.[10]

In sum, the absence of clearly divided issue publics, the lack of a well-structured space in voters' mental maps of the partisan competition, and the anemic content of ideological left versus right orientation means that it is very unlikely that ideological or issue divisions affected vote choice (corroborated below).

Candidate Traits: Campaign Persuasion and Priming

Despite weakly divided issue publics, the voters did perceive important differences between the candidates' abilities to tackle pressing national problems. In particular, between October 2005 and May 2006, the Calderón campaign successfully persuaded voters that he was more capable of dealing with these problems and primed voters to think of candidate competence as more important in determining their vote choices. These shifts in perceptions help account for the vote swing away from López Obrador and toward Calderón during the campaign.

To begin with, it is important to note that there was relative consensus about the most pressing national problems, as well as quite a bit of aggregate stability in how voters ranked these problems over time. I organized answers to an open-ended question about the biggest problem facing the country into four categories: economic problems, such as poverty and unemployment; public security issues associated with crime and drug trafficking; political problems, such as corruption; and social problems, such as public services.[11] In all three panel waves in the 2006 survey, as well as in the final wave of the Mexico 2000 Panel Study, voters consistently perceived economic problems as the most important, and public safety as a close second. Political and social problems lagged far behind. Other data also demonstrate that the differences between each candidate's supporters over the importance of these issue areas were minor and not statistically distinguishable before the election.[12]

Voters disagreed, however, on which candidate was most capable of addressing pressing issues. I constructed strict preference orders to gauge whether voters thought that one of the candidates was clearly more competent than the others.[13] In October, voters split almost evenly between whether Calderón or López Obrador was best able to deal with the economy, public security, and corruption. The only significant disparity was over the question of poverty reduction, where some 4 percent more of the electorate thought López Obrador the most capable. Madrazo was a distant third on all issue areas. By May, voters continued to think of Madrazo as the least capable candidate, but their perceptions of Calderón, as compared to López Obrador, rose in all issue areas. Calderón was strictly preferred to López Obrador by 4.1 percent more of the electorate when it came to managing the economy, by about 3 percent regarding enhancing public security and reducing poverty, and by a whopping 8.1 percent on handling corruption.[14] Thus, not only was Calderón able to neutralize the

October 2005 assessments that López Obrador would be better at reducing poverty, but he also opened up a competence gap in other salient areas.

What makes this change in comparative assessments of the candidates' capacities even more important is that the October to May shifts had palpable effects on vote choices. Statistical models that include voters' October ratings (as well as a full compliment of control variables) show that candidate traits had no statistically significant impact on vote choices in July. It is only when the May ratings are used in models having the same explanatory variables that these effects emerge. Thus, voters' ratings changed in important ways between October and May.

Campaign Persuasion

What induced these shifts in voters' perceptions of candidate competence? Did Calderón's media blitz persuade voters? Or did the campaigns simply disseminate information that helped activate pre-existing partisan dispositions or issue preferences, such that market-oriented voters eventually rated Calderón as the most capable economic manager, while voters who preferred a substantial role for the state in economic development instead picked López Obrador as the best?

It is clear that the campaigns informed voters and increasingly focused attention on economic issues. Calderón was the least-well-known candidate in October, with just 26 percent of the voters able to attribute any focus to his campaign; by July, 65 percent of them perceived a specific focus. López Obrador's long pre-campaign made him a better-known quantity early in the campaign season, but by July, he was no better known than Calderón. Most voters remained uncertain about the focus of Madrazo's campaign.

Voters also increasingly believed that the Calderón and López Obrador campaigns were focused on economic issues. Whereas the plurality of voters who could distinguish a particular focus to the campaigns in October believed that the two leading candidates emphasized issues of political reform, by July, the overwhelming majority identified economic issues as central. This shift was particularly pronounced for Calderón supporters who likely responded to his attempt, beginning relatively late in the campaign season, to become the "jobs" candidate. Whereas voters believed that the two main candidates were focused on economic issues, the same cannot be said of Madrazo. In his case, most voters eventually believed that his main bailiwick was public security.

The lion's share of these changes in voters' perceptions of the campaigns' main themes occurred between October and May, rather than in the last two months of the election.[15] This may have resulted from the timing of the campaigns' investments in advertising. Data from the Media Monitoring Program of the Federal Electoral Institute (IFE) show that from January 19 through the end of April, López Obrador's airtime was just 60 percent of Calderón's, when measured in seconds of radio and television coverage, and 73 percent when measured in the number of spots.[16] In the last two months of the campaign, López Obrador approximately doubled Calderón's television presence, but, as the vote swing section above implies, by then it was too late to recover the votes that had already flowed to Calderón.

To see whether and how the campaigns affected assessments of the candidates' abilities, I constructed models to predict the likelihood that a voter, in May, would rate each candidate as the person best able to deal with the economy, corruption, poverty, and public security.[17] I was particularly interested in the role of campaign awareness, which I measured with an index of television viewing, an index of political knowledge, and a dummy variable that coded whether a respondent thought that each campaign emphasized the capability under consideration or some other capacity. The models also controlled for three additional types of variables. First, they included the voters' economic policy preferences, to test whether voters who preferred state-led or market-led economic development were more likely to assess left-wing López Obrador or right-wing Calderón as the most capable. As it turned out, the voters' policy preferences had no statistically significant effect in any of the models. Second, I controlled for October 2005 assessments of the candidates' capabilities. As expected, the models showed a high degree of continuity in the voters' ratings. Finally, the models controlled for both the October and the May vote intentions. October vote intentions had no effect on the ratings, but the May intentions did. This implies that having made the decision to vote for a candidate, voters were naturally more likely to assess him as the best candidate to deal with each issue area. However, even when controlling for prior assessments and contemporaneous vote choices, voters were independently affected by campaign awareness. This indicates that rather than simply activating latent issue preferences by informing voters, the content of the advertising campaigns persuaded voters to change their assessments of the candidates' capabilities.[18]

Figure 13.2 uses the statistical model to show the predicted probability that an undecided voter in May, who did not previously rate any of the candidates as the most capable in October and who held average economic policy prefer-

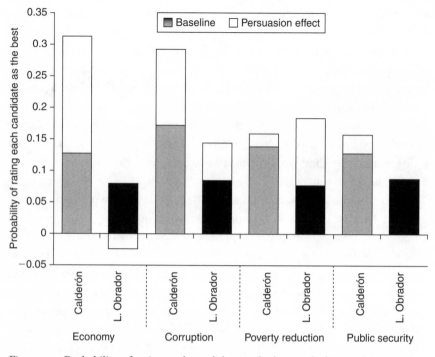

Figure 13.2 Probability of rating each candidate as the best at dealing with national problems.

Note: Figures are based on model predictions for an undecided voter in April/May. For details on model specification, see the Mexico Panel Study's supplemental materials for chapter 13 (http://web.mit.edu/polisci/research/mexico06/book.html).

ences, would rate each candidate as the most capable in May. The figure further distinguishes between the baseline effect for a voter who had a minimum level of campaign awareness (i.e., who watched very little television, had a low level of political knowledge, and did not think that the campaigns emphasized the issue area under consideration), and a persuasion effect for a voter who was the same in every way but had a maximum level of campaign awareness.

This figure provides evidence that campaign persuasion did occur and that it benefited Calderón much more than López Obrador in all areas except poverty reduction. An undecided voter with all the attributes mentioned above plus high campaign awareness was 19 percent more likely to think Calderón was the best economic manager in May than the same voter with low campaign awareness. At the same time, campaign exposure actually lowered voters' assessment of López Obrador by 2.3 percent on this issue.

The campaigns also persuaded voters with regard to other areas of competence. Calderón got a 12.2 percent bump from campaign awareness on the ability to combat corruption, while López Obrador benefited from a more modest 6.2 percent increase. As a result, the gap in favor of Calderón for voters with high campaign awareness hit 16 percent, instead of the 9 percent gap for those with low campaign exposure. On the question of public security, López Obrador got no campaign bounce at all, while Calderón benefited from a modest 3 percent rise. The one area where López Obrador outpolled Calderón was on the ability to reduce poverty. Campaign awareness raised the likelihood of rating López Obrador as the most capable by 11 percent, compared to just 2.1 percent for Calderón, but even with this bump, the gap between the two candidates remained low on this issue.

Overall, by May, ratings of the candidates' abilities swung in favor of Calderón, and the swing was much more substantial among voters whose exposure to the media made them more aware of the content of the campaigns. Although the panel data were collected too infrequently to allow us to pinpoint exactly when and why campaign awareness benefited Calderón, it seems likely that his April media blitz—dedicated to damaging López Obrador's character and presenting himself as the "jobs" candidate—was largely responsible for the change.

Campaign Priming

The Calderón campaign also raised another question associated with campaign competence. Aware of rising concern across the region with populist leaders—including Venezuela's Hugo Chávez, Argentina's Nestor Kirchner, and Bolivia's Evo Morales—Calderón's April advertisements, and those of his allies in the business community, warned that López Obrador's economic policy proposals were so irresponsible that, if elected, he would cause an economic crisis equivalent to the free-falls experienced in 1982 and 1994. The May poll found that 38.4 percent of the voters agreed, 46.8 percent disagreed, and the rest were uncertain. These assessments were naturally associated with vote choices. Nearly two-thirds of Calderón's May voters, and about half of Madrazo's voters, expressed concern that López Obrador would cause a crisis. Just 9 percent of López Obrador's voters (about 2.3% of the electorate) followed suit; however, among these cross-pressured supporters, the final vote choice for López Obrador was about 30 percent lower than among voters who did not think he would cause a crisis. Thus, raising the specter of a possible populist-inspired crisis *may* have cost López Obrador a small but ultimately quite important group of supporters.

The design of the panel survey made it impossible to discern whether the Calderón campaign persuaded more voters to fear that López Obrador would cause a crisis during the last two months of the campaign,[19] but there is evidence that the campaign successfully primed the crisis issue. I follow Bartels in conceptualizing priming as a "systematic change in the weights attached to prospective voters' attitudes and perceptions in the formulation of vote intentions over the course of the campaign" (2006, 82).[20] Although priming this particular issue would not necessarily persuade more voters to fear a López Obrador victory, it would make those who were already worried about a crisis put more weight on that factor in deciding how to cast their vote. Thus, a voter who agreed in May that López Obrador posed a risk but still planned to vote for this candidate, due to his or her attitudes on other factors, could have been pushed by priming to vote for Calderón in July.

To test for priming, I used the method suggested by Bartels (2006) and Lenz (2006) and compared the coefficients for substantively interesting explanatory variables in two regression models where pre-election vote intentions and post-election vote reports were the dependent variables. Any change in the explanatory effect of the independent variables between the models indicated that, on average, voters changed (i.e., reweighted) the importance they attached to previously held attitudes during the course of the campaign.

Fully specified models of vote choice (see the next section for details) naturally show that predictions that López Obrador would cause a crisis lowered voters' probability of choosing him and raised the likelihood of selecting Calderón. But the weight attached to this variable increased by 60 percent between May and July.[21] Thus, although voters were not necessarily persuaded to believe that López Obrador would cause a crisis, they were primed to think of their existing beliefs as significantly weightier influences in making their voting decisions.

Overall, attempts to persuade voters to change their assessments of the candidates' capabilities and prime them to weight economic competence more heavily in their vote choices appeared to have paid off. What remains to be seen is how much perceptions of competence mattered in final vote choices when stacked up against issue preferences, retrospective evaluations of the Fox administration, and other traditional elements in models of voting behavior.

Choosing Mexico's President in 2006

By the official start of the presidential campaign in 2005, historical trends and initial partisan maneuvering created three "facts on the ground" that set the stage for each candidate's strategy. First, the PRI was the only party with a nationwide organization. Although it had weakened since losing the presidency in 2000, it was larger than either the PAN or the PRD, both of which were regionally strong but nationally weak. As a result, some 35 percent of the electorate remained independent and unidentified with any party. Second, PRI voters were the most ideologically heterogeneous, and although PAN and PRD identifiers were less clearly ideological than they had been in the past, these parties' core voters were still spread to the right and left, respectively (see Greene 2007 and chapter 6 in this volume). Finally, López Obrador had a substantial lead in the polls, and he had already staked out his strategy of campaigning on the economic injustices of the past and mobilizing support behind a program for change squarely focused on redistribution, an expanded social safety net, and protection of domestic industry. He promised a populist nationalism that would be, as his slogan went, for the good of all, beginning with the poor.

Given these conditions, Calderón and Madrazo tried to shape the race in their own fashions. Madrazo, in order to win, would have to build on the PRI's traditional vote, but without focusing on issues that would alienate one or another of the party's traditional wings. Thus he stuck to vague policy statements that seemed to split the difference between Calderón and López Obrador and cast him as the responsible and competent centrist. To the extent that he focused on any issues, they were associated with public security concerns that naturally tended to evoke more consensus than disagreement. For his part, Calderón would have to bring down López Obrador without benefiting Madrazo. To do so, he tried to portray López Obrador as reckless, unpredictable, and ultimately unable to reduce poverty. At the same time, he presented himself as a competent economic manager who would continue the stable, if unspectacular, economic growth under Fox and, beginning in April, he argued that the resulting steady economic expansion under this policy would create more jobs.

How successful were each of these strategies? Was López Obrador able to turn the race into a competition over positional issues and different world views? Was Calderón able to dent López Obrador's personal appeal and cast doubt on the prudence of his economic policy proposals, thus shifting the race to retrospective issues and candidate traits? Was Madrazo able to rule the middle ground and appear as the responsible, experienced, and trustworthy centrist?

To analyze voters' decisions, I used data from all three waves of the panel survey and incorporated five sets of explanatory variables in a statistical model. The first was party identification, taken from the first survey wave in October 2005. These variables should have gone a long way toward accounting for final vote intention just nine months later. Nevertheless, since 30.7 percent of respondents changed their vote intention during this period, other variables associated with the campaigns must have been at work.[22]

The second set of variables focused on candidate traits, that is, voters' perceptions of which candidate would be the best at handling the economy, tackling corruption, enhancing public security, and reducing poverty. As discussed above, these measures tapped voters' strict preference for one of the three candidates on each issue, while the "excluded" category comprised the large group of respondents who did not have a strict preference, either because their ratings were not transitive or because they rated two or more candidates as tied. This set also included a somewhat different kind of candidate trait—whether the respondents thought that electing López Obrador would cause an economic crisis. Each candidate trait was measured in May, well before the July election but after the survey data showed substantial shifts in voters' assessments due to campaign persuasion over the previous nine months.

The third set of variables concerned retrospective evaluations of the incumbent's performance in office (Fiorina 1981), including a standard indicator of presidential approval, measured in May 2006, as well as an indicator of sociotropic (i.e., national) economic well-being, measured in October 2005. While these workhorse variables typically have a major impact on voting behavior in the United States (Tufte 1978), we might expect them to have less of an effect in a new democracy, where voters can only evaluate the incumbent party's performance over a single term rather than its accumulated performance over their lifetimes.

The fourth set of variables dealt with positional issues. To cast as wide a net as possible, they encompassed all of the positional issues measured in the panel study, whether or not the descriptive analysis above showed potentially meaningful differences by vote intention: privatization of the electricity sector, commercial relations with the United States, poverty reduction, the extent of the social safety net, abortion, and the death penalty.[23]

The final set of variables included demographics, an index of political knowledge based on a set of factual questions asked of survey respondents, and a variable that tapped respondents' assessments of the probability that Madrazo would win the election. Such probability assessments underlie the strategic decision to defect from trailing candidates in a multicandidate contest.[24]

I estimated the model using multinomial logit;[25] however, instead of presenting the difficult-to-interpret regression coefficients, I show results in the substantively more interesting form of predicted probabilities of voting for each candidate.[26] When all variables are set at their mean or mode, the baseline predicted probabilities are 41.76 percent for Calderón, 41.11 percent for López Obrador, and 17.14 percent for Madrazo.[27] These predictions come remarkably close to the actual 0.56 percent difference between Calderón and López Obrador. Even though they underpredict support for Madrazo by about 5 percent,[28] they are close enough to the real final outcome to give confidence in the model.

To appreciate the impacts of the explanatory variables, we can examine their individual effects on the predicted probability of supporting each candidate by moving each variable from its empirical minimum to its maximum, while holding all other variables at their means or modes. These first differences are detailed in table 13.1.

Scanning the table for significant changes in the probability of choosing each candidate gives the overall impression that the race was more candidate- than party-centric. Specifically, the outcome was shaped most strongly by candidate traits, somewhat by retrospective evaluations of the Fox administration, and virtually not at all by positional issues or demographics. Although party identification in October 2005 had a large impact on vote choices in July 2006, these variables were far from determinative. Some 35 percent of the electorate counted itself as independent and, even with controls for partisanship, campaign-related variables played important roles. Yet Madrazo was largely absent from this fight. Other than identification with the PRI, most of the main variables at play neither benefited nor hurt Madrazo. Even the statistically significant effects of candidate traits are of smaller magnitude for Madrazo than for the other candidates. This suggests that PRI voters were relatively more immune to campaign effects. The one major exception concerns (dwindling) assessments of Madrazo's chances of winning the election that encouraged defection (see chapter 10 in this volume). Since Madrazo voters were less persuadable, and because there were fewer of them, the race centered on a fight between Calderón and

Table 13.1 Change in the predicted vote choice for the explanatory variables

Variable type	Variable	Calderón	López Obrador	Madrazo
			Change in the predicted probability of voting for	
Party identification	PAN ID, w1	.33*	−.25*	−.08
	PRD ID, w1	−.30*	.38*	−.08
	PRI ID, w1	−.07	−.20*	.27*
Candidate traits	Calderón best for economy, w2	.17*	−.17	−.01
	Madrazo best for economy, w2	−.06	−.11	.17*
	López Obrador best for economy, w2	−.19	.19*	−.01
	Calderón best on corruption, w2	.15*	−.16*	.01
	López Obrador best on poverty, w2	−.28*	.40*	−.12*
	López Obrador will cause a crisis, w2	.28*	−.38*	.10*
Retrospective	Presidential approval, w2	.36*	−.14	−.22*
	Evaluation of national economy, w1	.28*	−.15	−.14
Prospective positional issues	Poverty reduction, w2	.40*	−.37*	−.03
	Privatization of electricity, w2	.04	−.05	.01
	Commercial relations with U.S., w2	−.06	.05	.01
	Extent of social safety net, w2	.04	−.12	.08
	Death penalty, w2	.01	−.00	−.01
	Abortion, w2	.04	−.04	.00
Other	Probability Madrazo wins, w2	−.06	−.59**	.65*
	Political knowledge, w1	.02	.11	−.13
	Age	.04	−.16	.11
	Education	.05	−.11	.06
	Religiosity	.01	−.08	.06
	Income	.09	−.04	−.05
	Male	−.11	.05	.05

Note: Entries are first differences, showing the effect on the probability of voting for each candidate if each explanatory variable is moved from its minimum to its maximum while holding all other variables constant. The dependent variable was vote choice in wave 3 (July 2006) of the Mexico 2006 Panel Study. W1 refers to wave 1 of the panel (October 2005); w2 refers to the April/May 2006 wave. For details on the analysis and the variables included in it, see the Mexico 2006 Panel Study's supplemental materials for chapter 13 (http://web.mit.edu/polisci/research/mexico06/book.html).

*Significant at the 95% level.

López Obrador, primarily for undecided voters and secondarily for each other's core constituents.

López Obrador's attempt to make the campaign into a referendum on the Fox administration's free-market economic policies and associated questions of social justice appears to have failed. Astonishingly, negative assessments of national economic progress did not help López Obrador. When voters thought that the economy was doing well, they rewarded Calderón as the bearer of continuity in free-market policies, but when they thought that the economy had tanked, they were not wooed by López Obrador's promise of economic nationalism to benefit the poorest. Along the same lines, only one of the four positional economic policy issues included in the model had any effect on final vote choices.[29] As expected, a preference for reducing poverty through increased distribution, rather than investment, hurt Calderón and helped López Obrador. Yet despite this effect, positional issues played such a small role in the race that even though the candidates' campaigns may have focused on economic issues, this election was clearly not about economic *policy*.

Voters' more abstract retrospective assessments of the Fox administration, irrespective of their evaluations of the national economy and their policy preferences, similarly helped Calderón but not López Obrador. Voters who liked Fox had a 35.6 percent greater likelihood of choosing Calderón, and since 64 percent of the respondents to the panel surveys approved of Fox, this was an important benefit for the PAN's candidate. Voters who disapproved of Fox were no more likely to choose López Obrador. That Calderón benefited at all from evaluations of the sitting president is notable for two reasons. First, positive retrospective evaluations of President Zedillo (1994–2000) did not help the PRI's candidate, Francisco Labastida, in the previous election (Magaloni 2006; see also Poiré 1999). Second, the link between Fox and Calderón was much vaguer than an analogous relationship would have been in other democracies. Fox's relations with the PAN were often strained (see Shirk 2005 and chapter 7 in this volume), and a combination of campaign restrictions, Fox's weak record, and Calderón's attempts to establish himself as his own man put distance between his candidacy and the Fox administration. Nevertheless, the analysis here shows that voters made the connection between Fox and Calderón, albeit in the vaguest way, that is, excusing economic policy performance and rewarding the outgoing president's positive image.

Despite the notable effects of the variables discussed above, Calderón's and López Obrador's fortunes hinged most significantly on candidate traits that were independent of retrospective performance evaluations and prospective policy concerns.[30] The Calderón campaign was so successful at persuading voters of its candidate's abilities that his October deficit in competence ratings turned into a May surplus. In addition, voters were primed to weigh the possibility of an economic crisis under a López Obrador presidency more heavily in their final vote choices.

These perceptions of competence strongly influenced vote choices. For the smaller proportion who thought López Obrador was the most competent, he benefited dramatically. An independent voter who was average in every way but perceived López Obrador as the most competent in all areas had an 88.5 percent chance of voting for him and just a 3.3 percent chance of choosing Calderón. Calderón also benefited handsomely from positive evaluations. If we take the same voter, but change the profile so that he or she thinks Calderón is the most competent candidate across the board, then the likelihood of that person voting for Calderón increases to 71.2 percent and the chance of choosing López Obrador falls to 6.4 percent. This slightly lower bump for Calderón implies that López Obrador benefited from a competency advantage whenever he could convince voters of his credentials. Thus, had Calderón's perceived competence been damaged, his candidacy would have suffered. Yet since López Obrador focused more on positional issues, Calderón largely escaped scrutiny on the question of competence.

Assessments of the candidates' traits played a key role for voters who identified one candidate as more capable than the others. Nevertheless, since the majority of voters did not have such a strict preference ordering when it came to competence, these variables had no effect on a large portion of the electorate. A related concern that affected all voters included in the model was whether they believed that López Obrador would spark an economic crisis if elected. Much was made of this claim during the campaigns, with Calderón launching vicious attack ads that compared López Obrador to Chávez and implying that the PRD candidate would cause painful currency devaluations. So what was the independent impact of this factor alone? In models that sought to predict vote choice in May 2006, this variable had no discernible effect. What a difference two months made! During that time, Calderón and his allies continued to hammer López Obrador, and findings from the model presented here indicate that this strategy finally worked. Perceptions that López Obrador would spark a crisis made it 28 percent more likely that an independent voter who was typical of survey respondents in every other way would choose Calderón and 38.4 percent less likely that he or she would vote for López Obrador.[31] Intense concern about López Obrador even increased the likelihood of voting for Madrazo by 10.4 percent, even though just 8.9 percent of the voters thought of him as the most competent economic manager. Thus, although this variable was not a magic bullet, it contributed significantly to Calderón's victory.

If perceptions of competence and evaluations of whether López Obrador would cause an economic crisis are taken into account, an average independent voter who assessed López Obrador positively had a whopping 94.6 percent probability of voting for him. A similar voter who instead perceived Calderón as the most competent and feared an economic crisis under the leftist party's candidate had a 78.1 percent probability of voting for Calderón. Thus, the combined effect of variables associated with managing the tasks of office had a major bearing on final vote choices.

In sum, this fully specified model of vote choice shows that images triumphed over issues in Mexico's first "normal" democratic presidential election. Voters were not induced to take sides and line up in ideological terms with candidates who sent clear cues through their campaign rhetoric. Instead, perceptions of the candidates' capacities to solve pressing national problems were crucial factors in determining the election's outcome. To drive this point home even further, for the voting public on the whole, these capacity ratings were not linked to proposed solutions to national problems, but instead rested at least in part on the images the candidates projected in the mass media.

Mexico's 2006 presidential race was no boring affair pitting Tweedledee against Tweedledum. Rather, the leading candidates outlined alternative futures for Mexico based on different world views. López Obrador built his image around a campaign for a profound change in Mexico's economy, one that would protect domestic industry, provide a broad social safety net, expand the role of the state in economic development, and redistribute benefits to the poor. Calderón, on the other hand, pledged to maintain the free-market-oriented status quo, albeit while also continuing to fund targeted welfare programs. Unlike the substantially more center-seeking presidential candidates six years earlier (see Greene 2007), these candidates were polarized on the issues.

Yet the voters did not bite. Vote choice turned on perceptions of candidate competence and presidential approval, not on distinct policy visions. Calderón benefited from Fox's popularity, appeared relatively unhurt by Fox's failures, and successfully projected an image of competence that attracted voters to his side.

As the campaign wore on and negative advertising took its toll, voters increasingly thought of López Obrador as less capable; an important minority even believed that his election would spark an economic crisis. López Obrador was not able to counter this slide effectively by priming economic policy issues because, according to the data presented here, these issues were never the primary source of his popularity. By election day, López Obrador's long-time lead had eroded to the point where Calderón, according to the official results, slightly surpassed him.

Presidential campaigns the world over invest massive amounts of resources in advertising that typically focuses on candidate images. Yet research on established democracies shows that image management rarely persuades voters and only occasionally primes their perception of the candidates enough to shift their vote choices (Finkel 1993). One of the reasons for such minimal effects may be the strong and widespread party identification that exists in these systems. This identification ties voters to parties and encourages them to transfer many aspects of the parties' accumulated reputations to the candidates (Hayes 2005; Petrocik 1996). As a result, only a small group of independents are available for conversion (Campbell et al. 1960). But in Mexico's new democracy, the lower level of party identification and the parties' weaker accumulated reputations leave more room for campaign priming and persuasion (Lawson and McCann 2005). These effects were especially felt in the area of candidate image. All three campaigns invested heavily in advertising, with Calderón spending the most in the apparently decisive first phase of the campaign. These outlays paid off by persuading a greater number of voters that Calderón was capable of dealing with national problems and by priming them to consider the potential risk that López Obrador represented.

The findings presented in this chapter also help forecast aspects of Mexico's political future. If issue polarization were at work, then the virtual tie between López Obrador and Calderón would reflect deep and precariously balanced partisan differences that could result in contentious national debates waged in the legislature and in the streets, leaving Mexico without policy solutions to vexing problems. This might have been a worrisome combination for Mexico. After all, it was not so long ago that polarized legislative politics under presidential systems in South America led to a politics of outbidding that stalled legislative output and eventually led to the breakdown of democratic regimes (see Collier and Collier 1991).

However, since polarization appears to have been driven by partisan elites alone, postelectoral antagonisms may fade and, if the political class can produce compromisers, legislative gridlock may be avoided. In addition, these findings suggest that the PRD's spectacular growth in this election was not fueled by newfound social support or the rise of a durable new left-wing movement, but rather by López Obrador's personal appeal. As a result, the PRD finds itself in a much weaker position, and the PRI will be better able to reclaim left-leaning voters and remain a viable party (see Greene 2008). Further, the absence of polarization among voters means that Mexico is not undergoing a durable electoral realignment; voters have not come to match their personal interests with political options, and campaigns are likely to continue to turn on personality rather than on issues. Finally, since the candidates earned votes not from their platforms but from their images, voters sent them to office with virtually no specific mandate, so politicians will have wider latitude to pursue their own interests in office. Thus, the striking absence of issue polarization leaves us with two impressions: Mexico may be saved from contentious battles that strain its representative institutions, but the temporary custodians of those institutions will have fewer clear signals about what the voters want them to do while in office.

CHAPTER FOURTEEN

Ideology in the 2006 Campaign

James A. McCann

During the 2006 presidential elections in Mexico, Felipe Calderón, Andrés Manuel López Obrador (often referred to by his initials, AMLO), and Roberto Madrazo spent little time debating the finer points of foreign policy. Mexico's relations with its major trading partners in North America are of paramount importance, of course, as are its connections to Central America, the Caribbean nations, and, increasingly, the Southern Cone of Latin America, the Far East, and the European Union. To the extent that the candidates discussed issues, however, they gave nearly all their attention to domestic concerns—increasing economic growth, alleviating poverty, rooting out corruption, reducing crime, and maintaining the nation's infrastructure.[1] When foreign policy came up, the candidates focused nearly exclusively on retaining tariffs for Mexican corn and beans that had not yet been phased out under the North American Free Trade Agreement (López Obrador), increasing Mexico's economic competitiveness (Calderón), and protecting Mexican migrants in the United States (all three candidates).

That the three leading contenders would avoid foreign policy issues is understandable, given public opinion in Mexico. When asked to name the most important problem facing the country, Mexican voters rarely bring up international affairs. In the second wave of the Mexico 2006 Panel Study,[2] for instance, only six out of 1,177 mentioned an issue that could be construed as an international issue (in these cases, either immigration or drug trafficking). Consequently, Calderón, López Obrador, and Madrazo would have seen little reason to speak about the intricacies of the North American Free Trade Agreement or other hemispheric concerns. "Foreign policy doesn't give you any votes in Mexico," noted Jorge Montaño, a former Mexican ambassador to the United States, in an interview three weeks before the July 2 election. "The candidates have been extremely practical."[3]

Yet actors and symbols from abroad did manage to find their way into the campaigns. One noteworthy example was the appearance of José Maria Aznar, the former prime minister of Spain, at the National Action Party (PAN) headquarters in February 2006. Aznar praised both President Vicente Fox and Calderón, adding that he hoped a representative of the incumbent party would again win the Mexican presidency in July.[4] Later in the campaign, the PAN began airing commercials implicitly comparing López Obrador to Venezuela's President Hugo Chávez. Chávez did not formally endorse the Party of the Democratic Revolution (PRD)'s candidate, but he made no secret of his antipathy toward the Fox administration. Shortly thereafter, Chávez used his weekly television program in Venezuela to attack the PAN and ridicule the Mexican election.[5] López Obrador's own criticisms of Chávez—and the marked dissimilarity of their policy proposals—received far less attention.

In this chapter, I examine how Mexican voters evaluated well-known foreign leaders and how these attitudes in turn shaped presidential preferences at home. I do not attempt to gauge whether Aznar's endorsement of Calderón or attack ads featuring Chávez had an effect on electoral behavior. Rather, I explore the factors underlying popular reactions to international figures like Chávez. My findings demonstrate that feelings toward three very different heads of state in countries close to Mexico—specifically, Chávez, Fidel Castro, and George W. Bush—cluster with each other and with left-right self-identification in such a way as to indicate a coherent ideological orientation. Furthermore, these orientations were significant predictors of vote choice. Far from being ideologically unconstrained, Mexicans appear capable of espousing firm and stable leftist, rightist, or centrist positions—and acting on these attitudes—even if they do not actively use terms like Left and Right.

In the following section, I discuss mass-level political ideology, as conceived of in terms of personal identifications and evaluations. I then explore the question of attitude structure and stability. To what extent do ratings of Presidents Bush, Chávez, and Castro, coupled with positions along a left-right continuum, stem from a central ideological perspective? Are these attitudes malleable, as preferences on most specific issues appear to be, or should they be thought of as *core* dispositions for voters? Finally, I explore voting decisions in the July 2 presidential election. Did ideological orientations ultimately help shape choices at the ballot box? And what part did the 2006 presidential campaign play in forging connections between left-right dispositions and votes?

Theoretical Background: Are Mexicans Ideological?

In popular accounts of party politics in Mexico, competition is often described in ideological terms, with the PAN tilting heavily toward the Right and the PRD on the Left (see chapter 6 in this volume). Members of the PRD generally wish to see the public sector expanded and oppose privatizing the electricity sector, while PAN partisans accept the main premises of neoliberal reform: opening up more of the economy to private investment, relaxing governmental regulations, lowering taxes and tariffs, and allowing employers greater liberty in managing their workforce (Moreno 2000).[6] The two parties also have predictable differences on cultural issues, such as abortion.

Are these patterns found at the mass level? At first glance, much as Converse (1964) discovered in his classic study of belief systems in the United States, public opinion in Mexico did not appear to be constrained by firm ideological principles.[7] When asked where they fell on a left-right scale (typically a continuum of five, seven, ten, or eleven points, ranging from "strongly left" to "strongly right"), a sizeable number of citizens gave no response (Moreno 2007, table 1).[8] Moreover, left-right positioning is fairly unstable over time, and seemingly dependent on cues from parties, candidates, and the mass media. In the mid-1980s, fewer than 10 percent of the public claimed to be on the left; a decade later, this percentage had more than doubled. Since the 1980s, the number of self-placements on the right has also grown, rising to a high of 49 percent following Fox's election in 2000. This trend toward somewhat greater ideological differentiation at the mass level no doubt reflects the consolidation of a multiparty system in Mexico, with the Institutional Revolutionary Party (PRI) being eroded by the Left (the PRD) and Right (the PAN).

Analyses based on panel survey data collected over a much shorter period of time show pronounced patterns of ideological instability. Between February and May 2000, as that Mexican presidential campaign became more intense, left-right self-placements proved to be fairly volatile. Even when random errors in the measurement of the respondents' ideologies were taken into account, positions along the left-right continuum were significantly less stable than party identification and presidential approval ratings (McCann and Lawson 2003).

This portrait of a largely nonideological and reactive public surfaces again in assessing preferences regarding major policy controversies. When asked for their opinions on the importation of foreign goods, the repayment of the national debt, the maintenance of state-owned industries, and other pressing issues, most Mexicans offered a response. These responses, however, did not overlap in such a way as to suggest a firm and coherent pro-neoliberal or anti-neoliberal disposition, or any other discernable ideological position (C. Davis 1998; Domínguez and McCann 1996; Lawson 1999, note especially table 6.1).[9] As was the case with the left-right self-placement scale, beliefs about policies also appear to be highly malleable. Indeed, during the 2000 presidential campaign, public opinion concerning two issues (whether a "heavy hand" should be used to deal with Mexico's crime problems and whether the electrical industry should be privatized) changed far more than positions on the left-right scale (McCann and Lawson 2003).

The contrast in Mexico between ideologically minded elites and apparent ideological innocence at the mass level is potentially troubling. At its best, voting in a democracy rests on a combination of retrospective considerations and forward-looking mandates (Anderson and Dodd 2005; Fiorina 1981; Key 1966). A typical voter in a typical democracy might ask both "Am I better off now (or is the country better off) than when the incumbent officeholders first took power?" and "Should policymakers move the country more in one direction or another in the future?" Much of the work on Mexican public opinion implies that voters could be capable of addressing the first question on retrospective assessments but might have serious difficulty on the second. In the pretransition environment (prior to 2000), the crucial concern for voters was whether the ruling party remained uniquely capable of managing the state and governing society (Domínguez and McCann 1996; Paolino 2005). Mexican citizens today face more issues and partisan choices. An ideological commitment to the Left, Right, or Center could help simplify these decisions and allow the electorate to steer the government—but only if Mexican voters did in fact take such stands.

Is public opinion in Mexico as ideologically unconstrained as prior studies suggest? As Conover and Feldman (1981) note, there is more to ideological attitudes than simply placing oneself along a left-right axis or offering support for particular policies. Politics is filled with individuals and groups who, by intention or circumstance, grow to symbolize what political scientists think of as the Left or Right. Reasoning about these ideologies involves both affective reactions (Do I have positive or negative feelings about specific public officials and social movements on the right or left?) and cognitive understandings concerning abstract principles (Do I agree with what they stand for?). Information about policy issues and the implications of ideological stands may be difficult for many Mexicans to acquire, retain, and express, because (1) vigorous Right versus Left partisan competition is such a new phenomenon in Mexico; (2) Mexican voters, like so many citizens in developing countries, lack the resources to become knowledgeable about leftist or rightist approaches to governing; or (3) seven-, ten-, and eleven-point scales in survey questionnaires are, at best, highly imperfect instruments to capture general political orientations. It might still be possible, however, for meaningful ideological stances to develop around impressions of prominent, ideologically identified figures. "Many in the mass public lack a firm understanding of political abstractions. All the same, many know whom they like, and, equally important, they also know whom they dislike. If coherent, these likes and dislikes can supply people with an affective calculus" (Sniderman et al. 1994, 94).[10]

In many countries, common symbols—such as big business, the rich, the poor, the workers, or unions—elicit strong feelings that correlate with other ideological beliefs (Conover and Feldman 1981). For Mexicans, the ideological overtones of such labels might be less certain, given that business elites, the rich, unions, poor peasants, and other major social and economic groups were historically incorporated in one way or another into the ruling party.[11] Not far from Mexico, however, are three familiar heads of state who symbolize dramatically different approaches to governing—Fidel Castro and Hugo Chávez in the socialist-statist mold, and George W. Bush, representing the quintessential liberal model. Positive and negative feelings toward these deeply polarizing figures could serve as a critical foundation for prospective ideological decision-making in national elections, even if specific information about right-wing or left-wing stands on the issues is lacking. Mexicans who disliked Chávez, for example, could simply have cast a vote on July 2 for the contender who appeared least likely to emulate the Venezuelan. During Mexico's 2006 presidential campaign, the major parties, candidates, and political groups certainly encouraged symbolic linkages of this sort.[12]

If Mexican citizens evaluate Castro, Chávez, and Bush in an ideological manner rather than simply by personal affect, we would expect these ratings to be highly correlated; those with a good opinion of Chávez, for instance, should feel positive toward Castro but dislike the American president. These three items should also overlap, at least to some degree, with self-descriptions—that is, those identifying with the ideological Right would feel more positive toward Bush but negative toward both Chávez and Castro. If correlations among these scores were low or incorrectly signed, we would have further evidence of ideological innocence within the Mexican mass public. These three leaders have been in the public spotlight for years or, in the case of Castro, many decades. Their governing principles and values are liable to be widely known, but so, too, are their personality traits, physical appearance, family members, and life stories. It is thus possible that when Mexicans offer opinions on such figures, ideological considerations are not uppermost in their minds because of these latter kinds of information.

Analysis and Findings

In each wave of the Mexico 2006 Panel Study, respondents were asked to rate a long list of actors and organizations, using a scale ranging from zero ("very bad") to 10 ("very good"). In the first wave (October 2005), respondents rated both Bush and Castro. In the second (April and May 2006) and third (July 2006) waves, Hugo Chávez, Fidel Castro, and George W. Bush were included in the battery, although Chávez appeared only on the smaller, independent, cross-sectional surveys. In all panel waves, respondents also reported their general ideological leanings in a branching format: they first reported whether they considered themselves a leftist, rightist, or centrist, and then indicated the degree of their commitment (e.g., very much on the left, or only somewhat on the left). The result was a seven-point scale.[13]

The first impression from these items was that Mexicans expressed rather negative opinions about all three world leaders.[14] Ratings of Bush were consistently higher over the course of the panel than those for the other two, but his averages (4.16, 3.73, and 4.17) remained well below the scale midpoint of 5.0. Evaluations of Chávez were the lowest, with average scores falling below 3.0; those for Castro fell in between the other two leaders. Nevertheless, there was a great deal of variation among respondents. In all three survey waves, Bush's rating at the 25th percentile was nearly six points below the 75th percentile score. The ranges in scores for Castro and Chávez were not as wide but, at approximately five points, they were still sizeable.

With respect to ideological self-placements, as chapter 6 in this volume makes clear, Mexicans appeared to hug the center. Throughout the panel study, the average score fell nearly at the scale midpoint (4.0), the pure centrist position. As with the Bush, Castro, and Chávez evaluations, there was an appreciable amount of variation around these means, though rather few Mexicans situated themselves near the ends of the ideological continuum. This may signal a truly middle-of-the-road orientation toward politics, which public officials would be well advised to heed. On the other hand, if left-right positioning was largely a matter of ill-informed guesswork (what Converse labeled "non-attitudes") or indifference, we still might expect to find Mexicans hugging the center. On its own, it is difficult to interpret the meaning of the left-right scale. In combination with other survey indicators, however, we can probe its validity as a marker for true ideological orientations.

Factor Structure

To address this issue, the relationship between each survey item and this hypothetical factor could be formalized as

evaluation$_{it}$ (respondent i's attitude at time t) = λ (latent ideological disposition$_{it}$) + e_{it} (a unique residual component that is not linked to one's ideological leanings).

Research on the measurement properties of feeling thermometers suggests that ratings of Bush, Chávez, and Castro might be susceptible to response set, that is, the tendency for survey participants to give consistently high or low marks to the persons and groups being considered (D. Green 1988; D. Green and Citrin 1994; Zeller and Carmines 1980). For this reason, the above equation for these three items is expanded to

evaluation$_{it}$ = λ_1 (latent ideological disposition$_{it}$) + λ_2 (response set$_{it}$) + e_{it}.

Estimates for the λ coefficients can be calculated via confirmatory factor analysis, provided that the factor structure is identified. To achieve identification, the impact of response set was assumed to be consistent for the Bush, Castro, and Chávez ratings. I also assumed that if an underlying ideological disposition truly existed, evaluations of the three figures would have been equally valid reflections of this disposition; in absolute terms, the λ_1 values were constrained to be the same for the three measurements. No such constraint was placed on the λ value for the left-right self-placement. The e_{it} terms for each attitude measure were further assumed to be uncorrelated with the unique variation for the other survey items. Finally, response set was assumed to be uncorrelated with the latent ideological dimension.[15]

Figure 14.1 reports the results from two confirmatory factor analyses, one for the second wave and another for the third. The results indicate that a significant latent ideological dimension—scaled so that the higher values reflect

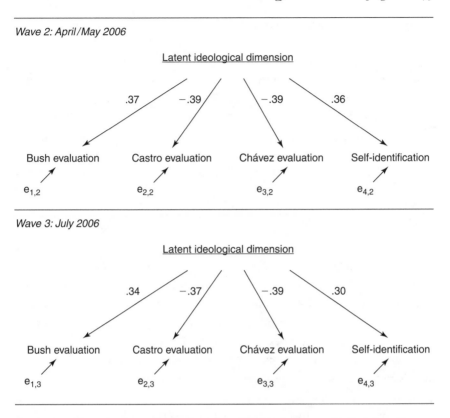

Figure 14.1 Factor structure for evaluations of foreign leaders and left-right self-identifications.

Note: These coefficients are standardized estimates calculated via AMOS 5.0 (SPSS, Chicago, IL), with all cases included. For details, see the Mexico 2006 Panel Study's supplemental materials for chapter 14, table 14.A, http://web.mit.edu/polisci/research/mexico06/book.html. In absolute terms, the regression weights linking the Bush, Castro, and Chávez evaluations to the latent ideological dimension were constrained to be equal; a response set measurement parameter for the three items in each wave was also estimated, but it is not shown, in order to simplify the presentation. χ^2_2 = 2.40 in wave 2 (p = 0.30) and 3.55 in wave 3 (p = 0.17). Variance estimates for the latent ideological dimension are highly significant: 1.35 (se = 0.19) in wave 2 and 1.16 (se = .17) in wave 3.

more positive feelings toward George W. Bush—did indeed condition both the respondents' evaluations of the three figures and their personal identifications with the Left, Center, or Right.[16] As shown here, however, the standardized factor loadings are far from 1.0. Although the ratings for Castro, Chávez, and Bush, coupled with the right-left scale, constituted a valid set of indicators for ideological dispositions, it is also the case that a large amount of variance was left out of this factor. Much of this remaining variation could be linked to response set, as anticipated.[17]

Systematic and random measurement errors notwithstanding, it is safe to say that Mexican citizens grasped the ideological competition taking place across the hemisphere. Through their evaluations of the three heads of state and their left-right self-placements, they took a stand. Being pro-Bush implied negativity toward Castro and Chávez, and vice versa. Furthermore, the structure of the respondents' feelings and beliefs changed little between April and May 2006 (a period of intense political mobilization) and July (in the aftermath of the election).[18]

Individual-level Stability

Panel surveys are designed to track the ebb and flow of positions over time, as candidates are nominated for office, debates are staged, the environment becomes saturated with political messages, and voters head to the polls. Much changed between the first and third waves of the Mexico 2006 Panel Survey. During this nine-month period, how volatile were ideological dispositions? As it turns out, these attitudes were exceedingly stable. Regressing the latent ideological factor from April and May on the scores from wave 1 resulted in an unstandardized stability coefficient of .70 (with a standard error of .04); the standardized coefficient—the correlation between the factors—was a striking .91. Attitude dispositions became even firmer between the second and third waves; the unstandardized stability coefficient rose to 1.0 (with a standard error of .06) and the correlation to .93. For all practical purposes, positions along this factor were locked into place during the final months of the campaign.[19] In other words, Mexicans did indeed hold firm ideological views, instincts, or values that had not been properly captured in earlier measurements. However, the same cannot be said for their personal evaluations of the three main Mexican presidential contenders.

Ideological Dispositions and the Vote

If left-right dispositions are truly relevant to politics, they would presumably affect voting preferences. To explore this issue, candidate choices reported in the postelection wave of the panel survey were modeled as a function of each respondent's ideological stand (a composite measure of evaluations of Bush and Castro combined with left-right self-identifications) plus a number of controls:

party identification, approval rating for Fox, education level, gender, age, and region.[20] These latter predictors were included so that the direct impact of political ideology could be isolated from potential confounding factors.[21]

The Model

The multinomial logistic regression coefficients for this model are given in the supplemental materials for the Mexico 2006 Panel Study.[22] On the whole, the predictors exerted quite substantial effects; the pseudo-r^2 was over 50 percent, with the most significant independent variables being partisanship and judgments regarding Fox. Even in the presence of these powerful controls, however, ideological attitudes were significant and operated in the expected direction: those on the right tended to support Felipe Calderón over Madrazo and López Obrador, while left-leaning voters preferred AMLO.[23] As shown in figure 14.2 (first plot), leftists were more than three times more likely to back López Obrador over Calderón (a probability of approximately .7 versus .2). This difference is equally great on the rightist side of the continuum, with these voters having nearly a 70 percent chance of supporting Calderón. As one would expect, given the traditional stance of the PRI and the tenor of its 2006 campaign, ideological considerations did not influence the vote for Roberto Madrazo.

Most Mexicans did not, of course, fall on either end of this spectrum. Indeed, as noted for figure 14.2, the average score for the composite index (0.51) is just a hairbreadth from the midpoint, and the standard deviation is only .16.[24] For the more numerous centrist voters, it appears that Calderón enjoyed a slight edge. In an election that was decided by only a handful of votes, this small margin undoubtedly paid handsome political dividends.

Campaign Effects

If left-right orientations were fairly stable from one panel wave to the next, the candidates still might not have been judged in such ideological terms at all points in the contest. Early on in election campaigns, there may be a great deal of uncertainty about the candidates' credentials, their stands on policy issues, and the teams that they would bring into government if elected. One key function of campaigns in a democracy is to bring clarity to such weighty matters (Gelman and King 1993). As the second plot in figure 14.2 shows, ideological positions influenced voting preferences far less in the first wave of the survey. During this period, Madrazo and Calderón were securing their nominations, and the most significant conflict was intra- rather than interpartisan, at least for

General Election Choices, July 2006

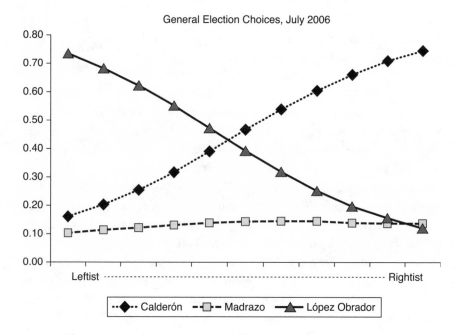

Leftist -- Rightist

··◆·· Calderón --□-- Madrazo ▲ López Obrador

Presidential Preferences, October 2005

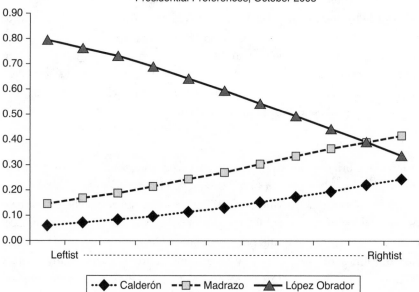

Leftist -- Rightist

··◆·· Calderón --□-- Madrazo ▲ López Obrador

the PRI and the PAN. (On the presidential selection processes, see chapters 7, 8, and 9 in this volume.)

With controls in place for party identification (in October 2005), presidential approval ratings (again in October 2005), and the same demographic variables from the earlier voting choice model, this second plot indicates that in the early months of the campaign, well before its official start in January 2006, only leftists had found a home. The great majority in this bloc leaned toward López Obrador. On the right side of the continuum, the contest was a toss-up, with Calderón, Madrazo, and—interestingly—López Obrador all being about equally competitive. The distribution of ideological attitudes at this time was largely the same as in July 2006 (m = .50, sd = .17). What changed dramatically was the relevance of these stands. Berelson et al. (1954), who pioneered the use of panel surveys to study vote choice, would not be surprised by the contrast between the two probability plots in figure 14.2. Using their terminology, the 2006 campaign in Mexico activated the ideological dimension in the national debate, thereby tightening up the connections between latent left-right views and presidential votes.

In a candidate-centered political environment dominated by broadcast television, this activation would come about through position-taking and appeals through the mass media by the main contenders. Candidates in democracies around the world often avoid taking clear positions on specific policies; some degree of ambiguity can be advantageous when reaching out beyond the traditional party rank-and-file. Nevertheless, over the course of the Mexican campaign, each candidate had no choice but to articulate his platform in relation to those of his opponents.[25] In the public mindset, López Obrador and Calderón,

---

Figure 14.2 Predicted probabilities of presidential vote choice by ideological disposition.

Note: The predicted values were calculated using CLARIFY (Tomz et al. 2001), based on multinomial logistic regression models with controls for party identification, presidential approval, age, gender, education, and place of residence. The regression coefficients themselves, standard errors, and measures of model fit are given in the Mexico 2006 Panel Study's supplemental materials for chapter 14 (http://web.mit.edu/polisci/research/mexico06/book .html). In the model of general election choices (top), all predictors were taken from the second survey wave; when modeling presidential preferences in October 2005, the predictors were from the first wave. Left-right positions (bottom) were gauged by putting ideological self-identifications and evaluations of Castro (reverse coded) and Bush on a 0–1 scale and averaging. In the model of general election choices, the mean of this composite ideological index is 0.51, with a standard deviation of 0.16. The contours of left-right ideology are nearly identical in the October survey wave.

as the standard-bearers for the PRD and the PAN, were evaluated in increasingly ideological terms as their campaigns moved forward. "Campaigns matter, because they tend to produce congruence between fundamental political conditions and predispositions on the one hand and vote intentions on the other" (Bartels 2006, 79–80).

Evidence for these effects surfaces when examining voters' perceptions of the contenders' personal traits and leadership skills. In fall 2005, survey respondents offered their assessments of each candidate's ability to manage the economy, fight poverty, and reduce crime, based on four-point scales (1 = not at all capable, 4 = very capable). Prospective judgments like these are an integral part of political reasoning, especially where parties have not yet developed strong reputations for governing, and ideology can inform these perceptions. As candidates take more recognizable positions on the left or right, the voter's own ideological leanings will shape inferences about these politicians' governing capabilities. A contender who is pushing for a larger role for the state in regulating business and providing public services will be seen by those on the left as likely to lead the country toward greater prosperity and tranquility if elected. Those on the right would anticipate failure should such a candidate take power.

This is what is found in the data. In the first panel wave, ideological dispositions were only weakly correlated with the respondents' impressions of the candidates' likely governing prowess, measured through factors based on all three survey items.[26] Individuals on the left were slightly more inclined to hold López Obrador in high regard, while those on the right were more optimistic about Calderón and Madrazo. Several months later, at the height of the campaign, the correlations between left-right dispositions and expectations regarding the PAN and PRD leaders were far larger, while beliefs about Madrazo's potential efficacy as president became even less linked to ideology.[27]

These dynamics were probed more deeply via regression analysis, where leadership assessments for Calderón, López Obrador, and Madrazo solicited late in the campaign were regressed on ideological dispositions and candidate ratings from the first wave. This design, presented in figure 14.3, posits that largely static left-right positions can cause changes in voters' perceptions of the contenders as the electorate moves into a more politicized environment. The connections between ideological stands and candidate appraisals are potentially reciprocal, that is, ideology aids citizens as they judge politicians' governing capabilities, but we should be mindful of persuasion effects. Voters could be drawn to a contender for reasons that have nothing to do with their positioning

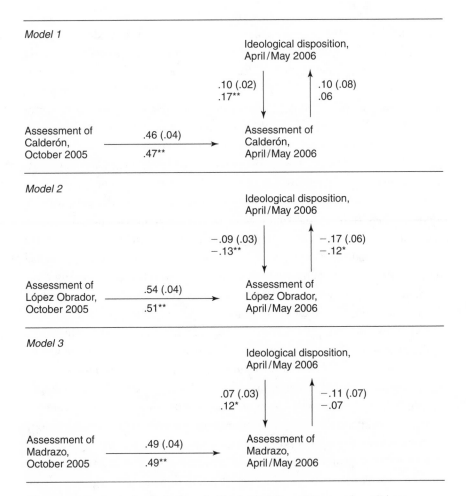

Figure 14.3 Reciprocal causal effects in ideological dispositions and candidate assessments.

Note: Unstandardized regression coefficients are presented, followed by standard errors (in parentheses) and standardized effects, calculated via AMOS 5.0 (SPSS, Chicago, IL) with all cases included. * = $p < 0.05$; ** = $p < 0.001$. Left-right positions from the first wave were included as a predictor of ideological dispositions in April/May to identify the simultaneous equations. Candidate assessments are factors based on three judgments of their abilities: to manage the economy, to reduce poverty, and to fight crime.

along the left-right continuum. Once convinced that their candidate is capable of managing the economy, helping the poor, and fighting crime, respondents, in turn, might revise their ideological leanings to reflect the stances of the nominee. The converse also might well occur; voters could be repelled by a candidate for some reason—for example, a gaffe during the campaign, a poor performance in a debate, televised attack ads, or news of a scandal—and move away from his or her ideological positions. Even though left-right dispositions in Mexico appear to have been remarkably consistent between October 2005 and July 2006, such feedback is certainly possible and should be taken into account.

The estimated regression findings in figure 14.3 confirm the primacy of ideology. Beliefs about the candidates' likely effectiveness as president were relatively fluid; stability scores between the first and second waves only ranged between .46 and .54.[28] For all three office-seekers, left-right stands shaped opinions of their governing capabilities. Mexicans who leaned to the right, for example, significantly increased their faith in Calderón while growing more pessimistic about López Obrador ($p < .001$). Ideological dispositions also affected the respondents' perceptions of Madrazo, though not as strongly. In two of the models, there was only mixed evidence that the candidates altered voters' ideologies; assessments of Madrazo and Calderón in these critical weeks of the campaign had only an insignificant effect on left-right attitudes. Evaluations of López Obrador, however, did move respondents along the ideological continuum. This effect, while slightly less pronounced than the impact of ideology on perceptions of the PRD nominee, was statistically significant. This implies that left-right dispositions in Mexico are not set in stone.[29] As candidates attract or push away voters during a campaign, they can reshape, to a degree, the core underpinnings of public opinion.[30] Such persuasion effects, however, are outweighed by the activation of latent ideological beliefs.

Only a dedicated minority of Mexican citizens engages in issue voting and takes comprehensive ideological positions. Mexicans are hardly alone in this respect. The earliest survey research in political science confirmed what Walter Lippmann (1922) had foreseen in the 1920s, that citizens across the established western democracies were often blissfully innocent regarding current events and issues. At this pivotal time in Mexico's transition to multiparty democracy, it is plainly unreasonable to expect citizens to follow public affairs closely and communicate ironclad policy mandates to elected officials.

This fact need not imply that elections are mainly about expressing partisan identifications and "throwing the rascals out" (or retaining the rascals if they are performing well). For as we have seen, citizens who possess only a loose understanding, or no understanding at all, of the minutia of government can still express their thoughts about ideological symbols and identifications. Come the day of the election, these sentiments help move voters into one of the partisan camps.[31]

Does this movement constitute a substantive mandate? In Mexico in 2006, neither the electorate's collective feelings regarding Presidents Bush, Castro and Chávez, nor the voters' stands along a left-right scale, provided specific guidance for lawmakers. However, the distribution of these attitudes was stable when analyzed as a set. Ideological orientations also overlapped quite significantly—and reasonably—with perceptions of the major candidates. For these reasons, we can conclude that ideology is a very real orientation within the Mexican mass public.

These outlooks could well serve to clarify the governing parameters for Mexico's post-transition democracy. Should officeholders aspire to govern as neoliberals in the American mold, with an emphasis on individualism and free trade? Or should they adopt contrasting values in the spirit of the Castro and Chávez regimes? In 2006, the Mexican electorate on the whole signaled no preference for one pole or the other. But this outcome is *not* because these citizens lacked an appreciation for the ideological discourse taking place both abroad and at home. Rather, the results of the election indicated a persistent division in Mexico that split the country almost evenly along ideological lines.

CHAPTER FIFTEEN

Conclusion

The Choices of Voters during the 2006
Presidential Election in Mexico

Jorge I. Domínguez

Mexico has experienced several close presidential elections in its history, but a
veil of fraud had shielded those outcomes from the public view.[1] Never, before
2006, had electoral authorities published election results that showed the election to be almost a tie. In the final count announced by the Tribunal Electoral
del Poder Judicial de la Federación (TEPFJ), or Federal Electoral Court, Felipe Calderón, candidate of the National Action Party (PAN), won 14,916,927
votes and was elected president of Mexico. He defeated Andrés Manuel López
Obrador, candidate of the Party of the Democratic Revolution (PRD), by a margin of 233,831 votes; López Obrador garnered 14,683,096 votes. Calderón also
prevailed over Roberto Madrazo, candidate of the Institutional Revolutionary
Party (PRI), who received 9,237,000 votes. Small parties and null votes account
for the remainder of the 41,557,430 total votes cast, which formed the basis of
the court's official tally (Instituto Federal Electoral 2006, 72; see also table 1.1
in this volume).

The 2006 presidential election was also distinctive in another sense. For the
first time in the country's history, the vote recount and postelectoral dispute
over the conduct of the election were carried out under the public glare of the
state's newly transparent electoral institutions, the mass media, and the international community, confirming that, yes, the voters had chosen Felipe Calderón
to become Mexico's next president.

A comparison between the aggregate votes cast for president and those cast
for the Chamber of Deputies[2] shows that López Obrador ran well ahead of his
partisan coalition, getting over 2.7 million more votes than the PRD coalition's
federal deputy candidates, who garnered 12,013,360 votes. Calderón, too, ran

over one million votes ahead of the 13,845,122 ballots cast for the PAN's candidates for these posts. In contrast, Madrazo lagged over 2.4 million votes behind his partisan base, as measured by the 11,676,598 votes that PRI-led federal deputy coalition candidates won (Instituto Federal Electoral 2006). The PRI's showing in the simultaneous legislative election demonstrated that it remained a powerful party, notwithstanding its bad choice of Madrazo as its presidential candidate or its past as the "party of the state" in a long-lasting authoritarian regime. López Obrador's and Calderón's vote counts, outperforming their respective parties, also demonstrate the salience of candidate traits in the choices made by Mexican voters.

In this chapter, I compare aspects of the 2000 and 2006 presidential elections and present them, in some detail, as an approach to thinking about how Mexican voters made their electoral decisions in 2006. I highlight some salient findings from the Mexico 2006 Panel Study[3]and argue that the 2006 presidential election edged Mexico closer to the patterns of public opinion and voting behavior that are familiar in well-established democracies. Partisanship, attitudes toward the incumbent, economic voting, the leading candidates and their campaign strategies, valence issue voting, mass-media reporting, and negative advertising were quite consequential. Clientelist practices, and the kind of strategic voting that mattered as part of Mexico's transition from authoritarian to democratic politics between the late 1980s and 2000, declined in prominence; positional issue voting and the demographic characteristics of voters have never mattered much in Mexican elections (for past electoral behavior, see Domínguez and Lawson 2004; Domínguez and McCann 1996). The outcome of Mexico's election, moreover, bore some important similarities to trends elsewhere in the larger Latin American countries.

From the 2000 to the 2006 Presidential Elections in Mexico

The 2006 election campaign showed several similarities with the Mexican presidential elections of 1988, 1994, and 2000. In these elections, the three big parties, and only these three—the PAN, the PRI, and the PRD—could put up credible candidates for the presidency. This structured Mexican party system arose from the 1988 election and has proven resilient (Greene 2002; Klesner 2005). In neither the 2000 nor the 2006 elections did a single party win an outright majority in either the Senate or Chamber of Deputies. Since 1997, democratic

Mexico has experienced a divided government, where the president lacks a governing majority in Congress.

The 2006 election was the second consecutive Mexican presidential contest during which the candidate who led in the early public opinion polls came in second on election day. In the 2000 election, Francisco Labastida, the candidate of the ruling PRI, had been ahead in the campaign's early stages but, in the end, lost to Vicente Fox, the PAN candidate. In 2006, the PRD's López Obrador was similarly in front in the early part of the campaign but, in the end, was defeated by the PAN's Calderón.

In the *poll of polls* (an average of surveys conducted by different firms) in January 2000, Labastida held a lead of about ten percentage points over Fox (Lawson 2004b). In December 2005, López Obrador's lead over Calderón exceeded that margin, and it held, with little change, through February 2006 (see both chapter 10 and figure 1.1 in this volume). The reasons for each outcome differed, however. In 2000, Labastida, the candidate with strong structural advantages that underpinned his front-runner status at the start of the campaign, turned out to be the loser on election day. In 2006, López Obrador, although holding an early lead as the campaign started, had this same array of structural circumstances stacked against him, thus making the prospects of his victory on election day even less certain.

In 2000, there were four good reasons to expect a victory by the ruling party's candidate. First, both the PAN and the PRD had fielded presidential candidates, thus dividing the opposition vote. Second, the PRI retained a strong partisan base, so the party itself was one of Labastida's assets. However, in 2000, the PRI would win more votes for its congressional candidates than Labastida did in his presidential run. Third, in the late 1990s, the economy had performed well in each year but the first of President Ernesto Zedillo's six-year term. The PRI had won past elections by drawing support from voters who were averse to turning the government over to less-experienced parties, even if they had held negative short-term retrospective assessments of its economic stewardship (Magaloni 1999). And fourth, in the months preceding the election, the public had a positive assessment of Zedillo's performance as president. All four factors should have helped Labastida to win.

In 2006, López Obrador's early lead was a tribute to his personal skill and ability to overcome obstacles. First, voters had a higher opinion of the presidential candidate than they did of his party; in the first wave (October 2005) of the 2006 panel study, 49 percent of the voters thought favorably of López

Obrador, but only 41 percent responded similarly to the PRD. Hence the party was one of López Obrador's liabilities, and it would remain so on election day. Second, the Mexican economy had grown slowly during the first three years of the Fox presidency, but it made much quicker strides during the second three years. Unemployment, which reached a peak in the third quarter of 2004, fell steadily through the eve of the July 2006 election, and in 2006 gross domestic product per capita grew 4.8 percent (Economic Commission for Latin America and the Caribbean 2007). These trends were not helpful to a challenger seeking to unseat the PAN from the presidency. Third, throughout the campaign, a substantial majority of the voters held the PAN's Vicente Fox in high regard—making him more popular than any of the presidential candidates seeking to replace him (Loaeza 2006; Rottinghaus and Alberro 2005). All three factors helped Calderón, the PAN's presidential candidate, and would make it more difficult for López Obrador to win.

In 2006, as in past presidential elections, partisanship mattered, a point Francisco Flores-Macías brings out forcefully in chapter 10 of this volume. Approximately half of the respondents in the panel survey's three waves were standpatters, that is, they kept their same choice for president in all three waves—October 2005 and May and July 2006—of the panel's public opinion polling of the views of the same individuals. Party identification was thus a powerful explanation for these unvarying decisions. This finding also means that half of the respondents changed their minds at least once during the course of the presidential election campaign. The campaign thus mattered significantly, thanks in large measure to the roles that the candidates and the mass media played. In this way, the 2006 presidential election resembled the 2000 contest and amplified the factors that had been crucial to the outcome of that race.

Campaign strategies played a role, therefore, in both elections. In 2000, Labastida made several important decisions that had adverse consequences. Although he was the establishment candidate, his campaign chose to emphasize his commitment to enacting change—an issue that a party in power for seventy-one years surely did not own. Labastida maintained some distance from Zedillo and did not utilize the solid performance of the economy at the end of the 1990s as a reason to vote for the PRI yet again in a presidential race. Instead of choosing a stance favorable to his party, Labastida felt compelled to operate under an agenda established and owned by his opponents, which placed him at a disadvantage—as U.S. elections also show (Damore 2004)—and contributed to his failure.

Calderón, in contrast to Labastida, ultimately rode to victory on an issue that he owned, but he had to experiment with different issues until he found the winning one. As Alejandro Moreno shows in chapter 11, Calderón won the PAN presidential primary election in 2006 by running as an honest man with "values and passion for Mexico." In the primary, he beat President Fox's preferred candidate, former minister of government Santiago Creel. At first, Calderón could not have capitalized on positive reactions to President Fox and the economy's performance because he was opposing Fox's choice for a successor. In the weeks that followed his primary victory, Calderón, a Roman Catholic, stuck with his "values" campaign and, in February 2006, took a socially conservative stance on issues such as abortion and contraception. His campaign failed to advance, so he changed his message. He moved ahead in the polls only after he had changed to another issue to which he could potentially lay claim, namely, a sound economy.

During the closing months of the campaign, Calderón at last embraced the Fox presidency's record of recent economic growth and promised to continue it. Calderón also crafted a strong negative campaign toward the opposition, labeling López Obrador a "danger to Mexico." Thus Calderón's second-stage campaign was the opposite of Labastida's in 2000. Calderón recognized, albeit belatedly, his three key assets: the popularity of an incumbent president from his own party, an economy that was performing well recently, and his party's strong base in the electorate. This candidate's message was not change, but continuity.

What about the utility of the PAN for Calderón? In the October 2005 panel survey, favorable opinions of the PAN exceeded favorable opinions of Calderón by 47 to 28 percent. By the April/May and July 2006 polls of the study, Calderón's popularity had risen to become essentially the same as the PAN's. On election day, Calderón outpolled his party's congressional candidates by over a million votes. Calderón thus won the election because he made a midcourse campaign strategy correction to align his message with the political environment encountered during the campaign.

In the latter stages of the campaign, Calderón staked his claim as the owner of the economic growth issue, doing so in a manner quite similar to that of successful presidential candidates in U.S. elections (Petrocik 1996). By aligning himself with the Fox presidency and its recent record of economic growth, Calderón gained credibility in his promise to enact no change that would put Mexico's prosperity at risk. Yet while he campaigned on behalf of the same set of policies that Fox and his team had pursued, Calderón now implied that they would be implemented more effectively. The government would work. He proceeded to emphasize the salience of this issue in order to activate those voters who agreed with him, as Moreno rightly argues in chapter 11. Calderón convinced these voters to turn out to vote for him on election day.

Kenneth Greene, in chapter 13 and jointly with Kathleen Bruhn in chapter 6, deepen our understanding of the Calderón campaign. They tell us that Calderón ran two simultaneous campaign strategies, one with his party's congressional candidates and another by himself.

In what I will call campaign 1, Calderón joined in the PAN's congressional strategy to focus on center-right positional issues. This campaign, Bruhn and Greene demonstrate, found little favor with Mexican voters. On issues such as abortion, the privatization of the electricity sector, the state's responsibility for the welfare of its citizens, and relations with the United States, Mexican voters were systematically centrist, in contrast to the highly polarized candidates from the PAN and the PRD. Calderón's choice of positional issues did not get him elected president of Mexico. On July 2, the PAN's candidates for federal deputies ran on campaign 1 and garnered over a million fewer votes than Calderón.

In campaign 2, Calderón emphasized valence issues—salient problems for the voters on which he could claim superior competence, a long-standing practice in U.S. elections (D. Stokes 1963). Calderón embraced the Fox administration's record of economic growth and painted López Obrador as economically incompetent, even dangerous. The PAN candidate primed the issue that electing López Obrador would lead to an economic crisis. Priming encourages voters to attach greater importance to a particular issue as they choose for whom to vote (Bartels 2006). In the 2006 Mexican elections, priming did not entail persuading more voters to fear López Obrador's economic management. Rather, it made those voters who were already somewhat concerned about this valence issue put more weight on it as a factor in their vote choice, and it possibly also increased their likelihood of turning out on election day. Greene shows that this campaign 2, valence-issue strategy worked well for Calderón. His voters were not particularly right-wing in positional terms, so campaign 1 had much less utility for Calderón as a potentially winning platform. However, as time went on, Calderón came to be considered more effective on economic issues, combating corruption, and enhancing public security. Campaign 2, "I'm more competent," helped to elect Calderón president of Mexico.

López Obrador responded to the challenge to his fiscal skills by priming economic policy issues, but these were not the reason why voters had once preferred him. Thus his strategy of priming positional issues failed, as Greene points out. In the end, López Obrador came to rely disproportionately on support from PRD backers and on agreement generated over only one of the prospective positional issues that he emphasized successfully, namely, the reduction of poverty. Yet, even on election day, the PRD dragged down his vote.

What might López Obrador have done differently? Bruhn provides clues in chapter 9. One basis for López Obrador's early and ongoing popularity had been his political moderation, relative to both his own party and the positions of the other candidates and parties. López Obrador's views were well to the right of the PRD, Bruhn shows, and not that different from those of the average citizen. She also demonstrates that other factors in López Obrador's popularity were his skillful management of his public image and, as mayor of Mexico City, his construction of a cross-class coalition, notwithstanding the fact that he thwarted attempts to introduce greater transparency into the governance of the capital city (Wirth 2006). Some of the popular features of López Obrador's city government, for example, were the monthly stipends provided to all city residents above the age of seventy, as well as loans for small businesses and scholarships for all public school children.

Yet part of López Obrador's instinct in managing political crises had been to stay quiet until the furor died down. When the Calderón campaign's advertising turned sharply negative in mid-March 2006, López Obrador did little to counter its charges of populism and radicalism. When an opportunity to respond came up via the first televised presidential debate, held on April 25, López Obrador chose to skip the debate altogether. The PAN and the PRI highlighted his absence, displaying a vacant chair for the missing candidate. Most Mexicans did not watch the debate, but they did learn that the PRD candidate was absent. As Bruhn concludes, López Obrador's overconfident reaction to the negative campaign gave Calderón an uncontested field, and Calderón surged ahead.

Issue ownership and negative advertising worked to help elect both Vicente Fox in 2000 and Felipe Calderón in 2006 as presidents of Mexico. In 2000, this approach enabled Fox to undermine Labastida's important strengths at the start of the campaign. In 2006, it allowed Calderón to capitalize on the underlying strengths that any PAN candidate would have had going into the election—a bigger partisan base, Fox's popularity, and an economy that had begun to grow.

Candidates and their campaigns matter. Roberto Madrazo is a good example; he brought to his presidential campaign a reputation for abuse of power that was too difficult to surmount. Yet static candidate traits do not suffice to explain outcomes. López Obrador started the 2006 campaign with higher personal approval ratings than his party. Calderón might have lost the 2006 election had he not ended what this chapter calls his campaign 1. Thus the candidates themselves matter, especially because of the strategic choices that they make during their campaigns. Fox in 2000, and Calderón in 2006, demonstrated how to be effective candidates, while Labastida in 2000, and López Obrador in 2006, showed how to run a campaign badly enough to ensure defeat.[4]

The Mexican Voter Prepares to Choose in 2006

In research for this and previous studies of public opinion and voting behavior, the authors of the various chapters in this book have come to believe that Mexicans are much less unique, esoteric, or labyrinthine in their political beliefs and choices than some older scholarly or journalistic writings had implied. There is analytical and descriptive value in emphasizing that Mexicans share traits with citizens of other democratic countries. The following stylized account of voter choice in the 2006 election highlights the common features between Mexico's and other democracies' polities.

The invisible hand of the past weighed on the process of choice for Mexican voters, and in this respect Mexico had long differed from the North Atlantic democracies. As recently as 1960, half of all Mexicans lived in communities that housed fewer than 2,500 people; many other Mexicans resided in towns and small cities. Yet the second half of the twentieth century witnessed an ecological realignment in Mexico. In 2000, only one-quarter of all Mexicans inhabited communities with fewer than 2,500 people. Between 1970 and 2000, the number of cities with a population above one million jumped from three to eight (Aguayo 2000). The PRI's power as a ruling party had long depended on its control of rural Mexico. However, rural Mexico was vanishing, and so was much of the PRI vote.

In terms originally used to explain conservative party declines in Italy and Japan, there were "changes in the relative size of one or more social groups or economic strata. In this case, the bases of party support do not necessarily undergo marked changes. Rather, the relative size of various demographic or attitudinal groups changes" (Dalton et al. 1984, 96). Wayne Cornelius and Ann Craig (1991) were among the first to call attention to the long-term impact of the decline of the rural sector on the PRI's capacity to prevail.

Urbanization, economic development, and education all weakened the power of the PRI (Klesner 1993, 2001, 2005; Magaloni 2006). In chapters 2 and 3, Roderic Ai Camp and Joseph Klesner demonstrate that in the 2006 election, PRI candidate Roberto Madrazo performed better in rural areas, among less-well-educated voters, and among older Mexicans. One need not hypothesize that rural voters were sincerely pro-PRI, though many may have been. The PRI had prevailed in poor rural areas by fair means or foul.

Mexico's demographic transformation in the recent past is, therefore, the first step in understanding how voters made their choices in the 2006 election. The PRI's "green vote" reservoir had been drained. Many hitherto rural Mexicans migrated to cities or to the United States. For some who had never chosen to vote for the PRI but whose votes had been counted as if they had, urbanization enabled them to exercise a real choice for the first time. Others who had genuinely favored the PRI simply declined in number. The invisible hand of urbanization contributed to make Mexican politics freer and the PRI weaker in a fair election.

Yet this large-scale social change should be kept in perspective. In this book, urbanism/ruralism explains little with regard to Mexican public opinion or voter behavior (once standard statistical controls are included), because the PRI lost support in both urban and rural areas. Mexico's ecological realignment (i.e., the transition from rural to urban) was supplemented with an electoral repositioning as voters, regardless of their place of residence, flocked to parties other than the PRI. This fact does not render these environmental changes unreal or unimportant. On the contrary, migration from the countryside altered the face of Mexico and made it less likely that the old political regime could be sustained. The key point is that ecological realignment is only the start of an analysis of the process of electoral choice.

Mexicans approach presidential campaigns in ways that are not unlike those that scholars have observed for U.S. campaigns (Gelman and King 1993; Holbrook 1996). Mexicans have experiences, preferences, networks of friends, and hopes for the future. Many of these sentiments and views congeal in their preferences for a political party and are activated during campaigns. As already noted, half of all respondents in the panel surveys had made their choice for the July 2006 presidential election as early as October 2005, before the interparty presidential campaign got under way. Partisan identification—itself the synthesis of many other long-term factors—was a key explanation both for that very early choice and for sticking with that choice. Partisanship has been a powerful explanation for every Mexican election since the start of Mexico's democratic transition in 1988, and its significance has been well documented in other works (Domínguez and Lawson 2004; Domínguez and McCann 1996).

A second important explanation for Mexicans' voting choices was political knowledge and campaign attentiveness. Highly politically aware voters in the United States "resist information that is inconsistent with [their] basic values or partisanship" (Zaller 1992, 266). So, too, in Mexico in 2006; the better-informed voters sought more political information, but they did so in order to confirm their prior beliefs, In chapter 10, Flores-Macías posits that more knowledgeable voters are less likely to switch electoral preferences. Something similar had happened in Mexico in the 2000 presidential election; high-exposure voters who watched the televised campaign debates strengthened their pre-existing electoral preferences as a result of this newly obtained information (Lawson 2004c). In Mexico, as in other countries, this dynamic makes better-educated and more knowledgeable voters less open to persuasion and increasingly prone to discuss politics with those who are like-minded.

Belief formation is not an asocial process, nor does it begin with an election campaign. One's family, school, occupation, and friendships help to create, refine, and sharpen individual beliefs. In chapter 4, Andy Baker's innovative research examines a powerful mechanism for belief formation, namely, discussion networks. He observes, as have many others, that region seems to describe the salient features in the outcome of the 2006 Mexican presidential election. Calderón swept the northern Mexican states, while López Obrador won those in southern Mexico; only in central Mexico was there a more mixed outcome. Madrazo, it should be noted, failed to win a single state.

And yet, Baker rightly asks, what accounts for such regional effects? He shows that variance in the arena in which one engages in interpersonal conversations explains why individuals with identical traits and beliefs exhibit different voting behavior patterns, ones that correspond to their region of residence. People discuss politics and deliberate over their choices with family and friends. Their beliefs are constructed and consolidated in embedded social networks. Therefore, PAN supporters in a region full of PAN adherents mutually reinforce each other. An identically profiled PAN supporter in a region full of PRD partisans may, however, switch.

Baker finds that discussion networks explain the regional effects in 2006; that is, regional effects stop being statistically significant explanations of the vote once the ramifications of discussions are taken into account. Flores-Macías (chapter 10) further discovered that voters who switched away from their initial candidate preferences in 2006 had more individuals in their discussion networks that disagreed with them; standpatters were more likely to participate in discussion networks with like-minded individuals.

Discussion effects build upon partisanship and individual traits and explain a voter's choice for president. Not only do these discussions have an impact prior to the start of an election campaign, but, as the campaign unfolds, they also serve as a filter for voters. Homogeneous networks strengthen the beliefs that its members share. Heterogeneous networks, in contrast, facilitate the possibility that some of its members will switch their choices. Discussion effects, as an explanation for region, reinforce Klesner's point in chapter 3, that contemporary patterns of political competition are built on past patterns of opposition party development, thus rooting the lasting effects of discussion networks in the past and empowering them for the future.

Opinions about the president's performance were another salient variable in the 2006 presidential election, just as they had been in the past. These impressions are generally formed prior to the start of the campaign, although they can also be affected by events as the campaign progresses. In chapter 13, Greene brings out the importance of presidential approval, which he uses, along with partisanship, as control variables to enable him to study the impact of issues during the election. Views of a president's performance develop during the course of a presidential term, and Vicente Fox spent a great deal of time during his presidency shoring up his personal presidential popularity. Therefore, voters who thought well of Fox were much more likely to prefer Calderón; voters who thought badly of Fox were the least likely to support the PAN's candidate.

Ecological realignment, partisanship, opinions of President Fox's performance, levels of education as they affect one's degree of political knowledge, and discussion networks all set the stage for the 2006 election prior to the start of the campaign. They identified the core supporters of each candidate as well as those voters most susceptible to persuasion. During the campaign itself, partisanship, levels of political knowledge, and discussion networks would continue to filter information, consolidate and activate core voters, and allow other voters to make initial judgments or modify the opinions that they may have formed at first.

The 2006 Campaign

The settled political habits that voters carry in their hearts and minds may be unsettled at the start of a campaign, when parties choose their candidates; this disruption happened for about half of the voters in the 2006 election. Yet at the start of the process it seemed as if these exogenous shocks would hardly matter. López Obrador had been the long-time favorite in the polls for several years, well ahead of all other potential presidential contenders. Thus Bruhn rightly describes the start of the campaign as the "prelude to a coronation" (see chapter 9), that is, the process whereby the PRD would ratify López Obrador as its candidate and the voters would confirm him as president.

Similarly, Madrazo seemed well positioned to become the PRI's presidential candidate. David Shirk (in chapter 7) and Joy Langston (in chapter 8) document how Madrazo, following the end of the last PRI presidency in 2000, became the PRI's leader, seized control of the party machinery, and prepped the PRI for an impressive round of victories in the 2003 nationwide congressional election and in the majority of gubernatorial elections. A coalition of PRI governors, led by state of México Governor Arturo Montiel, challenged Madrazo for the PRI's nomination but, through negative advertising, cunning, and luck, Madrazo prevailed when Montiel withdrew his scandal-plagued candidacy.

The PAN had a more complex process for their choice, because several internal candidates were viable presidential contenders. As Shirk shows in chapter 7, former minister of government Santiago Creel, President Fox's favorite, appeared well placed to win the PAN internal primary election. Yet Felipe Calderón, the former PAN president, turned out to have greater popularity within a party that credited him with its growth in the 1990s and still felt somewhat ignored during the Fox presidency.

After these three presidential candidates were selected, Madrazo fell to third place in public opinion polls, never to do any better. Starting in March 2006, Calderón's campaign strategy outmaneuvered López Obrador's. In what way, however, did voters respond to the strategies sketched out earlier in this chapter? Ideology, the activation of views about the economy, the construction of candidate issue ownership, and the support generated by specific government policies help formulate answers to that question.

Ideology mattered, although that point has been difficult to study in Mexico. Earlier efforts suggested that Mexican voters operated at a relatively modest to low level of ideological thinking (Domínguez and McCann 1996). Here, the chapter by Bruhn and Greene shows that Mexican voters were much less polarized across an array of issues than federal deputy candidates. However, James McCann, in chapter 14, gives us a tool to unlock the possible role of ideology during the campaign. He found that Mexican voters' perceptions of George W. Bush, Fidel Castro, and Hugo Chávez worked as proxies for the electorate's broad perspectives. Ideology became activated during the election campaign, thereby tightening up the connection between latent left-right views and presidential votes—just as the pioneers of such panel studies in the United States would have expected (Berelson et al. 1954). Ideology played both affective and cognitive roles; namely, it enabled the voters to determine whether candidates were likable and whether voters agreed with their general political stances. These findings built a bridge between what I have called Calderón's campaign 1 and campaign 2.

Voters' views of the Mexican economy have mattered in every election since 1988, and the 2006 race was no exception (for a similar analysis in Canada, see Alvarez et al. 2000). In chapter 11, Alejandro Moreno further argues that economic voting counted in 2006 in a way that it had not done before. As in the past, the governing party benefited from favorable views and suffered from negative views about the economy—classic economic voting. The novelty in the 2006 election was Calderón's success, not at persuading an increasing number of voters that the country's economy was doing well, but at convincing those who already thought so to cast a vote for him. His triumph in this arena accounts for the discrepancy between the standings of the candidates in the early polls and the final election results, a dynamic that has also been documented in the United States (Gelman and King 1993).

Calderón's support among economically optimistic voters leapt from 35 percent in October 2005 to 57 percent in July 2006. The key shift was among independents, that is, those voters who did not identify with any party. In October 2005, Calderón trailed López Obrador by fifteen percentage points among independents with positive views of the economy; in July, Calderón was ahead of López Obrador by fourteen points among economically satisfied voters. The change during the campaign was Calderón's success in activating this part of the electorate, resulting in an upswing of votes for himself.

The mechanism for this campaign achievement becomes apparent in chapter 13. Greene controls for pocketbook (or personal) economic evaluations as well as for sociotropic (or national) ones. These general assessments turn out to not be significant in explanations of voting choice. Does that contradict Moreno's findings in chapter 11? In his analysis, Greene includes variables for partisan identification and presidential approval, which are statistically significant, as is usually the case in Mexican elections. He then tests for the impact of economic voting, both through prospective positional issues (views for or against specific issue decisions) and what he calls "candidate traits." In this latter category, Greene tests for valence issues, which wed perceptions of the candidates to voters' opinions about issues.

Greene demonstrates that among the positional issues, only poverty was a statistically significant explanation of the vote—*not* the privatization of electricity, trade with the United States, the extent of the social safety net, or views regarding the death penalty or abortion. Greene shows that poverty also worked as a valence issue for López Obrador, that is, voters thought López Obrador more competent to address the scourge of poverty. Yet voters who also thought that Calderón would be best at managing of the economy or who worried that López Obrador would cause an economic crisis were significantly less likely to vote for the PRD candidate. Calderón's ownership of the economic valence issue is the mechanism that helps validate Moreno's argument, namely, that the activation of voters with positive perceptions of the economy worked to Calderón's benefit on election day.

In chapter 12, Alberto Díaz-Cayeros, Federico Estévez, and Beatriz Magaloni provide the last piece of the puzzle. PRI governments, in power for a long time, often appealed to voters on the basis of clientelist favors: jobs for individuals, payments in cash or in-kind, gifts, explicit or implicit threats about loss of benefits, and the like. PRI governments did not emphasize building support for universalistic, social-policy government programs for citizens who would then qualify for them on the basis of public, transparent, and well-specified empirical criteria. Mexico's poor benefited from the shift from politically selective handouts to clearly delineated rules that made them eligible for support and protected them, without regard to political affiliation, from losing benefits.

Díaz-Cayeros, Estévez, and Magaloni confirm what Cornelius (2004) had found was already the case for the 2000 election, namely, clientelist strategies (i.e., handouts) had become much less effective at generating voter support. The novelty in the 2006 election was that voters who benefited from the universalistic programs of the developing Mexican welfare state—conditional cash transfers through Oportunidades, and health insurance with Seguro Popular—rewarded the PAN presidential candidate with their support in a clear example of positive retrospective voting. As happens in other democratic polities, voters backed those who had served them well.

Political Change and Pending Matters

Democratic politics have come slowly to Mexico over the past couple of decades, but they have come. Early in this century, as Camp shows in chapter 2, strong majorities of Mexicans believe that the country's political system is democratic. They worry less now about the nature of the political regime and more about serious public issues, such as the lack of public security or the persistence of unemployment. Mexico's most committed democrats are economic optimists, adherents to some religious faith, young, better-educated, and more likely to be residents of northern Mexico. That leaves a significant minority of Mexicans who do not hold these beliefs. Camp's findings suggest not only that Mexican leaders in government, business, education, and the churches face a challenge in improving the performance of democratic politics, but that the instruments to do so are also evident—economic growth, improvements in personal safety, more and better schooling, and properly functioning democratic institutions. None of these is easy; each is possible.

More effective remedies to the one remaining major instance of Mexican voter disenfranchisement—the country's wholly flawed procedures to enable its citizens who live outside of Mexico to vote in the presidential election—should also be possible. While Mexico should provide its expatriates with better means for absentee voting, in chapter 5 James McCann, Wayne Cornelius, and David Leal argue for realistic expectations as Mexico approaches such reforms. Contrary to either high hopes or worries that Mexicans outside of Mexico would vote in such large numbers in Mexican elections that they could determine the outcome, these authors provide reasons why voter turnout among expatriate Mexicans would likely remain relatively low even if absentee-balloting procedures were to be improved. Such Mexicans, like people everywhere, care the most about the circumstances of their lives, and those of their families, in the place where they live. For these expatriates, life in the United States matters a great deal, and national elections in Mexico suggest remote solutions, at best. There is room to improve upon the extremely low level of participation among expatriates in 2006, but no one should expect that the turnout rate from abroad would come close to matching that within Mexico proper. Nonetheless, Mexican politicians ought to make it possible for Mexican citizens living outside of

Mexico to vote in their country's elections. Such democratic reforms are worth undertaking, but the results of these efforts may well be modest, as they have been in other countries.

Principal Findings

First, Mexico's 2006 presidential election confirmed some patterns discernable in analyses of Mexican presidential elections ever since the first reasonably competitive one in 1988. In 2006, as in past elections, partisanship, evaluations of the incumbent president's performance, and economic voting helped explain the attitudes and behavior of voters. In these respects, electoral politics in Mexico conformed well to democratic practices common to constitutional democracies worldwide. Yet demographic factors, both in the last as well as previous Mexican elections, had little or no impact on the formation of opinions and on voting behavior. This persistent finding has made Mexican politics somewhat different from European or Asian democracies, where certain social cleavages have resulted in a rather more structured electorate. Nevertheless, ecological realignment—the emigration of rural Mexicans to more urban environments—continued unabated. In addition, attitudes toward positional issues explained little about voter choice; such results vary a good deal between democratic countries.

Second, the research reported in this book has shown that some factors that had counted for less in previous presidential elections mattered considerably more in the 2006 and 2000 elections. In both 2006 and 2000, attitudes toward candidates were quite significant, with campaign strategies, mass-media reporting, and negative advertising helping to explain public opinions and voter choices. Both elections dramatically demonstrated how candidates' campaign decisions might advance or hinder their prospects for election; the "good" candidate is an effective strategist. Cognitive processes common to citizens in other democracies operate in Mexico, too. Campaigns activate the public's preferences and remind cross-pressured citizens where their strongest leanings would lead. The most knowledgeable voters are the least susceptible to being persuaded by campaign messages, even though they are the most likely to listen to those messages. In this indirect sense, education matters—that is, the best-educated voters are the most resistant to acquiring information from the campaigns and changing their views. For good or ill, electoral politics in Mexico resembles its counterparts in democracies elsewhere.

Third, two salient factors in earlier Mexican elections were less so in 2006. Clientelist practices, such as vote-buying or coercion, have been less common and less effective in elections in this decade. Only a few voters cast their ballots "strategically" in past Mexican elections, but they had mattered because their numbers often exceeded the margin of victory between the winner and the first runner-up. Between 1988 and 2000, such voting had been important for some of those opposed to the then-ruling PRI; they privileged defeating the PRI over "sincerely" voting for the opposition party that was their true preference. By the 2006 presidential election, the democratic regime question no longer structured voter choice; we found little evidence of strategic voting.

Fourth, by means of research that had not been carried out in Mexico before, this book explains some elements of public opinion and voting behavior in that country:

1. Broad ideological perspectives help structure public opinion, even if these orientations are not always captured in survey questions that use the words "left" and "right."

2. Priming the salience of an issue and mobilizing voters who care about that issue help explain voter shift during a campaign. In 2006, we called it the economic activation of voters.

3. Valence issues play a significant role in elections, even if positional issues do not. Candidates who own a valence issue—"I am more competent than you at advancing a goal that all citizens share"—will outperform their opponents. Issue ownership is the key mechanism for issue priming and voter activation.

4. Region had seemed to be a demographic factor that mattered, but—at least in part—it turns out to have been a proxy for the effects of discussion networks that reinforced the preferences of citizens in politically homogeneous settings and may lead to a change in preference in more heterogeneous settings.

5. In 2006, voters rewarded the government's universalistic social policy programs. They behaved as democrats should, supporting public servants who performed well.

Mexico's 2006 presidential election, in some respects, resembled that country's presidential election of 1994 more than the one in 2000. In both 1994 and 2006, the candidate with the strongest structural underpinnings for victory won the election. Ernesto Zedillo in 1994, and Felipe Calderón in 2006, had an advantage in terms of partisan preference, the popularity of an incumbent president from their own party, and public perception of a robust economy. In each of these two elections, opposition to the governing party was split. The purpose of the Zedillo and Calderón presidential campaigns was to activate their underlying structural advantages so as to rally their supporters and ride their ownership of valence issues—prosperity in particular—to a presidential victory. Victory in 2000 went to Vicente Fox, who overcame his candidacy's structural disadvantages by persuading voters to rally strategically for democracy above any of their other attitudinal preferences, rise above partisanship, imagine a better economic future, and vote for change. In 1994, as in 2006, the victory went to Ernesto Zedillo and Felipe Calderón, the candidates who promised not only continuity, but also greater effectiveness in implementing the good policy intentions that they inherited. Only time will tell whether voters were right.

Comparative Perspectives

The victory of the PAN presidential candidate in the 2006 Mexican presidential election was part of a broader trend across large Latin American countries[5] in the middle years of the first decade of the twenty-first century; parties that had held the presidency won the presidential elections that took place in these years. The victories went to incumbents on the left, such as Venezuela's President Hugo Chávez; the right, like Colombia's President Álvaro Uribe; and the center, such as Brazil's President Luiz Inácio Lula da Silva. Victories also went to governing parties or coalitions where the incumbent president could not or did not run for re-election, such as the Partido Justicialista in Argentina, the Concertación Democrática in Chile, and the PAN in Mexico. The effect of a growing world economy made it possible for ruling parties to claim credit for economic good times. Impressive as Felipe Calderón's personal achievement was in 2006, his victory was part of a broader Latin American pattern.

Latin America's many electorates were not, moreover, particularly leftist in their political attitudes. Jason Arnold and David Samuels (2008) have shown conclusively that there was no "left turn" in the Latin American public as the twenty-first century began. Few Latin Americans self-consciously identify as leftists, and the proportion of those who do did not increase for the continent as a whole. More importantly, the left-right scale does not distinguish well between the political attitudes of Latin America's Left and non-Left. There is only one dimension on which the Latin American political Left stands out clearly, namely, opposition to the Bush administration. In all of these respects, our findings for Mexico coincide with the general Latin American pattern. As McCann shows in chapter 14, attitudes toward the United States stand out distinctively in Mexico, but other elements of the left-right divide are not helpful in understanding either the 2006 Mexican electorate or the Latin American electorate in mid-decade.

Throughout this chapter, I have illustrated how Mexican voters are similar in many ways to voters in the United States or other North Atlantic democracies. Comparable factors shape the voting choice in Mexico and in these other democracies—among them, partisanship, economic voting, attitudes toward the incumbent president, discussion networks, and valence issues. The general importance of competence should also be underlined as an effective valence issue. Felipe Calderón won on competence, but so too did the Peronists in Argentina, the Center-Left in Chile, and conservative President Uribe in Colombia. Mexicans behave as democrats do everywhere.

There is one important difference, however, between Mexican elections and those in the longer-established North Atlantic democracies—campaigns matter much more in Mexico. Thus the candidates, mass-media coverage, negative advertising, and general campaign strategies have been essential in explaining the outcome in Mexico's two presidential elections during the current century. This is as should be expected in a country whose party system, though resilient, is young and where the transition to full constitutional democracy dates from the 2000 election. Mexico's democratic consolidation remains, therefore, an ongoing project as citizens argue, contest, change, and seek to shape a better future for themselves and their families.

Notes

ONE: Introduction

I am grateful to Francisco Flores-Macías, Kenneth Greene, Andy Baker, Jorge Domínguez, James McCann, and my other colleagues from the Mexico 2006 Panel Study for their trenchant comments on earlier versions of this chapter. I also received valuable advice from Henry Tom and Francisco González on the entire volume. Special thanks are due to Mike Myers and Kathleen Hoover for extensive editorial assistance on this and other chapters in this volume.

1. Most of the data analyzed in this volume are drawn from this project. Senior Project Personnel for the Mexico 2006 Panel Study include (in alphabetical order): Andy Baker, Kathleen Bruhn, Roderic Camp, Wayne Cornelius, Jorge Domínguez, Kenneth Greene, Joseph Klesner, Chappell Lawson (principal investigator), David Leal, Beatriz Magaloni, James McCann, Alejandro Moreno, Alejandro Poiré, and David Shirk. Funding for the study was provided by the National Science Foundation (SES-0517971) and *Reforma* newspaper. Fieldwork was conducted by *Reforma*'s polling and research team, under the direction of Alejandro Moreno. The core of the Mexico 2006 Panel Study is a three-wave, three-tier survey of ordinary Mexicans. The first wave of interviews was conducted in October 2005, just after the candidates were selected; it covered 2,400 ordinary Mexicans chosen from over 200 polling sites across the country. The second wave, carried out in late April and early May of 2006, reinterviewed as many people from the first wave as could be contacted—a total of 1,776 respondents. The third wave repeated this procedure just after the election in July 2006, reaching 1,594 respondents from the original sample. The original sample of 2,400 people comprised three separate groups of respondents: a nationally representative sample of 1,600 adults, an oversample of 500 adults in the Federal District, and an oversample of 300 adults from selected rural areas. The Mexico 2006 Panel Study also included two separate cross-sectional surveys of fresh respondents ($N = 305$ and $N = 400$, respectively); these were conducted contemporaneously with the second and third panel waves, at the same polling sites chosen for the panel study's national sample. Data from the study, and further details about it, are publicly available at http://web.mit.edu/polisci/research/mexico06/. All data in this chapter are taken from the national sample of the panel study.

2. The conventional wording for survey questions on partisanship in Mexico, used in the Mexico 2006 Panel Study, encourages self-identification with a major party. It reads: "In general, would you say you identify with the PAN, the PRI, or the PRD? [After response:] Would you say you identify strongly with the . . . or only somewhat with the . . . ?" In Spanish, the question reads: "*Generalmente, usted se considera panista, priísta, o*

perredista? [Insistir:] Se considera usted como muy . . . o algo . . . ?" Parties are listed in this question in the order in which they appear on the ballot.

3. ESPN Sports, "Roberto Madrazo allegedly cheated his way to marathon victory," October 9, 2007, http://abcnews.go.com/Sports/Story?id=3708478&page=1/.

4. Author's interviews.

5. In Mexico's electoral system, three-fifths of the lower house of Congress is chosen through first-past-the-post elections in single-member districts; the rest are selected through closed-list proportional representation from five circumscriptions. Three-quarters of the Senate are chosen from a first loser system, in which the winning party in a state claims two seats and the second-place party claims one; the rest of the seats in the Senate are chosen through proportional representation based on the parties' shares of the national vote. This system produces the peculiar result that one-quarter of senators do not represent a state.

6. Indeed, draft surveys for the first wave of the Mexico 2006 Panel Study prepared in late September originally omitted questions about Calderón entirely.

7. Mexico 2006 Panel Study, waves 1–3.

8. The lines were calculated using the nonparametric simple regression technique known as *lowess* (locally weighted least squares). Lowess fits a regression line to a scatter plot but uses only a moving "window" of data points at each observation. Hence it is local rather than general. A bandwidth of 0.5 was used in figure 1.1, although the general trend is unchanged using any bandwidths between 0.3 and 0.9. The percentages from the polls refer to the actual reported vote; that is, undecideds are not removed prior to calculating the percentages. The statistical analysis was conducted by Francisco Flores-Macías, and in chapter 10 he discusses conclusions drawn from it.

9. The states in question were Durango, Hidalgo, Nuevo León, Sinaloa, and Sonora.

10. This now-notorious spot showed López Obrador telling Fox to *cállate chachalaca* (stop squawking and shut up) at a March 15 rally in the southern state of Oaxaca.

11. A number of these advertisements were ruled out-of-bounds by Mexico's electoral authorities, but such rulings generally came after the spots had already run their course.

12. These "issue ads" were of dubious legality in Mexico. On the one hand, they never used the names of the candidates or words like "vote" or "election." On the other hand, Mexican law explicitly reserved the exclusive right to purchase airtime for messages "oriented toward influencing the vote" to political parties. These spots figured prominently in López Obrador's postelectoral challenge before the Federal Electoral Court, which—in its ruling after the election—declared such advertising to be illegal.

13. Author's interviews.

14. Author's interviews.

15. As experts on Mexican politics—and, in several cases, as foreign observers—none of the contributors to this volume find reasonable grounds to dispute the official result. (I observed the election in the small town of Santiago Tlacotepec, state of México, and witnessed nothing untoward.) After trailing for most of the race, Calderón eked out a narrow victory in a free, fair, and broadly inclusive contest.

16. This index represented a weighted average of responses to the question "How much are you following the presidential campaign: a lot, some, little, or none?" "None" was coded as 0, "little" as 1, "some" as 2, and "a lot" as 3. The index of political interest was computed in the same way, based on the question "How much interest do you have

in politics: a lot, some, little, or none?" About half of the increase in both political interest and campaign attention occurred between October 2005 and May 2006; the other half occurred between May 2006 and July 2006.

17. For Calderón, 6 percent felt that he wanted to restrict commercial relations with the United States, 25 percent believed that he wanted to keep them as they were, and 11 percent did not know. For López Obrador, the analogous figures were 29 percent, 28 percent, and 16 percent.

18. This item was not asked in the third panel wave.

19. Data include only those who participated in all three panel waves. The Mexico 2006 Panel Study employed a 0–10 feeling thermometer scale on which respondents rated the main candidates.

20. On the conditions under which voters may be risk averse or risk seeking, see Weyland 2002.

TWO: Democracy Redux?

1. In November, 1999, 33 percent of the voters preferred Fox, 53 percent Labastida, and 10 percent Cárdenas. The actual results of the July 2, 2000, election were Fox 42.5 percent, Labastida 36.1 percent, and Cárdenas 16.6 percent.

2. Mexico 2006 Panel Study, first wave. Unless otherwise noted, all data are from the national sample of the Mexico 2006 Panel Study (for details, see chapter 1, note 1 and http://web.mit.edu/polisci/research/mexico06/). For comparisons with other Latin American countries, see MUND Americas, "Mexico and democracy in Latin America," *Opinion Report* 14, Series 4, November 3, 2005.

3. "Divide su voto 1 de cada 5," *Reforma*, February 20, 2006, 6. The survey, with 565 respondents nationwide, was conducted on February 11–12, 2006.

4. For a comparison between Mexico and the United States, see Sekhon 2004.

5. Mexico 2006 Panel Study, first wave. Sixty-seven percent expressed little or no interest in politics and 55 percent rarely or never spoke about politics with other individuals.

6. "Elecciones 2003," *Reforma*, April 28, 2003, based on a national sample, 498 respondents, April 12–14, 2003. In his analysis of the 2000 election, Chappell Lawson concluded that "increasing access to political information is often fatal for PRI support" (2003, 79).

7. MUND Americas, *Opinion Report* 13, Series 4, October 21, 2005.

8. Consulta Mitofsky, "Confianza en instituciones, encuesta nacional de viviendas, estudio de opinión," April 2005, 4, from a national sample, 1,000 respondents, March 28–30, 2005.

9. Bruhn and Greene 2006, survey of 161 candidates for Congress, June 6–30, 2006.

10. Most analysts would probably suggest that "right" combined a preference for free markets with a preference for the regime status quo, while "left" combined economic statism with democracy. Data are from the Mexico 2006 Panel Survey, third wave.

11. In 2000, 36 percent of the actual voters identified themselves as being on the right and 21 percent on the left. The PAN captured 50 percent of the voters on the left, and the PRI captured 57 percent of the voters on the right. These figures come from Alejandro Moreno (personal communication), using information from pre-election and exit polls, *Reforma*, June and July, 2000.

12. For a discussion of ideological effects in 2000, which were minimal, see Magaloni and Poiré 2004. For a discussion of the evolution of ideology through 2003, see Moreno 2003b.

13. For an up-to-date analysis of the confusions surrounding ideology and public policy preferences, see Estrada and Parás 2006.

14. Emilio Salim Cabrera (2005) found that 83 percent of Mexicans were dissatisfied with democracy and an equal number viewed the country as pursuing the wrong path. Satisfaction with democracy in 2000 was 36 percent, declining to 26 percent the following year. In 2002 and 2003, degrees of disillusionment had already reached current levels.

15. Mexicans still believe democracy is the best system, regardless of its problems, by a large margin. For a detailed comparison over time, see Moreno 2005.

16. *Reforma* exit poll, 5,803 voters, July 2, 2006; Mexico 2006 Panel Study, third wave.

17. "Cada vez más fuerte el clamor por el cambio," *Diario de Yucatán*, June 23, 2000, www.sureste.com.mx.

18. There is little likelihood that the PAN and the PRD will be able to negotiate compromises on fundamental policy issues. For example, among the congressional candidates, 99 percent of PAN nominees believed private investment should be allowed in the electricity sector, compared to 67 percent of PRD nominees who thought it should remain entirely under government auspices (Bruhn and Greene 2006). Nevertheless, Bruhn and Greene (2007) present a convincing argument that the PRD's intransigence may push the PRI to form an alliance with the PAN, since it often is in a middle position between the two parties' policy preferences.

19. Consulta Mitofsky, "Así van . . . la carrera por la presidencia de México," June 2006, www.consulta.com.mx, 1,400 respondents, June 8–11, 2006. After the election, however, the figures evened out between the PAN and the PRD, with 26 and 24 percent respectively, followed by a significant decline among PRI partisans at 19 percent (Mexico 2006 Panel Study, third wave). By September 2006, 32 percent, 21 percent, and 19 percent claimed to be PAN, PRD, and PRI partisans, respectively (Consulta Mitofsky, "Posicionamiento y valor de los partidos políticos al final del sexenios de Fox," November 2006).

20. By 2004, the distribution of state legislators was 46 percent PRI, 29 percent PAN, and 17 percent PRD (Varela 2004a).

21. "Divide su voto 1 de cada 5"; Consulta Mitofsky, "Así van," June 2006, 14.

22. Consulta Mitofsky, "Así van . . . la carrera por la presidencia de México," March 2005, 15.

23. Consulta Mitofsky, "Gráficos presentados el 29 de mayo en el noticero de Joaquín López Dóriga en el canal 2 de televisa," June 23, 2005, www.consulta.com.mx.

24. For additional data on crime, see Vázquez (2003); see also Consulta Mitofsky, "La violencia en México," 2005. Fifty-eight percent in the panel survey considered it an urgent issue to address in 2006.

25. Some of the reasons why this might be the case are linked to citizen perceptions of corruption, a complex conceptual issue explored carefully by Bailey and Parás (2006).

26. Alejandro Moreno, "El viraje de las urnas," *Reforma*, July 13, 2003, www.reforma .com. Independents composed 28 percent of the electorate in 2003, and their support for the PAN declined to 39 percent, while increasing to 43 percent for the PRI.

27. BIMSA, "Encuesta nacional: Rumbo al 2006," November 15, 2005.

28. Opinión Pública y Mercados, "Encuesta nacional electoral—febrero 2006," survey of 1000 residents nationwide, February 10–16.

29. Carlos Ordóñez, "AMLO baja 4 percent; suben Calderón y Madrazo," *El Universal*, April 17, 2006. Based on a national survey of 1500 respondents, April 5–8, 2006. See *El Universal* online, "Encuesta nacional los presidenciables," www.eluniversal.com.mx/graficos/animados/presid-jun2-06.html.

30. Alejandro Moreno and María A. Mancillas, "Revierten independientes," *Reforma*, May 3, 2006, survey of 2,100 respondents, April 28–30, 2006.

31. Consulta Mitofsky, "Así van . . . la carrera por la presidencia de México," March 2006. Those voters expressing no party preference actually increased since November, reaching a three-year high of 44 percent in March, with 24 percent opting for the PRI, 17 percent for the PAN and 13 percent for the PRD.

32. Dan Lund, MUND Americas, "Is there a 'hot button' issue in the current presidential race?" *Opinion Report* 7, Series 5, March 8, 2006. Lund wisely noted that "AMLO has the space to develop a popular definition of the economic key driver: namely jobs. He speaks of construction of infrastructure and jobs, reforestation and jobs, you name it and jobs" (4).

33. "Divide su voto 1 de cada 5."

34. Consulta Mitofsky, "Así van," March 2006. The negative images for all three parties have essentially remained unchanged since November 2005.

35. Carlos Ordóñez, "AMLO baja 4 percent; suben Calderón y Madrazo." The percentage of voters who said they would never vote for López Obrador after this incident increased dramatically, by 60 percent, going from 12 to 20 percent. Thirty-five percent said the same about Madrazo, decreasing from 42 percent in March, and only 10 percent said that about Calderón, with his approximate percentage figure remaining stable throughout the campaign. Also, more than any other candidate, Calderón was viewed as the most popular second choice if a voter were to change his or her mind.

36. Interestingly, when asked to describe the three candidates as something other than a politician, in response to the question "Who would be the best . . . ?" (given five occupations), López Obrador was identified most strongly as a ship captain and teacher, Calderón as a teacher and priest, and Madrazo as a gambler and boxer. *Reforma* survey, 1,515 voters, November 11–14, 2006, www.terra.com.mx/presidenciables2006/.

37. Cinthya Sánchez, "Jóvenes, motor de las elecciones en México," *El Universal*, February 9, 2006; "Numeralia del IFE," www.eluniversal.com.mx/notas/.

38. CIDAC, *CIDAC electoral 2006*, May 8, 2006, 3.

39. Consulta Mitofsky, "Así van . . . la carrera por la presidencia de México," November 2005, 14.

40. "Puntea AMLO preferencia electoral: Encuesta," *El Universal*, February 16, 2006.

41. Mexico 2006 Panel Study, second wave.

42. The reasons voters participated in the 2000 election were as follows: change, 43 percent; candidate's proposals, 22 percent; the candidate, 9 percent; custom, 7 percent; other, 6 percent; party loyalty, 5 percent; least bad, 4 percent; obligation, 2 percent; don't know, 2 percent (Camp 2004).

43. Klesner expresses it differently: "The major cleavage running through Mexican politics before the 2000 elections revolved around attitudes about the regime. On the

antiregime side of the divide could be found those who considered the regime to be undemocratic and prone to electoral fraud. They showed a willingness to accept risk" (2004, 118–19).

44. In an analysis of the importance of issues among voters in waves 1 and 2 of the Mexico 2006 Panel Study, Kenneth Greene (2006) concluded that they were unimportant and that contrary to common perceptions, Mexican voters are not strongly polarized on the basis of campaign issues.

45. James C. McKinley, Jr., "Leftist outsider's campaign surges in Mexico," *New York Times*, March 19, 2006.

46. For a detailed analysis supporting this interpretation, see Greene (chapter 15 in this volume).

47. Ulises Beltrán and Alejandro Cruz Martínez, "Se cierra la contienda," Beltrán & Associates, national survey, 1,200 respondents, March 24–27, 2006.

48. Alejandro Moreno and Roberto Gutiérrez, "Bajo AMLO, sube Calderón," *Reforma*, April 25, 2006, national survey, 2,100 respondents, April 20–22, 2006. *Reforma's* poll, which shows Calderón ahead of López Obrador by 38 to 35 percent, also supports the dramatic change among independent voters. Nearly half of those voters backed the PRD candidate in January, February, and March, but their support dropped precipitously in April (to only 38%) while increasing equally dramatically (from 29% to 37%) in favor of Calderón.

49. Ibid.

50. See Lawson (chapter 1 in this volume); Héctor Tobar, "Candidates try to close gap in Mexico debate," *Los Angeles Times*, April 26, 2006, A20; and James C. McKinley, Jr., "In Mexico, race tightens for presidency, new polls show," *New York Times*, April 26, 2006.

51. Francisco Abundis Luna and José Alberto Vera, "Electores, entre el debate y la descalificación," *Excélsior*, April 25, 2006, based on a poll by Parametría, national survey, April 20–23, 2006.

52. Alejandro Poiré has noted, in an insightful observation, that in the ad campaign promoting López Obrador's own candidacy, his team did not use him to deflect the "fear" theme used by the PAN's strategists (personal communication, May 2, 2006.) Other Mexican observers have criticized López Obrador and his campaign team for not understanding the importance of the media in a democratic political context, despite attempts by some strategists to persuade them otherwise. See Héctor Tobar, "López Obrador loses big lead but not his nerve," *Los Angeles Times*, May 7, 2006, A28.

53. *Crónica*, survey of 1,200 respondents, May 31–June 3, 2006, www.cronica.com .mx. For example, *Crónica* reported that the PRD quadrupled its ads in May, leading to a decline (from 60% to 44%) from May to June among those citizens who viewed Calderón as honest. This campaign also produced an effect, although not as dramatic, on voter perceptions of his ability to create new jobs.

54. A study of one hundred of the poorest counties where the Oportunidades program maintained a significant presence, however, indicated that López Obrador won 76 of them, Madrazo 18, and Calderón only 6. See "Ganó AMLO en zonas beneficiadas por Fox," www.mileno.com/mexico/. In those congressional districts with the highest levels of marginalization, the PRD won 66 to the PAN's 39, mostly in south and south-central Mexico. On the other hand, the PAN won 65 districts versus 45 for the PRD in states with more moderate levels of marginalized populations.

55. See Will Weissert, "Growing Mexican economy could help ruling party candidate in close presidential race," *San Diego Union Tribune*, June 7, 2006. For additional discussions of economic voting, see chapter 11 in this volume by Alejandro Moreno and chapter 12 by Alberto Diaz-Cayeros, Federico Estévez, and Beatriz Magaloni.

56. Zogby International, "Tightrope? As election looms, Mexican future up in air among decided voters," June 19, 2006. The survey consisted of 1,489 respondents to obtain 1,000 likely voters, June 10–15, 2006.

57. Alejandro Moreno and Alicia Martínez, "Cambia imagen de candidates," *Reforma*, June 4, 2006, 6.

58. Parametría, "Por quien, cómo y dónde votaron, la historia de una elección cerrada," 6000 interviews, July 2, 2006, www.parametria.com.mx.

59. Consulta Mitofsky, "Posicionamiento y valor," November 2006. Those attributes included ability, honesty, good government, most democratic, and concerned with poverty.

60. An outstanding description of the Federal Electoral Court's responsibilities and its accomplishments can be found in the presentation at the Center for Strategic and International Studies by the president of the court (Orozco-Henríquez 2006), as well as Berruecos (2003).

61. Parametría, "Los mexicanos apuestan por la institucionalidad," 1,000 interviews, July 22–25, 2006, www.parametria.com.mx. An equal percentage shared a similar opinion of IFE (see BIMSA, "Encuesta nacional post-electoral, Mexico 2006," July 27, 2006, national survey, 1,000 respondents, July 21–24, 2006). In September, when the court validated Calderón's election, 74 percent of Mexicans approved its decision, and 72 percent of the population classified its decision as just and fair. Furthermore, 68 percent believed its decision strengthened democracy (*Reforma*, September 6, 2006, 12, interviews with 450 adults, September 5, 2006).

62. BIMSA, "Encuesta nacional post-electoral."

63. Carta Parametría, "Divide a mexicanos 'el efecto 2 de julio,'" 1,200 respondents, November 17–20, 2006.

THREE: A Sociological Analysis of the 2006 Elections

Thanks are due to Jorge Domínguez and Chappell Lawson, who offered many suggestions that improved the analysis in this chapter. I also thank Francisco Flores-Macías for his efforts in assembling the aggregate data that complement the Mexico 2006 survey data, and Alejandro Moreno for kindly sharing the dataset from *Reforma*'s exit poll. I remain responsible for any errors herein.

1. In addition to Alejandro Moreno's exit poll data, see also table 2.2 in this volume.

2. For an overview of the Mexico 2006 Panel Study, see chapter 1, note 1.

3. In contrast, in the national sample of wave 3 of the Mexico 2006 Panel Study, a significant difference emerged between Calderón and Madrazo among union and nonunion families, with Calderón gaining about a 12 percent higher share of nonunion than union votes, while Madrazo had a 12 percent greater vote share coming from union than nonunion ones.

4. Overt partisan appeals by religious figures are illegal in Mexico.

5. Skin color is a marker of class status in Mexico, with whiter-skinned persons typically enjoying higher education levels, living standards, and social status. An interviewer's

coding of skin color cannot, of course, establish a respondent's self-perception of where he or she fits into racial categories. In general, though, those with darker brown skin are more likely to be of indigenous parentage.

6. Since many PRI voters obviously split their ballots, my analysis here does not take into account the full PRI voter base, especially those voters who might have voted strategically in the presidential race.

7. For some representative examples, see Aziz Nassif 2006; CIDAC 2006; and Lopez-Bassols 2006. For contrary views, see Díaz-Cayeros 2006 and Merino et al. 2006.

8. The PAN's colors are blue and white; it also uses orange in some material. The PRD's colors are yellow with a black Aztec sun. The PRI's colors are those of the Mexican flag—red, green, and white. In the popular press, areas won by the PRI are typically shown in green, those by the PRD in yellow, and those by the PAN in blue.

9. The PRD also controls the Federal District.

10. Díaz-Cayeros (2006) offers a county-level analysis that shows pockets of PRI support spread across the nation.

11. For a much more detailed study of ballot-splitting and crossover voting, and their meaning for electoral alignment, see Moreno and Méndez 2007.

12. A detailed analysis of these individuals can be found in the Mexico 2006 Panel Study's supplemental materials for chapter 3 (http://web.mit.edu/polisci/research/mexico06/book.html).

13. The supplemental materials show a multiple regression analysis of municipal-level data.

14. See the supplemental materials, which include a graphical presentation of predictions from the municipal-level analysis.

15. Coefficients and goodness-of-fit statistics for these models are reported in the supplemental materials.

16. The supplemental materials report predicted vote shares for the major candidates, given particular characteristics (e.g., being female or being from a union household). CLARIFY (Tomz et al. 2001) uses STATA regression results as input into a Monte Carlo simulation program designed to produce more readily interpretable output.

17. The income measure I use is an average of the self-reported income in the May and July waves of the panel study. Hence it is a continuous variable. Similar results emerge if an index of major household possessions is used instead.

18. The education measure I use is an average of the respondent's self-reported schooling across all three waves of the panel study.

19. These and the following predictions are based on the basic multinomial logit model that uses individual-level variables only.

20. For an analysis of the North and some of its self-perceptions in the period of the Revolution, see Carr 1973. The classic study of Mexican regionalism is Simpson 1941 (and many subsequent editions).

21. The Cristero War, fought after the Mexican Revolution was already over, claimed tens of thousands of lives.

22. See the studies in Randall 1996.

23. The northerners surveyed in the *México y el Mundo* study (2004) had traveled abroad on average ten times in their lives, in contrast to a national figure of about three times (see Klesner 2006).

24. For arguments that explore the diffusion of PAN and PRD governance at the mu-

nicipal level in concentrated regions of Mexico, see Lujambio 2001; Hiskey and Bowler 2005; Hiskey and Canache 2005.

25. I develop this argument more fully in Klesner 2005.

FOUR: Regionalized Voting Behavior and Political Discussion in Mexico

I wish to thank Chappell Lawson and Jorge Domínguez for their valuable comments on previous drafts.

1. Pundits chose these color designations to match the two parties' symbolic colors.

2. For details on the Mexico 2006 Panel Study, see chapter 1, note 1. Data from the study is available at http://web.mit.edu/polisci/research/mexico06/.

3. A fifth factor that scholars offered in the 1990s was that residents of some northern states had lived under non-PRI governors, so this could have lowered the perceived risks entailed in opposition governance (Poiré 1999). In fact, however, Mexico's regional cleavages sharpened in the elections occurring after 2000, that is, after political turnover at the federal level and in most states.

4. This same battery asked respondents how they were related to each discussant.

5. Comparative networks data are still rare, because name generators have only been administered in a few countries. The eight nations are Brazil (from Baker et al. 2006), Bulgaria, Hungary, Poland, Russia, Spain, the United States (all from Gibson 2001), and Mexico. An apples-and-oranges issue exists, however, as some countries in the sample requested the names of those with whom the respondent discussed "important matters," while others queried exclusively "political" discussants. The wording of the former question (asked in Bulgaria, Hungary, Poland, Russia, Spain, and the United States) obviously queries a much larger pool of discussants than the latter (Brazil, Mexico, and South Bend, Indiana [Huckfeldt and Sprague 1995]), although research shows that these measurement differences are not as consequential as one might think (Huckfeldt et al. 2004).

6. The results are for all possible dyads, even though this means counting many respondents (with multiple discussants) more than once.

7. Only dyads in which *both* members had a known preference are used in the analysis. In other words, dyads in which either the respondent or the discussant had no preference (as a result of abstention or indecision) and cases where the discussant's preference not known are omitted.

8. Although Brazil has a much more fragmented party system than does Mexico, the probability of random agreement was actually higher in Brazil, because one candidate, eventual winner Luiz Inácio Lula da Silva, received a near majority of the four-candidate vote share in 2002. Mexico's three-candidate race in 2006 was, by comparison, much more balanced. Brazilian results are based on the election returns in two cities, Caxias do Sul and Juiz de Fora, while those for Mexico are based on nationwide results.

9. Another dimension of networks measured in the panel study is network intimacy, or the extent to which networks are comprised of family members. Intimacy is high when individuals tend to hold discussions only with spouses, blood relatives, and other relatives. In contrast, intimacy is low when most conversations take place among friends, coworkers, acquaintances from civil society groups, and other nonfamily members. To measure intimacy, panel respondents were asked to describe their relation to each named discussant. In both waves, 50 percent of the named discussants were nonfamily members, and this figure did not vary at all between urban and rural areas. Interestingly, 50 percent

places Mexico in the least insular half of countries with available network data and means that Mexicans were less likely than people in the United States (60%) to name family members at this point. In short, Mexican citizens are not abnormally segmented into insular, familial groups when they engage in interpersonal political exchanges.

10. Of course, only two of these three variables can be used in any particular model, since knowledge of two for a given state is enough to identify the value of the third. Using all three would induce near-perfect collinearity.

11. See http://web.mit.edu/polisci/research/mexico06/book.html.

12. Hermosillo is far from being the most PAN county (which was San Julian, at 72%), or even the most PAN city (León, at 67%, and Celaya, at 66%). I chose counties that were not maxima (or minima) so as to avoid skewing or exaggerating the results with outliers. That said, all three examples are around the 99th percentile.

FIVE: Absentee Voting and Transnational Civic Engagement among Mexican Expatriates

We thank Chappell Lawson and Jorge Domínguez for helpful comments.

1. México, Consejo Nacional de Población, unpublished data, July 2004.

2. See also Chris Kraul, "Hopes of office lure migrants home," *Los Angeles Times*, July 4, 2004; Ginger Thompson, "Mexico's 'Tomato King' seeks a new title," *New York Times*, July 5, 2004; Associated Press, "Mexico elects a woman as governor," *New York Times*, July 6, 2004; Associated Press, "Fresno professor picked to run for state legislature in Mexico," *San Diego Union-Tribune*, August 3, 2004.

3. Only about 67,000 Mexican nationals applied to their government for dual nationality during the initial, five-year application period, out of more than 15 million eligible first- and second-generation Mexican-origin persons living in the United States. The small number of applicants may reflect poor informational efforts, as well as a perception that the material benefits of dual nationality are very limited.

4. The cross-national evidence suggests that expatriate voting has never come close to affecting national electoral outcomes in any country that allows it. About sixty countries currently permit expatriates to vote in home-country elections, either by mail or by visiting a consulate or embassy. They include Argentina, Brazil, Colombia, Honduras, and Peru. But in none of these cases does absentee voting yield a tidal wave of votes. The largest number—over 61,000—was cast by Colombian expatriates in their country's 2006 presidential election. Thus, the importance of absentee balloting is mostly symbolic in these electoral systems.

5. According to surveys administered in 1998, 10 percent of Colombians, 13 percent of Dominicans, and 8 percent of Salvadorans were members of a home-country political party, and significantly more reported at least occasional engagement in home-country electoral politics.

6. Funding for the 2006 Mexican Expatriate Study was provided by the Carnegie Corporation of New York, the Public Policy Institute at the University of Texas at Austin, the College of Liberal Arts at Purdue University, and the University of California–San Diego (information is available from the authors). Nearly all interviews were conducted in Spanish, and on average lasted just over twenty minutes. Two modes of survey administration—telephone and in person—were used to safeguard against sampling biases. Undergraduate students trained by McCann carried out the initial polling in Indiana

between February and May; professional firms conducted the June interviews, with a cooperation rate of 89 percent by telephone and 78 percent in person. The demographic profiles of respondents contacted by the students are quite comparable to those polled by professional interviewers. By region, N = 478 (Indiana), 126 (San Diego), and 500 (Dallas). All respondents were Mexican-born adults over eighteen.

7. For details, see chapter 1, note 1 and http://web.mit.edu/polisci/research/mexico06/.

8. The panel study's figures—implying that 92 percent of the country's residents intended to vote—were, of course, an overestimate of turnout on the day of the election in Mexico.

9. Question wordings and response distributions are given in the Mexico 2006 Panel Study's supplemental materials for chapter 5 (http://web.mit.edu/polisci/research/mexico06/book.html).

10. These authors found that demographic variables such as education and age significantly shape transnational civic engagement among Colombians, Dominicans, and Salvadorans. Social networks also play a part, as does time spent in the United States. Interestingly, however, whether or not the Colombian, Salvadoran, or Dominican was a U.S. citizen had little to do with the incidence of transnational engagement.

11. Respondents who favored a minor candidate, were unsure of their preferences, or would not take part were not included in the models.

12. CLARIFY (Tomz et al. 2001) was used to calculate these point estimates and confidence intervals (see also King, Tomz, and Wittenberg 2000). The multinomial regression coefficients themselves, standard errors, and model fit diagnostics appear in table 5.B in the supplemental materials for chapter 5 (http://web.mit.edu/polisci/research/mexico06/book.html). As noted in that table, Hausman tests indicate that the independence from irrelevant alternatives (IIA) assumption is tenable in both samples.

13. As discussed in chapter 14 of this volume, left-right scales may contain a substantial amount of measurement error, which could result in insignificant findings such as these. The similarities between expatriates and Mexicans living in Mexico suggest that, to the extent the instrumentation is error-ridden, the amount of error does not vary greatly across the two countries.

14. One reason for the discrepancy in the case of Madrazo could be that among respondents who had a good opinion of the PRI, expatriates were slightly less inclined than Mexicans in Mexico to give the party a strongly positive evaluation. The two samples do not differ in this way with respect to ratings of the PAN and the PRD. This finding implies that PRI identifiers in the United States were somewhat less committed to and personally identified with the former ruling party, compared to PRI supporters south of the border.

SIX: The Absence of Common Ground between Candidates and Voters

We are particularly grateful to Chappell Lawson and Jorge Domínguez for their close and careful reading of drafts of this chapter, as well as to the other members of the Mexico 2006 Panel Study for their insightful comments and suggestions at various points along the way.

1. Luna and Zechmeister's (2005) excellent study on elite-mass linkages in Latin America includes Mexico; however, it relies on only a small number of responses on the

elite side, and it employs different questions on the elite and mass surveys. Data for that study were collected before the PRI's loss of power in 2000, which changed the competition space (see the introductory chapter to this volume).

2. Bruhn collected the electoral platforms, coded them, and analyzed the results. She requested the full code books plus training manuals from the Comparative Manifestos Project, or CMP (see www.wzb.eu/zkd/dsl/projekte-manifesto.en.htm for information about this project), and passed their intercoder reliability test prior to coding. She particularly wishes to thank Dr. Andrea Volkens, who provided assistance and advice in the early phases of coding. Any errors remain the responsibility of Bruhn alone.

3. Coders break down literal sentences into quasi-sentences if the sense of the sentence changes significantly (for instance, where a platform lists several intended policies separated by semi-colons). Country coders can create new categories for issues specific to their countries, but they are discouraged from doing so in order to enhance the comparability of the data. In these cases, after consultation with the CMP, it was necessary to create only one new category—focusing on the need to develop checks and balances against presidential power—which fell outside of the areas of concern of the European/U.S. parties.

4. To transform the scores on coding categories into aggregated ideological positions, we first express the data in percentage terms, that is, as the relative emphasis for each category with respect to the total number of sentences in the platform. To calculate the ideological placement of parties, the coder sums the total percentages of "right" items (as described by Budge and Robertson 1987) and subtracts the total percentages of "left" items. Positive scores indicate more conservative ideological placements, while negative scores indicate more leftist ideological ones.

5. As coded by Bruhn (see Bruhn 2004).

6. This category also includes wage and tax policies to stimulate private enterprise.

7. In the CMP coding instructions, the education category covers a basic education provision at all levels. Educational expenses, defined in terms of "training and research"— as applied to the modernization of industry, for example—fall under the technology and infrastructure category. Thus the CMP categories attempt to distinguish between education as a human capital investment explicitly designed to improve economic performance and education as a fundamental social right.

8. Two types of theoretical statements predict advantages to centrism in three-party competition. First, under deterministic spatial voting, the classic result predicts cycling in unidimensional competition (Cox 1990); however, in any one round, the peripheral parties still have an incentive to "squeeze" toward the center. Convergence is also an equilibrium if the interior party cannot leapfrog out of the center. Second, under the assumption of probabilistic voting, three-party competition may lead to convergence on the minimum-sum point, regardless of the dimensionality of the competition space (Lin et al. 1999).

9. The principal investigators were Kathleen Bruhn and Kenneth F. Greene (listed in alphabetical order). The project was funded by the University of Texas at Austin and the University of California–Santa Barbara. We split the sample into a telephone survey and a web survey, but we only report the results of the larger telephone survey here. The telephone survey was administered by Data OPM, Mexico City. The authors particularly want to thank Pablo Parás, Luis Estrada, and their intrepid survey team for carrying out this work, as well as Chappell Lawson for important input on the survey design.

10. Our telephone sample included 84 responses from PAN candidates and 77 from PRD candidates. Our contact lists for the telephone survey contained 176 PAN candidates and 166 PRD candidates (note that we held back 100 of the 300 PAN candidates for the web survey; the PRD list had many missing contacts, principally for candidates from other parties that participated in the Coalition For the Good of All). Based on our initial contact lists, our response rate was 47.7 percent for the PAN and 46.4 percent for the PRD. The uniqueness of our survey means that we lack comparative data; however, considering that the survey was administered in the hectic last days before the election, we consider our response rate to be quite good. Based on the universe of candidates for single-member-district races in the lower house, our response rate is still quite respectable, at 28 percent for the PAN and 25.7 percent for the PRD.

11. $t = 5.8$, $p < .001$, two-tailed test.

12. $t = 3.5$, $p < .001$, two-tailed test.

13. For details, see the Mexico 2006 Panel Study's supplemental materials for chapter 6 (http://web.mit.edu/polisci/research/mexico06/book.html).

14. We used CLARIFY (Tomz et al. 2001) to compute the predicted probabilities.

15. For details on the Mexico 2006 Panel Study, including data and question wording, see http://web.mit.edu/polisci/research/mexico06/. Chapter 1, note 1 provides an overview of the survey design. All mass-level data in this chapter are taken from that project.

16. The knowledge variable used data from wave 3 of the Mexico 2006 Panel Study and asked respondents to identify the three branches of government (executive, legislative, and judicial). Low-knowledge respondents (65.1%) correctly identified none or one of the branches, while high-knowledge respondents (34.9%) identified two or all three.

17. It is also possible that low-knowledge respondents are truly less in favor of expanded commercial relations with the United States. In the Mexico 2006 Panel Study (see note 15), knowledge is correlated with education at .46. Public opinion studies often show that more-educated voters prefer free trade, and although the correlation between the two variables is not terribly high, the knowledge gap may be picking up an education gap. If this were the case, then measurement error would not bias the results.

18. For the PAN, the data matching yielded 24 candidate-voter district dyads on the question of privatization and 26 on the question of abortion. For the PRD, it yielded 18 on privatization and 17 on abortion. Details of the analysis are available on the Mexico 2006 Panel Study website at http://web.mit.edu/polisci/research/mexico06/book.html.

19. For details on the analysis, see the Mexico 2006 Panel Study's supplemental materials for chapter 6 (http://web.mit.edu/polisci/research/mexico06/book.html).

20. The PAN's issue profile is also similar to that of Republicans in the United States; however, whereas Republicans typically favor capital punishment, the PAN candidates oppose it.

21. See "The Latinobarómetro poll," *Economist*, November 15, 2007.

SEVEN: Choosing Mexico's 2006 Presidential Candidates

This chapter was originally presented as a paper at the American Political Science Association conference held in Philadelphia on August 31, 2006, and at the Working Group Meeting on Mexico's 2006 Elections hosted by the Weatherhead Center for International Affairs at Harvard University (November 30 to December 2, 2006). I gratefully acknowledge the useful comments and suggestions from Jorge Domínguez, Federico Estévez, Chappell Lawson, Jay McCann, Alejandro Poiré, David Samuels, Alexandra Webber, Thomas Webber, Steve Wuhs, and Francisco González, the reviewer for this volume.

1. In contrast, only three U.S. presidential races in the last six decades (1988, 2000, and 2008) involved an open contest between two nonincumbent candidates. Hence, when attempting to assess the impacts of open and divisive primaries, it is difficult to control for the incumbency advantages and the particular considerations of sitting presidents in most U.S. presidential races (Atkeson 2000).

2. Poiré (2003) argues that a major motivator for the opening of PRI candidate selection rules has been a desire to prevent costly defections by strong contenders.

3. Prominent potential contenders with ties to the incumbent Fox administration included former comptroller Francisco Barrio, former senator Carlos Medina Plascencia, then foreign relations secretary Luis Ernesto Derbez, and then first lady Martha Fox, although each ultimately declined to run.

4. Thirteen presidents emanated from the ruling party from 1928 to 2000, with eight former ministers being nominated to this post, owing largely to the minister of government's role as the president's right-hand man. Francisco Labastida, the only one not handpicked by the sitting president, was the sole member of this group who failed to win the presidency.

5. Creel had strong credentials as a journalist and civic leader before serving as a citizen representative for the Federal Electoral Institute (1994–96). Although his family had a history of participation in the PAN, Creel himself was nonetheless relatively new to the party. See David Aponte and Salvador Frausto, "Yo no compito con nadie," *Cambio*, September 22–28, 2002.

6. An engineer and urban planner, Cárdenas Jiménez's political career began in the state of Jalisco, where he was elected mayor of Ciudad Guzmán (1992–94). After his term as governor of Jalisco (1995–2000), Cárdenas Jiménez served as Mexico's national forestry commissioner (2001–3) and secretary of the environment and natural resources (2003–5).

7. Several prominent members of Fox's own 2000 campaign staff signed on as part of Cárdenas Jiménez's team, including Carlos Rojas Magnon, Joaquín Fortín, Fernando González, Sergio García de Alba, and Lino Korrodi (implicated in the Fox campaign finance scandal that cost the PAN nearly three million U.S. dollars in 2003). See Jorge Herrera, "Acusan panistas a Ebrard de simular la indagatoria," *El Universal*, March 13, 2004.

8. Calderón had also served as a federal deputy in 1991–94.

9. In order to obtain a PAN candidacy or leadership position, one must first become a member of the party, collect a nominal number of signatures from active party members in support of one's campaign, and then win during multiple rounds of voting in the party's caucuses or conventions.

10. See www.pan.org.mx.

11. Author's estimates, based on the PAN membership registry. There were approximately 53 and 71 million registered voters in Mexico in 2000 and 2006, respectively (www.idea.int).

12. Data for the United States from www.centerforpolitics.org and www.census .gov. Reliance on the number of registered voters obviously neglects eligible voters. There are useful estimates for the actual number of eligible voters in the United States

through the U.S. Elections Project, developed by George Washington University professor Michael McDonald, which is available at http://elections.gmu.edu/.

13. In 2008, the total number of Republican presidential primary voters was nearly 21 million; the total number of Democratic voters exceeded 35 million (www.realclear politics.com). A total of 136.6 million voters participated in the 2008 general presidential election (Seth Boren, "Voter turnout best in generations, maybe a century," Associated Press, November 5, 2008).

14. The Election Commission comprised eight national commissioners, named by the party's National Council. At the state level, local commissions—comprising 160 members appointed by the National Council (five from each of Mexico's thirty-two state entities, including the Federal District)—oversaw the implementation of the party primary (www.pan.org.mx).

15. The first round of primaries (on September 11, 2005) included ten north-central states (Durango, Guanajuato, Hidalgo, México state, Nuevo León, Querétaro, San Luis Potosí, Tamaulipas, Tlaxcala, and Zacatecas). The second round (on October 2, 2005) comprised eight southeastern states (Campeche, Chiapas, Oaxaca, Puebla, Quintana Roo, Tabasco, Veracruz, and Yucatán). The final round (on October 23, 2005) covered the populous Federal District and thirteen states (Aguascalientes, Baja California, Baja California Sur, Chihuahua, Coahuila, Colima, Guerrero, Jalisco, Michoacán, Morelos, Nayarit, Sinaloa, and Sonora). See CEN-PAN (Comité Ejecutive Nacional-Partido Acción Nacional), "Reglamento para la elección del candidato a la Presidencia de la República del Partido Acción Nacional," www.pan.org.mx.

16. "Center-right Partido Acción Nacional spurns President Vicente Fox's candidate, re-elects incumbent to top leadership post," *SourceMex*, March 13, 2002.

17. Calderón benefited from strong support in the states of Campeche (the home state of Juan Camilo Mouriño, his closest campaign advisor and later his chief of staff) and Yucatán (where he had close ties to sitting governor Patricio Patrón and the state party apparatus).

18. "Mexico's 2006 presidential race comes into focus," *SourceMex*, October 26, 2005.

19. Cárdenas's only strong showing of support (indeed the only state in which he won a majority) was in Jalisco, where he polled 52 percent to Calderón's 40 percent.

20. According to Calderón, "On the one hand, I'm the candidate of the governing party. At the same time, I don't need to take on the burden of being the government's candidate. People know that my candidacy developed not only outside the government but in spite of the government." Quoted in Dudley Althaus, "Mexico's presidential race: 'Disobedient son' works to strike balance," *Houston Chronicle*, February 15, 2006.

21. Calderón Vega authored several books on the PAN, politics, and religious issues (see, for example, Calderón Vega 1992 and Calderón Vega and Vicencio Acevedo 1978).

22. Calderón Vega lived to see Felipe take office as a member of the Mexico City assembly, but he died shortly thereafter in 1989. Donald Mabry provides a compelling and deeply personal account of Luis Calderón Vega's life and his relationship with his family in his online encyclopedia of Mexican politics, "Father of a Mexican President: Luis Calderón Vega," www.historicaltextarchive.com.

23. Building a career as a journalist and an activist within the party's structures in his home state of Yucatán, Castillo Peraza embodied the image of the righteous and quixotic PAN crusader, running in numerous seemingly futile campaigns for public office: mayor of Mérida (1984), governor of Yucatán (1988), and mayor of Mexico City (1997).

24. In some races, notably in Sinaloa and Oaxaca in 2004, the PRI was also bolstered by the failure of the PRD and PAN to negotiate electoral alliances. See Javier Cabrera Martínez, "Ven pocas posibilidades a coalición en Sinaloa," *El Universal*, March 15, 2004; Alberto López Morales, "Se tambalea alianza PRD-PAN en Oaxaca," *El Universal*, March 15, 2004.

25. Madrazo had also followed in the footsteps his father by serving as governor of Tabasco in the late 1950s. The younger Madrazo tried to capitalize on his father's reputation as a reformer within the PRI; the elder Madrazo was allegedly forced to resign from the PRI due to his efforts to combat corruption and later died in a mysterious airplane crash.

26. In the words of one high-ranking PRI party official, in the past "there was a custom that the president set the direction for the party. Now that we no longer have the presidency, we ourselves will have to set the direction." Quoted in James F. Smith, "Mexico's PRI feeling rejuvenated at massive party congress," *Los Angeles Times*, November 21, 2001.

27. Proposals to adopt new candidate selection regulations (which empowered activists at the grassroots level) were believed to favor Madrazo's eventual takeover of the party presidency. Changes made at the convention also provided for greater representation in the party for women and younger people, two groups deemed to have drifted from the PRI to Fox in 2000 (see Smith, "Mexico's PRI feeling rejuvenated," November 21, 2001).

28. Fernando Mayolo López, "Se decide Paredes, va por dirigencia," *Reforma*, January 9, 2002.

29. Claudia Guerrero, "Buscan priístas candidatura única," *Reforma*, January 9, 2002.

30. Paredes alleged that the vote was manipulated in several states, favoring Madrazo by inflating the results and suppressing turnout among her supporters through various forms of deception. See "Bitter internal election threatens to split former governing Partido Revolucionario Institucional," *SourceMex*, February 27, 2002.

31. "Bitter internal election," February 27, 2002.

32. "Center-right Partido Acción Nacional," March 13, 2002.

33. Andrés Becerril, "Madrazo-Elba Esther: Huele a divorcio en el PRI," *Cambio*, September 1–7, 2002; "Mr. Fox and Ms. Fix," *Economist*, August 28, 2003. The SNTE is often described as the largest union in the hemisphere.

34. After later bolting the party, signs of Gordillo's wrath included her support for the New Alliance Party (PANAL) candidacy of Roberto Campa—who devoted much of his campaign to attacking Madrazo—as well as overtures to Calderón.

35. See Chris Aspin, "Loser cries fraud in Mexico state election," Reuters News Service, August 2, 2004.

36. The process for determining the TUCOM candidate relied on the results of polls, conducted by three major firms, among respondents drawn from professed party members and a representative sample of the general electorate.

37. Gordillo later filed a claim with the Federal Electoral Court, but was unsuccessful. Notimex, "Regresará Gordillo a su cargo en el PRI: Campa," *El Universal*, June 4, 2005.

38. See chapter 1, note 1 and http://web.mit.edu/polisci/research/mexico06/ for further details.

39. Julia Preston, "At a hopeful moment, feud tears at Mexico's Left," *New York Times*, July 15, 1999, 3.

40. Counter mobilizations and maneuvering by Madrazo prevented federal intervention in the Tabasco elections. For a full discussion, see Eisenstadt 2004.

41. Alberto Cuenca and Héctor Molina, "De las ruinas del 85 edificó su carrera," *El Universal*, May 13, 2004.

42. Francisco Arroyo, "Negocian PRI y PAN en lo oscuro: Padierna," *El Universal*, April 26, 2000; Sam Dillon, "Bid to disqualify a key Mexican candidate," *New York Times*, April 21, 2000; Ella Grajeda, "Buscan descalificarnos a la mala, sostiene AMLO," *El Universal*, April 26, 2000.

43. Dillon, "Bid to Disqualify," April 21, 2000.

44. See Ella Grajeda, Alejandro Torres, and Felipe de Jesús González, "Se defiende López Obrador," *El Universal*, May 4, 2000.

45. Ella Grajeda, "Emplea AMLO a compañeros de lucha," *El Universal*, January 24, 2004; Icela Lagunas, "Según Bátiz, el nepotismo es una falta administrativa," *El Universal*, January 24, 2004.

46. In a series of "video-scandals" involving PRD members, footage was released to the media that showed René Bejarano and Carlos Ímaz, the PRD delegate representing Tlálpan, receiving money from Carlos Ahumada, a businessman with ties to the PAN. Gustavo Ponce Meléndez, the Mexico City finance minister who was alleged to have indirectly accepted $3 million in bribes from Ahumada, was apprehended in March 2004 after being identified by security cameras at a high-stakes table of the Bellagio casino in Las Vegas. See Ricardo Alemán, "AMLO, la 'telecracia' y los videos." *El Universal*, March 14, 2004; "Un video destapa fraude por 30 millones de pesos contra el GDF," *La Jornada*, March 2, 2004.

47. Ginger Thompson, "Hundreds of thousands in Mexico march against crime," *New York Times*, June 28, 2004, 6.

48. Calls to remove Mexico City police chief Marcelo Ebrard first came in the wake of the video-scandals, on the grounds that the mayor and police chief were not thoroughly investigating the crimes within his administration. Ebrard was finally removed in the months that followed after three federal police officers were beaten—and two ultimately burned to death—while local police looked on. See Herrera, "Acusan panistas a Ebrard," March 13, 2004.

49. Sergio Jiménez and Jorge Teherán, "Procede el desafuero," *El Universal*, April 2, 2005.

50. Cárdenas proposed dissolving the party's internal factions, removing all eighteen members of the party's National Executive Committee (CEN), and appointing a new list of CEN members. Party president Leonel Godoy Rangel also criticized the mayor's lack of communication with the party. See Jorge Ramos, "Desdén y regaños en la inauguración," *El Universal*, March 27, 2004; Nayeli Cortes, "Propone Cárdenas refundar al PRD," *El Universal*, March 23, 2004; Jorge Ramos, "Temen perredistas cambios simulados," *El Universal*, March 27, 2004.

51. Ricardo Alemán, "Cambiar sin cambios," *El Universal*, March 29, 2004; Periodistas de *El Universal*, "La crisis del PRD," *El Universal*, April 14, 2004.

52. "Retoma Cárdenas lucha por candidatura," *El Universal*, May 20, 2005.

53. Jorge Ramos, "Elegir candidato y evitar fractura, el reto," *El Universal*, May 5, 2005.

54. Jorge Ramos and Lilia Saúl, "Facilitan candidatura para López Obrador," *El Universal*, April 24, 2005.

55. Cota's triumph as PRD party president prompted criticisms that the pro-AMLO New Leftist Current, the reincarnated Bejarano faction, had employed machine tactics to elect him. See "Controversy surrounds election of new PAN & PRD leaders," *SourceMex*, March 30, 2005.

56. Cuauhtémoc Cárdenas, "Carta de declinación (texto íntegro)," *El Universal*/Redacción online, July 5, 2005.

57. In the initial negotiations with the PRD, the PT requested a total of thirty seats (including eleven Senate seats, compared to four offered by the PRD). Later, under the terms of their agreement, the PRD evidently offered a total of seventeen Deputy seats to Convergence. Jorge Octavio Ochoa, "Negociación entre PRD y PT sigue entrampada," *El Universal*, November 13, 2005; Jorge Octavio Ochoa, "Ven en PT riesgo de escisión por candidatura," *El Universal*, November 17, 2005; Jorge Ramos, "Anuncian 70 por ciento de avance para alianza entre PRD y PT," *El Universal*, November 23, 2005; Jorge Ramos, "Cierran PRD y PT alianza hacia 2006," *El Universal*, November 24, 2005; Jorge Ramos and Lilia Saúl, "El PRD y Convergencia confirman la coalición," *El Universal*, December 1, 2005.

58. For example, the PAN's decision to maintain a relatively closed nominations process reflected the party leaders' desire to have a candidate who was representative of the party's program and ideals, having learned the pitfalls of the alternative under Fox. In the PRD, López Obrador essentially pursued a de facto Fox-style strategy of outward-bound campaigning that eclipsed his own party in the process.

59. In recent years, major exceptions have included Bolivia, the Dominican Republic, Ecuador, and Peru.

60. During the same period (November 2005 to December 2006), only three countries had incumbent presidential candidates who sought and won their parties' nominations during this same period: Brazil, Colombia, and Venezuela. In 2008, the United States experienced the first presidential race since 1954 where there was no incumbent presidential or vice-presidential candidate, producing one of the most competitive party primaries in history for both parties and dramatically increasing voter participation.

EIGHT: The PRI's 2006 Presidential Campaign

I would like to thank Jorge Domínguez, Federico Estévez, and Chappell Lawson for their comments and criticisms of the chapter.

1. Los Pinos is the name of the presidential compound, i.e., Mexico's White House.

2. However, over the entire six-year term of the PAN presidency, the PRI also lost several states for the first time ever: Morelos, San Luis Potosí, Chiapas, Yucatán, Michoacán, and Guerrero.

3. Five hundred federal deputies and 128 senators are elected concurrently with the president. Three hundred deputies are elected in single-member districts, and 200 are chosen by proportional representation based on their party's share of the national vote. Three-quarters of the senators are chosen on binominal closed-list tickets in each state, where the winning party in that state earns two seats and the party that finishes second wins one; the remaining one-quarter are chosen by proportional representation. Party lists for the Senate and the Chamber of Deputies are closed, in the sense that voters

cannot strike out or alter the order of candidates on the list. On July 2, 2006, voters in Jalisco, Morelos, the Federal District, and Guanajuato also elected governors. Chiapas and Tabasco choose governors in the months following the presidential elections.

4. These three sectors include (1) organized labor, (2) peasant associations, and (3) middle-class, professional, and other occupational groups—each of which is dominated by a single peak-level association.

5. Former party leaders who had left politics, retired, or died were excluded from the sample. State party leaders other than governors were also excluded, as they have more limited spheres of influence and are normally tied to a national leader. For information on state-level leaders, see chapter 6 in this volume.

6. Thanks in large part to Madrazo's complaints and threats during the course of 1998 and 1999, the then president of Mexico, Ernesto Zedillo, organized an open-party primary to nominate the PRI's 2000 presidential candidate, instead of simply imposing his favored candidate. Madrazo lost the primary and voiced protests over about the process's unfairness, but he did not leave the party. The entire episode gave him enormous credibility with PRI members who were angry about the takeover of the party by "technocrats" under President Carlos Salinas (1988–94).

7. TUCOM's leaders included former governors Enrique Martínez y Martínez of Coahuila, Tomás Yarrington of Tamaulipas, Miguel Alemán of Veracruz, Arturo Montiel of the state of México, and Manuel Ángel Nuñez Soto of Hidalgo, as well as sitting governors Natividad González Paras of Nuevo León and Eduardo Bours of Sonora. Enrique Jackson, former leader of the PRI delegation in the Senate, was also a prominent member. See also chapter 7 in this volume.

8. "Cuestionan priístas honestidad de Montiel," *Reforma*, October 17, 2005. This telephone poll interviewed 605 PRI sympathizers.

9. Raymundo Riva Palacios, "Estrictamente personal," *El Universal*, November 11, 2005.

10. According to the PRI's statutes, the National Political Council decides on the method of candidate selection for the presidential race, and it has two options: either a primary (which can be open either to all registered voters or only PRI sympathizers) or a delegate convention (Articles 23 and 25 of the *Reglamento para la elección de dirigentes y postulación de candidatos*, www.pri.org.mx). Half of the delegates for the convention must be made up of national councilors, and the other half of state councilors (Article 28).

11. Personal communication with the former president, Mexico City, May 13, 2002.

12. The Madrazo media team came out with a spot questioning AMLO's honesty that was ruled out-of-bounds by the Federal Electoral Court (after the spot had run its natural course and had already been taken off the air).

13. The PRI candidate was nervous: his eyes shifted back and forth, his voice was hoarse, he made rude attacks on a minor candidate, and when he held up a piece of paper to make a point, his hands shook visibly. Madrazo even dropped one of the papers and momentarily disappeared from the camera's view when he bent down below the podium to retrieve it. Calderón, meanwhile, was calm, smiling, and well spoken. Roberto Campa, the candidate of Gordillo's New Alliance Party, spent most of his allotted time criticizing Madrazo and ended the debate by accusing him of not having paid his taxes in the last few years.

14. Palacios, "Estrictamente personal," November 11, 2005.

15. "Madrazo ofrece limpiar al gobierno de corrupción," *El Universal*, June 26, 2006.

16. Madrazo had an almost pathological inability to arrive at events on time, and often the attendees had begun to leave by the time he showed up. Sparse attendance was reported everywhere. For example, in Guanajuato, see Ciro Pérez Silva, "Yo no busco en la política un salario; vivo de mis rentas," *La Jornada*, May 31, 2006.

17. Consulta Mitofsky, "Encuesta nacional en viviendas: Segunda quincena de junio 2006," www.consulta.com.mx (accessed June 23, 2006; article no longer available). *Reforma* polls had Madrazo in third place in March at 25 percent, trailing Calderón (at 31 percent) and AMLO (at 41 percent). By April, Calderón had climbed to 38 percent and first place, with AMLO dropping to second at 35 percent, and Madrazo 15 percent behind the front-runner, at only 23 percent. See Alejandro Moreno and Roberto Gutiérrez, "Pelean por votos volatiles," *Reforma*, May 24, 2006.

18. For information on the Mexico 2006 Panel Study, see chapter 1, note 1 and http://web.mit.edu/polisci/research/mexico06/.

19. In the aftermath of the elections, only 9 percent of nonidentifiers were willing to admit they had voted for Madrazo (data from the Mexico 2006 Panel Study, wave 3).

20. Pérez Silva, "Yo no busco," May 31, 2006.

21. Mexico 2006 Panel Study, waves 1 and 2.

22. José Gil Olmos, "Arranca el tricolor su campaña '20 con Madrazo,'" *Proceso*, May 15, 2006.

23. Mario Gutiérrez Vega, "Replantea PRI estrategia," *El Norte*, March 26, 2006.

24. This became a popular refrain by May. See "Carrera por presidencia se cierra en dos opciones contrapuestas," Agencia EFE, June 7, 2006. Before the June 6 debate, Madrazo announced that the other two candidates would surely attack him; in fact, both largely ignored him, as he was not considered to be a contender.

25. According to the PRI's statutes, candidates can be chosen either in a party primary or through district level conventions, or by customary law for indigenous municipalities (see Article 25 of the PRI statutes). However, these rules do not hold if the party runs in an alliance, as it did with the PVEM in 2006.

26. For more on the alliance with the PVEM, see "Dictamen al acuerdo del órgano de gobierno de la coalición 'Alianza por México' por el que se elaboran las propuestas de candidatos a senadores de la República y Diputados Federales al Congreso General," www.pri.org.mx.

27. For example, Jesús Murillo Karam stated that in Hidalgo, his party should concentrate on doing well in the congressional races, not on saving Madrazo's campaign.

28. Senator Mario González Zarur was plotting openly in June to help ensure the CEN presidency for his ally Jackson.

29. Governor Enrique Peña Nieto apparently organized a group of governors to this end, but ultimately they failed.

30. In San Luis Potosí, the PAN nominated an ex-member of the PRI and leader of the state's SNTE to an elected post. In the state of Jalisco, federal deputy Gonzalo Moreno Arévalo from the PRI was named the campaign chief for the PAN's gubernatorial candidate. In Chihuahua, a member of PRI-led state government was nominated to a Senate candidacy for the PRD. A leader of the PRI in Chiapas left the party when he was denied the gubernatorial nomination. Members of the PRI's peasant wing in Yucatán threatened to leave the party. The party's candidate for governor in Guanajuato declined his candidacy when his ally was denied the Senate nomination. And so forth.

NINE: López Obrador, Calderón, and the 2006 Presidential Campaign

I would like to thank Jorge Domínguez, Chappell Lawson, Joy Langston, the other project participants in the Mexico 2006 Panel Study, and Francisco González (the reviewer from the Johns Hopkins University Press) for comments on earlier drafts of this chapter, as well as Michael Myers for editorial assistance.

1. Heather Murphy, "The presidential candidates," *Washington Post*, June 9, 2006, www.washingtonpost.com/wp-dyn/content/article/2006/06/09/AR2006060900814 .html.

2. Gustavo Ponce Meléndez was filmed gambling in Las Vegas on the government's dime. René Bejarano was filmed stuffing his pockets with cash provided by Argentine businessman Carlos Ahumada, who had received several lucrative construction contracts from the Mexico City government.

3. Parametría, "Felipe Calderón aventaja a López Obrador (May 06)," May 5–8, 2006, www.parametria.com.mx/carta-parametrica.phtml?id=4017&text1=2006.

4. The government charged him with violating a court order requiring him to stop building a new road to a hospital, pending a decision on whether the municipal government could legally expropriate the land. The PRI and PAN representatives cooperated to strip López Obrador of his legal immunity as mayor of Mexico City so that he could be charged. According to Mexican electoral law, anyone charged with a violation of federal law cannot be a candidate for president.

5. Parametría, "Felipe Calderón aventaja."

6. Author's confidential interview with a CEN member.

7. Coders assign each sentence in a platform to one of fifty-six common categories, according to the sense of that sentence (or part of a sentence, if it contains multiple ideas). The data is expressed in percentage terms as the relative emphasis for each category with respect to the length of the platform. Coded sentences can be grouped according to issue areas (domains) or summed together to create scales on specific dimensions (e.g., left-right placement). The left-right scale developed by Budge and Robertson (1987) on the basis of European party platforms includes thirteen right emphasis items and thirteen left emphasis items from the list of categories. To calculate the left-right position of any party, one sums the total percentages of the right items and subtracts the total percentages of the left items. To enhance the comparability of the data, I obtained the full code books and training manuals from the Comparative Manifestos Project (see www.wzb.eu/ zkd/dsl/projekte-manifesto.en.htm for information about this project) and passed their intercoder reliability test. In the initial phases of coding, I received assistance and advice from Dr. Andrea Volkens as I came across problems. I wish to thank the Comparative Manifestos Project, and Dr. Volkens in particular, for their generous assistance.

8. Figures for these results can be found in the Mexico 2006 Panel Study's supplemental materials for chapter 9 (http://web.mit.edu/polisci/research/mexico06/book .html).

9. Parametría, "Felipe Calderón aventaja."

10. For details on the Mexico 2006 Panel Study, see chapter 1, note 1. For data from the study, see http://web.mit.edu/polisci/research/mexico06/.

11. Georgina Saldierna, "Trajo el PAN a Aznar para promover el voto en favor de Calderón Hinojosa," *La Jornada*, February 22, 2006, www.jornada.unam.mx/ 2006/02/22/014n1pol.php.

12. Parametría, "Felipe Calderón aventaja."

13. Jorge Ramos Pérez y Sergio Javier Jiménez, "AMLO y Calderón reprueban ataque de Chávez a Fox," *El Universal*, November 11, 2005, www.eluniversal.com.mx/nacion/131921.html.

14. Article 38 of Mexico's Procedures Code, the *Código Federal de Instituciones y Procedimientos Electorales* (COFIPE). Cited in Alonso Urrutia, "Piden PRD, PT y Convergencia al IFE retire tres espots *ofensivos* de Madrazo." *La Jornada*, March 15, 2006, www.jornada.unam.mx/2006/03/15/index.php?section=politica&article=006n1pol/.

15. Martín Diego Rodríguez, "Retira AN espot sobre Chávez y López Obrador," *La Jornada*, March 27, 2006, www.jornada.unam.mx/2006/03/27/index.php?section=politica&article=008n2pol/.

16. Alonso Urrutia, "Se retracta el PAN; decide mantener el espot contra López Obrador," *La Jornada*, March 28, 2006, www.jornada.unam.mx/2006/03/28/index.php?section=politica&article=013n1pol/.

17. The Executive Council is chaired by the president of the IFE's General Council and is composed of the heads of the technical sections within it, such as the registry of voters. As a body of professional electoral specialists, the Executive Council has formal responsibility for "monitoring the fulfillment of norms applicable to political parties." It can recommend sanctions to the General Council, but it requires the latter's approval to implement them. See http://www.ife.org.mx/portal/site/ifev2/Acerca_del_IFE/;jsessionid=5/.

18. Mariusa Reyes, "Primer debate presidencial en México," April 25, 2006, http://news.bbc.co.uk/hi/spanish/latin_america/newsid_4941000/4941718.stm.

19. Andrea Becerril Enviada, "López Obrador demanda al IFE investigar espots pagados por el PAN," *La Jornada*, April 8, 2006, www.jornada.unam.mx/2006/04/08/index.php?section=politica&article=011n1pol/.

20. Jaime Aviles Enviado, "Nos van a seguir atacando, eso significa que vamos muy bien: López Obrador," *La Jornada*, April 24, 2006, www.jornada.unam.mx/2006/04/24/index.php?section=politica&article=006n1pol/.

21. Parametría, "El presidente Vicente Fox aprobado por los mexicanos," May 5–8, 2006, www.parametria.com.mx/es_cartaext.php?id_carta=137/.

22. Reyes, "Primer debate presidencia," April 25, 2006.

23. Claudia Herrera and Ciro Pérez, "Calificativos y ofensas, lo destacado del debate," *La Jornada*, April 26, 2006, www.jornada.unam.mx/2006/04/26/index.php?section=politica&article=012n1pol/.

24. Alonso Urrutia, "Se emparejan los promocionales de candidatos en medios electrónicos: IFE." *La Jornada*, May 18, 2006, www.jornada.unam.mx/2006/05/18/index.php?section=politica&article=020n1pol/.

25. IFE, "Gastos en radio y televisión: Informes anticipados, 2006," http://www.ife.org.mx/portal/site/ifev2/Informes_Anticipados_Radio_y_TV/;jsessionid=q1knJhzcjKkmGXjTLdYydlkQXodvGQowFwq6z1x2QW1Qbng2CMGZ!1714953953!210818381/.

26. Alonso Urrutia, "Mantiene el PAN espots calumniosos, dice Duarte." *La Jornada*, May 22, 2006, www.jornada.unam.mx/2006/05/22/index.php?section=politica&article=007n1pol/, and Urrutia, "Se emparejan los promocionales," May 18, 2006.

27. In demonstrating how to vote, the DVD showed a sample ballot marked for the PAN.

28. 2006 Mexico Panel Survey, wave three.

29. In 1994, López Obrador ran for governor of his home state of Tabasco against Roberto Madrazo. Madrazo won the official count amid charges of electoral fraud and violating campaign spending limits. As he would do in 2006, López Obrador organized a series of protests culminating in a "march for democracy" from Tabasco to Mexico City. Unlike 2006, he had concrete evidence, having obtained several boxes of documents and cancelled checks confirming Madrazo's expenses. When an independent investigation ordered by President Zedillo validated his charges, López Obrador succeeded in negotiating a deal with Zedillo; Zedillo would not attend Madrazo's gubernatorial inauguration and would pressure him to step down. Madrazo simply refused to step down and threatened to mount a protest campaign of his own. At this point, absorbed in the peso crisis which had erupted a month after the disputed election, Zedillo chose prudence over valor. Needing the oil-rich state of Tabasco to keep producing and exporting petroleum, he caved in and backed Madrazo.

30. See, for instance, Secretaría de Derechos Humanos del PRD, *En defensa de los Derechos Humanos* (México, DF: Grupo Parlamentario del Partido de la Revolución Democrática, 1994).

31. Jorge Alonso, "Repoliticizing the Electoral Institute: A severe setback for Mexican democracy," www.envio.org.ni/articulo/2185/.

32. Roberto Garduño, "Imponen PRI y PAN el nuevo consejo del IFE," *La Jornada*, November 1, 2003, www.jornada.unam.mx/2003/11/01/003n1pol.php?origen=politica .php&fly=1/.

33. Claudia Herrera Beltrán, "El próximo domingo López Obrador registrará su candidatura ante el IFE," January 4, 2006, www.jornada.unam.mx/2006/01/04/index.php? section=politica&article=007n1pol/.

34. Andrea Becerril Enviada, "AMLO propone acuerdo migratorio con EU que genere empleos en México," January 27, 2006, www.jornada.unam.mx/2006/01/27/index .php?section=politica&article=012n1pol/.

35. "El IFE y los espots," June 28, 2006, www.jornada.unam.mx/2006/06/28/index .php?section=opinion&article=002a1edi/.

36. Jaime Aviles, "El plantón espera hoy un triunfo o más sacrificios," September 4, 2006, www.jornada.unam.mx/2006/09/04/index.php?section=politica&article=005n1 pol/.

37. Ibid.

38. Jesús Ortega, López Obrador's campaign manager, lost a primary election to López Obrador's favorite, Marcelo Ebrard. The fact that López Obrador came out of the PRI, whereas Jesús Ortega came out of the Communist Left, exacerbated the problem.

TEN: Electoral Volatility in 2006

I wish to thank Chappell Lawson, Jorge Domínguez, and all the members of the Mexico 2006 Panel Study for their helpful suggestions and intellectual support. I thank as well Keith Edwards, Gustavo Flores-Macías, and Paul Staniland for their comments on earlier versions of this draft.

1. *El Universal* online, "8 encuesta nacional los presidenciables." www.eluniversal .com.mx/graficos/animados/presid-nov05.html.

2. James McKinley, "Leftist outsider's campaign surges in Mexico," *New York Times*, March 19, 2006, A12.

3. An appropriately titled front-page story at this time was by James McKinley, "Now in attack mode, a rightist surges in Mexico," *New York Times*, May 23, 2006, A1.

4. See, for example, Klesner 2004, 98 [table]; Moreno 2003a, 32 and 33 [table].

5. For details on the Mexico 2006 Panel Study, from which most of the data in this chapter are drawn, see chapter 1, note 1 and http://web.mit.edu/polisci/research/mex ico06/. All statistics from the panel presented in this chapter use only respondents from the national sample who participated in all three waves.

6. For more information on the video scandals, see, for example, "Sacuden videos al DF," *El Universal*, March 4, 2004. www2.eluniversal.com.mx/pls/impreso/noticia .html?id_nota=57626&tabla=ciudad.

7. The impeachment was triggered by López Obrador's violation of a court order in a minor case. The process, had it been carried to its full conclusion, would have prevented him from competing in the 2006 presidential race, and most political observers and ordinary Mexicans saw it as a transparent effort to do just that. López Obrador orchestrated massive protests in downtown Mexico City, and the Fox administration backed down. For more information on the impeachment process and its consequences, see chapter 9 in this volume. Also see, among others, Ángel Bolaños, "Ni los más sucios políticos podrán manchar la política: López Obrador," *La Jornada*, April 25, 2005. www.jornada.unam .mx/2005/04/25/003n1pol.php.

8. Although Key focused on people who switched across presidential elections rather than during a single campaign, his conclusion has been generalized to a single election context.

9. Key used this term to refer to voters who did not switch preferences during the time period under study.

10. See Lazarsfeld et al. 1944, chapter 7.

11. D. Green et al. (2002) have proposed a similar theory of switching, but apply it to changes in party identification across several years—not, as is the case here, in terms of vote choice in a single election. The central idea is that there may be regional snowball effects concerning switching; once more people have switched, those left behind feel pressure not to be different from others in their community, many of whom they may look up to. Green and his colleagues use their model to explain the shift in party identification in the American South from the Democratic to the Republican Party. In the Brazilian context, Baker et al. (2006) do focus on voter volatility within a single election and conclude that citizens are highly reliant on their immediate social context in making vote choices. Their theoretical approach underscores the importance of social cues among the less educated, which may help explain why Mexico City, with its high level of schooling, seemed to defy the sociological model in the 2006 election.

12. For a critique of the two-step model, see Paolino 2005.

13. Moreno (1999a) measures campaign awareness using an index based on the ability of respondents to recall campaign slogans. In this chapter, such a measure is labeled "reception of information," while attention to the campaign is measured using respondents' self-reported assessments.

14. For information on and data from the Mexico 2000 Panel Study, see www.icpsr .umich.edu/cocoon/ICPSR/STUDY/03380.xml and web.mit.edu/polisci/research/mexi co06/Assets/Explanation%20of%20data.pdf.

15. These percentages take into account changes to and from the undecided category, which includes those who did not express a preference or who did not vote. Initial sup-

porters of Bernardo de la Garza of the Green Ecologist Party (PVEM), which ultimately formed an electoral coalition with the PRI, were treated as not having switched if they supported Madrazo in both wave 2 and wave 3 ($n = 4$).

16. These percentages differ from those of the paragraph above, because waverers and party changers only allow the undecided category to be an intermediate stage, but not an initial or a final one. For that reason, I make the distinction between returners—who go back to their original state, including being undecided—and waverers, which follows the definition of Lazarsfeld et al. (1944) as those who supported a candidate early on. Interestingly, the amount of switching in the 2006 presidential campaign appears to be slightly smaller than that which occurred six years earlier, when Vicente Fox won the election. The Mexico 2000 Panel Study differed somewhat in design from the 2006 study, so that direct comparisons for switching are not straightforward. Yet in 2000, the total number of party changers—those who preferred one party at the time of wave 1 and ended up voting for someone else—was 26 percent, slightly greater than the 22 percent of 2006.

17. Nevertheless, 35 percent of the disenchanted supported López Obrador in wave 1, suggesting that there is much more to voter turnout than the candidates' perceived electoral prospects.

18. Percentages refer to the overall sample—both switchers and standpatters—in each demographic or political subgroup.

19. These percentages differ from those of all of the PRI switchers in table 10.1. The reason is that not all PRI identifiers supported Madrazo in the first round of the panel.

20. For a recent descriptive study on nonpartisans in Mexico, see Estrada 2006.

21. For a study on late-deciding voters in the United States, see Gopoian and Hadjiharalambous 1994.

22. See http://web.mit.edu/polisci/research/mexico06/book.html. Because the dependent variable in both instances can have only two values, switching or not switching, each model is run as a binary probit. Robust standard errors are used, in order to account for the clustering of the observations in the panel survey.

23. These probabilities refer to model 1.

24. The analysis that follows relies on descriptive statistics. Multivariate regression analysis is not advisable in this case, since the low number of observations for each hypothesis does not support the asymptotic assumptions of maximum-likelihood estimation.

25. Blanche Petrich, "Al desnudo, la intriga contra Lydia Cacho," *La Jornada*, February 14, 2006. www.jornada.unam.mx/2006/02/14/003n1pol.php.

26. The effect of these campaign events is assessed only for respondents who had initially supported the candidate in question or were undecided. The idea is that those who were already supporting other candidates would be predisposed to have a stronger adverse reaction to these events.

27. A dummy variable for whether a respondent had watched or listened to at least part of the debate was added as an independent variable in models 1 and 2, described above; it was not a statistically significant predictor of switching in either case.

28. For an example of a sophisticated statistical analysis of the effectiveness of negative advertising in Mexico, using data from the Mexico 2000 Panel Study, see Moreno 2004.

29. A sizable literature exists on strategic voting. In the Mexican context, see Mag-

aloni and Poiré 2004. For a nuanced analysis on what it means to vote strategically, albeit in a Westminster-style parliamentary system, see Johnston et al. 1992, 1998.

30. Other items in the questionnaires for the panel study could have been used, such as the respondents' second-choice preference in wave 2 or their expectation (at the time of wave 2) that their preferred candidate would lose the election. Yet very few respondents provided a second-choice preference or admitted that their top choice would be likely to lose the election, rendering it virtually impossible to construct an index inclusive of all these variables. It is worth mentioning, however, that of 73 people that provided a valid response to the question on who was their second choice for president in wave 2—and who did not choose Calderón as their first selection in the same wave—52 percent named Calderón as their second choice. This contrasts with 24 percent of 84 respondents who did not choose López Obrador as their first choice in wave 2 but for whom he was their second choice. The interpretation is that, in fact, Calderón was the number-two choice for more voters. Yet ultimately voting for the candidate who was ranked second at an earlier point is not evidence, by itself, of strategic voting, since voters may have been genuinely persuaded during the remainder of the campaign.

ELEVEN: The Activation of Economic Voting in the 2006 Campaign

I thank Arturo Alvarado, Wayne Cornelius, Jorge Domínguez, Federico Estévez, Alberto Gómez, Nydia Iglesias, Chappell Lawson, Gabriel Lenz, and Alejandra Sota for their comments, and María Teresa Martínez for her skillful research assistance.

1. For a brief description of the Mexico 2006 Panel Study, see chapter 1, note 1. For data, survey instruments, and field notes, see http://web.mit.edu/polisci/research/mexico06/.

2. "A Survey of Mexico," *Economist*, November 18, 2006, 9. This article reports a loss of 700,000 jobs, mainly in the *maquiladora* sector.

3. Variations between the panel study and the exit poll may reflect not only differences in the composition of both the voting population and the electorate at large, but, more importantly, a disparate set of timeframes in the question itself. The exit poll asked respondents how they thought economic conditions then compared with those during the previous year, whereas the panel study asked about economic conditions during the Fox administration. In the July 2006 survey wave, this latter question elicited a 42 percent positive economic response, versus favorable judgments from only 33 percent of the voters in the exit poll that same year.

4. Similar questions on the economy were not included in the second round of interviews, conducted in April/May 2006.

5. The aggregate stability in the Mexico 2006 Panel Study does not allow us to see the individual-level variations that are always expected in panel design. In this case, economic evaluations from 63 percent of the respondents in waves 1 (October 2005) and 3 (July 2006) remained stable, 18 percent indicated improvement, and 19 percent were worse. The latter two sets of opinions cancel each other out.

6. From then on, Calderón's campaign constantly referred to better living standards— *para que vivamos mejor* (so that we live better).

7. These and other collections of political ads for the 2006 presidential election can be seen at www.youtube.com.

TWELVE: Welfare Benefits, Canvassing, and Campaign Handouts

1. Díaz-Cayeros was commissioned to analyze the evaluation survey.

2. For example, the National Solidarity Program (Programa Nacional Solidaridad, or Pronasol)—the hallmark poverty-relief program of the Salinas government (1988–94)—was extremely discretionary, resulting in insufficient allocations based on poverty criteria, highly partisan skews in benefit flows, and transient welfare improvements for benefited localities (Díaz-Cayeros et al. 2008).

3. Elite- and mass-based survey evidence for the PAN's rightist stance on fiscal and redistributive issues in the late 1990s can be found in Magaloni (2006) and Estévez and Magaloni (2000).

4. In the same vein, inferring the effects of other social programs (such as Progresa) on support for the former ruling party by simply employing respondents' reported benefits as an independent variable could lead to erroneous conclusions because of strong endogeneity, given the fact that the rural poor who were selected to participate in the program already disproportionately supported the PRI. For a full discussion of this problem, and an analysis of the effects of the National Solidarity Program and Progresa on voting behavior that corrects for endogeneity, see Díaz-Cayeros et al. 2008.

5. The conditions of Wantchekon's (2004) fascinating study of Benin are very hard to replicate.

6. The different findings might also be related to econometric strategies. Tina Green (2005) uses a regression-discontinuity framework, while De la O (2006) estimates a first-differences regression model.

7. This is a classic problem of selection bias that is not generated by the research design, but rather by the observational, as opposed to the experimental, nature of the data being studied.

8. In this technique, assumptions of linearity are not necessary, because matching is done nonparametrically. The challenge is to find a scale (i.e., the *propensity score*) under which the assumption of nonconfoundedness holds (Imbens 2003). There is no direct test that can assure that this assumption holds. We follow common practice in making sure that the propensity score of the treated and the control groups have a similar distribution (what is known as the *balancing test*).

9. See chapter 1, note 1. Data from the Mexico 2006 Panel Study, and further details about it, are available at http://web.mit.edu/polisci/research/mexico06/.

10. For details, see the Mexico 2006 Panel Study's supplemental materials for chapter 12 (http://web.mit.edu/polisci/research/mexico06/book.html).

11. Ibid.

THIRTEEN: Images and Issues in Mexico's 2006 Presidential Election

I thank Chappell Lawson, Jorge Domínguez, James McCann, and Andy Baker for comments on earlier drafts. All errors are, of course, my own.

1. Chapter 1, note 1 provides a short description of this project. For details and data, see http://web.mit.edu/polisci/research/mexico06/.

2. This figure includes those respondents who switched to and from "undecided," as well as those who initially supported a candidate but failed to vote. Approximately one-

third of the sample made a hard switch, that is, changed from one to another of the three main candidates.

3. The third (postelection) wave of the panel study overrepresents Calderón's final vote. With the available data, it is difficult to know precisely how much is due to overreporting and how much to respondent attrition in the panel study. Nevertheless, the vote swing reported in the main text represents an impressive amount of change.

4. Finkel (1993), Gelman and King (1993, 412) and Bartels (2006, 94, 97) show that models of vote choice two months before elections in the United States predict final vote choice very well.

5. Evidence of issue leadership and the independent causal effect of issue preferences among the strongest party identifiers come from models included in the Mexico 2006 Panel Survey's supplemental materials for chapter 13 (http://web.mit.edu/polisci/research/mexico06/book.html).

6. It should be noted that using data from the third wave of the Mexico 2006 Panel Study did produce two issue dimensions that mirrored those of the candidates. However, it is not clear whether this postelectoral structure was caused by voters eventually absorbing cues from the candidates or was instead informed by post hoc rationalizations of vote choices made for other reasons.

7. For details on the Mexico 2000 Panel Study, conducted during the presidential campaign of that year, see www.icpsr.umich.edu/cocoon/ICPSR/STUDY/03380.xml and links at http://web.mit.edu/polisci/research/mexico06/. See also Domínguez and Lawson 2004.

8. McCann and Lawson (2003) found that voters' left-right dispositions and attitudes on crime and privatization in 2000 were unstable over time, although the authors did not examine vote choice.

9. Voters who did not consider Mexico to be a democracy had a greater, albeit substantively small, propensity to identify as leftists; those who thought of Mexico as a democracy placed themselves somewhat further to the right.

10. For further discussion of the relationship between ideology and attitudes toward particular leaders, see chapter 14 in this volume. McCann's analysis relies on attitudes toward foreign leaders, rather than domestic contenders, to construct an ideological issue dimension.

11. Economic issues include unemployment, inflation, the economy, poverty, privatization, and Pemex. Public safety covers drug trafficking, crime, and kidnapping. Political issues encompass corruption, the need for good politicians, public works, the Fox administration winning the presidency, political parties, and the tone of the campaigns. Social issues include the environment, education, public health, public transit, public services, eldercare, women's rights, social/community problems, and the countryside/Chiapas. Nonresponses and don't know responses were excluded.

12. Wave 1 and wave 2 assessments of the country's biggest problem were independent of wave 3 vote choice. Chi-squared tests failed to reach statistical significance, even at the 90 percent level. Contemporaneous relationships between Mexico's biggest problem and vote choice for all three waves were statistically different at the 99 percent level. Thus immediate pre-election assessments may have affected election day choices; however, the panel data were collected too infrequently to know for certain.

13. Magaloni and Poiré (2004a) used this measurement technique to tap competence in their analysis of the Mexico 2000 Panel Study data.

14. A remarkably large number of voters did not have a strict preference for one candidate over the other two. This result may, in part, be an artifact of the limited four-point scale offered to survey respondents and reflect the fact that many voters rated two candidates as tied. Nevertheless, using strict preference orders captures the essence of what appear to be strongly held divisions between the Calderón and López Obrador camps.

15. A table that details these findings is available in the Mexico 2005 Panel Study's supplemental materials for chapter 13.

16. The raw data are available at http://www.ife.org.mx/. The percentages are the author's calculations that represent paid advertising, including spots paid by the IFE, but do not include earned coverage on news programs.

17. These models are available in the Mexico 2006 Panel Survey's supplemental materials for chapter 13.

18. For an analysis of persuasion in the 2000 elections due to television viewing habits and negative campaigning, see Lawson (2004d) and Moreno (2004), respectively.

19. The panel survey did not repeat the crisis question in the July wave, both because it was necessarily phrased prospectively and because López Obrador's postelection protest would likely have introduced substantial bias.

20. For survey-based empirical studies on priming effects in campaigns, see Berelson et al. (1954), Johnston et al. (1992), and Krosnik and Kinder (1990), among others.

21. Specifically, the logit coefficients of the crisis variables were 1.04 in the pre-election model and 1.65 in the postelection model. Coefficients were statistically significant at the 99 percent level in both models.

22. Just over 22 percent of the October 2005 party identifiers reported voting for a different party in July 2006.

23. When voters' issue preferences were measured as distances from the candidates' perceived stands, they had an important impact on the vote in Mexico's 2000 elections (Greene 2007). Similar measures were available for just two economic policy issues in 2006, which only used crude directional measures that fall short of the nuances available in the 2000 surveys. Nevertheless, voter-candidate distance on commercial relations with the United States did reach statistical significance at the 95 percent level when included in fully specified models of voting behavior for 2006. I leave more complicated tests to determine whether this finding results from projection or issue effects for another analysis.

24. Inter-item correlations were generally very low, and no two variables were correlated at more than .51, suggesting that although various measures of economic evaluations and candidate traits are related to each other, each included variable measures a substantively distinct underlying attitude.

25. Alvarez and Nagler (1998) argue that multinomial probit (MNP) should be used to examine vote choice in multiparty elections because, unlike multinomial logit (MNL), it does not assume that choices are independent across alternatives (the independence of irrelevant alternatives, or IIA, assumption). As a result, MNP should produce better estimates; however, Dow and Endersby (2004) argue that MNP models are often weakly identified and return coefficients and standard errors that are indistinguishable from MNL without a very large number of observations. In addition, they argue that the problems associated with IIA are exaggerated and may not obtain when elections feature a stable number of competitors, as they did in Mexico in 2006.

26. The full statistical model is available in the Mexico 2006 Panel Survey's supplemental materials for chapter 13.

27. I used CLARIFY (Tomz et al. 2001) for all postestimation predictions.

28. This deviation likely resulted either from the fact that respondents often underreport voting for the loser in postelection surveys or from panel attrition among Madrazo voters.

29. Positional issues package together at too low a level of aggregation in voters' minds for use as indexes or latent factors in the vote-choice model. Neither a combination of the six positional issues featured in the model, nor just one of the four economic policy issues, are jointly statistically significant for Calderón versus Madrazo or Calderón versus López Obrador.

30. The highest level of correlation between voters' strict competence ratings of the candidates and any positional issue preference is 0.13; between competence ratings and retrospective evaluations, it reaches just 0.27.

31. If the perception that López Obrador would cause a crisis is incorporated into a simulation that shifts all candidate trait variables together in favor of Calderón, then the crisis variable alone has the more modest effect of making an independent average voter 16.3 percent more likely to vote for Calderón and 18.1 percent less likely to vote for López Obrador. The difference between the independent effect of the crisis variable and its effect when incorporated into various voter profiles is due to the curvilinear nature of logistic regression models. As a voter becomes much more or much less likely to choose one candidate, each additional variable has a smaller independent effect.

FOURTEEN: Ideology in the 2006 Campaign

Earlier versions of this chapter were presented at the Bi-National Conference on Voters and Parties in Mexico's 2006 Elections, University of Texas–Austin, February 3, 2006; the 26th International Congress of the Latin American Studies Association, San Juan, Puerto Rico, March 15–18, 2006; the Politics and Society in Contemporary Latin America Regional Workshop, University of Notre Dame, May 16, 2006; and the Political Communication Workshop, Purdue University, November 10, 2006. I thank Chappell Lawson, Jorge Domínguez, Francisco Flores-Macías, Andy Baker, Kenneth Greene, Elizabeth Zechmeister, Scott Mainwaring, Michael Coppedge, Frances Hagopian, Katsuo Nishikawa, Charlie Stewart, Abby VanHorn, and Philo Wasburn for helpful comments.

1. Rachel Gisselquist and Chappell Lawson, "Preliminary findings from content analysis of television spots in Mexico's 2006 presidential campaign," http://web.mit.edu/polisci/research/mexico06/ContentAnalysis—ads.doc.

2. See chapter 1, note 1 and http://web.mit.edu/polisci/research/mexico06/. All survey data used in this chapter are taken from that project.

3. Manuel Roig-Franzia, "In Mexico, migration issue gets no traction," *Washington Post*, June 15, 2006, A14.

4. The PAN was eventually fined for encouraging Aznar to make this endorsement, a violation of Mexican electoral law. See James C. McKinley, Jr., "Mexico's enforcers take on election-year mudslingers," *New York Times*, June 12, 2006, A1.

5. Jeremy M. Martin, "The Chávez effect in Latin American politics," *San Diego Union-Tribune*, June 20, 2006, 8–9.

6. See also Kathleen Bruhn and Kenneth F. Greene, "Mexico 2006 candidate and party leaders survey," unpublished manuscript, 2006; preliminary results are available from the investigators upon request.

7. Cross-national research in the 1960s and 70s found that Converse's conclusion applied to many other western democracies as well (D. Butler and Stokes 1969; Barnes and Kaase 1979).

8. In pilots for the Mexico 2006 Panel Study, half of the respondents indicated that the terms "left" and "right" were not helpful to them. Genuine dispositions may nevertheless lie underneath public opinions.

9. Even if a substantial amount of potential random error in measurement (which could depress correlations among survey items) is taken into account, issue opinions still appear to be only loosely connected (McCann 1998).

10. See also Levitin and Miller 1979; D. Green 1988.

11. Mexicans at the elite level, however, may be adept at linking such symbols to contemporary leftist or rightist ideology (see Zechmeister 2006).

12. In one particularly blunt television commercial, images of Hugo Chávez were accompanied by a dire voice-over warning prospectively minded voters who might be fearful of a leftward turn that "in Mexico, you don't have to die to defend your future—you only have to vote!" See Manuel Roig-Franzia, "Chávez's image becomes tool for attack in Mexican presidential race," *Washington Post,* June 28, 2006, A14.

13. The items on Bush, Castro, and Chávez were designed to be comparable to the 101-degree feeling thermometer measurements that electoral researchers have used for many years in democracies around the world. The left-right scale is quite similar to the liberal-conservative questions commonly used in American National Election Study surveys.

14. The Mexico 2006 Panel Study's supplemental materials for chapter 14, table 14.A contains descriptive statistics for left-right self-placements and evaluations (http://web .mit.edu/polisci/research/mexico06/book.html).

15. With these elements in place, the factor structure has two degrees of freedom, which allows for fit diagnostics to be calculated.

16. As the χ^2 values indicate, the model specification leads to a reasonable fit in each wave (Kline 2005).

17. Over half of the variance in the evaluations of Bush, Chávez, and Castro in each wave was tied to response set, implying that survey participants strongly tended to favor one part of the scale consistently when rating the three figures. For some, a very positive evaluation might have been, say, a nine; for others, an equally positive rating would be a five or six.

18. It is worth noting that left-right self-identifications and attitudes toward George W. Bush and Fidel Castro clustered together in a coherent ideological dimension years before the 2006 presidential election. In the fifth wave of the Mexico 2000 Panel Study, which was fielded in May 2002 under the direction of Alejandro Poiré, Alejandro Moreno, Federico Estévez, and colleagues at the Instituto Tecnológico Autónomo de México, respondents positioned themselves along a ten-point, left-right continuum and evaluated Bush and Castro using feeling thermometers. A confirmatory factor analysis of these three items yields coefficients that are quite comparable to those in figure 14.1.

19. The findings on individual-level stability are presented in greater detail in the supplemental materials for chapter 14.

20. The composite measure of ideological stands was formed by rescaling the items on Bush, Castro, and left-right self-descriptions so that scores fall between 0 and 1 (without standardizing responses) and then averaging. Comparable findings emerge in the regression model if factor scores are used instead to measure ideological leanings.

21. The predictor variables were all taken from the second wave, to avoid any possibility that partisanship and the other attitude measures would be contaminated by post-election rationalization. Regrettably, this meant that feelings toward Hugo Chávez could not be part of the composite measure of ideology. When calculating this index, attitudes toward Bush and Castro and self-placements on the seven-point ideological continuum were equally weighted. This model of the vote is far from fully specified, and I do not attempt to trace any indirect effects of ideological positions. The central task here is to explore whether ideology matters more than might have been expected, given previous studies of Mexican electoral behavior, and whether its effect is robust when put alongside other predictors that are known to exert strong influences on voting choices.

22. See table 14.B in the supplemental materials for chapter 14.

23. Nonvoters and those few respondents who backed one of the minor presidential candidates are not included in the model. It is worth noting that if the summary index of ideological attitudes (feelings toward Castro and Bush coupled with left-right self-placements) is dropped, and the self-placement item is entered on its own as a predictor, ideology would appear to have no significant effect on candidate choice. This echoes the findings from figure 14.1. The left-right self-placement scale is a valid indicator of ideological leanings, but this item contains a great deal of measurement error which, if not taken into account, could bias causal inferences.

24. Such centrism is widely shared throughout Latin America. See "Latinobarómetro poll: Latin Americans, despite stereotypes, are political moderates," Program on International Policy Attitudes, University of Maryland, January 10, 2007, www.worldpublic opinion.org.

25. To illustrate this point, when asked in October 2005 whether the major candidates favored or opposed more private investment in Mexico's electrical energy sector, the modal response was "not sure." Among those offering a judgment, 38 percent believed that Calderón favored private investment, and 30 percent thought López Obrador did, as well. In the April–May panel survey wave, these figures changed to 53 percent and 33 percent, respectively.

26. Beliefs about a candidate's ability to manage the economy and lessen poverty and crime cohere into a very solid factor, with loadings above .70 for each contender.

27. In the first wave, the correlations between the latent ideological factor and the candidate trait assessments were .09 (Calderón), –.14 (López Obrador), and .15 (Madrazo). Six months later, these coefficients were .26 (Calderón), –.31 (López Obrador), and .11 (Madrazo).

28. Ideological positions from the first wave were included as a predictor for ideology in the April–May wave of the panel survey to identify the simultaneous equations.

29. If left-right self-placements were largely endogenous to candidate support, we would expect to find the largest impact regarding leadership traits in the evaluations of Madrazo (whose standing in the polls dropped markedly between the first and second waves), and the least with López Obrador (whose share of the vote changed little). The fact that it is the reverse further suggests that ideology is indeed more a cause than an effect of candidate support.

30. The complete results from these models and the preceding analyses are available from the author upon request (mccannj@purdue.edu). When cross-lag rather than synchronous coefficients are used to assess the causal relationships between ideology and candidate trait impressions, substantively identical findings emerge. The left-right positions significantly shape leadership appraisals for all three contenders, while perceptions of López Obrador, in turn, have an effect on ideology, though this effect is not as significant as the impact of ideology on trait ratings for the PRD's standard-bearer.

31. Mexico's election was, of course, but one of many presidential contests held in Latin America in 2006. Partisan competition was especially fierce in Colombia, Costa Rica, Nicaragua, Peru, and Ecuador. Given the prominence of Presidents Bush, Chávez, and Castro across the hemisphere, ideological orientations linked to assessments of these figures might well have helped shape voting blocs in other electorates.

FIFTEEN: Conclusion

This chapter draws extensively and explicitly from the chapters in this book. I am deeply grateful to my colleagues. All the good ideas belong to them; all the mistakes are mine alone. I am especially grateful to Roderic Ai Camp, Jason Lakin, Chappell Lawson, and James McCann for comments on previous versions. Harvard University's Weatherhead Center for International Affairs provided general research support.

1. The presidential elections held in 1940 and 1988 may have been extremely close, but the published election results affirmed the victory of the ruling party by a very wide margin.

2. The Chamber of Deputies has 500 members, of whom 300 are elected by plurality in single-member districts, and 200 are elected by closed-party-list proportional representation in large districts. The election of deputies in single-member districts is likely to be affected by local factors beyond the scope of this chapter. For a discussion of how these deputies behaved, see chapter 6 in this volume.

3. For details, see chapter 1, note 1. Data from the Mexico 2006 Panel Study, and further information about it, are available at http://web.mit.edu/polisci/research/mexico06/.

4. I am grateful to Nirmala Ravishankar for comments on this paragraph.

5. Peru is the only large Latin American country where the president's party nearly disintegrated, so there was no incumbent party continuity.

Bibliography

Achen, Christopher. 1978. "Measuring representation." *American Journal of Political Science* 22 (3): 475–511.

Aguayo, Sergio, ed. 2000. *El almanaque mexicano*. México, DF: Editorial Grijalbo.

Albo, Andrés. 2003. "The balance and consequences of July 6." *Review of the Economic Situation of Mexico* 79 (931): 288–92.

Aldrich, John H. 1980. *Before the convention: Strategies and choices in presidential nomination campaigns*. Chicago: University of Chicago Press.

Alesina, Alberto, and Nouriel Roubini. 1999. *Political cycles and the macroeconomy*. Cambridge, MA: MIT Press.

Alianza Cívica. 2006. "Observación del proceso electoral federal 2006." www.alianza civica.org.mx/informes.html (accessed January 2, 2007; article no longer available).

Alvarez, R. Michael. 1998. *Information and elections*. 2nd ed. Ann Arbor: University of Michigan Press.

Alvarez, R. Michael, and Jonathan Nagler. 1998. "When politics and model collide: Estimating models of multiparty elections." *American Journal of Political Science* 42 (1): 55–96.

Alvarez, R. Michael, Jonathan Nagler, and Jennifer Willette. 2000. "Measuring the relative impact of issues and the economy in democratic elections." *Electoral Studies* 19 (2–3): 237–53.

Ames, Barry, Andrew Baker, Marilia Mochel, and Lucio Renno. 2006. "Party identification in third wave democracies: Brazil's 2002 election." Paper presented at the Midwest Political Science Association, 64th Annual National Conference, April 20–23, Chicago.

Anderson, Leslie E., and Lawrence C. Dodd. 2005. *Learning democracy: Citizen engagement and electoral choice in Nicaragua, 1990–2001*. Chicago: University of Chicago Press.

Angell, Alan, and Cristóbal Reig Salinas. 2007. "¿Cambio o continuidad? Las elecciones chilenas de 2005/6." In *Las elecciones chilenas de 2005: Partidos, coaliciones y votantes en transición*, ed. Carlos Huneeus, Fabiola Berríos, and Ricardo Gamboa, 11–28. Santiago: Catalonia.

Arnold, Jason, and David Samuels. 2008. "Public opinion and Latin America's 'left turn.'" Paper prepared for the "Latin America's Left Turn" conference, Weatherhead Center for International Affairs, April 4–5, Cambridge, MA.

Arriola, Carlos 1994. *Ensayos sobre el PAN, las ciencias sociales*. México, DF: Grupo Editorial Miguel Ángel Porrúa.

Asch, Solomon E. 1951. "Effects of group pressure upon the modification and distortion of judgement." In *Groups, leadership and men*, ed. Harold Guetzkow, 177–90. Pittsburgh, PA: Carnegie Press.

Atkeson, Lonna Rae. 1998. "Divisive primaries and general election outcomes: Another look at presidential campaigns." *American Journal of Political Science* 42 (1): 256–71.

———. 2000. "From the primaries to the general election: Does a divisive nomination race affect a candidate's fortunes in the fall?" In *Pursuit of the White House 2000: How we choose our presidential nominees*, ed. William G. Mayer, 285–312. New York: Chatham House.

Aziz Nassif, Alberto. 2006. "Nuevo mapa electoral." *El Universal*, July 4. www.eluniver sal.com.mx/editoriales/34800.html.

Bada, Xóchitl, Jonathan Fox, and Andrew Selee, eds. 2006. *Invisible no more: Mexican migrant civic participation in the United States*. Washington, DC: Woodrow Wilson Center and Department of Latin American and Latino Studies, University of California–Santa Cruz.

Bailey, John, and Pedro Parás. 2006. "Perceptions and attitudes about corruption and democracy in Mexico." *Mexican Studies/Estudios Mexicanos* 22 (1): 57–82.

Baker, Andy. 2003. "Why is trade reform so popular in Latin America? A consumption-based theory of trade policy preferences." *World Politics* 55 (3): 423–55.

Baker, Andy, Barry Ames, and Lucio R. Renno. 2006. "Social context and campaign volatility in new democracies: Networks and neighborhoods in Brazil's 2002 elections." *American Journal of Political Science* 50 (2): 382–99.

Bakker, Matt, and Michael P. Smith. 2003. "El Rey del Tomate: Migrant political transnationalism and democratization in Mexico." *Migraciones Internacionales* 2 (January–June): 59–83.

Barnes, Samuel H. 1977. *Representation in Italy: Institutionalized tradition and electoral choice*. Chicago: University of Chicago Press.

Barnes, Samuel H., and Max Kaase, eds. 1979. *Political action: Mass participation in five western democracies*. Beverly Hills, CA: Sage.

Barraza, Leticia, and Ilán Bizberg. 1991. "El Partido Acción Nacional y el régimen político méxicano." *Foro Internacional* 31 (3): 418–45.

Bartels, Larry M. 2006. "Priming and persuasion in presidential campaigns." In *Capturing campaign effects*, ed. Henry E. Brady and Richard Johnston, 78–112. Ann Arbor: University of Michigan Press.

Berelson, Bernard R., Paul F. Lazarsfeld, and William N. McPhee. 1954. *Voting: A study of opinion formation in a presidential campaign*. Chicago: University of Chicago Press.

Bernstein, Robert A. 1977. "Divisive primaries do hurt: U.S. Senate races, 1956–1972." *American Political Science Review* 71:540–45.

Berruecos, Susana. 2003. "Electoral justice in Mexico: The role of the Electoral Tribunal under New Federalism." *Journal of Latin American Studies* 35 (3): 801–25.

Bonfil Batalla, Guillermo. 1996. *México profundo: Reclaiming a civilization*, trans. Philip A. Dennis. Austin: University of Texas Press.

Boyd, Richard W. 1989. "The effects of primaries and statewide races on voter turnout." *Journal of Politics* 51 (3): 730–39.

Brooks, David, and Jonathan Fox, eds. 2002. *Cross-border dialogues: U.S.-Mexico social movement networking*. La Jolla: Center for U.S.-Mexican Studies, University of California–San Diego.

Brown, Clifford W., Lynda W. Powell, and Clyde Wilcox. 1995. *Serious money: Fundrais-*

ing and contributing in presidential nomination campaigns. New York: Cambridge University Press.

Bruhn, Kathleen. 1997. *Taking on Goliath: The emergence of a new left party and the struggle for democracy in Mexico.* University Park: Pennsylvania State University Press.

———. 2004. "Globalization and the renovation of the Latin American Left: Strategies of ideological adaptation." Paper presented at the Midwest Political Science Association, 62nd Annual National Conference, April 15–18, Chicago.

Bruhn, Kathleen, and Kenneth F. Greene. 2006. "Mexico's 2006 Candidate and Party Leaders Survey." Unpublished data, University of California–Santa Barbara and University of Texas at Austin.

———. 2007. "Elite polarization meets mass moderation in Mexico's 2006 elections." *PS: Political Science and Politics* 40 (1): 33–38.

Budge, Ian, and David Robertson. 1987. "Do parties differ, and how? Comparative discriminant and factor analyses." In *Ideology, strategy, and party change: Spatial analyses of post-war election programmes in 19 democracies,* ed. Ian Budge, David Robertson, and Derek Hearl, 388–416. Cambridge: Cambridge University Press.

Butler, David, and Donald E. Stokes. 1969. *Political change in Britain.* New York: St. Martin's.

Butler, Roger Lawrence. 2004. *Claiming the mantle: How presidential nominations are won and lost before the votes are cast.* Dilemmas in American Politics. Cambridge, MA: Westview Press.

Calderón, Felipe. *Para que vivamos mejor: Discursos de Felipe Calderón, campaña 2006.* México, DF: Partido Acción Nacional.

Calderón Chelius, Leticia, ed. 2004. *Votar en la distancia.* México, DF: Instituto Mora.

Calderón Vega, Luis. 1992. *Memorias del PAN, 1946–1950,* vol. 2. 3rd ed. 5 vols. México, DF: EPESSA.

Calderón Vega, Luis, and Gustavo Vicencio Acevedo. 1978. *Memorias del PAN.* 2nd ed. México, DF: Editorial Jus.

Calvo, Ernesto, and Maria Victoria Murillo. 2004. "Who delivers? Partisan clients in the Argentine electoral market." *American Journal of Political Science* 48 (4): 742–57.

Camarena, Salvador, and Jorge Zepeda Patterson. 2007. *El presidente electo.* México, DF: Planeta.

Camp, Roderic Ai. 2001. *Citizen views of democracy in Latin America.* Pittsburgh, PA: University of Pittsburgh Press.

———. 2003. "Learning democracy in Mexico and the United States." *Mexican Studies/Estudios Mexicanos* 19 (1): 3–27.

———. 2004. "Citizen attitudes toward democracy and Vicente Fox's victory in 2000." In Domínguez and Lawson 2004, 25–47.

Campbell, Angus, Philip E. Converse, Warren E. Miller, and Donald Stokes. 1960. *The American voter.* New York: Wiley.

Carey, John, and John Polga-Hecimovich. 2006. "Primary elections and candidate strength in Latin America." *Journal of Politics* 68 (3): 530–43.

Carr, Barry. 1973. "Las peculiaridades del norte mexicano: Ensayo de interpretación." *Historia Mexicana* 22 (3): 321–46.

Chand, Vikram K. 2001. *Mexico's political awakening.* Notre Dame, IN: University of Notre Dame Press.

CIDAC (Centro de Investigación para el Desarrollo AC). 2006. "Un pueblo con dos

proyectos." *CIDAC Electoral 2006* 6 (August 2): 1. www.cidac.org/vnm/pdf/pdf/
CIDACelectoral 2006-6.pdf.

Cleary, Matthew. 2007. "Electoral competition, participation, and government responsiveness in Mexico." *American Journal of Political Science* 51 (2): 283–99.

Collier, Ruth Berins, and David Collier. 1991. *Shaping the political arena: Critical junctures,
the labor movement, and regime dynamics in Latin America.* Princeton, NJ: Princeton
University Press.

Conover, Pamela Johnston, and Stanley Feldman. 1981. "The origins of liberal/conser-
vative self-identifications." *American Journal of Political Science* 25 (4): 617–45.

Converse, Philip E. 1962. "Information flow and the stability of partisan attitudes." *Public
Opinion Quarterly* 26 (4): 578–99.

———. 1964. "The nature of belief systems in mass publics." In *Ideology and discontent*,
ed. David Apter, 206–61. New York: Free Press.

Converse, Philip E., and Roy Pierce. 1986. *Political representation in France.* Cambridge,
MA: Harvard University Press.

Cornelius, Wayne A. 2002. "La eficacia de la compra y coacción del voto en las elecciones
mexicanas de 2000." *Perfiles Latinoamericanos* 20 (June): 11–31.

———. 2004. "Mobilized voting in the 2000 elections: The changing efficacy of vote
buying and coercion in Mexican electoral politics." In Domínguez and Lawson 2004,
47–65.

Cornelius, Wayne A., and Ann Craig. 1991. *The Mexican political system in transition.*
Monograph Series 35. La Jolla: Center for U.S.-Mexican Studies, University of California–San Diego.

Cornelius, Wayne A., and Jessa M. Lewis, eds. 2006. *Impacts of U.S. border enforce-
ment on Mexican migration: The view from sending communities.* Boulder, CO: Lynne
Rienner / Center for Comparative Immigration Studies, University of California–San
Diego.

Cox, Gary. 1990. "Centripetal and centrifugal incentives in electoral systems." *American
Journal of Political Science* 34 (4): 903–36.

Cronin, Thomas E. 1982. *Rethinking the presidency.* Boston: Little, Brown.

Dalton, Russell H. 1985. "Political parties and political representation: Party supporters
and party elites in nine nations." *Comparative Political Studies* 18:267–99.

———. 2002. *Citizen politics.* Chatham, NJ: Chatham House.

Dalton, Russell H., Scott Flanagan, and Paul Allen Beck, eds. 1984. *Electoral change in
advanced industrial democracies.* Princeton, NJ: Princeton University Press.

Damore, David F. 2004. "The dynamics of issue ownership in presidential campaigns."
Political Research Quarterly 57 (3): 391–97.

Davis, Charles L. 1998. "Mass support for regional economic integration: The case of
NAFTA and the Mexican public." *Mexican Studies / Estudios Mexicanos* 14 (1): 104–30.

Davis, Diane E. 1994. *Urban Leviathan: Mexico City in the twentieth century.* Philadelphia:
Temple University Press.

De la O, Ana Lorena. 2003. "Do poverty relief funds affect electoral behavior? Evidence
from a randomized experiment in Mexico." Ms, MIT.

Díaz-Cayeros, Alberto. 2006. "Blue state, yellow state." www.stanford.edu/~albert
od/2006elections2.html.

Díaz-Cayeros, Alberto, Federico Estévez, and Beatriz Magaloni. 2008. "Strategies of vote
buying: Social transfers, democracy, and welfare in Mexico." Ms, Stanford University.

Dixit, Avinash, and John Londregan. 1996. "The determinants of success of special interests in redistributive politics." *Journal of Politics* 58 (November): 1132–55.

Domínguez, Jorge I. 1997. "Latin America's crisis of representation." *Foreign Affairs* 76 (1): 100–113.

———. 2004. "Conclusion: Why and how did Mexico's 2000 presidential election campaign matter?" In Domínguez and Lawson 2004, 321–55.

Domínguez, Jorge I., and Chappell Lawson, eds. 2004. *Mexico's pivotal democratic election: Candidates, voters, and the presidential campaign of 2000.* Stanford, CA: Stanford University Press.

Domínguez, Jorge I., and James A. McCann. 1995. "Shaping Mexico's electoral arena: The construction of partisan cleavages in the 1988 and 1991 national elections." *American Political Science Review* 89 (1): 34–48.

———. 1996. *Democratizing Mexico: Public opinion and electoral choice.* Baltimore: Johns Hopkins University Press.

Domínguez, Jorge I., and Alejandro Poiré, eds. 1999. *Toward Mexico's democratization: Parties, campaigns, elections, and public opinion.* New York: Routledge.

Dow, Jay, and James Endersby. 2004. "Multinomial probit and multinomial logit: A comparison of choice models for voting research." *Electoral Studies* 23:107–22.

Downs, Anthony. 1957. *An economic theory of democracy.* New York: Harper and Row.

Echegaray, Fabián. 2005. *Economic crises and electoral responses in Latin America.* Oxford: University Press of America.

Economic Commission for Latin America and the Caribbean. 2007. *Preliminary overview of the economies of Latin America and the Caribbean, 2006.* New York: United Nations.

Edelman, Murray. 1964. *Symbolic uses of politics.* Champaign: University of Illinois Press.

Eisenstadt, Todd A. 1999. "Electoral Federalism or abdication of presidential authority? Gubernatorial elections in Tabasco." In *Subnational politics and democratization in Mexico,* ed. Wayne A. Cornelius, Todd A. Eisenstadt, and Jane Hindley, 269–93. La Jolla: Center for U.S.-Mexican Studies, University of California–San Diego.

———. 2004. *Courting democracy in Mexico: Party strategies and electoral institutions.* New York: Cambridge University Press.

Encarnación, Omar. 2003–4. "The strange persistence of Latin American democracy." *World Policy Journal* 20 (4): 30–40.

Escobar, Cristina. 2007. "Extraterritorial political rights and dual citizenship in Latin America." *Latin American Research Review* 42 (3): 43–75.

Estévez, Federico, and Beatriz Magaloni. 2000. "Legislative parties and their constituencies in the budget battle of 1997." Documento de Trabajo WPPS 2000-01, Political Science Department, Instituto Tecnológico Autónomo de México (ITAM).

Estrada, Luis. 2006. "Determinantes y características de los independientes en México." *Política y Gobierno* 13 (1): 149–73.

Estrada, Luis, and Pablo Parás. 2006. "Ambidiestros y confundidos: Validez y contenido de la izquierda y la derecha en México." *Este País* 180 (March): 51–57.

Finifter, Ada. 1974. "The friendship group as a protective environment for political deviants." *American Political Science Review* 68:607–25.

Finkel, Steven E. 1993. "Reexamining the 'minimal effects' model in recent presidential campaigns." *Journal of Politics* 55 (1): 1–21.

Finkel, Steven E., and Peter R. Schrott. 1995. "Campaign effects on voter choice in the German election of 1990." *British Journal of Political Science* 25:349–77.

Fiorina, Morris P. 1981. *Retrospective voting in American national elections.* New Haven, CT: Yale University Press.

Fitzgerald, David. 2002. "Rethinking the 'local' and 'transnational': Cross-border politics and hometown politics in an immigrant union." Working paper 58 (August), Center for Comparative Immigration Studies, University of California–San Diego.

Fox, Jonathan, and Gaspar Rivera-Salgado, eds. 2004. *Indigenous Mexican migrants in the United States.* La Jolla: Center for Comparative Immigration Studies and Center for U.S.-Mexican Studies, University of California–San Diego.

Fundar. 2006. "Monitoreo de programas sociales en contextos electorales." Resumen General (February). www.fundar.org.mx/programassociales/1RgeneralMps.pdf.

Galderisi, Peter F., Marni Ezra, and Michael Lyons. 2001. *Congressional primaries and the politics of representation.* Lanham, MD: Rowman and Littlefield.

Gelman, Andrew, and Gary King. 1993. "Why are American presidential election campaign polls so variable when voters are so predictable?" *British Journal of Political Science* 23 (4): 409–51.

Gibson, James L. 2001. "Social networks, civil society, and the prospects for consolidating Russia's democratic transition." *American Journal of Political Science* 45 (1): 51–68.

Gopoian, J. David, and Sissie Hadjiharalambous. 1994. "Late-deciding voters in presidential elections." *Political Behavior* 16 (1): 55–78.

Granovetter, Mark. 1973. "The strength of weak ties." *American Journal of Sociology* 78 (6): 1360–80.

Gray, Lee Learner. 1980. *How we choose a president: The election year.* 5th ed. New York: St. Martin's.

Green, Donald Philip. 1988. "On the dimensionality of public sentiment toward partisan and ideological groups." *American Journal of Political Science* 23 (3): 758–80.

Green, Donald Philip, and Jack Citrin. 1994. "Measurement error and the structure of attitudes: Are positive and negative judgments opposite?" *American Journal of Political Science* 38 (1): 256–81.

Green, Donald Philip, and Alan S. Gerber. 2004. *Get out the vote!* Washington, DC: Brookings Institution Press.

Green, Donald Philip, Bradley Palmquist, and Eric Schickler. 2002. *Partisan hearts and minds: Political parties and the social identities of voters.* New Haven, CT: Yale University Press.

Green, Tina R. 2005. "Do social programs affect voter behavior? Evidence from Progresa in Mexico, 1997–2000." Working paper, University of California, Berkeley.

Greene, Kenneth F. 2002. "Opposition party strategy and spatial competition in dominant party regimes: A theory and the case of Mexico." *Comparative Political Studies* 35 (7): 755–83.

———. 2006. "Issues and voting behavior in Mexico's 2006 elections." Paper presented at the American Political Science Association annual meeting, August 31, Philadelphia.

———. 2007. *Why dominant parties lose: Mexico's democratization in comparative perspective.* New York: Cambridge University Press.

———. 2008. "Dominant party strategy and democratization." *American Journal of Political Science* 52 (1): 16–31.

Gutiérrez, Alexis, and Miguel Ángel López. 2007. "Factores explicativos de la conducta electoral de los chilenos." In *Las elecciones chilenas de 2005: Partidos, coaliciones y votantes en transición*, ed. Carlos Huneeus, Fabiola Berríos, and Ricardo Gamboa, 177–96. Santiago: Catalonia.

Gutmann, Amy, and Dennis Thompson. 2004. *Why deliberative democracy?* Princeton, NJ: Princeton University Press.

Hayes, Danny. 2005. "Candidate qualities through a partisan lens: A theory of trait ownership." *American Journal of Political Science* 49 (4): 908–23.

Hernández Vicencio, Tania. 2001. *La experiencia del PAN: Diez años de gobierno en Baja California.* Tijuana: Plaza y Valdés.

Hill, Kim Quaile, and Patricia A. Hurley. 1999. "Dyadic representation reappraised." *American Journal of Political Science* 43 (1): 109–37.

Hillygus, D. Sunshine, and Simon Jackman. 2003. "Voter decision-making in election 2000: Campaign effects, partisan activation, and the Clinton legacy." *American Journal of Political Science* 47 (4): 583–96.

Hillygus, D. Sunshine, and Todd Shields. 2008. *The persuadable voter: Strategic candidates and wedge issues in presidential campaigns.* Princeton, NJ: Princeton University Press.

Hiskey, Jonathan T., and Shaun Bowler. 2005. "Local context and democratization in Mexico." *American Journal of Political Science* 49 (1): 57–71.

Hiskey, Jonathan T., and Damarys Canache. 2005. "The demise of one-party politics in Mexican municipal elections." *British Journal of Political Science* 35 (2): 257–84.

Ho, Daniel E., Kosuke Imai, Gary King, and Elizabeth Stuart. 2007. "Matching as nonparametric preprocessing for reducing model dependence in parametric causal inference." *Political Analyses* 15:199–236.

Holbrook, Thomas. 1996. *Do campaigns matter?* Thousand Oaks, CA: Sage.

Hondagneu-Sotelo, Pierrette, Genelle Gaudinez, Hector Lara, and Billie C. Ortiz. 2004. " 'There's a spirit that transcends the border': Faith, ritual, and postnational protest at the U.S.–Mexico border." *Sociological Perspectives* 47:133–59.

Huckfeldt, Robert, Ken'ichi Ikeda, and Franz Urban Pappi. 2005. "Patterns of disagreement in democratic politics: Comparing Germany, Japan, and the United States." *American Journal of Political Science* 49 (3): 497–514.

Huckfeldt, Robert, Paul E. Johnson, and John Sprague. 2004. *Political disagreement: The survival of diverse opinions within communication networks.* Cambridge: Cambridge University Press.

Huckfeldt, Robert, and John Sprague. 1988. "Choice, social structure, and political information: The information coercion of minorities." *American Journal of Political Science* 32 (2): 467–82.

———. 1995. *Citizens, politics, and social communication: Information and influence in an election campaign.* Cambridge: Cambridge University Press.

Hunter, Wendy, and Timothy J. Power. 2007. "Rewarding Lula: Executive power, social policy, and the Brazilian elections of 2006." *Latin American Politics and Society* 49 (1): 1–30.

Imai, Kosuke. 2005. "Do get-out-the-vote calls reduce turnout? The importance of statistical methods for field experiments." *American Political Science Review* 99 (2): 283–300.

Imbens, Guido. 2003. "Semiparametric estimation of average treatment effects under exogeneity: A review." Ms, University of California, Berkeley.

Instituto Federal Electoral. 2006. *Encuestas y resultados electorales.* México, DF: Instituto Federal Electoral.

Johnston, Richard, André Blais, Henry E. Brady, and Jean Crête. 1992. *Letting the people decide: Dynamics of a Canadian election*. Stanford, CA: Stanford University Press.

Jones, Mark, Miguel De Luca, and María Inés Tula. 2002. "Back rooms or ballot boxes? Candidate nomination in Argentina." *Comparative Political Studies* 35 (4): 413–36.

Jones-Correa, Michael 1998. *Between two nations*. Ithaca, NY: Cornell University Press.

Katz, Elihu, and Paul F. Lazarsfeld. 1955. *Personal influence*. Glencoe, IL: Free Press.

Key, Valdimer Orlando. 1966. *The responsible electorate: Rationality in presidential voting, 1936–1960*. Cambridge, MA: Harvard University Press.

Kinder, Donald R., and D. Roderick Kiewiet. 1981. "Sociotropic politics: The American case." *British Journal of Political Science* 11 (2): 129–61.

King, Gary, Emmanuela Gakidou, Nirmala Ravishankar, Ryan T. Moore, Jason Lakin, Manett Vargas, Martha María Téllez-Rojo, Juan Eugenio Hernández Ávila, Mauricio Hernández Ávila, and Héctor Hernández Llamas. 2007. "A 'politically robust' experimental design for public policy evaluation, with application to the Mexican universal health insurance program," *Journal of Policy Analysis and Management* 26 (3): 479–506.

King, Gary, Michael Tomz, and Jason Wittenberg. 2000. "Making the most of statistical analyses: Improving interpretation and presentation." *American Journal of Political Science* 44 (2): 347–61.

Kitschelt, Herbert, Zdenka Mansfeldova, Radoslaw Markowski, and Gabor Toka. 1999. *Post-Communist party systems: Competition, representation and inter-party cooperation*. New York: Cambridge University Press.

Kitschelt, Herbert, and Steven Wilkinson. 2007. *Patrons or policies*. Cambridge: Cambridge University Press.

Klesner, Joseph L. 1993. "Modernization, economic crisis, and electoral alignment in Mexico." *Mexican Studies / Estudios Mexicanos* 9 (2): 187–223.

———. 1995. "The 1994 Mexican elections: Manifestation of a divided society?" *Mexican Studies / Estudios Mexicanos* 11 (1): 137–149.

———. 1999. *The 1998 Mexican state elections: Post-election report*. Western Hemisphere Election Study Series 17, Study 1. Washington, DC: Center for Strategic and International Studies.

———. 2001. "The end of Mexico's one-party regime." *PS: Political Science and Politics* 34 (1): 107–14.

———. 2004. "The structure of the Mexican electorate: Social, attitudinal, and partisan bases of Vicente Fox's victory." In Domínguez and Lawson 2004, 91–122.

———. 2005. "Electoral competition and the new party system in Mexico." *Latin American Politics and Society* 47 (2): 103–42.

———. 2006. "Economic integration and national identity in Mexico." *Nationalism and Ethnic Politics* 12 (3/4): 481–507.

———. 2007. "The 2006 Mexican elections: Manifestation of a divided society?" *PS: Political Science & Politics* 40 (1): 27–32.

Kline, Rex B. 2005. *Principles and practice of structural equation modeling*. New York: Guilford Press.

Koelble, Thomas. 1992. "Recasting social democracy in Europe: A nested games explanation of strategic adjustment in political parties." *Politics and Society* 20:51–70.

Krosnik, Jon, and Donald Kinder. 1990. "Altering the foundations of support for the president through priming." *American Political Science Review* 84:497–512.

Lago, Ignacio, José Ramón Montero, and Mariano Torcal. 2007. "Introducción: Modelos de voto y comportamiento electoral." In *Elecciones generales 2004*, ed. José Ramón Montero, Ignacio Lago, and Mariano Torcal, 15–29. Madrid: Centro de Investigaciones Sociológicas.

Lakin, Jason. 2005. "Opportunities and constraints: Health and policymaking in democratic Mexico." Ms, Harvard University.

Langston, Joy. 1997. *Why rules matter: The formal rules of candidate selection and leadership selection in the PRI*. México, DF: División de Estudios Políticos, Centro de Investigación y Docencia Económicas.

———. 2003. "Rising from the ashes? Reorganizing and unifying the PRI's state party organizations after electoral defeat." *Comparative Political Studies* 36 (3): 293–318.

Lawson, Chappell. 1999. "Why Cárdenas won: The 1997 elections in Mexico City." In Domínguez and Poiré 1999, 147–173.

———. 2000. "Mexico's unfinished transition: Democratization and authoritarian enclaves." *Mexican Studies/Estudios Mexicanos* 16 (2): 267–87.

———. 2003. "Voting preferences and political socialization among Mexican-Americans and Mexicans living in the United States." *Mexican Studies/Estudios Mexicanos* 19 (1): 65–79.

———. 2004a. "Building the Fourth Estate: Media opening and democratization in Mexico." In Middlebrook 2004, 473–501.

———. 2004b. Introduction to Domínguez and Lawson 2004.

———. 2004c. "Mexico's great debates: The televised candidate encounters of 2000 and their electoral consequences." In Domínguez and Lawson 2004, 211–41.

———. 2004d. "Television coverage, media effects, and the 2000 elections." In Domínguez and Lawson 2004, 187–209.

———. 2006. "Preliminary findings from the Mexico 2006 Panel Study: Blue states and yellow states". http://web.mit.edu/polisci/research/mexico06/Region_and_demographics8.doc.

Lawson, Chappell, and Joseph Klesner. 2001. "Adiós to the PRI? Changing voter turnout and Mexico's political transition." *Mexican Studies/Estudios Mexicanos* 17 (1): 17–39.

Lawson, Chappell and James A. McCann. 2005. "Television coverage, media effects, and Mexico's 2000 elections." *British Journal of Political Science* 35 (1): 1–30.

Lazarsfeld, Paul F., Bernard Berelson, and Hazel Gaudet. 1944. *The people's choice: How the voter makes up his mind in a presidential campaign*. New York: Columbia University Press.

Lean, Sharon F. 2007. "The presidential and parliamentary elections in Nicaragua, November 2006." *Electoral Studies* 26 (4): 828–32.

Lengle, James I. 1980. "Divisive presidential primaries and party electoral prospects, 1932–1976." *American Politics Quarterly* 8:261–77.

———. 1981. *Representation and presidential primaries: The Democratic Party in the post-reform era*. Westport, CT: Greenwood Press.

Lengle, James I., Diana Owen, and Molly Sonner. 1995. "Divisive nominating mechanisms and Democratic Party electoral prospects." *Journal of Politics* 57:370–83.

Lenz, Gabriel. 2006. "What politics is about." PhD diss., Princeton University.

Levitin, Teresa, and Warren Miller. 1979. "Ideological interpretations of presidential elections." *American Political Science Review* 73 (3): 751–71.

Levy, Santiago. 2006. *Progress against poverty*. Washington, DC: Brookings.

Levy, Santiago, and Evelyn Rodriguez. 2005. *Sin herencia de pobreza*. México, DF: Planeta.

Lewis-Beck, Michael S. 1988. *Economics and elections: The major western democracies*. Ann Arbor: University of Michigan Press.

Lin, Tse-min, James Enelow, and Han Dorussen. 1999. "Equilibrium in multicandidate probabilistic spatial voting." *Public Choice* 98:59–82.

Lippmann, Walter. 1922. *Public opinion*. New York: Harcourt, Brace.

Lipset, Seymour Martin, and Stein Rokkan. 1967. "Cleavage structures, party systems, and voter alignments: An introduction." In *Party systems and voter alignments: Cross-national perspectives*, ed. Seymour Martin Lipset and Stein Rokkan, 1–64. New York: Free Press.

Listhaug, Ola. 2005. "Retrospective voting." In *The European voter: A comparative study of modern democracies*, ed. Jacques Thomassen, 213–34. Oxford: Oxford University Press.

Loaeza, Soledad. 1999. *El Partido Acción Nacional: La larga marcha, 1939–1994, oposición leal y partido de protesta*. México, DF: Fondo de Cultura Económica.

———. 2006. "Vicente Fox's presidential style and the new Mexican presidency." *Mexican Studies/Estudios Mexicanos* 22 (1): 1–32.

Lopez-Bassols, Hermilo. 2006. "El México dividido." *El Sol de México*, July 14. www.oem.com.mx/elsoldemexico/notas/n5358.htm.

Lujambio, Alonso. 2000. *El poder compartido: Un ensayo sobre la democratización mexicana*. México, DF: Oceano.

———. 2001. "Democratization through Federalism? The National Action Party strategy, 1939–2000." In *Party politics and the struggle for democracy in Mexico: National and state-level analyses of the Partido Acción Nacional*, ed. Kevin J. Middlebrook, 47–94. La Jolla: Center for U.S.-Mexican Studies, University of California–San Diego.

Luna, Juan, and Elizabeth Zechmeister. 2005. "Political representation in Latin America: A study of elite-mass congruence in nine countries." *Comparative Political Studies* 38 (4): 388–416.

Mabry, Donald J. 1974. *Mexico's Acción Nacional: A Catholic alternative to revolution*. Syracuse, NY: Syracuse University Press.

Madrazo, Roberto, and Manuel Garrido. 2007. *La traición*. México, DF: Planeta.

Magaloni, Beatriz. 1999. "Is the PRI fading? Economic performance, electoral accountability, and voting behavior in the 1994 and 1997 elections." In Domínguez and Poiré 1999, 203–36.

———. 2006. *Voting for autocracy: Hegemonic party survival and its demise in Mexico*. New York: Cambridge University Press.

Magaloni, Beatriz, and Alejandro Moreno. 2003. "Catching-all-souls: The PAN and the politics of Catholicism in Mexico." In *Christian democracy in Latin America*, ed. Timothy Scully and Scott Mainwaring, 247–74. Stanford, CA: Stanford University Press.

Magaloni, Beatriz, and Alejandro Poiré. 2004a. "The issues, the vote, and the mandate for change." In Domínguez and Lawson 2004, 293–319.

———. 2004b. "Strategic coordination in the 2000 Mexican presidential race." In Domínguez and Lawson 2004, 269–92.

Mainwaring, Scott, Ana María Bejarano, and Eduardo Pizarro Leongómez, eds. 2006. *The crisis of democratic representation in the Andes*. Stanford CA: Stanford University Press.

Marcelli, Enrico, and Wayne A. Cornelius. 2005. "Immigrant voting in home-country elections: Potential consequences of extending the franchise to expatriate Mexicans residing in the United States." *Mexican Studies/Estudios Mexicanos* 21 (2): 429–60.

Marshall, Thomas R. 1981. *Presidential nominations in a reform age: American political parties and elections.* New York: Praeger/Eagleton Institute of Politics, Rutgers University.

Mayer, William G., ed. 2004. "The basic dynamics of the contemporary nominations process: An expanded view." In *The making of the presidential candidates 2004,* 83–132. Lanham, MD: Rowman and Littlefield.

McCann, James A. 1998. "The changing Mexican electorate: Political interest, expertise, and party support in the 1980s and 1990s." In Serrano 1998, 15–37.

———. 2004a. "The emerging international trend toward open presidential primaries." In *The making of the presidential candidates 2004,* ed. William G. Mayer, 265–94. Lanham, MD: Rowman and Littlefield.

———. 2004b. "Primary priming." In Dominguez and Lawson 2004, 157–83.

McCann, James A., and Chappell Lawson. 2003. "An electorate adrift? Public opinion and the quality of democracy in Mexico." *Latin American Research Review* 38(3): 60–81.

———. 2006. "Presidential campaigns and the knowledge gap in three transitional democracies." *Political Research Quarterly* 59 (1): 13–22.

Meinke, Scott R., Jeffrey K. Staton, and Steven T. Wuhs. 2006. "State delegate selection rules for presidential nominations, 1972–2000." *Journal of Politics* 68 (1): 180–193.

Merino, José, Marco Morales, and Roberto Ponce. 2006. "México 2006: El mito del país dividido." *Este País* (September): 27–35.

"México y el mundo: Visiones globales 2004." http://mexicoyelmundo.cide.edu/2004/.

Mexico 2006 Panel Study. http://web.mit.edu/polisci/research/mexico06/.

Middlebrook, Kevin J. 1995. *The paradox of revolution: Labor, the state, and authoritarianism in Mexico.* Baltimore: Johns Hopkins University Press.

———. 2001. "Party politics and democratization in Mexico: The Partido Acción Nacional in comparative perspective." In *Party politics and the struggle for democracy in Mexico: National and state-level analyses of the Partido Acción Nacional,* ed. Kevin J. Middlebrook, 3–46. La Jolla: Center for U.S.-Mexican Studies, University of California–San Diego.

———, ed. 2004. *The dilemmas of change in Mexican politics.* London: Center for U.S.-Mexican Studies, University of California at San Diego and the Institute of Latin American Studies, University of London.

Miller, Warren E., and Donald Stokes. 1963. "Constituency influence in Congress." *American Political Science Review* 57:165–77.

Mizrahi, Yemile. 1993. *Rebels without a cause?: The politics of entrepreneurs in Chihuahua.* México, DF: División de Estudios Políticos, Centro de Investigación y Docencia Económicas (CIDE).

———. 1997. *The costs of electoral success: The Partido Acción Nacional in Mexico.* México, DF: División de Estudios Políticos, Centro de Investigación y Docencia Económicas (CIDE).

———. 2003. *From martyrdom to power: The Partido Acción Nacional in Mexico.* Notre Dame, IN: University of Notre Dame Press.

Molinar Horcasitas, Juan. 1991. *El tiempo de la legitimidad: Elecciones, autoritarismo y democracia en México.* México, DF: Cal y Arena.

Moreno, Alejandro. 1998. "Party competition and the issue of democracy: Ideological space in Mexican elections." In Serrano 1998, 38–57.

———. 1999a. "Campaign awareness and voting in the 1997 Mexican Congressional elections." In Domínguez and Poiré 1999, 114–46.

———. 1999b. *Political cleavages: Issues, parties, and the consolidation of democracy.* Boulder, CO: Westview Press.

———. 2000. "The public and its representatives: Mass and elite opinion in Mexico." Working paper WPPS 2000-02, Instituto Tecnológico Autónomo de México (ITAM).

———. 2003a. *El votante mexicano: Democracia, actitudes políticas y conducta electoral.* México, DF: Fondo de Cultura Económica.

———. 2003b. "Left-right orientations and party support in Mexico, 2000–2003." Ms, Instituto Tecnológico Autónomo de México.

———. 2004. "The effects of negative campaigns on Mexican voters." In Domínguez and Lawson 2004, 243–68.

———. 2005. *Nuestros valores: Los Mexicanos en México y en Estados Unidos al inicio del siglo XXI.* México, DF: Banamex.

———. 2006. "Choosing a president Right . . . or Left? Mexico's changing ideological dimensions and voting in 2000 and 2006." Paper presented at the American Political Science Association annual meeting, August 31, Philadelphia.

———. 2007. "The 2006 Mexican presidential election: The economy, oil revenues, and ideology." *PS: Political Science and Politics* 40 (1): 15–19.

Moreno, Alejandro, and Patricia Méndez. 2002. "Attitudes toward democracy: Mexico in comparative perspective." *International Journal of Comparative Sociology* 43 (3–5): 350–67.

———. 2007. "La identificación partidista en las elecciones presidenciales de 2000 y 2006 en México: ¿Desalineación o realineación?" *Política y Gobierno* 14 (1): 43–75.

Morris, Stephen D. 2005. "Mexico's long-awaited surprise." *Latin American Research Review* 40 (3): 417–28.

Mutz, Diana C. 2006. *Hearing the other side: Deliberative versus participatory democracy.* New York: Cambridge University Press.

Mutz, Diana C., and Paul S. Martin. 2001. "Facilitating communication across lines of political difference: The role of mass media." *American Political Science Review* 95 (1): 97–114.

Nicolau, Jairo. 2008. "The presidential and congressional elections in Brazil, October 2006." *Electoral Studies* 27 (1): 170–75.

Noelle-Neumann, Elisabeth. 1984. *The spiral of silence: Public opinion—our social skin.* Chicago: University of Chicago Press.

O'Donnell, Guillermo. 1994. "Delegative democracy." *Journal of Democracy* 5:55–69.

Orozco-Henríquez, Jesús. 2006. "The Mexican Electoral Court of the Federal Judiciary and the 2006 presidential election." Speech given at "Administering Mexico's 2006 Federal Elections," a Center for Strategic and International Studies (CSIS) Mexico Project event, May 18, Washington, DC. www.csis.org/media/csis/events/060518_orozco.pdf.

Paolino, Philip. 2005. "Voter behavior in democratizing nations: Reconsidering the two-step model." *Political Research Quarterly* 58 (1): 107–17.

Petrocik, John R. 1996. "Issue ownership in presidential elections with a 1980 case study." *American Journal of Political Science* 40 (3): 825–50.

Pitkin, Hanna Fenichel. 1967. *The concept of representation.* Berkeley: University of California Press.

PNUD (Programa de las Naciones Unidas para el Desarrollo). 2006. *Encuesta nacional sobre protección de los programas sociales federales.* México, DF: Programa de las Naciones Unidas para el Desarrollo.

Poiré, Alejandro. 1999. "Retrospective voting, partisanship, and loyalty in presidential elections: 1994." In Dominguez and Poiré 1999, 24–56.

———. 2003. "Why primaries?" Paper presented at the Midwest Political Science Association, 61st Annual National Conference, April 2–6, Chicago.

Portes, Alejandro, Cristina Escobar, and Renelinda Arana. 2007. "Divided or convergent loyalties? A report on the political incorporation of Latin American immigrants in the United States." Working paper, Center for Migration and Development Working Paper Series, Princeton University.

Powell, G. Bingham. 2004. "Political representation in comparative politics." *Annual Review of Political Science* 7:273–96.

Powell, Linda W. 1982. "Issue representation in Congress." *Journal of Politics* 44:658–78.

Przeworski, Adam, and Henry Teune. 1970. *The logic of comparative social inquiry.* New York: Wiley.

Putnam, Robert. 2001. *Bowling alone.* New York: Touchstone.

Randall, Laura, ed. 1996. *The changing structure of Mexico: Political, social, and economic prospects.* Armonk, NY: M. E. Sharpe.

Reveles Vázquez, Francisco. 2003. "La lucha entre fracciones priístas en la selección de candidatos presidenciales." In *Partido Revolucionario Institucional: Crisis y refundación,* ed. Francisco Reveles Vázquez, 79–152. México, DF: Universidad Nacional Autónoma de México / Gernika.

Reyes, Marisol. 2004. "Patterns of non-voting in Mexico: An aggregate analysis of the local and federal elections from 1991 to 2003." In *LASA 2004: Latin American Studies Association XXV International Congress, Las Vegas, Nevada, October 7–9, 2004,* ed. Latin American Studies Association, 1–25. Pittsburgh, PA: LASA Secretariat.

Reynolds, John F. 2006. *The demise of the American convention system, 1880–1911.* Cambridge: Cambridge University Press.

Rodríguez, Victoria E., and Peter M. Ward, eds. 1995. *Opposition government in Mexico.* Albuquerque: University of New Mexico Press.

Rosenbaum, Paul R., and Donald B. Rubin. 1983. "The central role of the propensity score in observational studies for causal effects." *Biometrika* 70:41–55.

Rosenstone, Steven J., and John Mark Hansen. 1993. *Mobilization, participation, and democracy.* New York: Macmillan.

Rothstein, Jeffrey S. 2005. "Economic development policymaking down the global commodity chain: Attracting an auto industry to Silao, Mexico." *Social Forces* 84 (1): 49–69.

Rottinghaus, Brandon, and Irina Alberro. 2005. "Rivaling the PRI: The image management of Vicente Fox and the use of public opinion polling in the 2000 Mexican election." *Latin American Politics and Society* 47 (2): 143–58.

Salim Cabrera, Emilio. 2005. "Autoritarismo irreflexivo o gobernabilidad democrática." *Este País* 166 (January): 41–44.

Scarrow, Susan. 1997. *Parties and their members: Organizing for victory in Britain and Germany*. Oxford: Oxford University Press.

Schattschneider, E. E. 1975. *The semisovereign people: A realist's view of democracy in America*. Hinsdale, IL: Dryden Press.

Scott, John. 2006. "Seguro Popular incidence analysis." In *Decentralized service delivery for the poor: Vol. 2, background papers*, ed. World Bank, 147–65. México, DF: World Bank.

SEDESOL (Secretaría de Desarrollo Social). 2005. "En marcha programa de blindaje social para elecciones de 2006; SEDESOL y onu firman acuerdo." Boletin 56 (November 17). México, DF: SEDESOL. See also CITCC (Comisión Intersecretarial para la Transparencia y el Combate a la Corrupción), "Blindaje electoral." www.blindajeelectoral.gob.mx/Secretarias/sedesol_pnud/sedesol%20fepade.htm.

Sekhon, Jasjeet S. 2004. "The varying role of voter information across democratic societies." Paper presented at the Latin American Studies Association XXV International Congress, Las Vegas, Nevada, October 7–9, 2004.

Serrano, Mónica, ed. 1998. *Governing Mexico: Political parties and elections*. London: Institute of Latin American Studies.

Shirk, David A. 2000. "Vicente Fox and the rise of the PAN." *Journal of Democracy* 11 (4): 25–32.

———. 2005. *Mexico's new politics: The PAN and democratic change*. Boulder, CO: Lynne Rienner.

Simpson, Lesley Byrd. 1941. *Many Mexicos*. Berkeley: University of California Press.

Smyth, Regina. 2006. *Candidate strategies and electoral competition in the Russian Federation: Democracy without foundation*. New York: Cambridge University Press.

Sniderman, Paul M., Richard A. Brody, and Philip E. Tetlock. 1994. *Reasoning and choice: Explorations in political psychology*. New York: Cambridge University Press.

Solinger, Dorothy J. 2001. "Ending one-party dominance: Korea, Taiwan, Mexico." *Journal of Democracy* 12 (1): 30–42.

Stevenson, Randolph T., and Lynn Vavreck. 2000. "Does campaign length matter? Testing for cross-national effects." *British Journal of Political Science* 30 (2): 217–35.

Stokes, Donald. 1963. "Spatial models of party competition." *American Political Science Review* 57:368–77.

Stokes, Susan. 2005. "Perverse accountability: A formal model of machine politics with evidence from Argentina." *American Political Science Review* 99 (3): 315–25.

Tomz, Michael, Jason Wittenberg, and Gary King. 2001. CLARIFY: Software for interpreting and presenting statistical results, Version 2.0. Cambridge, MA: Harvard University. http://gking.harvard.edu.

Trelles, Alejandro, and Héctor Zagal. 2004. *AMLO: Historia política y personal del jefe de gobierno del D.F.* México, DF: Plaza Janés.

Tufte, Edward. 1978. *Political control of the economy*. Princeton, NJ: Princeton University Press.

Varela, Carlo. 2004a. "The balance of the 2004 electoral year." *Review of the Economic Situation of Mexico* 80 (947): 448–51.

———. 2004b. "The electoral processes have begun." *Review of the Economic Situation of Mexico* 80 (941): 220–24.

Verba, Sidney, Norman Nie, and Jae-on Kim. 1978. *Participation and political equality*. New York: Cambridge University Press.

Von Sauer, Franz A. 1974. *The alienated "loyal" opposition: Mexico's Partido Acción Nacional.* Albuquerque: University of New Mexico Press.

Walters, Ronald W. 1988. *Black presidential politics in America: A strategic approach.* SUNY Series in Afro-American Studies. Albany: State University of New York Press.

Wantchekon, Leonard. 2004. "Clientelism and voting behavior: Evidence from a field experiment in Benin." *World Politics* 55 (3): 399–422.

Ware, Alan. 2002. *The American direct primary: Party institutionalization and transformation in the North.* Cambridge: Cambridge University Press.

Wattenberg, Martin P. 1990. *The decline of American political parties, 1952–1988.* Cambridge, MA: Harvard University Press.

Weissberg R. 1978. "Collective versus dyadic representation in Congress." *American Political Science Review* 72:535–47.

Weyland, Kurt. 2002. *The politics of market reform in fragile democracies: Argentina, Brazil, Peru, and Venezuela.* Princeton, NJ: Princeton University Press.

White, John Kenneth, and Jerome M. Mileur. 1992. *Challenges to party government.* Carbondale: Southern Illinois University Press.

Wirth, Clifford J. 2006. "Democracy in Mexico City: The impact of structural reforms." *Mexican Studies/Estudios Mexicanos* 22 (1): 153–73.

Wlezien, Christopher, Mark Franklin, and Daniel Twiggs. 1997. "Economic perceptions and vote choice: Disentangling the endogeneity." *Political Behavior* 19 (1): 7–17.

Wuhs, Steven. 2002. "Political parties and the failure of representation in Mexico." Presentation for the Center for U.S.-Mexican Studies Seminar Series, La Jolla, CA.

———. 2006. "Democratization and the dynamics of candidate selection rule change in Mexico, 1991–2003." *Mexican Studies/Estudios Mexicanos* 22 (1): 33–55.

———. 2008. *Savage democracy: Institutional change and party development in Mexico.* University Park: Pennsylvania State University Press.

Zaller, John. 1992. *The nature and origins of mass opinion.* New York: Cambridge University Press.

———. 1996. "The myth of massive media impact revived: New support for a discredited idea." In *Political Persuasion and Attitude Change,* ed. Diana C. Mutz, Paul M. Sniderman, and Richard A Brody, 17–78. Ann Arbor: University of Michigan Press.

Zaller, John, and Stanley Feldman. 1992. "A simple theory of survey response: Answering questions versus revealing preferences." *American Journal of Political Science* 36:579–616.

Zechmeister, Elizabeth. 2006. "What's Left and who's Right? A Q-method study of individual and contextual influences on the meaning of ideological labels." *Political Behavior* 28 (2): 151–73.

Zeller, Richard A., and Edward G. Carmines. 1980. *Measurement in the social sciences: The link between theory and data.* Cambridge: Cambridge University Press.

Contributors

Andy Baker is an assistant professor of political science at the University of Colorado at Boulder. He is the author of *The market and the masses in Latin America* (2009). His publications on political economy and public opinion have appeared in *World Politics*, *American Journal of Political Science*, and *Electoral Studies*.

Kathleen Bruhn is a professor of political science at the University of California, Santa Barbara. She is the author of *Taking on Goliath: The emergence of a new left party and the struggle for democracy in Mexico* (1997), and *Urban protest in Mexico and Brazil* (2008).

Roderic Ai Camp is the Philip M. McKenna Professor of the Pacific Rim at Claremont McKenna College. He is the author of more than twenty books on Mexican politics. His most recent work includes *Politics in Mexico, the democratic consolidation* (2007), *Mexico's military on the democratic stage* (2006), and *Mexico's mandarins, crafting a power elite for the twenty-first century* (2003).

Wayne A. Cornelius is the Theodore E. Gildred Distinguished Professor of Political Science and U.S.-Mexican Relations, director emeritus of the Center for U.S.-Mexican Studies, and director of the Center for Comparative Immigration Studies at the University of California–San Diego. With David Shirk, he coedited and coauthored *Reforming the administration of justice in Mexico* (2007). With Jessa M. Lewis, he coedited and coauthored *Impacts of border enforcement on Mexican migration* (2007).

Alberto Díaz-Cayeros is an assistant professor of political science at Stanford University.

Jorge I. Domínguez is the Antonio Madero Professor of Mexican and Latin American Politics and Economics and vice-provost for international affairs at Harvard University. With Chappell Lawson, he coedited and wrote for *Mexico's pivotal democratic election: Candidates, voters, and the presidential campaign of 2000* (2004). With James McCann, he is coauthor of *Democratizing Mexico: Public opinion and electoral choices* (1996).

Federico Estévez is a professor and researcher of political science at the Instituto Tecnológico Autónomo de México (ITAM).

Francisco Flores-Macías is a Ph.D. candidate in Political Science at the Massachusetts Institute of Technology.

Kenneth F. Greene is an assistant professor of government at the University of Texas at Austin. His book, *Why dominant parties lose: Mexico's democratization in comparative perspective* (2007), received the 2008 best book award from the comparative democratization section of the American Political Science Association.

Joseph L. Klesner is a professor of political science at Kenyon College. He has written extensively on Mexican electoral politics. His most recent work has focused on political culture and participation in Latin America. His articles have appeared in journals such as the *Latin American Research Review*, *Latin American Politics and Society*, *Mexican Studies*, *Comparative Politics*, and *Electoral Studies* and in various edited volumes.

Joy Langston is a professor of political science at the Centro de Investigación y Docencia Económicas (CIDE). She specializes in political parties in Mexico and has published in *Comparative Politics*, *Comparative Political Studies*, and *Party Politics*.

Chappell Lawson is an associate professor of political science at the Massachusetts Institute of Technology. He was a principal investigator for the Mexico 2006 Panel Study, the Mexico 2000 Panel Study, and the 1997 Mexico City Panel Study.

David L. Leal is an associate professor of government at the University of Texas at Austin. His primary academic interest is Latino-Hispanic politics, and his work explores a variety of questions involving public opinion, political behavior, and public policy. He has published over three dozen journal articles and book chapters and is a coeditor of *Immigration policy and security* (2008) and *Latino politics: Identity, mobilization, and representation* (2007).

Beatriz Magaloni is an assistant professor of political science at Stanford University. Her book, *Voting for autocracy: Hegemonic party survival and its demise in Mexico* (2006), was a corecipient of the 2007 Leon D. Epstein Book Award, given by the political organizations and parties section of the American Political Science Association. It also received the 2007 best book award of the comparative democratization section of the association.

James A. McCann is a professor of political science and graduate placement director in the Department of Political Science at Purdue University. With Wayne A. Cornelius and David L. Leal, he conducted the 2006 Mexico Expatriate Study. With Jorge I. Domínguez, he is coauthor of *Democratizing Mexico: Public opinion and electoral choices* (1996).

Alejandro Moreno is an associate professor of political science at the Instituto Tecnológico Autónomo de México (ITAM) and head of the department of polling at the newspaper *Reforma*, both in Mexico City. He has published over 40 academic articles in journals and edited volumes, and over 500 journalistic articles based on public opinion polls. He has authored or coauthored six books, including *El votante mexicano* (*The Mexican voter*, 2003). Moreno was responsible for fieldwork in the 2000 and 2006 Mexico Panel Studies, the 2000 and 2005 World Values Surveys (WVS) in Mexico, and the Comparative National Election Project (CNEP-III), also in Mexico, in 2006.

David A. Shirk is an assistant professor of political science and director of the Trans-Border Institute at the University of San Diego. His recent publications include *Police and public security in Mexico* (2009), *Contemporary Mexican politics* (2008), and *Reforming the administration of justice in Mexico* (2007).

Index

Page numbers in *italics* indicate figures and tables.